HOW TO
BUY/SELL YOUR OWN HOME
WITHOUT A BROKER OR LAWYER

The National Home Sale And Purchase Kit

By Benji O. Anosike, B.B.A., M.A., Ph.D.

New Way to CUT Home COSTS!

(Revised Edition)

Copyright © 1997, 2000 by Benji O. Anosike

Library of Congress Cataloging-in-Publication Data

Anosike, Benji O.
    How to buy/sell your own home without a broker or lawyer : the national home sale and
purchase kit : usable in all 50 states / Benji O. Anosike.-- Rev. ed.
        p. cm.
    Includes bibliographical references and index.
    ISBN 0-932704-50-6 (paper : alk. paper)
    1. Vendors and purchasers--United States--Popular works. 2. House buying--United
States. 3. House selling--United States. I. Title.

KF665.Z9 A56 2000
346.7304'37--dc21
                                                                99-059362

Printed in the United States of America
ISBN: 0-932704-50-6
Library of Congress Catalog Number:

Pu...
Do-It-Yourself Legal Publishers
60 Park Place,
Newark, NJ 07102

LI NEW

Special Dedication...

In Fun Memory of:

...DAD

DAVID NWOKOLIE ANOSIKE,
**WHO TAUGHT ME A GREAT DEAL ABOUT OWNERSHIP, RESPECT,
AND APPRECIATION OF REAL PROPERTY**

The Publisher's Disclaimer

It remains for us, the Publishers, to assure our readers that we have diligently researched, checked and counterchecked every bit of the information contained in the manual to ensure its accuracy and up-to-dateness. Nevertheless, we humans have never been noted for our infallibility, no matter how hard the effort! Furthermore, details of laws, rules and procedures do change from time to time. And, with specific respect to real estate home selling or buying, and the like, the specific details of rules of procedures (though generally not the law or the broad basic principles themselves) often differ from one state to another. Nor is this relatively short manual conceivably intended to be an encyclopedia on the subject, containing the answers or solutions to every issue on the subject. THE READER IS THEREFORE FOREWARNED THAT THIS MANUAL IS SOLD AND DISTRIBUTED WITH THIS DISCLAIMER: The publisher (and/or the editors or author) does not make any guarantees of any kind whatsoever, or purport to engage in rendering professional or legal service, or to substitute for a lawyer, an accountant, financial or estate planner, a tax expert, or the like. Where such professional help is legitimately called for in your specific or other cases, it should be sought accordingly.

—Do-It-Yourself Legal Publishers

ACKNOWLEDGMENTS...

Our profound thanks and gratitude to the following: Julius Blumberg, Inc., the New York legal forms printers, whose forms are reproduced in the manual for purposes of illustrations; Washington D.C.'s HALT, Inc., the national legal reform organization, and their authors ("Real Estate"); author Harley Bjelland ("How To Sell Your House Without A Lawyer"), and his publisher, the Cornerstone Library; authors Martin M. Shenkman and Warren Boroson ("How To Sell Your House In A Buyer's Market") and their publisher, John Wiley & Sons, Inc; real estate analyst and author Robert Irwin ("The For Sale By Owner Kit," Dearborn Financial Publishing); author Edward Siegel ("How To Avoid Lawyers"), and his publishers, Fawcett Crest; the U.S. Department of H..U.D., Washington, D.C., and the authors of its superb manual ("Home Buyer's Information Package: A Guidebook for Buying and Owning a Home"); and many others too numerous to mention herein.

All of the above named (and many others too numerous to mention) have, in one way or the other, by their prior deed, pioneering works and/or research in the field—and by their ever unselfish readiness to share and disseminate the fruits of that—made the present undertaking both more purposeful and easier for the present author and publisher.

CREDITS TO...

Amy R. Feigenbaum and Suzanne Feigenbaum of *Rivanne Advertising* Creative Desktop Publishing Services, Brooklyn, NY, for art direction, design, typesetting, and illustration.

SPECIAL THANKS TO...

Finally, the author would like to remind you, the reader, of this: please note that I continue to love hearing from you on your real estate ideas, aspirations and experiences. Please continue to send us all those comments, information, opinions, thoughts, or suggestions that you might have regarding this manual or its subject matter. As always, just drop us a few lines through the publisher's offices (written communications are preferred, please!). With us, YOU, the reader, are the KING or QUEEN! We value and welcome your feedback—always!

Thank You, again.

Table of Contents

CHAPTER 1
MUST YOU NECESSARILY BUY/SELL A HOUSE WITH A LAWYER OR BROKER?

CHAPTER 2
ARE YOU BUYING? FIRST DETERMINE THE TYPE OF HOUSE
AND NEIGHBORHOOD YOU CAN ACTUALLY AFFORD

CHAPTER 3
LET'S SEARCH FOR THE PROPER HOUSE, NEIGHBORHOOD, AND/OR BROKER FOR YOU

CHAPTER 4
ON YOUR FINDING THE HOUSE TO BUY, NEGOTIATE THE TERMS OF SALE WITH SELLER

CHAPTER 5
BUYING A HOUSE YOURSELF: HERE'S THE COMPLETE STEP-BY-STEP PROCEDURES, FROM START TO FINISH

APPENDICES

CHAPTER 6
ARE YOU SELLING? HERE ARE THE COMPLETE STEP-BY-STEP
PROCEDURES, FROM START TO FINISH

FOREWORD:
THE PUBLISHER'S MESSAGE

To All our Dear Readers:

THE TRAUMA OF HOME BUYING IN AMERICA

Yes. You may already have heard it or even guessed it right. FOR MOST AMERICANS, THE PROCESS OF PURCHASING A HOME WINDS UP BEING ONE OF THE MOST TRAUMATIC EXPERIENCES OF THEIR LIVES— SECOND ONLY TO THE GRIEF THEY SUFFER FOR THE LOSS OF A LOVED ONE! A countless array of formal studies, as well as all manners of indices, have consistently shown this. The results, for example, from a 1974 tabulation of the questions (they were about 3,000,000) sent to the research division of Encyclopedia Brittannica by the American public, was consistent with this long-perceived trend: home buying was right at the top of the list of items about which most Americans were concerned or worried—in second place only to questions on careers!

CAUSES OF THE TRAUMA IN HOME BUYING

It is not just the kind of expenditures involved in buying a home, the fact that for most this will probably be the largest single purchase they'll ever make. But, more importantly, it is the fact that the formalities and procedures involved in physically translating the 'American dream' of owning a home to reality—of bringing about the transfer of real property from citizens to citizens—have come to rank among the most intimidating, bureaucratized, unnecessarily complicated and expense-fraught in America. [It is the exceptional, rather than the average home buyer, who shall have had a working comprehension of such mysterious terms as 'discounts,' 'points,' 'abstracts,' 'equity,' 'closing,' 'escrow,' 'balloon payments,' and the like!]

On the other side of the matter, is the fact that on top of all these, yet little or no concrete information or education is made available to the average home buyer or seller about the basics, the knots and bolts of real property or real property transfer. A CENTRAL PURPOSE—AND MISSION —OF THIS MANUAL IS TO HELP IN FILLING THIS ALL-IMPORTANT VOID.

'PROFESSIONAL MIDDLEMEN' AS THE PROBLEM

At the heart of the problem, many analysts agree, is the proliferation of "professional middlemen" in real estate transfer transactions—persons from various trades and disciplines who serve as "providers" of different services and must, in the process, extract their respective "cuts" of fees and charges and impose various procedural demands and requirements along the way. As the study *by* HALT Inc., the Washington D.C. legal reform organization, appropriately sums it up, "Paying large fees to professional middlemen is perhaps the most aggravating aspect of home buying."

The professional middlemen of real estate transfers include title search and title insurance companies and their agents, escrow agents, financial institutions, mortgage brokers, real estate brokers, and lawyers.

This manual concentrates on the roles of the two principal and most dominant middlemen in the business—the real estate lawyer and the real estate broker. It's not just that the lawyer's fees (an average of $5,000-$7,000 for representations alone on both sides) are among the highest of all middlemen charges. But, even more importantly, the role played by the lawyer in real estate transfer deals is often pivotal, acting to set the tone of, and to set in motion much of the host of formalities and redtapes in the process, and their associated price tags. As for the real estate brokers, not only does the broker's commission (typically 6 or 7 percent of the actual home selling price) invariably constitute one of the heaviest "cash" expenditures the home seller makes, but the real estate broker is also agreed to be "often the most influential actor in the entire process of transferring real estate."

WHAT THIS MANUAL DOES FOR YOU

This manual provides, primarily for the use and benefit of the non-lawyer and non-broker (though such professionals could equally benefit from it), the tools and knowledge by which to comprehend the home transfer process in a comprehensive and systematic way, and the tools and knowledge by which the common man and woman can undertake the home purchase or sale procedures by themselves. As a home buyer or seller, you shall have acquired the capability and knowledge to completely rid yourself of the need to use the attorney or the broker (and their associated fees and charges) in home transfer deals! Or, if and when you must for one *reason or the other use their services—or those of other 'middlemen'* in the real estate industry—you *shall have had the capability and knowledge to at least get your* money's worth from them!

True, the deck is extremely stacked against the home buyer (or seller) under the present prevailing system, and per- haps nothing (other than the complete overhaul of the law and the proce- dures by an act of Congress and state legislatures) would probably let you avoid totally having to deal with at least some of the army of "profession- als" who run the vast, hugely lucrative real estate industry. However, with a relatively minimal amount of effort, you can, through the rare access afforded you by this book into the most closely guarded real estate industry 'trade secrets,' achieve something close to exactly that: the freeing of yourself, through knowl- edge, from exploitation or abuse; an ability to beat down (or, in situations where it might be to your advantage otherwise, to increase) the home purchase price, or the assortment of fees and costs involved in "closing" and "settlement" services. Above all, you shall have at the very least acquired a sound knowledge of your legal rights, of what is reasonable and prudent, and of how to bargain and comparison-shop for better prices and better quality services. In deed, of this much you can rest assured: *with a good mastery of the contents of this book, you shall have known in as much as, and in many respects probably more than, the average attorney or real estate broker on the subject—the concepts, procedures, terminologies, trade short cuts, trade tricks, money-saving tips of real estate transfer deals.*

YOU ARE JUST AS CAPABLE. YOU CAN DO AS GOOD A JOB OF REPRESENTING YOURSELF IN SELLING/BUYING YOUR HOME

Much has conventionally been made of the role of the two principal professionals discussed in this book in real estate transfers, though more so with respect to the lawyer. An elaborate folklore has been orchestrated—and the lawyers have enjoyed fostering and keeping it alive—that the lawyer's role in real estate transfer deals is indispensable. An often heard (but never proven!) rationale particularly advanced by lawyers, is that the lawyer's role in real estate transfers is necessary because of the (supposed) need for the lawyer to give legal "protection" to the home buyer or seller, and that persons who attempt to undertake the formalities and the "legal" paperwork of real estate transfers on their own without the lawyer's participation, necessarily confronts grave, even certain financial risks and consequences! And the real estate broker has similarly staked out a similar, though lesser, claim to the indispensability of his role in home buying or selling.

That bogey of the lawyer or the broker playing a unique role or being indispensable to you in the buying or selling of a home, is adequately laid to rest by this manual, once and for all. (See Chapter 1, pp. 1-5). The conclusive reality that is of relevance from a preponderance of actual evidence is crystal clear : *lawyers and brokers do not necessarily have to be used in the transaction of routine real estate transfers; though a layman, you too can do just as good or safe a job (perhaps even a better one!) transacting these matters by yourself, as you'll generally get hiring a lawyer or a broker to do it for you. And, it'll be at huge savings, too, to you!*

NEED FOR CONSUMER EDUCATION
PROGRAM AS THE KEY

How many American home buyers or sellers know, for example, that most settlement charges are not fixed, and that except for a few of them (such as taxes), most such charges vary considerably among lenders or providers, while others are negotiable? Not very many!

A 1980 government-sponsored report prepared by the prestigious accounting firm of Peat, Marwick, Mitchell and Company for the H.U.D., found that private home buyers and sellers seldom negotiated or shopped for more favorable terms, and concluded that a major reason why costs for settlement services were higher than they should be is because there was no active price competition among the providers of such services and because there was lack of comparison shopping among private home buyers and sellers. And four years later, a May 1984 staff report by another federal government agency, the Federal Trade Commission, pretty much found the same situation in its survey: that private home buyers and sellers were paying more than they had to because of practices within the real estate industry and lack of knowledge and sophistication on the part of the people entering real estate transactions. Sellers are paying too much, the report added, because they are unaware that there are alternative (i.e., discount) brokers who charge less than the 6 or 7 percent standard industry commission, and that even full-service brokers are frequently willing to negotiate and accept lower fees. And buyers are paying too much, the report said, because they fail to recognize that the broker who helps them find their house is not "representing" them but is actually acting on behalf of the seller and in his (the broker's) own self-interest, and not on the buyer's, nor is he necessarily interested in getting the lowest price for the buyer.

To be sure, there has been no want of outcries or expressions of concerns in America over the state of affairs in the costs of real estate transfers and about excessive 'settlement' costs. *Certainly, laws abound, many of them good and well-meaning. But the basic problem, we find, has been that consumers just aren't adequately informed about them, or given ready access to them.* Take, for example, the experience with the Real Estate Settlement Procedures Act (RESPA). Passed by Congress in 1974, the law required mortgage lenders to provide loan applicants with a "good faith" estimate of settlement costs, and further required that lenders give buyers a special H.U.D.-prepared information booklet that explains settlement charges and consumer rights, and gave applicants the right to examine the actual settlement statement the day before the closing. The hope of Congress had been that once consumers were informed about costs before a closing took place, they would comparison-shop and that the resulting competition will bring settlement prices down.

The actual experience so far? An abysmal one, according to the Peat Marwick report. The law, the report found, has been able to induce only 1 out of 10 buyers to shop for better terms. Buyers did actively look for the best mortgage terms but when it came to selecting a title-insurance company, a mortgage insurance provider, or a lawyer, buyers merely accepted referrals from real estate brokers and from lenders. Sellers who used brokers almost always used "full-service" brokers instead *of* "discount" or "flat-fee" concerns, meaning having to pay a full brokerage commission of 6% or 7% of the sale price of the house.

These long-standing but continuing realities in America's real estate industry, underscores, in our view, the critical need for greater and wider dissemination of pertinent facts and information, and for a book such as the present one to begin to fill the gaping void in consumer education and knowledge among American home buyers and sellers, albeit on a more comprehensive and sophisticated basis.

THE ULTIMATE SOLUTION: JUNK THE PRESENT LAWYER-INSPIRED
LAND "RECORDING" SYSTEM AND USE A LAND "REGISTRATION" SYSTEM, INSTEAD

Analysts have often pointed out that the use of most middlemen in real estate transfer deals would be less costly—and, in many cases, even unnecessary—if only just one measure could be undertaken, namely, simplification of the procedures for transferring and recording real estate. A mere institution of a simplified procedure, many analysts have contended, will drastically reduce the cost of many of the services which are now required in real estate deals, such as title insurance, title search reports and survey reports, and may eliminate even the need for some of the services and the associated costs.

Perhaps the most frequently mentioned simplification method is the use of land "registration" (in place of the common present system of land "recording"), more particularly one version of the registration system—the **TORRENS LAND REGISTRATION SYSTEM (TLRS).** A system long in use in the Western industrialized world, here's how the Torrens registration system will basically work. Under it, a single title certificate would be issued as a public document by the office of the recorder of deeds for each parcel of property, with the certificate showing the present legal owner of the land. All pertinent information concerning the parcel (e.g., its ownership, liens, judgments, easements) would, by law, be entered on that certificate. Any subsequent changes in the original issuance of a certificate would also have to be entered on the certificate. Thus, all the information that must be considered to buy, sell, or mortgage the property, would be readily accessible in one place, and, if placed on a computer, could be called up at the touch of a button. To transfer a property, all that the seller needs do is to sign the certificate over to the buyer—much as one now does when one signs over title to an automobile!

Now given the obvious superiority, in terms of costs and simplicity, of the Torrens system over the bureaucracy-fraught and costly 'recording' system that most Americans are now burdened with, the obvious logical question is, of course: Why not? Why hasn't there been a mad rush across the country to implement such a system? One report on the subject summed up what has been the obstacle this way:

> "...most land registration proposals have been sternly opposed by a multi-billion dollar title industry composed of title lawyers, title companies, and property insurance companies.... [This proposed new] method of recording and exchanging property would eliminate the current 'need' for expensive title searches.... No need [would further exist] for expensive title insurance policies to cover non-existent risks.... Lawyers and other title industry people would lose very lucrative business opportunity—and you could purchase your home for considerably less in anxiety and in settlement costs."*

We are all too aware of the reality, therefore, that the implementation of a land registration system, though most desirable and urgently needed, is not about to become a reality in much of America in the foreseeable future! In the meantime, American consumers will, of course, continue to buy and sell homes, and those consumers will therefore continue to need help.

IN THE MEANTIME, THE 'HIRING' OF THIS BOOK COULD SAVE YOU $$ THOUSANDS RIGHT OFF THE BAT!

It is for that reason that this manual is conceived and written, and to such consumers that the manual is primarily commended: to guide and inform you competently and comprehensively through the current real estate marketplace and its realities, and to help you find your way through the maze of professionals, middlemen, legal procedures, and financial arrangements which have come to surround the essentially simple process of transferring real property in America.

No exaggeration is meant here. But, quite easily, even merely at the standard lawyers' going rates and brokers' commission (not to speak of all the other middlemen!) in real estate transfers, it should be obvious how and why the proper use of this book could save you, not hundreds, but literally an average of several thousands of dollars over the course of a few years or less.

Here, you need no fancy calculation to make this fact obvious: Let's take just the broker's commission alone. Let's say you sold your home for $100,000 without using a broker. Then, your savings, the broker's standard commission charge of 6 percent or 7 percent of the $100,000 selling price, comes to, not one or two thousands of dollars, but at least SIX THOUSAND, and possibly SEVEN THOUSAND DOLLARS ($6,000-$7,000)!! And this is only on a house selling for just $100,000, mind you. But wait a minute! Imagine what you'd be saving if the house in question is higher priced—say, $200,000, $500,000, $1,000,000 or greater!!

---

*This quotation, and much of the substance of this subject matter, is from HALT's booklet, "Real Estate," at pp. 40-41.

THE NATIONAL SCOPE—AND GOAL—OF THIS MANUAL

But that's not all. The financial benefits—and import—of this manual is not limited just to the individual home buyer or seller alone. It is diverse and potentially national in scope. There are an estimated 91 million parcels of real property in the United States, and about 9 million of that are transferred each year. In fact, one out of every five families moves every year. Hence, what it boils down to, is that as a practical matter, selling your home at the best price often goes hand in glove with buying a new one, later to be again sold for another home purchase to repeat the cycle over and then over and over again.

Fortunately for you, as a reader of this manual, and as a potential user of it in undertaking a home purchase or sale transaction, there's one not-always-available but comforting fact in this instance: the basic principles and procedures which govern the process involved in the subject matter at issue are essentially national in scope, essentially identical from state to state across the nation. Hence, this book has been carefully designed to be used, and is largely usable in, the buying or selling of any piece of real property in any state or locality in the nation.

HOW YOU SHOULD USE
THIS MANUAL

But one or two words of caution are called for. First, you must read through the manual, every word of every chapter (including the footnotes, especially!) from the beginning to the end, if you are to derive the most benefit from this publication. Do not just glance through or hastily skim around it or some select portions. Secondly, keep the book handy, get acquainted with and master its contents, and freely refer to it often, even after you've bought or sold the house in question. The point to always remember is that, fundamentally, much of this book is designed not so much to help you "solve" problems after they're underway, but to help you (through advance knowledge) "prevent" and "avoid" them—by not letting the problems arise at all, in the first place. (It's always good to be able to solve a problem, but much much better not to have to face the problem at all!)

LIST OF TABLES, CHARTS & FORMS: WHERE TO FIND THEM

Chapter 1

MUST YOU NECESSARILY BUY/SELL A HOUSE WITH A LAWYER OR A BROKER?

A. The Supposed Roles of the Lawyer and Broker in Real Estate Transfers

To begin with, what functions and purposes are the real estate lawyer and broker, respectively, meant to serve a buyer or seller?

In theory, at least, the rationale commonly advanced by real estate lawyers and other professionals in the field as justification for employing a lawyer in real estate transactions, is for the reason that the home buyer or seller needs to get some "legal advice" from the lawyer by which to "protect" oneself against the potential of falling into some financial and/or legal "pitfalls" in such a gigantic financial investment and commitment. Proponents and enthusiasts of the idea of using a lawyer in real estate transfer transactions would invariably note that, for most people, the purchase of a home would likely be the biggest investment they'll make in their lives, or at least the biggest one they've ever made to that date. And to hear the real estate lawyers and their enthusiasts tell it, just considering that fact alone is a sufficient justification warranting that everyone who contemplates buying (or

Illustration credit to Bill Kresse.

selling) a house should first run out and hire himself (or herself) a lawyer before venturing into it. Why? Because only by so doing, they say, can the buyer or seller ensure adequate "protection" from falling into some potential traps in a financial transaction of such awesome magnitude!

Robert G. Natelson, a Denver Colorado practicing real estate attorney and an obvious exponent of the great value of using a lawyer in real estate deals, sums up the conventional rationale this way: "...you are making one of life's larger purchases. You are locking yourself into a home or an important investment. You are subjecting yourself to an obligation (the mortgage loan) likely to last thirty years. Does it make any sense to be un-represented by counsel?"* Natelson added that the lawyer is necessarily needed in such transactions to "negotiate and draft non-standard documents and clauses, to review all documents for legal sufficiency and errors (preferably before the closing), and to attend the closing itself where he helps to guide it and explains to his client what is happening."

And as for the real estate broker? His classic function is primarily said to be that of acting as a 'go-between' between the prospective seller and the prospective buyer, that of bringing a "ready, willing and able" purchaser together with a seller and thereby making it possible for them to find each other to transact business in the buying or selling of a piece of real property. Nevertheless, in the same vein as the real estate lawyers, the real estate brokers, though not quite arrogating to themselves the same level of significance or sense of indispensability that the real estate lawyers ascribe to themselves in real estate deals, have come to promote the general professional idea that they, too, should—and must—necessarily be employed in the buying and selling of real estate, again all for the supposed buyer's or seller's own "protection' and best interest!!

Those are the conventional rationale, the "official line" traditionally advanced by advocates for the use of these two principal "professional middlemen" in real estate transactions. What, though, is the actual truth about it, about the usefulness—or indispensability—of these two middlemen in the buying or selling of real property? To put it slightly differently, what, if any, does one truly stand to lose—and, what is even more relevant, how likely is it that such a loss will actually occur in the average instance—when one goes it alone without using a lawyer, or without using a broker?

The best way to assess this central question is by answering these ones: What role do these middlemen, respectively, play in real estate transfers; where and when are they typically best-suited and most effective in real estate transfer matters, and where and when, on the other hand, are they not so endowed? And, just as relevantly, couldn't you find alternative channels that could serve you the same needs and just as effectively and competently—but at less cost and expense, and with less bureaucratic involvements?

B. Non-Lawyers Have Been Just as Competent in Providing Real Estate Services

As for the lawyer, this much is the commonly acknowledged and undisputed fact: that, by custom and by practice (and in some states, by law), the role of the lawyer in real estate transfers differs in varying parts of the nation; that while in some states and localities, (notably in the Eastern part of the country) the lawyers for both sides pretty much run the entire process from start to finish, *in other states and localities (notably in parts of the West, among them, states like Arizona, Arkansas, Michigan, Missouri, Minnesota, New Mexico, and Wisconsin) it is not the lawyers, but other non-lawyer entities such as brokers, financial institutions, and title companies, who actually run the real estate transfer show*—who prepare the deed, sales contract and other key legal documents, and undertake most negotiations and settlement tasks, and dominate the closings. As one study** summed it up, in such localities the "lawyer never gets any closer to the actual proceedings than drawing up a one-time, standard contract form for use by the realtor."

A study prepared by the reputable national accounting firm of Peat, Marwick, Mitchell & Company for the U.S. Department of Housing and Urban Development (H.U.D.) and released in October 1980, pretty much

---

*Cited from "How to Buy and Sell a Condominium" (Simon & Schuster), 1981, pp. 46 & 47.

**"Real Estate," by HALT, Inc., (1980), p. 6.

suggested that the role of the attorney in real estate transfers is by and large redundant and superfluous at least in certain parts of the country, and that alternatives abound which could—and do —provide the same services the lawyers provide just as competently and effectively.   Noting that the services provided by attorneys are principally in three general areas of the real estate settlement process: title assurance, conveyancing services (such as document preparation, settlement or closing, and escrow), and contract negotiations, the study* states that:

> ".other types of participants often perform all of these services. In fact, attorneys usually play little or no role in the real estate transfer process in the Western states.   However, in most Eastern states, their role is significant .... While many home buyers undoubtedly hire an attorney before they sign a contract, attorneys often enter the process only to perform title assurance and routine conveyancing services ... [and] these same services are often performed by non-attorneys such as title assurance companies, real estate brokers, and lenders...
> The report concluded: "We believe that attorneys have a unique role in providing advice and consultation to home buyers and sellers in their sales contracting.   However, other professionals can and do provide title assurance and conveyancing services in many market areas."

Fundamentally, for our purposes here, the truly relevant issue here, anyway, should not be what role the lawyer (or the broker) typically or traditionally plays—or would like to play— in the real estate transfer process. Rather, **the real question should be this:** WHETHER OR NOT THE LAWYER (OR THE BROKER) IS, IN FACT, SOLELY, UNIQUELY, AND MOST COST EFFECTIVELY BEST SUITED TO PLAY THE ROLE HE HAS TRADITIONALLY PLAYED TO DATE. Whether, in other words, you cannot yourself attain the same basic ends of buying or selling your home through alternative channels that would be just as effective in affording you all the necessary legal "protection"—while probably being less expensive and less involved?

The answer to this is rather simple. Look at it this way: isn't it an agreed fact—a reality—that in a significant portion of the country, it is not the lawyers, but the non-lawyer entities who handle almost all the so-called "legal" as well as non-legal work involved in real estate transfers? *And yet, for several generations after generations of such practice, the home-buyers and sellers in those areas of the country have never been heard to complain about not having been legally "protected," or about their having suffered any special risks or financial losses therefrom!* Obviously, then, this reality alone automatically gives the lie to the fiction typically bandied around by the real estate attorneys—to the effect that their participation in real estate deals supposedly provides some unique or special legal "protection" to the home buyer or seller.

As a **study by HALT,** a Washington D.C. legal reform organization, realistically sums it up, noting that most of the work involved in title searches and settlement is routinely performed by non-professionals and non-lawyers,

> "[the work involved] rarely consists of more than checklist verification and completion of standardized forms .... [Yet] despite the casual nature of the work actually performed [by professionals and non-professionals alike], **complications in property transfers rarely arise**... only a few percent of all property transfers develop complications, and those are usually resolved easily ... the incidence of complications in some areas is as low as 1 in 100,000."**

In deed, **in a famous November 1961 "test case" in the State of Arizona,** in which the State Bar of Arizona had earlier dragged one Mr. Ford Hoffman, then a Phoenix real estate broker and a non-lawyer, into court for supposedly committing the sin *of* "unauthorized practice of law" (he had drawn up for a home seller, free of charge, an Agreement of Sale, Warranty Deed, Quitclaim Deed, and Bill of Sale), the judges of **the state's Supreme Court,** though upholding the state bar's position against Hoffman and ruling that only lawyers could thereafter draft papers involved in the sale or purchase of real estate, nevertheless conceded that:

> "the record does not disclose any testimony regarding specific injury to the public from [these] practices [of non-lawyers drafting such documents"]***

---

*The Real Estate Settlement Procedures Act, Section 14a: The 1979-1980 Evaluation, Volume I: Executive Summary, (Peat, Marwick, Mitchell & Co.) pp. 111.10-111.12.

**"Real Estate," by HALT, Inc., Washington, D.C.: (1980), P. 40.

***Subsequent, however, to this ruling prohibiting lay persons from henceforth drafting such papers in Arizona, the people of the state were so outraged that they organized a voter-initiated referendum; the voters overwhelmingly overturned the decision of Arizona's highest court, and since November 1962, the Arizona realtors have had—and competently exercised — the authority to draft all legal papers in real estate transfers!

Then, there's another **similar later case decided in the State of New Mexico by** the state's **Supreme Court** in March 1978. There again, the State Bar of New Mexico had, as usual, dragged to court the state's Guardian Abstract & Title Company, Inc., a New Mexico abstract and title company which had for over 20 years done about 90% of all closings of real estate sales and loans in one county of the state, and had used non-lawyers to complete the standard printed forms of deeds, mortgages and other papers involved in the transactions. The lawyers' group charged the abstract company with the usual sin of engaging in "unauthorized practice of law." But there again, the New Mexico Supreme Court, though partially siding with the state bar's position against the abstract company on "the issue of giving legal advice" but not on the "issue of filling the forms," nevertheless admitted as follows:

> "There was no convincing evidence that the massive changeover in the performance of this service [of drafting the forms needed in real estate transactions] from attorneys to the title companies during the past several years, has been accompanied by any great loss, detriment or inconvenience to the public. **[On the other hand, actually] the uncontroverted evidence was that using lawyers for this simple operation considerably slowed the loan closings and cost the persons involved a great deal of money [more]."**

The point we make here is that there is nothing, absolutely NOTHING, particularly complex or intrinsic about real estate transfers which makes it necessary—or necessarily wiser or more advisable, from the standpoint of the relative costs and benefits— that a lawyer be generally used in such transactions. And the same can, of course, be just as forcefully said about the broker's place in real estate transfers: it's obvious that a house for sale cannot possibly be found only through a broker's listing, nor can a broker's listing be the only possible source through which a prospective seller can find a prospective buyer. Such could be—and are—just as easily accomplished daily across the nation by word of mouth *or* through newspaper ads, or through a sign out front, etc.—and at far less costs to the seller and buyer! The fact that the lawyer or the broker has come to be commonly employed in such matters all across the nation is simply a practice borne out of centuries of habit and custom—not to be mistaken as being out of any vital necessity. To put it another way, the fact that a given practice has, over a period of time, become a fixture or habit of society, does not, in and of itself, necessarily or automatically imbue that practice with validity, or make it a necessary or natural one!

C. The Areas of Legitimate Lawyer/Broker Usefulness in Real Estate Deals

It is not to say, though, that there are no instances where, or situations when, the lawyer or broker, respectively, may have a proper and legitimate role to play in the transfer of real estate; it is not to say that there aren't some tasks or aspects of the home transfer process in which these middlemen may be, and are often, genuinely useful. Not at all!

As a general proposition, depending on which other entities may be involved in a given real estate transaction, and what role such other entities (e.g., the title insurance underwriter, the broker, the escrow agent company, etc.) play on your behalf, an attorney—an experienced, real estate attorney!—can certainly play a genuinely legitimate and necessary role in the area of "looking over" or reviewing the key legal papers involved in property transfers— especially the Contract of Sale and deed documents, and in offering you his legal advise or opinion on the terms, conditions, and implications of the provisions contained therein in advance of the negotiations and signing. *When it comes, however, to such matters as picking the right home, setting a home's selling price, evaluating the structural quality of a home, negotiating the price and other conditions of sale, knowledge of available range of home financing plans and mortgage terms, and the like, the average lawyer who pretends to be knowledgeable in such matters, or chooses to arrogate to himself such duties, shall have ventured beyond his legitimate territory into an arena often beyond his scope of competence even for a lawyer with a modest practice in real estate transfers!*

A real estate broker, on the other hand, can be very useful in certain other areas of importance in home sale or purchase, quite aside from his services in helping you find a home or a buyer. More especially for the seller, the broker can be useful in the screening of prospective buyers to eliminate the ineligible or the non-serious ones; he can be very useful in the area of helping you set an attractive or more realistic asking price for the house, and advice you as to whether to accept a lower offer; he can assist you in arranging various kinds of financing to make a sale possible, and, inasmuch as the average practicing broker is typically a consumate salesman often possessing an intimate technical knowledge of the structure and market value of landed property, the broker may be able to present your property more attractively to prospective buyers than you could, highlighting its good qualities and minimizing the bad.

Most lawyers, even those experienced and actively engaged in real estate practice, concede that they generally lack much detailed technical knowledge of the real market conditions, and still less about the sales value of a property or other vital matters involved in the buying or selling of a home, such as the picking of a home or the financing of it.

As **Walter L. Kantrowitz,** a New York real estate lawyer, candidly put it, "Choosing your home is not something your attorney normally gets involved in—unless you happen to be married to one, the lawyer enters only after you've made up your mind."

Another view, a report widely respected and followed by legal professionals, is even more blunt in assessing the limits of the lawyer's range of competence in real estate transfers: "It is a better part of wisdom" the report advised, "for the attorney to refrain from expressing any opinions upon the business aspects of the transactions; whether the price is a good one, whether the house is well built, and questions of this kind are not only not the job but are generally beyond the scope of his competence."*

The real estate broker, on the other hand, is generally conceded by most professionals in the field to be the relative expert in the basic technical or market information vital in the conduct of real estate deals, and given the reality that the average person knows just about little or nothing about real estate, this is one area where the broker may be most useful to a buyer and/or a seller.

Certainly, then, both the lawyer and the broker have their legitimate places and areas of competence and usefulness in real estate transfer transactions. It is only when they refuse to confine themselves to such roles, or attempt to overstate the real value of their role, or to arrogate to themselves a status of indispensability or exclusivity in the transfer process, that they step beyond the bounds of legitimacy—and must be stopped!

---

*West McKinney's Forms, Real Estate Property Practice, Vol. II, (1967), Section 1.03, p. 8.

Chapter 2
ARE YOU BUYING? FIRST DETERMINE THE TYPE OF HOUSE AND NEIGHBORHOOD YOU CAN ACTUALLY AFFORD

A. First, Estimate The Home Price Range That's Right For Your Income Bracket: The Type Of House You Can Afford

How much can I afford to spend for a house? What home price range should I realistically aim my sight at? These are among the very first questions you should ask yourself—even before you start looking for a house, or looking at one. You should have a fairly good idea of the answers to these questions before anything else. And, armed with this knowledge, you will be saving yourself valuable time and effort in looking for a house to buy because you won't then have to even bother with those you can't possibly afford. Instead, you can just limit your efforts to those you can reasonably afford.

Indeed, this process—of determining in advance what type of home you can afford—is the flip side of what's known in the mortgage banking trade as "pre qualification": advanced determination of how large a mortgage you can probably afford. Consequently, both concepts—the question of how large a mortgage you'll require and the price of the home you can afford—will be treated as one and the same problem here, since having an idea of how large a mortgage you can afford will, in turn, directly determine the price of the home you can afford.

B. Some Rules-Of-Thumb Formulas

How do you determine how much home value you can afford?

There are many so-called "rules of thumb" which loan agents use to officially qualify buyers. And such rules, though by no means definitive but only a rough guideline, could be helpful in giving you a fairly realistic idea of the kinds of houses you can possibly afford.

1. Method One

One rule of thumb by which lenders, housing financiers, and real estate professionals have generally attempted to determine the kind of house a buyer can afford is this: a person can afford that kind of house which costs no more than 3 times the person's yearly gross (before tax) income. (Thus, for example, for someone [or a household] making a net income of $30,000 a year, the kind of house he could possibly afford, by this guideline, would be worth $30,000 x 3, or $90,000.)

2. Method Two

Another rule of thumb guideline is: the combined monthly payments on a house (the monthly mortgage payment, plus the monthly taxes, house insurance premium, and average insurance premium) should be less than 1 week's take home (after tax) income of the prospective homebuyer.

EXAMPLE: say you require a $120,000 mortgage, and that your terms of borrowing at the time are interest rate at 9 percent for a 30 year term. Hence, from the mortgage amortization payment tables (see Table 2.1 on p. 7) your monthly mortgage payment on $120,000 would be $866. Assume your projected or actual other expenses

FIGURE 2.1

EQUAL MONTHLY PAYMENT TO AMORTIZE A LOAN OF $1,000

Mortgage Factor Chart

Term Rate %	10 Years	15 Years	20 Years	25 Years	30 Years
4	10.13	7.40	6.06	5.28	4.78
4 1/8	10.19	7.46	6.13	5.35	4.85
4 1/4	10.25	7.53	6.20	5.42	4.92
4 3/8	10.31	7.59	6.26	5.49	5.00
4 1/2	10.37	7.65	6.33	5.56	5.07
4 5/8	10.43	7.72	6.40	5.63	5.15
4 3/4	10.49	7.78	6.47	5.71	5.22
4 7/8	10.55	7.85	6.54	5.78	5.30
5	10.61	7.91	6.60	5.85	5.37
5 1/8	10.67	7.98	6.67	5.92	5.45
5 1/4	10.73	8.04	6.74	6.00	5.53
5 3/8	10.80	8.11	6.81	6.07	5.60
5 1/2	10.86	8.18	6.88	6.15	5.68
5 5/8	10.92	8.24	6.95	6.22	5.76
5 3/4	10.98	8.31	7.03	6.30	5.84
5 7/8	11.04	8.38	7.10	6.37	5.92
6	11.10	8.44	7.16	6.44	6.00
6 1/8	11.16	8.51	7.24	6.52	6.08
6 1/4	11.23	8.57	7.31	6.60	6.16
6 3/8	11.29	8.64	7.38	6.67	6.24
6 1/2	11.35	8.71	7.46	6.75	6.32
6 5/8	11.42	8.78	7.53	6.83	6.40
6 3/4	11.48	8.85	7.60	6.91	6.49
6 7/8	11.55	8.92	7.68	6.99	6.57
7	11.61	8.98	7.75	7.06	6.65
7 1/8	11.68	9.06	7.83	7.15	6.74
7 1/4	11.74	9.12	7.90	7.22	6.82
7 3/8	11.81	9.20	7.98	7.31	6.91
7 1/2	11.87	9.27	8.05	7.38	6.99
7 5/8	11.94	9.34	8.13	7.47	7.08
7 3/4	12.00	9.41	8.20	7.55	7.16
7 7/8	12.07	9.48	8.29	7.64	7.25
8	12.14	9.56	8.37	7.72	7.34
8 1/8	12.20	9.63	8.45	7.81	7.43
8 1/4	12.27	9.71	8.53	7.89	7.52
8 3/8	12.34	9.78	8.60	7.97	7.61
8 1/2	12.40	9.85	8.68	8.06	7.69
8 5/8	12.47	9.93	8.76	8.14	7.78
8 3/4	12.54	10.00	8.84	8.23	7.87
8 7/8	12.61	10.07	8.92	8.31	7.96
9	12.67	10.15	9.00	8.40	8.05
9 1/8	12.74	10.22	9.08	8.48	8.14
9 1/4	12.81	10.30	9.16	8.57	8.23
9 3/8	12.88	10.37	9.24	8.66	8.32
9 1/2	12.94	10.45	9.33	8.74	8.41
9 5/8	13.01	10.52	9.41	8.83	8.50
9 3/4	13.08	10.60	9.49	8.92	8.60
9 7/8	13.15	10.67	9.57	9.00	8.69
10	13.22	10.75	9.66	9.09	8.78
10 1/8	13.29	10.83	9.74	9.18	8.87
10 1/4	13.36	10.90	9.82	9.27	8.97
10 3/8	13.43	10.98	9.90	9.36	9.06
10 1/2	13.50	11.06	9.99	9.45	9.15
10 5/8	13.57	11.14	10.07	9.54	9.25
10 3/4	13.64	11.21	10.16	9.63	9.34

FIGURE 2.2

Buyer Qualification Computation Chart

Enter the Purchase Price:_____ Mortgage Interest Rate:_____

			YEARS TO REPAY LOAN			
				20	25	30
DOWN	1. In Percent					
PAYMENT	2. In Dollars					
3. Loan Total (Home price, less the down payment)						
4. Monthly Payment on loan: [Work out from Fig. 2.1]						
5. Monthly Taxes and Insurance (From Fig. 6.9)						
6. Utilities, Monthly Average (Get from Fig. 6.9)						
7. Total Monthly Expenses [Add columns 4, 5 and 6]						
8. Yearly Payment (Housing Cost) [Column 7 x 12]						
9. The Required Buyer's Minimum Yearly Salary [Column 8 x 4]*						

The first column heading is blank so you can insert any specific payment period you may desire.
*Column 8 multiplied by 4.

are as follows: yearly taxes on the house $960; monthly utilities average $100; and yearly home insurance premium $480. Your monthly expense picture on the house would be as follows:

Mortgage payment per month	$866.00
Taxes per month ($960 divided by 12)	80.00
Utilities average per month	100.00
Insurance expense per month ($480 divided by 12)	40.00
	$1,086.00

Thus, under this guideline, to be able to afford the $120,000 mortgage, you (the home buyer) should be making a take home income of $1,086.00 per week, or better.

To apply this rule of thumb to any particular case (yours or anybody else's), first use the Fact Sheet (Figure 6.9 on p. 110) to assemble your figures on the relevant data (the tax expenses, utilities, insurances, etc...) on the house. Then simply use Figure 2.2 above to make the computation. From the mortgage amortization payment table (Figure 2.1 on p. 7), you find the amount a buyer must pay per month for each $1,000 of the loan amount, then multiply this amount by the number of thousands contained in Line 3 of Figure 2.2. Enter this in Line 4. Finally, the yearly payment on the house (Line 8) multiplied by 4, gives you the minimum yearly take-home income the buyer (borrower) must earn to be able to afford the house (Line 9).

Note that this qualification method can also be worked in reverse. First, you start with the proposed borrower's (buyer's) yearly income on Line 9 and divide by 4, you have Line 8. Divide Line 8 by 12, giving you Line 7, which is the total monthly expenses the party can afford. By subtracting Lines 5 and 6 amounts from Line 7, you get Line 4 — the monthly payment this party can afford on a house.

You may repeat this procedure a number of different times with different down payments and loan repayment periods for your available interest rate. You'll get the maximum loan a buyer can make and be able to buy a particular house based on the person's specific salary. This then gives you the down payment the prospective buyer has to come up with to be able to buy the given house.

3. Method Three

Another rule of thumb (guideline), probably the most common method used nowadays for roughly qualifying mortgage applicants, is something called the *"28/36 ratio" rule.* Under this rule, the "28" figure refers to how much (what percentage) of your gross income may be spent on your mortgage payment; and the "36" figure refers to the percentage of your monthly gross income that your total debts may not exceed. To put it another way, basically, this rule says, first, that only 28% (no more than 28%) of your monthly gross income may go towards the mortgage; and, second, that your total, combined debts—the mortgage payment, plus all your other major debts*—may not exceed 36% of your monthly gross income. (Where you don't know what the real estate taxes and insurance expense costs are, simply ask a knowledgeable Realtor in the area).

*The other debts which are usually includable in calculating the "total" debt, apart from the principal and interest on the mortgage loan, are the following: property taxes and insurance, auto loans, student loans, child support, alimony, and debts that will have more than 10 months to run. Credit card debts are usually not counted with this category (unless the party has a lot of them), and regular household costs, such as household utility bills or rents are also excluded.

To use this method to qualify any particular case, simply use the Pre-qualifier Worksheet (Figure 2.3) below, and the table on p. 7 (Table 2.1) to make the computation.

PRE-QUALIFIER WORKSHEET—Figure 2.3

(All figures are estimates rounded to the nearest dollar amounts).

1. Monthly Real Estate Tax and Homeowners Insurance Payments (annual amount divided by 12). $_____

2. Monthly Installment Payments (auto loans, child support, alimony, student loans,
   but not monthly household costs). $_____

3. Monthly Gross Income (including alimony and dividends for party or parties). $_____

4. Multiply the Monthly Gross Income (Line 3) by 0.28 ———>   = $_____
   Subtract the Monthly Real Estate Tax and Homeowners Insurance Payments (Line 1)—-—>   = $_____

5. ....*Amount A* = $_____

6. Multiply the Monthly Gross Income (Line 3) by 0.36 ———>   = $_____
   Subtract the total of the Monthly Real Estate Tax and Homeowners Insurance Payments
   and the Monthly Installment Payments (Lines 1 & 2). ————>   = $_____

7. ....*Amount B* = $_____

The lesser of the above two amounts, Amount A and Amount B, is the approximate monthly mortgage payment for which you can qualify.

4. Method Four

Another rule of thumb guideline, attempts to gauge the house "affordability" for a given buyer — the approximate home purchase price that you (a would-be buyer) can afford. The formula is the same principle as the so-called "28/36" ratio employed in Method Three above, but with a slight twist.

To use this method to pre qualify any particular case, simply use the Affordability Worksheet on p. 10 (Figure 2.4), along with the table on p. 7 (Table 2.1) to make the computation. Line 16 in Figure 2.4 gives the approximate purchase price the buyer can afford.

FIGURE 2.4
The Affordability Worksheet

(1) Enter your monthly gross income (yours and a co-borrower's combined) $_____

(2) Multiply the amount from line 1 by 0.28 $_____

(3) Multiply the amount from line 1 by 0.36 $_____

(4) Enter estimated monthly real estate tax (may get from Fig. 6.8 or inquire with area realtor
   or local tax assesor's office) $_____

(5) Enter estimated monthly homeowners insurance payment (may discuss $_____
   coverage needed with qualified insurance agents or get from Fig. 6.9)

(6) Enter other monthly installment payments (debts with 6 or more months to run, $_____
   e.g., auto loans, child support, major credit card or revolving credit balances. Exclude household costs
   (utilities, phone bills, etc.)

(7) Add lines 4 and 5 and round the result to nearest dollar amount $_____

(8) Add lines 6 and 7 and round the result to nearest dollar amount $_____

(9) Subtract line 7 from line 2 $_____

(10) Subtract line 8 from line 3 $_____

(11) Determine mortgage interest rates by asking your realtor, or lenders, $_____
   and then look at the Monthly payment table (Fig. 2.1). Use the interest rate
   in the Term Rate % column and follow across the page until you reach the
   Term that you prefer. Enter the monthly payment amount.

(12) Look at lines 9 and 10. Enter the amount of whichever line is less. $_____
   This is the approximate monthly payment that you can qualify for.

(13) Divide line 12 by line 11. Enter the number. $_____

(14) Multiply line 13 by 1000.00 and round the result to the nearest dollar amount $_____
   This is the approximate mortgage amount your lender will allow you to borrow.

(15) Enter amount available for down payment. $_____

(16) Add lines 14 and 15. The result is the approximate purchase price you can $_____
   afford.

can you afford it?

NOTE: Bear in mind that the results of these calculations, whichever of the above three methods used, is only a rough estimate. The final judgment and qualification must usually be made by a loan company to whom the prospective home buyer ultimately applies. The point of this "pre-qualification" calculation is primarily to have some idea, a reasonable measure, of your (the prospective buyer's) ability to borrow, how large a mortgage you can afford, at what rate, and how long. This way, the dreamers who cannot possibly qualify financially and have no business bidding on a house of a given value can be eliminated before hand!

FIGURE 2.5

Worksheet For Figuring Your Net Worth

WHEN YOU GO TO A LENDER TO APPLY FOR A MORTGAGE LOAN, YOU SHOULD BE PREPARED TO ANSWER A NUMBER OF QUESTIONS ABOUT YOUR FINANCIAL SITUATION. THIS WORKSHEET WILL HELP PREPARE YOU TO ANSWER SOME OF THOSE QUESTIONS.

INFORMATION ON YOUR ASSETS

LIST ALL YOUR ASSETS. Include any of the following:

<u>Assets</u>	VALUE
● Amount you now have in Savings Account(s)	$_____
● Cash on hand (in cash or checking account)	$_____
● Stocks, bonds, life insurance policies (give current market value or actual cash value)	$_____
● Real Estate you now own (give assessed market value or price paid)	$_____
● Automobile(s) (give the book value for make, model, and year of the car)	$_____
● Household furnishings (give the value of all items including furniture, silverware, carpets, paintings, T.V.'s, stereo, other appliances)	$_____
● Jewelry, antiques, furs (give appraised value)	$_____
● Other items of value (for example, boat, trailer, bike, etc.)	$_____
● Amount of money owed to you (IOU's, tax refunds, etc.)	$_____
● Other	$_____
TOTAL ASSETS	$_____

WHEN YOU KNOW THE APPROXIMATE VALUE OF YOUR ASSETS YOU WILL ALSO WANT TO KNOW WHAT YOUR LIABILITIES ARE; THAT IS, ALL THE OUTSTANDING DEBTS YOU OWE TO OTHER PEOPLE. SEE THE NEXT PAGE.

FIGURE 2.6

Worksheet For Figuring Your Liabilities

YOU WILL WANT TO LIST THE *TOTAL AMOUNT OWED* TO AN INDIVIDUAL CREDITOR
(BUT *NOT YOUR MONTHLY PAYMENT* TO THE CREDITOR).

Liabilities
PERSON OR INSTITUTION TO WHOM
MONEY IS OWED (CREDITOR)

	TOTAL AMOUNT NOW OWED
Personal loans from Banks or Finance Companies	$
Automobile loans	$
Installment Accounts (charge accounts, credit cards, department stores, revolving accounts)	$
Medical/dental bills due (including hospital)	$
School (tuition, education loan)	$
Real Estate loans	$
Personal loan from relatives or friends	$
Other debts now owed or bills not paid	$
TOTAL LIABILITIES	$

SUBTRACT THE AMOUNT OF YOUR *LIABILITIES* FROM YOUR TOTAL *ASSETS* (bottom of preceding page) TO ARRIVE AT THE FIGURE FOR YOUR *NET WORTH*.

TOTAL ASSETS (Fig. 2.5) $

less TOTAL LIABILITIES (above) $

equals NET WORTH $

THIS WILL GIVE YOU AN IDEA OF YOUR PRESENT INDEBTEDNESS,
AND HELP YOU DETERMINE HOW MUCH MORE FINANCIAL BURDEN YOU
CAN HANDLE.

Chapter 3
LET'S SEARCH FOR THE PROPER HOUSE, NEIGHBORHOOD, AND/OR BROKER FOR YOU

A. Consider What Kind of House and Neighborhood You Want

Having first figured out what kind of home price range you ought to have your sight on (the subject matter of the preceding Chapter 2), your next order of business—before you actually set about searching for a house—is to consider the kind of house, neighborhood characteristics, and other factors you can live with—within the limits imposed by the kind of price range you fall under.

HERE ARE THE MAJOR FACTORS TO BE CONSIDERED:

•The Nature of the Community

•Taxes (remember that taxes are determined by both the tax rate and the property valuation practices of the given locality's assessors alone, and that these rates and practices widely differ from locality to locality.)

•The area's zoning laws and practices.　[What type of houses—one-family or multiple-family, commercial or residential, or both, etc.—are permitted? Does the community permit easy variances in zoning laws?　Are industrial and commercial buildings permitted near your house? Are conversions allowed? Etc.]

•The neighborhood—the location, the surroundings, the type of people who live there and their economic/social level; accessibility of the location to schools, shopping centers, public transportation, etc. *[Experts assert that the 'neighborhood' factor is the single most important factor to consider in picking a home.]*

•Do you want a new or old house?　A single family house or one with rental units? Or a condominium?

[See Figure 3.1, "NEIGHBORHOOD INSPECTION CHECKLIST" on p. 20 below]

B. Now, Search for the Right House for You

Having determined the type of house you can afford (Chapter 2 at pp. 6-12), and considered the kinds of housing and neighborhood characteristics you can live with within your budget range (Section A above), you are now finally ready to begin THE SEARCH FOR THE RIGHT HOUSE TO BUY.

1. The Three Basic Channels for Searching for a House

There are various ways by which you could shop for a house that is right for you and your family. Among such ways, are these three principal avenues by which houses are found or sold:

 i) through real estate advertisements contained in newspapers and magazines;
 ii) through real estate brokers; and
 iii) through direct purchase from the home owner.

In so far as a buyer (as opposed to a seller) is concerned, it really wouldn't matter from which source he makes his purchase or his find, providing the house at issue is the right one for him, and the price and terms of purchase are right. For one thing, it wouldn't matter whether he uses a broker as his source for finding the house to buy, since he wouldn't have to pay any fees or commission for the service, anyway, as the common rule is that it is only the property seller that pays the broker's commission. A wise approach would be to use <u>all three</u> sources as fully as possible in searching for a house—you are exposed to more opportunities and to a wider variety and options, this way!

2. The Advantages Of Using A Good Real Estate Broker In Finding Your Prospective House

If, eventually, you must make your purchase through a broker—and chances are that you probably would, since the overwhelming majority of home purchases (about 80%) are ultimately made through brokers—it is most essential that you be prepared to pick the right broker, and that you use the broker's services wisely. In deed, for a buyer—a wise buyer—***THE USE OF A GOOD BROKER FOR HELP IN FINDING A HOUSE COULD BE VERY USEFUL AND ADVANTAGEOUS:*** the broker is often quite knowledgeable in the real property values of his area of operation and you can learn a lot from him about the general market conditions of the area's property, about what property is available and what they are really worth, about the general state and characteristics of the neighborhood, about what comparative property in the area has sold for in the recent past, and about what kinds of financing is available and where you stand in terms of being able to qualify for a purchase loan with the lenders, and much more.

Also, many of the larger brokers and brokerage chains provide an extensive, often computerized promotional and publicity networks, including newspaper and radio ads and, for those members which belong, the **Multiple Listing System (MLS).** Through such vast network systems (they include names like Match Maker, Electronic Realty Associates, Red Carpet, Better Homes & Gardens, Century 21, Partners, Re/Max, and Realty World), a prospective buyer in, say, New York, who wants to relocate to Houston, Texas, can learn of the listings in Houston without ever having left New York, thereby making for a wider, faster and easier matching of buyer and seller and on a national market.

Furthermore, since it is ultimately in the broker's interest that you make a purchase (he gets to collect his commission from the seller only if you make a purchase!), he frequently serves another important function which might prove just as relevant for you: that of helping you in the negotiating process with the seller, back and forth, on the terms and conditions of sale. Indeed, as we shall see in the chapters ahead [see, especially pp. 25-6], the role of a competent broker in being able to uncover and provide insight into the underlying "need to sell" situation of a home owner, the underlying needs that motivate him (or her) to put up his house for sale, is often crucial in enabling a buyer make intelligent negotiations with the home owner and to secure a property on a favorable and affordable financing or other terms. [See Chapter 4 and pp. 123-131, for the negotiations phase of the home purchase process, and for more on the role of the broker in that.]

don't hesitate, ask Questions!

*Finally, aside from every other consideration by the home-buyer, for most people buying under today's market conditions, **there has probably emerged one overriding consideration in making the selection of a broker: the broker's ability to aid you in your financing needs**—how much expertise, experience, and ability the broker commands in locating sources of financing, and in packaging and arranging a feasible financing deal for you, the home buyer!* One report* by the New York Times pointedly put it this way:

> "Because persistently high interest rates have put a crimp in the housing market, a home owner's choice of the right real estate agent can be crucial…Today, the best [real estate sales] agent may be someone who can skillfully maneuver buyers and sellers through the intricacies of 'creative financing'.*"

The report quoted a past president of the New Jersey Association of Realtors and Sales Manager of a Wayne, New Jersey real estate agency, Norman N. Kailo of the Soldoveri Agency: "There are at least 40 different ways of financing a sale [today], and if an agent can't name at least 10 right off the bat, you might want to find someone else."

In sum , in the final analysis, even as a buyer (or a seller), a good broker will save you both time and money in a host of ways. He will make one of the better efforts to discover your specific needs and could have the listings that will fit those needs. He will know about local financing sources and creative financial techniques, and will be able effectively to negotiate your needs with the seller or home owner, and to literally "sell" your offer to the home owner. He can help smooth the way in your dealings with appraisers, home inspectors, lawyers, town officials, escrow agents, home closing agents, and other parties that may be involved in a home sale arrangement.

3. General Pointers for Finding the Right House

Closely follow the following tips in looking for the proper house to buy or the proper broker to use, and you shall have likely selected the right house for yourself, in the end:

• In searching for property, peruse the advertisements in both the "classified ads" and the "real estate" sections of *two basic types* of newspapers: a large metropolitan newspaper covering the area (e.g., the N.Y. Times, the L.A. Times or the Washington Post), as well as a strictly local paper.

• The Federal Department of Commerce reports that 1 in 3 homes sell without the intervention of a broker. Hence, the point is that in searching for a house to buy (or to sell) you cannot afford not to take into account the great potential for business outside the traditional brokerage community. Look for the many sources of support and promotion of the for-sale-by-owner concept in your area for which there is a growing number in recent years. For example:
—there are those mortgage lenders who offer free marketing videos and help with qualifying prospective home buyers and arranging the loan.
—search through cable TV access channels for personally made videos, electronic billboards (like the one run by American Online and Prodigy) for sources of home-for-sale information.
—there has been an exploding growth of regional give-away publications exclusively geared to advertising for-sale-by-owner properties. In the New York-New Jersey Metropolitan regions, for example, they include: For Sale By Owner, based in Coram, L.I., Hill's For Sale By Owner, based in Poughkeepsie, N.Y., FSBO Homes of New Jersey, based in Toms River, N.J., and For Sale By Owner Connection, based in Canton, Conn. [Nationally, there are now over 150 such publications. The publishers' National Trade Group, called By Owner Real Estate Association of America, can be reached as follows: Picket Fence Productions, Burlington, Vt., (802) 660-3167.]

• Let your friends and neighbors know that you are house hunting. Then take your time in shopping the market.

• Visit as many houses as possible and compare prices, housing features, and neighborhood conditions.

• Take a Sunday afternoon drive or a walk through the neighborhoods you desire. You may locate a few "House for Sale" signs and model homes on display.

"How to Choose a Real Estate Agent," The N.Y. Times, Sunday, Oct. 18, 1981.

- Be thorough in your search, visit the house that appeals to you as many times as possible —two, three, four, or more times, and look it over and over.

- Inspect the house during the day, as well as at night (and also when it is raining, and/or snowing, if possible.)

- Check with all important sources of information—friends and relatives, real estate brokers, newspapers, people at work, neighborhood residents, supermarket bulletin boards, community organizations, City Hall (about taxes, schools, etc.), lenders in the area (for recent sales prices, etc.)

- *Ask questions, more questions, and still more questions* of the home owner, the seller or the broker, about the house—when it was built and bought, why the sale was being made, how long the house has been on the market, what major structural work have had to be done on the house and when and why, how much the owner had bought the property for, the major problems in the neighborhood, etc., etc?

4. General Pointers For Finding The Right Broker Who May Help You In Finding The Right House

- In looking for a good real estate broker, ask for recommendations by friends who have used the services of one, or call the mortgage officers of local banks and savings-and-loan associations. Notice which brokers run the most newspaper ads for the kind of houses you have in mind and in the desired neighborhood. (Of course, if all you are interested in is finding any real estate broker whatsoever, you can always find one in the local Yellow Pages under the heading "Broker" or "Real Estate"!)

- Remember, that, *as a buyer, the kind of sellers you are primarily interested in finding are sellers who are in a "need-to-sell" situation*—cases where the home owner/seller is under some degree of pressure to sell, such as a marriage, or business split-up, deteriorating physical health, job opportunities or relocation to another community, etc. Hence, your best prospect is to look for real estate brokers who are experienced in the specific geographical area you are interested in. Such a broker will usually have important exclusive listings and would be in a favorable position to hear about *need-to-sell* situations as they come on the market—in many cases even <u>before</u> they come on the market. But, be careful to make the proper distinction and selection. You've got to pick the big, successful, well-established brokerage firms. But, within the firms, themselves, you've also got to try to work with a broker or sales agent who has a depth of professional experience in both the area you're interested in and the type of housing situation you are looking for, rather than someone new to real estate or new to the community. (Pointer: simply ask the brokerage firm's manager for the name of the most successful real estate broker or salesperson in the organization, the top among the 20% of the sales force who usually make 80% of the sales. Such "crackerjack" salesperson is most likely to have the experience, know-how, or the drive, persistence, and negotiating skill to help you.)

  *For the particular agent you pick to work with in the firm, insist on a specific answer to the question of whether the agent sells property **full-time**. You want someone who puts in 40 hours a week or more, whose sole means of livelihood is real estate selling.*

- You can use the internal structure of a brokerage firm for a clue in gauging whether that's the kind of brokerage firm you should choose. The ideal one is a fairly large firm that has a large budget (this way it will be able to continue advertising in a slow market and not cut back); one that has lots of agents (the more agents, usually the more contacts and leads they will have, and the more homes and buyers and sellers they will have.) The firm should advertise a lot (a broker who advertises houses heavily week after week is sure to develop a list of prospective buyers than one who doesn't.)

  Visit any brokerage firm you're interested in. Is the office open at nights and on weekends? Are the agents actually working, or are they just reading newspapers or chatting around? Telephone the brokerage houses and inquire about the kind of house (describe it) you're interested in. Does the sales agent who comes to the phone try to sell you another house (as a good salesperson rightly should) if you say the house offered or advertised is too expensive or not to your liking?

- As stated above, as a buyer, your primary home buying need is to find a need-to-sell situation. In addition, you also want to be able to find an *affordable* house that will allow you some sort of creative financing. To be able to get this, you will be best served to work with many brokers—as many as you feel you can. By making your needs known to several brokers who have a depth of experience about the community you are interested in, as well as experience with creative financing and the art of negotiating, you directly multiply your chances of finding what you are looking for several times over.

- Check (ask the broker, if you have to), the type of listing arrangement a broker has on most houses he (she) has in his listing inventory—is it *"Exclusive Right To Sell"* arrangement, or *"Exclusive Listing,"* or *"Open Listing"*? ("Exclusive right to sell" listing means that the broker will have the exclusive right to sell the property, subject to the rate of the commission and conditions specified, and the broker will be entitled to a commission whether he sells the property or the home owner sells it; "exclusive" listing provides that the owner has the right to sell the property himself without having to pay a commission to the listing broker; and "open" listing is a listing that is as open to as many brokers as the home seller wishes).

  In the home sale business, houses for sale are a broker's stock-in-trade, and the listings are said to be "the very lifeblood" of a growing real estate office. Hence, if you find that a brokerage firm's listed inventory of homes consists mostly of Exclusive-Right-To-Sell listing, that's a good indication that the firm is probably a well-established broker since brokers who enter into such an arrangement are those with the financial security to plan a full-scale marketing program to sell the property. (The seasoned broker with exclusive listings on realistically priced property, will work hardest to sell property his own firm has listed (exclusive listing), since he doesn't have to share his commission with another firm. Furthermore, it's not just a matter of his trying to win the entire commission—it's a matter of pride.) If, on the other hand, a broker's listing consists mostly of the third type, the Open listings, or multiple listing or co-broker listings, or if the broker has next to nothing in the way of a listing inventory of homes for sale, that's not the kind of broker you should want to deal with— he (she) has been shut out of the all-important exclusive listings that invariably go to the established, respected local firms with a reputation for a solid sales performance, hence he probably is either too new or has some other problems preventing his firm from getting the all-important listing of the right type.

  Thirdly, if a brokerage firm doesn't belong to the local Multiple Listing Sevice, unless it can give you a good reason why it doesn't, you should pass it by. Such a firm won't have access to as many of the serious buyers in the area as will a firm that does belong to the multiple-listing service. A Multiple Listing Service is a system whereby agents from competing firms cooperate in selling all houses in the area in return for a sharing of the commission.

- Check the broker's listing in terms of its prices. Are the vast majority of his listings overpriced? If so, that's a good signal that that's the wrong broker for you. That's an indication either that there's a lack of knowledge on the broker's part about the current market values, or worse yet, that he might be one among the little crop of the overzealous but dishonest brokers, who, in their desire to get listings, will list a house well above current market prices in order to satisfy the sellers unrealistic desire to make a killing in the sale of his home.

- The agent or broker you need is not a high-pressure, promoter salesman type—one who is interested only in the "fast buck and the fast sale," and is interested in pushing the buyer (or even the seller) into something that fits his (the broker's) own needs, but not necessarily the buyer's needs. You need an agent who inspires confidence, but not necessarily by being a fast-talker.

  How do you make this differentiation? It's simple. If, for example, the buyer says "Hey, this house doesn't have a living room," the fast-talker type will say, "One less room for you to clean," explains one expert. The agent who inspires confidence will say, "That's true, and I know you'd prefer a house with a separate living room, rather than a combined living room/dining room, but that's why this house is so reasonably priced. You might pay $40,000 more for a house like this if it had a separate living room. That would make your monthly payments a lot higher, wouldn't it?' "

- Real estate is not unlike any other area of business. It has its own share of people who lack personal ethics and integrity. And it will be your task to seek out those brokers who not only have the needed experience, but possess integrity. There are several ways you can size up a broker concerning this. Simply look to the way he deals with you. Does he come on or across as a fast-talking promoter? Does he make exaggerated claims? Does he make deceitful or misleading statements or indicate devious or unethical tactics? For example, if a broker engages in what is generally known as "puffing"—i.e., overselling—beware. That's a red flag, as when a broker tells you, for example, that the schools in the district are "the best in the country," or that the house he's showing you is "the most fantastic buy" he'd ever handled. Double-check him! Visit the schools and talk to the principal, for example, or ask the neighbors. If you can, while you are in the broker's office, listen to what and how he (or others who work with him) say to other brokers or customers on the telephone. Is the broker one who is always advertising unbelievable home sales and financial deals that always seem to vanish when you (or other customers) get to his office—the old "bait and switch" tactic, where the prospect is lured in with a sweet offer and then switched into "the better model for you"!? Be warned. That's a red flag.

- Does the broker generally take the time to ask you questions about your needs? Or, does his main thrust simply seem to be to persuade you to buy (or to sell, as the case may be) where he can make the bigger commission, rather than to fit your own needs?

- When it comes time for you to visit some houses listed under a particular broker or agent, deliberately and freely raise some objections with different aspects of the property and be attentive to see how he reacts or responds. Does he (she) fight you when you bring up an objection? Does he give you a put-down kind of response, a "you're-wrong-on-that-point," or "how-stupid-of-you-to-have-asked that-question" kind of answer? If so, that's a good sign that you're probably dealing with an inexperienced broker. The experienced real estate salesperson, on the other hand, will minimize the effect of a buyer's objection; even when he isn't agreeing with you, he'll still acknowledge your objection and convey the impression that he's taken it under consideration. Instead of fighting you or giving you the how-could-you-ask-such-a-question attitude, he'll let you feel that your questions are welcome, that he is giving you new information that more than compensates for your objection. He'll use such phrases as "that's an interesting point," or "I know what you mean, but…" or, "I agree with your thinking; however, don't loose sight of…"

- Independently check out the broker's claims or reputation—is he (or she) licensed to sell real estate (ask to see the license) ; is he a member of any reputable professional organization [e.g., a Graduate of the Realtors Institute, (G.R.I.)], or a holder of a Certified Residential Specialist (CRS) designation, or a member of the National Association of Realtors; how long has he been on the job; how many houses has he sold in the last 6 months, etc?

     If he is a member of the National Association of Realtors, for example, qualifying him to be called a "Realtor," you'll at least know that he will be required to take certain training courses and to obey a strict code of ethics, and that if you ever have a complaint against the broker, you will have someone to complain to. But don't rely exclusively on the certificates. They are no guarantee that the agent who has them will necessarily be a great agent, but they're a plus. As one expert, Edith Lank, author of The Homeseller's Kit, accurately warns, "They [the certificates], mean you've at least got someone who invested some time and effort and is experienced." A GRI designation requires about 90 hours of study, and about 90% of all relators hold a GRI. A CRS designation, on the other hand, which is the more impressive qualification, requires a minimum number of transactions, a GRI or ten years experience, and extra hours of study; only about 3% of all Relators hold a CRS.

- Before you eventually settle on some three or more major and experienced brokers, visit several brokers and find out what is available in the given areas within your price range. Ask to see each **broker's 'listing book,'** and make copies of the information for the houses you desire.

- Make sure the broker tells you about all, not just some, of the houses available in your price range.

• When visiting a house, **ASK QUESTIONS of the broker** about the house and the neighborhood. [Honest brokers will tell you about the faults of a house (or a neighborhood), as well as its good points.   BUT TO GET IT, YOU'LL HAVE TO ASK—AND ASK THE RIGHT QUESTIONS! If a broker doesn't know or have answers to a particular question at the moment, make sure he gets the information for you. Don't let him brush it aside or forget it.

• *Perhaps most important in eventually picking the brokers to engage, does the broker possess expertise and experience in working out* **'creative financing'** *arrangements for the home buyer, and does he have a working relationship with banks, mortgage brokers, and creative financing sources?* Ask him and ask others he has done this kind of service for, and satisfy yourself sufficiently on this.

A WORD OF CAUTION ON PICKING A BROKER: In all you do, it is important that you remember, nonetheless,   NOT to rely solely or too heavily on the words or oral promises of the broker. Remember, the broker is not your partner; he is an independent third party. He is there, first and foremost, to NEGOTIATE for the highest possible price that you will pay and the lowest price the owner will accept; he is engaged by, and is therefore working principally for, the seller, and then for himself—<u>not</u> for you!

[Copies of the LISTING AGREEMENT with a broker, Form T486 [see sample on p. 104], are obtainable from the Legal Publishers. To order, see Order Form on p. 191]

FIGURE 3.1
Neighborhood Inspection Checklist

NEIGHBORHOOD QUALITY	YES	NO	NOT IMPORTANT
1. Are the homes well taken care of?	☐	☐	☐
2. Are there good public services (police, fire)?	☐	☐	☐
3. Are there paved roads?	☐	☐	☐
4. Are there sidewalks?	☐	☐	☐
5. Is there adequate street lighting?	☐	☐	☐
6. Is there a city sewer system?	☐	☐	☐
7. Is there a safe public water supply?	☐	☐	☐
8. Are the public schools good?	☐	☐	☐

NEIGHBORHOOD CONVENIENCE			
1. Will you be near your work?	☐	☐	☐
2. Are there schools nearby?	☐	☐	☐
3. Are there shopping centers nearby?	☐	☐	☐
4. Is there public transportation available?	☐	☐	☐
5. Will you be near child care services?	☐	☐	☐
6. Are hospitals, clinics, or doctors close by?	☐	☐	☐
7. Is there a park or playground nearby?	☐	☐	☐

NEIGHBORS			
1. Will you be near friends or relatives?	☐	☐	☐
2. Will you be near other children of your kids' age?	☐	☐	☐
3. Will you feel comfortable with the neighbors?	☐	☐	☐
4. Is there an active community group?	☐	☐	☐

DOES THE NEIGHBORHOOD HAVE ANY PROBLEMS, SUCH AS:			
1. Increasing Real Estate taxes?	☐	☐	☐
2. Decreasing sales prices of homes?	☐	☐	☐
3. Lots of families moving away?	☐	☐	☐
4. Heavy traffic or noise?	☐	☐	☐
5. Litter or pollution?	☐	☐	☐
6. Factories or heavy industry?	☐	☐	☐
7. Businesses closing down?	☐	☐	☐
8. Vacant houses or buildings?	☐	☐	☐
9. Increasing crime or vandalism?	☐	☐	☐

	GOOD	FAIR	POOR
WHAT IS YOUR OVERALL RATING OF THE NEIGHBORHOOD?	☐	☐	☐

Chapter 4

ON YOUR FINDING THE HOUSE TO BUY, NEGOTIATE THE TERMS OF SALE WITH THE SELLER

THE NEGOTIATIONS PHASE IS CRITICAL FOR BEING ABLE TO MAKE A BUY

O.K. You've considered the kind of house and neighborhood characteristics you want. You've looked for and found — with the help of an experienced, knowledgeable real estate broker and sales agent, and/or through other avenues — the right house you'd like to own, and you've calculated how much it will cost you to buy (as well as to maintain) the property. And now, you want to see if you can buy it, if the seller will sell it to you. What do you do next?

Your next order of business would be NEGOTIATIONS — to negotiate the purchase terms and conditions with the homeowner or his agent. This phase of the buying-selling process has been called "the most important element at your {a buyer's} disposal to help him buy an affordable house."* Experts explain the centrality of possessing good negotiating skills as a major determinant of whether you will be able to get the house in terms of the fact that unless you are first able to persuade the seller to accept the terms of your offer, there just will be no deal for you! The reasoning goes something like this: even if you have a first rate broker or sales agent, an excellent knowledge of how to work with brokers and of the different types of mortgages and creative financing techniques, and of how the banks work, and everything else, *if you don't know how to bargain and negotiate effectively on those things in order to get what you want, then all of that knowledge is only of limited value to you!* In a word, in the final analysis, only if you can persuade the seller to accept your terms for a purchase, will you be able to get a deal, and the house of your dream!

A. Different Issues That Could Be The Object Of Negotiations

The following are among the major issues that can often become the object of negotiations:
- the price of the house, the amount of cash down, the amount of cash to be paid at closing, the amount that might be paid at a later date [For some idea of this, see Step 3 of Chap. 6, at p. 90]
- whether the seller will give some financing, and if so, the amount of the purchase money mortgage that is required from the seller, the length of such a mortgage (preferably get a 5-year term or more)**, whether the purchase money mortgage is fully amortizing, how the purchase money mortgage payments are to be made (is it monthly, quarterly, semiannually, or annually?), and if the purchase money mortgage that is set up on a partially amortizing basis (meaning when only part of the principal is paid and there is a remaining "balloon" payment at the end of the term) requires interest-only payments, or amortizing, including regular interest payments. [See pp. 50, 99-100, for more on this].
- which items of personal property (e.g., air conditioners, refrigerators, washers and dryers) go with the sale
- the move-in date (the buyers may want to move in quickly, before the normal closing schedule, because their lease is almost up
- whether the seller will permit the buyers to rent for a while, with an option to buy

---

*Richard F. Gabriel, *How To Buy Your Own House When You Don't Have Enough Money*, p. 103.

** The reason for this is that anything less than five years means that the property will have to appreciate fast enough and the future financing costs must be reasonable enough for you to comfortably refinance the property to get sufficient money out of the property's increased equity in order to pay off your remaining balance on the purchase money mortgage and still handle the probable higher interest rates on the new larger first mortgage.

• whether the seller will pay certain closing costs that, in the area, are traditionally paid by the seller — e.g., the costs of title insurance [see pp. 41, 59-62, for more on this]

• whether the seller will contribute an amount of money to lower the buyer's mortgage interest rate

• when and where the closing will take place [see p. 57]

• how much "earnest money" deposit will be left with the seller [see pp. 29-31, 98, for more on this]

B. A Few General Principles of Negotiations

The following are among the important general elements, principles and techniques, for effectively negotiating a house purchase (or sale) with a broker or seller:

1. Try to do your negotiating on your turf, not on the other party's.

2. Don't negotiate on the phone—you'll want to negotiate face-to-face so as to watch for facial, eye, or body reaction to your points. Also, it is easier for someone to say no over the phone than it is in person.

3. Don't antagonize or be combative, argumentative or critical of the other person; you'll get better results if you can get the other person to like, or at least to accept you.

4. Keep your discussion focused on the issues, not on personalities.

5. In the negotiations, if you run into a negative respone to your offer, the way to view it is that this only means that the other party is looking for a different solution to the problem. Don't take the no as a rejection, but rather as a signpost that says,"Please take another road. Try a different approach."

6. When you've reached as far as you can go, by way of an offer or concession, don't issue some abrasive ultimatum such as, "That's as far as I can go; take it or leave it." Rather, say something more pleasant and less final, something like "I'd love to be in the position to offer you more, but I just can't afford to go beyond this point."

7. *Bear in mind that as a buyer, particularly in a buyer's market but even in a seller's market as well, you have several areas of power — you are, so to speak, more in the driver's seat —than the seller. You call the shots that get the entire game "into play."* For example, nothing happens, or can happen, until you make an offer on the property, or come back with a counteroffer. You, and you alone, know how much you're willing to pay for the property. The seller has to wait for someone to come by who's interested enough to make an offer. Most sellers, you should recognize, are usually more anxious to sell than prospective buyers are to buy; the average seller bedevils himself with a variety of worries: Will an interested buyer show up on a home viewing appointment? Will the buyer's initial offer be his best offer? And how much more will the buyer increase his offer? Has the buyer found another property that interests him? And so on and on. Hence, be patient and confident and don't be in a rush, but take full advantage of the powers you can have as a buyer.

8. Most sellers who are in a "need to sell" circumstance (i.e., circumstances wherein there's some pressure for them to sell), are generally nervous by virtue of the situation itself. The nervous seller, once you've expressed interest in the property and made an initial offer, is concerned that he not lose the sale. Therefore, your strategy should be to keep the negotiating process stretched out for as long as you can — for days, weeks, or even months, if necessary. The longer the negotiating process, the more time and emotion the seller gets invested and the more worried he gets as to whether he's ever going to get the sale completed or will ever get another buyer with the same level of interest, and the more likely he is to make concessions to you to consummate a sale.

The point is that time is one of the most potent forces you have as a negotiator: always try to put the clock on the other person, create as many clock cut-off dates as possible as a way of putting a sense of urgency into the other party's thinking and thereby place him at a disadvantage. [For example, you can make your offer but put it subject to hearing from the seller by a specified date, say, because, you "have to leave town on business by that date".]

9. In any offers or counteroffers, never make any concessions or give up something of value to the other party *unless* you get or extract a concession of equal (or greater) weight in return. To begin with, you must never do anything that would convey the impression that your offers or counteroffers are less than final or serious. Your initial offer or subsequent offers, must convey the impression that they are firm and final. However, if you decide to make other offers beyond the previous one, be careful always to say something like,*"I've had more opportunity to review your proposal again, and I'm prepared to do or give such and such if you, in turn, do or give such and such."*

10. A good practice is to write down the different points and issues on which you seek the owner's agreement or concession before you go into actual negotiations. Rank them in terms of which of those issues are most important to you, as well as which ones are most important to the seller. The strategy is to know at the start of the negotiations battle which issues to fight for, and which ones to sacrifice and use as a trade-off to get something you want, to lock onto an area that you know is important to the seller but not necessarily of equal importance to you.

Here's how this strategy works. You know, for example, from hearing the home owners say so when you were being shown through the house, that the home owners have a strong interest in taking with them a lovely sitting room chandelier. But you, nonetheless, include that chandelier as part of your purchase, along with the other conditions you want. And, naturally, as is usual in that kind of situation, the owners oppose you on the chandelier. But you, knowing the game you're after, keep insisting that the chandelier is part of the deal, but finally conceding it to the home seller if they will accept to keep that in exchange for something you actually want.

11. As the negotiations proceed over the course of time, write down concessions made by each side, if any, as they are made in the course of the negotiations so that you have a clear written record of what was agreed upon.

12. When negotiating on the price or money issues, try to determine if there is a certain kind of pattern to the amount of dollars contained in each subsequent counteroffer put forth by the seller. And if you can determine such a pattern, you could then pattern your own negotiating strategy after that, accordingly. For example, you notice that two total price reductions offered by the seller are each $1,000. Then you can pretty much guess from that that a third reduction might be the same and act accordingly.

13. As a rule, the biggest concessions are usually given in the earliest stages of the negotiations, and as the negotiating process moves along, there's a tendency with each party to become more and more entrenched and less giving in his position, probably more for emotional reasons and reasons of personal ego than anything else. The appropriate strategy for you should be to use your concessions conservatively and wisely in the beginning in order to get the proceeding off to a good-spirited, cooperative start. Then, later on in the negotiations, you can begin giving your concessions in smaller increments as things get tougher near the end.

14. If possible for you, bring with you any things that will substantiate your position or demand, anything that will support or bring credibility or a sense of legitimacy to your position. For example, it might aid your cause if you can show the seller (or the seller showing a buyer, as the case may be) some recent articles in newspapers, magazines, newsletters, or the like on, say, how creative financing is becoming an increasingly more common way to sell, how more home sellers are helping in the financing, how sellers can help buyers even by way of offering to help them at the mortgaging bank (say, as a co-signer or by persuading the real estate broker to take a promissory note for part or all of his commission), or some other documentation of relevance to real estate. [The reverse of this approach is, of course, true if and when the seller is the one supplying you all sorts of written or printed material in justification of his own position, then you'll have to be able to come up with your own set of papers or other means to counter that!]

15. Make a list of all the defects in the property, as well as any drawbacks concerning the area and its surrounding neighborhood — it's lack in convenience, proximity to shopping, schools, job, entertainment, transportation, etc. When you make your initial offer to the seller [STEP 4 on p.29], mention at that time a few of these defects concerning the house. However, do not mention all the defects concerning the house at the time of the initial offer; you should save some of them to use when you make your counteroffer as that approach better strengthens the impact of the counteroffer. [Something like: *'Well, we've reviewed our offer, and just to satisfy our conscience that we've done everything we should to get this house, we are willing to increase our offer by $___, but that's it. We can't possibly go beyond that, particularly in light of the fact that it just became clear to us that your garage is not going to be big enough to take the new car we are getting. That means additional expense of thousands of dollars for us'.*]

Indeed, the more effective version of this strategy is to use the drawbacks concerning the AREA and the NEIGHBORHOOD as the basis for raising the complaint or objection with the home seller. Use of the drawbacks of the area is the more effective bargaining tool and tactic because, while a house defect can always be repaired, an area or neighborhood defect is invariably uncorrectable.

16. Negotiations have been described in military terms as a "battle ground." You should enter into serious negotiations only when you are at your strongest, emotionally and mentally, for that's when you can best view things realistically.

Avoid being involved in any serious negotiations when you're either on an emotional "low" because of some loss or misfortune in your business, family or social life, or on an emotional "high" because of some good that's come your way.

17. Use the listing real estate brokers and agents as primary allies in your negotiation endeavors; the good, accomplished ones would also know how to "sell" your offer to the home owner, and how to overcome and/or moderate the objections of the seller to your offers. And they can often make excellent negotiators who can play a valuable role in the negotiations on your behalf because negotiating through them, rather than directly with a seller, avoids any emotions or irrational acts or statements by either side. He's invariably experienced in negotiations, he will know how to handle a seller in order to get the desired result, since, after all, he wants the sale as much as the seller wants to sell and you want to buy! [See pp. 25, 101, on the role of a broker in house purchase and negotiations.]

> **NOTE:** Note that it's not enough for you to simply turn the matter completely over to the broker and ask him to do the work all by himself and buy you a house at a good price and on good terms. To gain the full range of advantages, you need to be able to personally present your position in the transactions, even if you choose to handle it yourself, or authorize someone else (e.g., an experienced businessman knowledgeable in labor negotiating or real estate sales, or an experienced real estate investor) to represent you.

18. Have as many buying options available to yourself as possible, work with several brokers and have them bring you several good properties so that you can make many offers on several properties at the same time; but (this is legally permitted) just make certain, though, that you include in each written offer a clause making each offer "subject to advice of counsel," or use any other "subject to" condition that will give you an opportunity to back out of the deal. [By having several buying options, you wouldn't have to chase after a particular property and give the seller the impression that you are desparate to get the property and at all costs].

C. The Best Negotiating Situation: Find and Deal With a "Motivated" Seller

According to real estate sales experts, there are two important basic types or categories of house sellers (the same for buyers, as well):

1. "Unmotivated" sellers — meaning nonpressured house owner/seller selling primarily for profit; and
2. "Motivated" sellers — meaning pressured sellers involved in some need-to-sell situations wherein the house owner/seller is under some degree of pressure.

And, a fundamental strategy among professionals experienced in house buying in ensuring that they get the best deal, is to seek out the *"motivated"* seller and attempt to make a purchase from such a seller. If you are like most buyers, the likelihood is that you're probably looking for a house-buying deal wherein you can make a low out-of-pocket cash offer that is highly leveraged (mortgaged) on the property, and at a price below its offered market price.

Hence, real estate marketing strategists say, YOUR BEST APPROACH SHOULD BE TO SEARCH OUT SELLERS WHO HAVE A REAL NEED-TO-SELL SITUATION, as such sellers, it is said, are the ones most likely to be most responsive to the kind of creative financing terms you'll require to be able to meet your low-cash home-ownership needs. On the other hand, it is said, the home seller who is under no pressure whatsoever, is going to be a lot tougher to strike a deal with.

Broadly speaking, need-to-sell situations usually grow out of one or more of the following circumstances:
   1. a marriage and/or business split-up
   2. deteriorating physical health and the desire to get out from under home-ownership responsibilities
   3. need for retirement to a warmer climate
   4. job opportunities or transfer to another community
   5. strong interest in, or prior committment to another home
   6. imperative requirement for home repairs (because of neglect, fire, and so on) that the owner is not interested in undertaking
   7. estate sales occasioned by death in the family, or pending foreclosure sales occasioned by inability to keep up with the mortgage
   8. financial difficulties from an existing bigger house and a desire to downsize to a smaller house

The trick for landing a purchase on an affordable financing terms, then, is to "uncover" the seller's (each seller's) true motivation for wanting to sell his house, his or her specific need-to-sell situation, and then try to come up with an offer or a form of financing that will accomodate the seller's needs, as well as your own goals.

Richard F. Gabriel, a hugely successful real estate broker and author and respected expert in little-money-down home buying strategies, explains the essence of dealing with the motivated "seller" in negotiations this way:

> *"The single most important factor that will make the most impact on the negotiation process resides in one word: MOTIVATION.* People's emotional needs, which are at the basis of their motivation, will invariably play a larger role in the negotiation process than will the property itself. What this means to you as a cash-shy buyer looking for an affordable house in a market where prices are too high and the cost of mortgage money skyrockets, is that *only through your knowledge of the needs of the seller, coupled with your ability to couch your offer in terms that will attempt to fulfill those needs, will you be able to get what you want. If you can fulfill, or come close to filling, the needs of the other party, they in turn will then fulfill, or come close to filling your needs as a buyer...*
>
> This requires buyers to view things in terms of the other person's needs. [The underlying theory is that] *if you want to sell a home owner on selling his house to you on your terms, then you'll have to fulfill his needs.* You will have to fulfill his needs first because, as the buyer, you're the one that's taking the initiative — you're the one that's courting the seller — you are the suitor because they (the sellers) have something you want (that is, their house at a price and condition you can live with). Taking your mind off your own needs, separating limiting factors in your own ego or financial requirements, and concentrating a good amount of time, energy, and investigative talents in finding out about your seller, are the keys to getting the property you desire. If the negotiation process is similar to a battle, then it behooves you to do what every good general does: Learn everything you can about your "enemy" — their strengths, weaknesses, needs, hopes. Scout out the "enemy" to know what you'll be contending with [and then structure your strategies to meet those requirements.]"

D. Using Your Broker In Finding & Negotiating With The Motivated Seller

By what means and avenues do you gain insight into the needs of the seller, or find this all-important need-to-sell "motivated" seller?

One simple way is to work with your brokers on this. Put your brokers to proper use to accomplish this. Good salespersons are, as has been repeatedly said in this chapter and others, good negotiators, and can make or break a deal for you. *So, what you do, simply is to emphasize to each real estate broker or realtor you engage, that what you seek are strictly need-to-sell situations.* Be forthright with them. Tell them honestly but realistically what your needs are—in terms of the kind of property, price, neighborhood, you seek or can afford, the available cash and other resources you have, your interest in properties that are purchasable under creative financing arrangements, and the like. The more facts and information your broker knows about your realistic needs and limitations, the quicker, better and more effective help he can be to you.

Thereafter, armed with this knowledge and information, any good, experienced, topflight real estate professional with the proper sales know-how, will be able to seek out the listings and the need-to-sell situations that will fit your needs. Through his interviews with the home owner and other investigations, the real estate broker or agent would be able to sufficiently understand the underlying reasons — the "motivation" — which compel an owner to want to put his house up for sale.

There are some more visible 'red flags' or warning signs you may look to, which may be indicative that a home seller might be under some kind of underlying pressure to sell, aside from the more formal indicators, such as marriage or business breakup, deteriorating physical health, retirement or relocation for business, job or health purposes, expanding needs from a growing family, etc. You can make such a determination by finding the answers to questions or issues such as the following: Does the owner want (or must have, of necessity) a quick or a delayed sale, and why? How long has the property been on the market; has there been any other offers made on the property, and when; how long has the owner owned the property and what size of his equity is in the property; is the owner an experienced businessperson, himself, who is well seasoned in sales deals and negotiations, or only a first-time seller? Is he abrupt in his dealings and quick to come to decisions, or is he the type that takes his time and is slow in making a decision or is generally indecisive? And so on.

On your own part, as a buyer (or seller, as the case may be), having known the personality characteristics of the seller and his motivation for selling, you'll at least know what kind of general behavior to expect from the seller, and even more importantly, you will be in the position to use the valuable information on the seller's need-to-sell situation to negotiate more favorably with the seller, in that you can then structure your offers to fit and fill those needs of the homeseller. [See below for the negotiations phase of the home purchase process, when the buyer may employ his knowledge of the seller's need-to-sell situation to his own best advantage].

E. Negotiating With The Seller: Here's The Actual 'Haggling' Process And Procedures

Here is the scenario and tactics given by one expert, Richard F. Gabriel,* a widely experienced and accomplished real estate broker and negotiations specialist, on the actual negotiations process with the home seller:

> *"Quid pro quo* negotiating is a better way to refer to the negotiation process; this Latin phrase means 'one thing in return for another.' The negotiation process for acquiring a property comprises three stages. Stage One is the initial offer. Stage Two is the counteroffer to the seller's counteroffer. Stage Three is usually where the two parties finally reach a settlement, or not, as the case may be...
>
> [Assuming we're dealing with a seller in a need-to-sell situation, that you enter a subject-to-advice-of-counsel clause in all offers so that the buyer will have an avenue of escape in the event the seller accepts the initial offer with the high cash down payment, and that the seller will be taking back financing in the form of a purchase money mortgage, the initial offer] might consist of a high cash down offer and a low total purchase price for the property, coupled with small purchase money mortgage from the seller. The seller might like the cash down part of the offer, express unhappiness with the offered price of the property, and say he could "live with" the small, short-term second mortgage. After an appropriate lapse of time, the buyer might make a new offer reflecting a higher total price for the property but with less cash down and a slightly larger second mortgage and longer term at a lower interest rate. By now, the sellers are probably hooked. Most sellers have a tremendous drive to see that they get as full a price on their property as possible in order to confirm their self-image as astute businesspersons. Utilize this universal drive of all sellers as a stepping stone to get the most favorable financing. Remember that *conditions of sale are much more important than the price of the sale*.
>
> Subsequent offers and counteroffers will continue to raise the price of the property but lower the cash down commitment and increase the amount of the purchase money mortgage under more favored conditions (that is, the rate of interest and the size of the balloon payment). By the time the negotiations finally close, you may well have bought the property with as little of your own money as possible.

*op. cit., pp. 116-7, 120.

> *...The trick in much of these negotiations is caring but not caring too much*—which means wanting to buy the house but not wanting it so much that you can taste it. When you put yourself in that position, then you're too emotionally involved and, as a result, you will probably not make the best deal for yourself. It's only when you can convey a certain indifference as to the final outcome that you will do that much better for yourself in negotiating. If, after all, the broker gets the idea from you [and conveys it to the seller], and you in turn are perceived as "wanting the house in the worst way," then, frankly, you'll probably get it in the worst way possible because ... then the seller naturally will begin to take a more rigid position on both his price and conditions."

The following graph (Fig. 4.1) contains examples of a series of offers planned out before the first offer is made, and are presented herein for illustrative purposes. To be sure, each stage and each variable element in the stage, is not going to come out exactly as you would want or anticipate, but by preplanning the strategy and playing around with the elements of each subsequent offer, you will more often than not be able to come close to your ultimate goal of buying a home on the terms that are favorable and affordable.

FIGURE 4.1
SAMPLE PLANNED STAGES OF OFFERS

PROPERTY OFFERED AT: $72,000

1ST OFFER: $58,000	2ND OFFER: $64,000	3RD OFFER: $66,500	4TH OFFER: $68,500
Cash down —$21,000 1st mortgage from bank —$33,000 purchase money mortgage from seller —$ 4,000 • payable in 1 year • fully amortizing • 16 percent interest	Cash down —$15,000 1st mortgage from bank —$43,000 purchase money mortgage from seller —$ 8,000 • payable in 3 years • partially amortizing • 13 percent interest	Cash down —$ 9,000 1st mortgage from bank —$45,000 purchase money mortgage from seller —$12,500 • payable in 4 years • interest only • 12 percent interest	Cash down —$ 5,700 1st mortgage from bank —$48,000 purchase money mortgage from seller —$14,800 • payable in 5 years • interest only • 9 percent interest

Finally, it is very important for you that you always bear in mind that bargaining on the purchase of the home does not have to be on the issue of PRICE. Or on the issue of price alone. Quite to the contrary, you should remember that you can also use CASH SUBSTITUTES — you can just as well negotiate on other important things besides money, on the so-called "CONDITION OF SALE" ISSUES. In deed, according to some experts, such matters can often constitute the make or break issues that ultimately moves a tough negotiations round out of a deadlock into a breakthrough and a successful purchase.

Again, Richard F. Gabriel, the real estate sales negotiations specialist, provides an instructive scenario of this angle of the real estate sales-purchase negotiation process, this way:

> Another tactic for you to keep in mind is that all bargaining does not have to be in the area of PRICE. *Conditions of sale* are extremely important to the sucess of your negotiations. Conditions of sale can be used during the negotiating process as trade-off tools to reduce the price of the property. However, after you've been in the negotiation process for a while and you're coming down to the wire with the seller, you may find yourself at a stand-off. What do you do when you've gotten most if not all the conditions of sale you can realistically hope to get, yet the seller is firm at a total price that is above what you're willing to pay? Get your discussions away from price and get your seller to throw in some other asset he might have in lieu of the price diference — kind of a, "Well, I can see that you are absolutely firm on your price, which is certainly your privilege, and I in turn am just as firm in my price. In order for us to get this off dead center, I'd like to

suggest the following: I'll concede to you and buy at your price if you throw in the Ride 'Em Mower you have sitting in your garage and the snow blower."

Getting the seller to exchange some asset (it could be household equipment, a product, services, or a collectible) in place of a cash reduction of the total price, will sometimes loosen the logjam that's developed between you and the seller. It gives the seller a way of saving face and, in turn, it has given you a valuable asset that you can use or convert to cash.

Sometimes, after a long give-and-take exchange on price has taken place and both parties have become entrenched in their positions, the broker will need the patience of a saint, the insight of a mind reader, and the tact and patience of a United Nations representative to get the situation moving again. If the broker can, separately, get each side to start thinking about splitting the difference, he might save the situation and make himself a well-earned commission. "Splitting the difference" is a well-used last-ditch compromise that has moved many a stalled negotiation back into the mainstream and might prove helpful to you in your negotiations."

Gabriel adds the following counsel on the appropriate underlying philosophy that should guide your negotiations:

"Frankly, the best deals are the ones where both sides feel satisfied with the final results rather than where one side tries to blast the other side off the map and leave the adversary a bloody mess. Even if a general sense of fair play didn't dictate that the other side should also be left feeling satisfied, remember that some day, either directly or indirectly, your paths may cross again and it's better to leave them smiling and thinking well of you than frowning and speaking ill of you.

In essence, the man who drives the hard bargain and tries to get the last drop of blood isn't the best negotiator. In fact, this kind of person will invariably stimulate a combative and argumentative response that will probably make you say, "Hey, I'll show this guy a thing or two. He's not going to push me around!" The old saying is still true: You can catch more flies with honey than you do with vinegar. If the other side perceives you as generally reasonable and understanding of their needs, then they will take a more cooperative, sympathetic, and open approach to your needs. As a result, there will be a mutual area of trust, with both sides willing to make concessions in order to meet a common goal. When you run into roadblocks, you have to come up with fair alternatives. *If you go into battle with the "I have to win at all costs" attitude, there's a good chance that negotiations will never come to a satisfactory conclusion. On the other hand, if you're willing to make concessions in order to receive concessions and you are able to think creatively of alternative approaches when logjams arise, then chances are you'll have fruitful negotiations.* Let the other party know that you're interested in his problems. You will find that the other party is usually less defensive when he sees that you're not trying to jam your demands down his throat and are not interested in debating everything, but are trying to identify problems and work them out." [Emphasis added by the present writer].

Chapter 5

BUYING YOUR HOME YOURSELF: HERE ARE THE COMPLETE STEP-BY-STEP PROCEDURES, FROM START TO FINISH

A. General Guidelines On Using This Chapter

In this chapter, we deal with the complete procedures, legal and otherwise, for the "buying" part of home transfers. (The equivalent treatment for the "selling" part of home transfers is at Chapter 6, from p. 83).

The forms, information and instructions outlined in this chapter, are carefully arranged and organized in a system of orderly, simple **"STEPS"**—from Step 1 to Step 10. In each "step," you are told what to do (or to expect) and, where necessary, provided with sample forms along with instructions on how to complete or make use of them, and what to do. But a word of caution is necessary: to be able to fully get and make the most out of the invaluable information provided in this chapter, it is essential that you take the "STEPS" one (and only one) at a time, following them in <u>exactly</u> the same numerical order in which they are listed below in the chapter. <u>Do</u> not skip around from step to step, or from page to page (unless so instructed in the manual.)

B. And Here They Are, The 10 Simple Systematic Steps Involved In Your Home Buying Process:

STEP ❶: DETERMINE THE KIND OF HOME & NEIGHBORHOOD YOU CAN AFFORD TO HAVE YOUR SIGHT ON
(See Chapter 2, at pp. 6-12.)

STEP ❷: LET'S SEARCH FOR THE PROPER HOUSE, NEIGHBORHOOD & BROKER FOR YOU
(See Chapter 3, at pp. 13-20.)

STEP ❸: ON YOUR FINDING THE PROPER HOUSE TO BUY, NEGOTIATE THE TERMS OF SALE WITH THE SELLER
(See Chapter 4, at pp. 21-8.)

STEP ❹: MAKE AN OFFER TO SELLER, PUT UP 'GOOD FAITH' DEPOSIT, AND SIGN BINDER AGREEMENT

O.K. You've considered the kind of house and neighborhood characteristics you want; you've looked for and found the right house you think you can afford which you'd like to own, and you've calculated how much it will cost you (not only for buying but also for maintaining it), and now you want to bid for it. What do you do next?

Your next order of business would be to make an offer to the homeowner or his agent, such as his broker. The actual details or sequence of events involved in a particular case, state or locality, may differ. But, generally, the sequence runs roughly this way: Having deliberated and decided on how much you desire to pay for the property, you first make an initial offer to the seller (or his agent or broker) stating the price you propose to pay for the property, normally a price well below the price quoted you by the seller. The seller responds. If he rejects the initial offer (as he probably would!), he would probably come back with a **"counter-offer"** —that is, indicate a price (or other terms) he would accept or consider. You, in turn, will again pass word to the seller as to whether the seller's counter-offer is agreeable to you, or offer some modifications to the counter-offer. Now, a little later down the road, after the offers and counter-offers shall have been tossed back and forth between the parties by verbal communications, you'll make your **WRITTEN OFFER** to purchase, usually with some money, the so-called **"good faith" money** or **"earnest money" deposit**—the object of which is to signify to the seller your seriousness and earnestness about the deal, and to "bind" both parties to the deal in the meantime until a more comprehensive sales contract can be worked out and signed by the buyer and seller! [Samples of written offer and counter-offers are on p. 31].

At this stage, the written offer is still that—just an offer. However, at any time whenever the seller (or his agent or broker) happens to come back with the offer sheet with his signature on it, he has, in effect, agreed to your offer, and at that point what you and the seller now have becomes a binding agreement with each other—a so-called **BINDER AGREEMENT.*** [See a sample Binder (Agreement) on p. 32.]** This is a binding agreement or contract alright. But don't be mistaken—it is NOT the final or main contract. Not Yet. Basically, all that this agreement means is that it "binds" you (i.e., holds both the buyer and the seller) to the price stated, and assures you that you have the option to negotiate a binding, final contract with the seller before anyone else. You are, in effect, assured by this agreement that the seller will "hold" the house for you at the fixed, stated price, but only for a specified, limited period of time, say 3 days—until the time that more elaborate terms and details of a final purchase contract can be hammered out, prepared, agreed upon and signed.

The basic advantage of this exercise to you is this: that at least the price of the house is fixed and you can proceed to negotiate the other terms of the sale that will be detailed in the Purchase Agreement.

From the standpoint of the buyer, here are a few pointers on how best to protect your interest:

i) Even *before* you ever decide to sign a binder agreement or to give a binder deposit to a seller, first make sure that you've cleared a few key questions with the seller:

• The price. Is the asking price (and what you offer to pay) close to what you can afford? [Remember that it is not just the down payment money, or even the asking price of the house, that you have to come up with within a matter of weeks to finalize the deal, but all the other "closing costs" associated with buying a house —figure about 5% of the sales price, or $5,000 on a $100,000 house.]

• Exactly what is included in the price? ("Lighting fixtures," "built-ins," "appliances," etc.?) What, if any, will the seller remove or keep for himself?

don't sign or give E.M. deposit until you are sure of .....

Ernest Money Deposit $$

---

*It goes by different names in different localities: "a binder," an "offer and acceptance," "preliminary sales contract," "conditional sales contract," "agreement to buy and sell," etc.

**Copies of the BINDER AGREEMENT may be obtained from the Legal Publishers; see the Order Form on pp. 191.

- Are there tenants in the building (or is it owner-occupied)? What kind of lease, if any, do they have? What rent do they pay? Can they be made to leave? When?

- Exactly when will the house be available for you to move in?

- If there is an existing mortgage, what is the amount? How much is the interest rate? How much longer will it run? Is the mortgage assumable—i.e., can you take it over, instead of having to get a new one?

ii) Give as little binder deposit ("earnest money") as possible—from a buyer's standpoint, you want to give up as little cash as possible so that you will have less to lose if something should go wrong. (There is no set or standard amount for this. Binder deposits could be as little as, say, $50 or $100, or as much as the full down payment. The reasonable measure, though, is that the amount you give should be large enough to convince the seller that the buyer is really serious).

Generally, you are protected and should be able to recover your deposit, especially if the binder is an "agreement to agree" type of understanding, for such a binder will be made "contingent upon the ability of the buyer and seller to negotiate a full, formal contract of sale [or purchase] acceptable to both parties" —meaning, if there's no mutual agreement on the main contract within a short while, there'll be no keeping of the deposit by the seller! However, if you're not quite sure, you may assure absolute protection against the possibility of having to lose this deposit, by doing this: make every effort to see that a clause such as this (or one like it) is inserted—or already contained— in the binder agreement: "BUYER SHALL GET A REFUND OF DEPOSIT IF A FORMAL CONTRACT TO PURCHASE THE PROPERTY IS NOT AGREED TO OR ENTERED INTO BY THE PARTIES WITHIN____DAYS."

A SAMPLE WRITTEN OFFER

January 17, 19_____

To: Mr. & Mrs. Dow D. Dean
       129 Purchase Street
       New York, NY 10004

Dear Mr. & Mrs. Dean:

I herewith offer to purchase from you, free and clear of all encumbrances, the real property located at 129 Purchase Street, New York, New York, to include also the built-ins, curtains, drapes, carpeting, storm windows, swing set, and affixed shelving or bookcases, all light fixtures and all kitchen wares and appliances, all located at the said premised, for the total sum of $196,100. My down payment is to be 10 percent (i.e., $19,610).

This offer is to be considered valid for 3 days, and is contingent upon my being able to obtain a mortgage loan to finance the purchase deal.

Yours truly,
John Johnson

A SAMPLE COUNTER -OFFER

Date:_____

Dear Mr. Johnson:

I hereby accept your offer contained in your letter dated January 17, 19___, but with the following modifications:
                    The Purchase Price shall be $199,200.
                    The down payment is to be 20 percent.

The closing shall be concluded not more than 30 days from the date of this counter-offer, unless you and I both agree to extend the time. If you accept these terms, please sign below and return a copy to me.

Signed:_____
Dow D. Dean

I accept the foregoing counter-offer.
Signed:_____ Date:_____

B 122—Purchase offer, standard form: plain English: 11-78

32

OFFER TO PURCHASE (PURCHASE OFFER)

TO THE OWNER OR PERSON WHO   IS THE RIGHT TO SELL THE PROPERTY DESCRIBED BELOW:

Property

I (We) agree to purchase the following property situated in the village/city of New York
County of ....Kings............, State of ....New York................ known as ....(Street addr.?)
being a ......two-family residential brick house..
....
(for a more detailed description of the property reference is hereby made to the deed thereof) together with all lighting, heating and plumbing fixtures, window shades, screen and storm doors and windows, if any, water heater, water meter and all fixtures and fittings belonging to or used in the operation of the property and owned by you.

Price

AT THE PRICE OF...$

Dollars, payable as follows:

Deposit

$.....................cash deposited with (person to be appointed/entrusted?)....to be held until this offer is accepted, at which time it shall become part of the purchase price, or returned if not accepted.

Balance

$.....................cash on or before .... on passing of deed.

[ENTER HERE ANY OTHER STIPULATIONS/ CONDITIONS YOU MIGHT PREFER]

Searches, Taxes, Easements, Restrictions, Zoning, etc.

You are to deliver to me or my attorney, at least five (5) days before closing, a forty year abstract of title and ten year search or tax receipts showing the property free and clear of all liens and encumbrances, except as herein set forth, and except building and use restrictions, pole and wire easements of record, and subject to zoning ordinance and to any taxes for local improvements not now completed.

Deed

Transfer is to be completed at the office of..
....
on or before...or as soon thereafter as the abstracts can be brought to date. At that time you are to convey to me by... deed, good title to the property free of all liens and encumbrances, except as above set forth, subject to rights of tenants, if any.

Adjustments

Interest, insurance premiums, rents, and taxes shall be pro-rated and adjusted as of.................., 19......
....
City, State and County Taxes shall be adjusted and apportioned on a calendar year beginning Jan. 1, and ending Dec. 31. School Taxes outside the city shall be adjusted and apportioned for the fiscal year beginning July 1st and ending the following June 30th. and Village Taxes shall be adjusted and apportioned for the fiscal year beginning June 1st and ending the last day of May following or as otherwise provided by law.

Possession

Possession of premises shall be delivered on or before..................................19...... on passing of deed

Mortgage Expenses

Upon any purchase money mortgage given, I (We) agree to pay the usual mortgage tax and recording fee and Revenue stamps on bond where required.

Assignment

This offer may be assigned to an individual or corporation for the purpose of holding title thereto. However. I (We) shall remain responsible for the faithful performance of the contract.

Risk of Loss

The risk of loss or damage to the property by fire or other causes until the delivery of the deed is assumed by you.

[personal & business names of broker used], OR

Broker

I (We) represent that [e.g.: there's no broker used herein]..........is the broker in this transaction and that no other real estate broker or agent has helped to bring about this sale.

Persons Bound

This offer, when accepted shall be a binding contract. It shall bind the parties hereto and their respective executors. administrators. distributees, successors and assigns.

Dated.., 19....... (Signed) X Buyer ....(L. S.)

Witness.. (Signed) X Buyer ....(L. S.)

ACCEPTANCE (BINDER)

The undersigned hereby accepts this offer, agrees to sell on the terms and conditions set forth, and agrees to pay

....the authorized agent,................................commission.

The deposit made or as much as covers the commission may be applied to payment of the commission.

Dated................................., 19.......

(Signed) X Seller ....(L. S.)

Witness.............................. (Signed) X Seller ....(L. S.)

Salesmen are not permitted to change the regular rates of commission.

STEP ⑤ : ARRANGE FOR A FORMAL INSPECTION AND EVALUATION OF THE PROPERTY'S CONDITION

A. It's Advisable To Have An Inspection Done

No one (not the seller, the lender, broker, or what have you), would require you to actually do a formal inspection of the house you propose to buy as a condition for your being able to buy the house. [In instances where it might be necessary, e.g., in situations involving F.H.A. or V.A.-guaranteed mortgage loan, the agencies which require such inspections would themselves arrange and conduct it.] You'll probably be able to proceed with your home-buying transactions without one. Nevertheless, as a buyer, *a thorough, detailed, competent physical inspection of the house could be an important protection for you; it is probably the best way to guard against possibly dabbling into a costly but unwise purchase you'd later regret for a long time to come, and could often make the difference between deciding to buy or not to buy a house.*

Hence, if you haven't already gone so before now, NOW, at this stage in the process, is the time you had better found out, for sure, how good the house you'll soon commit your life savings to really is!

There are basically two routes to go. You may elect to conduct the inspection yourself. (For some pointers, see Appendix A, "Inspecting and Evaluating the Condition of a House," at pp. 143-9). Or, even better still, you may engage the services of a **professional home inspector** to do it for you. (The fee in New York area for such service ranges from $250 to $500 for an average-size home).

> <u>NOTE:</u> At the same time that you sign the Binder's Agreement with the seller and leave a good faith deposit with him (or, with some sellers, it's when the actual sales contract is signed), you should expect the seller to (he should) provide you as well with a *Property Disclosure Statement* describing the entire condition of the property and any problems, if any, in some great details. (See, Figure B-1 in Appendix B on p. 151 for a sample of such a statement). It's very important that you, as well as any inspector you employ, thoroughly study this statement as you go about the task of viewing the property and making the formal home inspection. The disclosure statement could serve as a very valuable supplemental tool to you and to an inspector in the conduct of the home inspection.

B. How do you find a professional inspector for your area?

One way of finding a local professional inspector is to look in your area's Yellow Pages or the Phone Directory. Look under "building inspection services" or "inspection bureaus." **But be forewarned:** Though most professional inspectors are probably faultless, not all are competent or reliable; it is essentially an unregulated business and, as a practical matter, anyone in fact can advertise in the yellow pages as a "house inspector". *It becomes essential, therefore, that you get the right type of inspector—if the inspection and the report you are to get are to be of any real value or reliability for your needs.*

The home inspection trade is one that has no officially designated national regulatory body, and it may be hard to screen out the technically qualified inspectors meeting a minimum standard of competence and professionalism for the given area. In some areas, local engineers, architects, or builders with some housing experience, may double as house inspectors. There have developed, though, some two or three private national organizations across the country which certify their members as meeting minimum qualifications to do home inspection work, and which, in the words of the executive director of the American Society of Home Inspectors, the nation's leading home inspection organization, try to "set some standards and to add some professionalism to a business that has no qualifications, no constraints, and no code of ethics." The American Society of Home Inspectors (ASHI), a non-profit organization formed in 1976 to develop formal inspection guidelines and professionalism, has today come to be recognized nationally by home inspectors and home owners alike, as the leading authority in the home inspection field. You may contact the organization for a list of its accredited home-inspectors for your designated state and locality, at:

American Society of Home Inspectors, Inc.
3299 K Street, N.W.
Washington, DC 20005
(202) 842-3096

You (the buyer) may want different kinds of inspection – termite inspection, housing inspection, roofing, asbestos, radon, or any of the dozen or so other kinds of inspections. [See Appendices A & B]. In addition, often the mortgage lender will independently require a termite clearance inspection before it may fund the loan.

C. Uses To Which You Can Put The Inspection Report

What happens if the "inspector's report" turned in by the inspector (or your own report, if you did your own inspection) were to turn up some really serious environmental or structural problems in the house? If the problems are so bad that they can't be corrected or you can't possible live with them, that's one thing. In such a case, there would, of course, be only one sensible thing to do — cancel out and pull out of the deal, and ask for your 'earnest money' deposit back. But if, on the other hand, the kinds of defects turned up by the inspection are such that you figure that, though bad enough, you can still live with them? Then here's the big value of this: you can use this new found professional data as an important "bargaining point" with the seller; you can use this to go back to him and bargain with him either to get the purchase price of the house down, or to have him do some interim repairs on the house at his expense. This may mean anything, ranging from fixing a broken window, to treating the house to remove termites. And chances would be that, if at all the seller is serious about making a sale, he's likely to be agreeable to any half-way reasonable compromise you might propose to remedy the uncovered defects, since the alternative might mean having the potential sale go right down the drain!

Here's how you go about it. Whatever the defects or flaws uncovered in the inspection, go get two or three written estimates from professionals of what it will cost to repair, replace, or correct them. Then confront the seller with these estimates, using and dwelling on those shortcomings as your basis for negotiation or renegotiation of terms ("Step 6" below).

STEP ⑥: NEGOTIATE PURCHASE TERM DETAILS AND SIGN THE PURCHASE/SALES CONTRACT WITH SELLER

Alright.   So you've taken a good, hard look at that dream house of yours (or, had a house inspector do that for you), and you feel its alright and now wish to go ahead with the buying of the house. What next? The next order of business is for you and the seller to work up and sign a **PURCHASE AGREEMENT** on the deal: The whole process involved in doing this is often referred to as **"going to contract."**

A. What Is A Purchase/Sales Agreement?

In a word, a Purchase Agreement (also called by other names, such as "Purchase and Sales Agreement," "Sales Agreement," "Sales Contract," "Contract of Sale," "Agreement of Sale," etc., depending on the state or locality), is simply a legal document or contract in which the seller agrees to sell a piece of property, and the buyer agrees to buy it, with the complete terms and conditions of the deal fully spelled out in the document and signed by both the buyer and the seller.   It is, in a word, the paper that documents a sale in real estate transfers, conveying all the terms and conditions of the sale.[See sample copy of pre-printed standard Purchase Agreement form on p. 43. As with most other matters involved in real estate transfers, a pre-printed standard form of this is often commonly employed for this purpose by most].

BY ALL ACCOUNTS, *THIS DOCUMENT IS THE SINGLE MOST IMPORTANT DOCUMENT IN THE ENTIRE REAL ESTATE TRANSFER DEAL.* Why? Because it specifies (or should do so!) the exact price of sale, what and what are exactly included in the sale (house, land, fixtures, appliances, etc.), the exact date of the sale ("Closing"), and when the owner is to move out of the house and you can move in, and under what conditions you can get out of the agreement and get your deposit back— in short, everything that is important about the sale and purchase of the property. *So, before ever you eventually 'sign on the dotted line' of this document, make sure you've first read and re-read it several times over (or have somebody else read and interpret it for you), and be sure that you understand the provisions and that they conform to what you can live with and have in mind agreeing to!*

B. Who draws up the document?

Customarily, the seller (or his attorney, if he is using one, or the real estate broker, in some parts of the country), prepares this document. Whoever it is, however, that physically draws up this document in a given instance, **WHAT IS IMPORTANT TO BE NOTED IS THIS:** the person will only draw up its provisions to reflect and spell out the terms and conditions of sale that are previously negotiated and agreed upon by both the seller   and the buyer.

May the FSBO (for-sale-by-owner) seller, himself, prepare this document? To hear the real estate lawyers talk about it, this document should never be prepared by anybody except a lawyer. However, in reality, there is really no valid reason — legally, practically, or otherwise — why a non-lawyer may not prepare it. The point, simply, is that it could just as easily, accurately, or competently and legally be prepared by a non-lawyer.* Essentially, the document is often a pre-printed form containing paragraphs for various contingencies, and all that the preparer of the form (be it the seller, the broker, buyer, and even the lawyer, etc.) will need to do, is to fill in the required information and details (the names of the parties involved, the property description, etc.), cross out certain clauses that may not apply, check and initial the appropriate paragraphs, and fill in the sales price, the loan amount, payment terms, etc. In many states, it is the real estate agents or organizations, who are generally non-lawyers, that usually prepare the contract forms for their agents and members to use, and large real estate franchise companies such as Coldwell-Banker or Century 21, have and prepare their own special forms. In fact, in some states and parts of the country, particularly the West, the use of real estate attorneys is *uncommon*, and it is the real estate broker and the non-lawyer FSBO seller who actually handle the preparation of the contract, usually in conjunction with title insurance and escrow officers. Finally, if you are going to use an escrow agent in your house closing (and most sellers often do), you have an additional safeguard in that while escrow officers would not actually help with the preparation of the Contract form, they will aid you in seeing that all its conditions are carried out after you shall have completed and signed the contract.

By and large, in most localities what is used for this contract is a pre-printed standard form obtainable from an area title company or legal stationery store, and all that the person drawing up the contract would do, would be merely to add, delete, or change around certain details or the other in the form, modifying the contents of the printed form to conform them to the particular specifics agreed upon by the given buyer and seller. [See same standard contract form reproduced on p. 43].

C. How to complete the sales contract or agreement

To prepare the Sales/Purchase Contract, the seller shall have, of course, first found a buyer who has committed, in writing, to buy (STEP 4 above). Next, you should complete (or the seller should, if applicable) the worksheet on p.37 (Figure 5.1). This gives you a clear written overview of the important points on which you (the seller) and the buyer are in agreement, as well as those that are still to be negotiated. Buy copies of the pre-printed Sales/Purchase Contract form from your local stationery store. (Oftentimes you may be able to borrow the applicable sales agreement forms from a local broker, or to have a broker who works in the area fill them out for you). More simply though, you may just order from the Legal Publishers one of the different kinds of CONTRACT OF SALE forms carried by it. See the Order Form on p. 191.

The Sales/Purchase Contract Worksheet (Figure 5.1 on p. 37) merely sets down in writing those things the buyer and the seller have agreed upon. It's not a binding contract and neither the buyer nor the seller will sign it. The main significance of using a worksheet (as opposed to merely listing the agreements from your head, or writing them on a sheet of paper), is that, with a worksheet format, you and the buyer can sit down together and put in writing exactly what the terms of the sale are, so that there can be no misunderstanding or misinterpretation of what is meant or agreed to prior to entering them in the contract. Or, even if you and the buyer do not exactly sit down to work out the terms in a worksheet, you can complete the worksheet and simply have it looked over by the buyer.

Once confirmed by the buyer, the seller would then use the contents to complete the sales contract form. Furthermore, it could be extremely useful as a negotiating tool in situations where there are still some points of disagreement still to be resolved between the parties. Using the worksheet, you can reasonably say to the buyer: "This is only a worksheet. It's not a binding agreement, neither you nor I will sign it. Let's sit down and put the numbers and the proposals down on paper and see if we can work it out."

---

*One expert opinion sums it up this way: "either the buyers or the sellers may draw up an agreement which includes standard safeguards, [but] they would be wise to buy a standard purchase agreement form at a stationery store…Having a lawyer draw up the agreement is another alternative, of course, one which may be necessary for more complicated transactions. Typically, on the West Coast, lawyers do not become involved in drafting purchase, sale, or exchange agreements unless circumstances, such as pending probate, a lawsuit, or divorce proceedings, complicate the matter. The real estate agent, the buyer, or seller normally draws up the agreement. On the East Coast, however, lawyers do play a large part in real estate transactions, in some areas drawing up the purchase agreement, examining the title, and preparing the necessary legal documents…" Sandy Gadow, in *All About Escrow*. (Express Publishers, El Cerrito, CA) at p. 24.

FIGURE 5.1
SAMPLE FSBO PRICE AND TERMS WORKSHEET

Address of property _____

_____

Buyer's name _____

Seller's name _____

Sale Price $ _____

Deposit $ _____

Cash down (down payment) $ _____

(in addition to deposit)

First mortgage $ _____

Assume _____ ?	New _____ ?
Interest rate _____ %
Fixed _____ ?	Adj. _____ ?
Term _____ ?	Pts. _____ ?

Second mortgage $ _____

Assume _____ ?	New _____ ?
Interest rate _____ %
Fixed _____ ?	Adj. _____ ?
Term _____ ?	Pts. _____ ?

Third mortgage $ _____

Assume _____ ?	New _____ ?
Interest rate _____ %
Fixed _____ ?	Adj. _____ ?
Term _____ ?	Pts. _____ ?

Total $ _____

(Must equal price)

Other conditions of sale

_____

_____

_____

_____

The date the escrow will close _____

The date the buyer gets occupancy _____

The real estate broker to be used (if any) _____

The title insurance company to be used _____

The escrow company to be used _____

TERMS OF SALE

- How long does the buyer have to qualify for the mortgage before there will be a close of escrow — the time when the title will transfer and the sale made and money paid. (Typically, financing can be arranged in 45 days).
- The date of occupancy when the buyer takes possession. (It's often the same date as the close of escrow, but it could be some other date atimes).
- What personal property will be included in the sale? (The seller may have a favorite chandelier in the living room, for example, which he may want to keep and not have included in the sale).
- What inspections are going to be done — structure of building, electrical, plumbing, heating and air conditioning, pool and spa, geological, flood control, termites and fungus, environmental, etc.

D. The General Procedures & The Terms And Conditions To Look For In Your Purchase Contract/Agreement

i) The Initial Provisions Contained in the Contract Document Are Absolutely Negotiable

Whatever the initial provisions contained in the contract document, or the format used, whether the document is a pre-printed standard form or otherwise, remember this: that *the document is merely a framework whose provisions are negotiable and adjustable, and is not by any means a finished, "final" document.* It's not one —*unless* and *until* you append your signature to it! Any and every clause whatsoever that is contained in the initial document may still be deleted or altered, or a new one added, to meet the needs and protect the interests of either party—as may be proposed, negotiated, and agreed to by both sides.

ii) Names and Addresses of the Seller(s) and Buyer(s)

Be sure to see that the Contract contains the correct and present (full) names and addresses of *all* the actual present owner or owners (get it as exactly set forth in the seller's deed), as well as *all* the buyers or buyer (if a single buyer, or husband and wife, or partners, it should be so reflected.)

iii) Description of the Property Involved

The property you have in mind buying should be fully and accurately described, and should include not just the street address, but also the *exact* and *accurate* official designation of the property as it is precisely contained in the seller's existing deed or building survey—the dimensions and location, the "block" and "lot" numbers, the map numbers, or other designations used under the local custom. [Generally, the survey document, or the seller's existing deed—see pp. 40 & 47—will provide the most complete and official description for this purpose, and should simply be copied.]

iv) The Purchase Price and Mortgage Terms

Money matters should be detailed in full in the contract: the total price of the property (is it accurate?); amount of the down payment; amount of your "earnest money" deposit; whether these amounts (especially the down payment) should be held in an "escrow account"* until the closing, and by whom; details about the mortgage, if applicable (the mortgage amount needed, the interest rate, number of years to repay, and whether an existing old mortgage will be "assumable" or not); and how and when the money will be paid.

IMPORTANT: Generally, in house sale or purchase transactions in which mortgage financing applies, a provision is made (or should be made) in the Purchase Agreement making the agreement "subject to" (i.e., contingent upon) the buyer being able to qualify for and to obtain a mortgage loan, while also requiring the buyer to make an honest, diligent effort to obtain such a mortgage loan. The agreement may specify that the buyer must *immediately* apply for a mortgage and that the lender must provide him a letter of preliminary loan approval within, say, 7 days to the date of the sales contact, or obtain the final loan approved within, say, 30 days thereof, providing the buyer makes

---

*Having someone else, an independent third party, such as an escrow agent, the buyer's attorney, or the real estate broker, hold the down payment in a special segregated account ("escrow account"), affords the buyer the best protection in that it makes it easier for him to get his money back in the event that the transaction falls through for one unpredictable reason or the other. Alternatively, you may arrange with a bank to serve as the escrow agent and hold the money in escrow for you.

every diligent effort in good faith to apply for and obtain the loan . Note, however, that with such a provision—which, by the way, you should ensure is included in your own agreement—you are protected in being able to recover your down payment, <u>although</u> you yourself (the purchaser) must also make an honest effort to obtain the loan. (If, for example, you were to seek to pull out without having made a legitimate effort to obtain the loan, say because you discovered some other property you like better, then in such event the seller may have the legal right either to compel you to go through with the deal or have you forfeit your down payment). A clause such as this suffices: *"If the buyer is unable, within _____ days from today, to obtain a mortgage for $____ payable over ____ years with interest at ____ percent or better, after making a diligent and good faith effort to obtain one from lending institutions,   this contract shall be null and void and the buyer shall be entitled to a return of his down payment, in full."*

Of course, if the existing mortgage is an "assumable" one, and if it is at all possible for you to obtain the seller's (or the bank's) consent to take over the old mortgage — in which case you'll then be buying the house "subject to the existing mortgage" —you should save yourself all the trouble and use that option! For one thing, given the high and fluctuating interest rates in recent years, you'd stand a chance to save yourself some big money in a lower interest mortgage, not to speak of the savings from not having to pay the mortgage recording fees and taxes, title insurance policy costs, bank attorney fees, and the like, all over again!!

v) Personal Property Items

Don't assume or take anything for granted in regard to what items are includable in the sale. You wouldn't, of course, want to sabotage the whole deal over a mere birdbath. But you (the buyer) should make sure that the contract specifically enumerates all the major "personal property" items you really care about and want to have included in the deal. Otherwise, a seller may possibly decide to remove a major "personal property" item that is not readily considered a structural part of the house after you've paid for the house! A good way to accomplish this objective is this: have a so-called **"general inclusion" clause** included in the agreement, whereby you specifically enumerate the important, applicable, personal property items you desire (e.g., refrigerator, stove, air conditioner, appliances, barbeque grill, chandelier, light fixtures, washing machine, carpeting, drapes, window blinds, fireplace andirons, etc.) as part and parcel of the house purchase you are making.

vi) Special Condition of the House at Time of Sale

Not only should the property be maintained in good condition until closing, subject to your inspection, but also all known violations of the building, electrical or plumbing codes, should be <u>expressly enumerated</u> in the contract, and the contract should specify who or at whose expense, yours or the seller's, such violations are to be repaired and within what time schedule.

What about any significant violations or defects that you may possibly discover, say, after a housing or termite inspection? Your best protection against this possibility is to exert your maximum effort to see that there's provided in the contract—often such is already contained in the standard form contract— some type of **"express warranty" or "contingency" clause.** Something that reads like this:

> "The seller represents that the heating, plumbing, and electrical systems are in good working order, and will be in good working order at the time of closing, and that the roof is in good repair and does not leak."

If, as it may happen in some jurisdictions or circumstances, the buyer goes to contract before the house is professionally inspected (STEP 5, at pp. 33-4 above), then be sure to have a clause in the Contract making the offer to buy contingent upon your getting a favorable report. Something like this:

"Buyer, providing he/she so chooses, has ___ days after the signing of this contract within which to have the house inspected for termite infestation, and for a structural inspection to be done by a qualified home inspection service or engineer, all at the buyer's sole expense. If the inspection reports indicate termite infestation and/or structural problem, the seller shall have the option either to eliminate the infestation or correct the structural problem at seller's expense or to deem the contract concelled, providing that the seller must give <u>notice</u> of such intent to cancel to the buyer within 10 days after seller's receipt of the said inspection reports."

NOTE: Don't accept a seller's (or broker's) verbal exhortation that a given defect will be corrected. If he tells you to 'take my word for it,' don't— unless you get it in writing.

Furthermore, don't forget that whatever the written "warranties" provided for in the contract, they will be of no further real practical use or value to you <u>after</u> the closing, since they will generally expire then—that is, unless you hurry and get the necessary inspections done and quickly act upon them <u>before</u> the closing.

vii) Deeds and Title; Type of Deed

The document called the "deed" is what signifies the ownership of the property, and at the closing of any real estate transaction, when the seller finally delivers and the buyer receives the deed, it's at that mementous moment that the "title" (the instrument symbolizing ownership) is deemed to be transferred from the seller (the "grantor") to the buyer (the "grantee").

There are basically THREE types of deeds. The particular type employable in a given transaction is generally determined by what is agreed to in the contract as well as by what is customary in the given area. **The three main types are:**

a) The Full Covenant and Warranty Deed

From the standpoint of a buyer, this type of deed (also known as a **"General Warranty Deed"**) is the best of the three types. However, in more recent times, with the increasing use of title insurance, this type of deed is not as commonly used in most transactions.

Essentially, by a Full Covenant deed, the seller says to the buyer, in effect: "Look, I guarantee that I lawfully own this property and that I have the right to transfer it; that this title (to the property) is absolute and clear, and that I'll defend it against any claim or attack made on it."

[A sample copy of the Warranty Deed, is reproduced on pp. 136-7. Blank copies of the deed forms are obtainable from the Legal Publishers. See the Order Form on p. 191].

b) The Bargain and Sale Deed

This type of deed, (also known as a **"special warranty deed"** and more routinely used in areas like New York City and many others), says to the buyer, in effect, "Look, I, the seller, guarantee that I pass absolute title to you and warrant that I have not done or permitted to be done, anything that would adversely effect that title, or reduce its value."

When used with the usual "covenants" made therein (as is customarily done in most instances when it's employed, as in the standard form reproduced on p. 138-9 of the manual), this deed—especially if coupled with title insurance from a reputable company—is said by one real estate legal expert to "be enough to satisfy even the most neurotic purchaser." [A sample copy of the Bargain and Sale Deed is reproduced on pp. xxx. Blank copies of the deed forms are obtainable from the Legal Publishers. See the Order Form on p. 191].

c) The Quitclaim Deed

This type of deed is regarded as the least desirable of the three. With a quitclaim deed, the seller does not vouch for the extent or legitimacy of his rights or interest in the property, but merely "quits" (i.e., transfers) to you any rights or interests he may have in the property—whatever those rights or interests may actually happen to be, if any.

The seller merely says to you, in effect, "Look, I'm guaranteeing you nothing about what specific rights or interests I actually have in this property, but whatever rights or interests they happen to be as of the time I convey this deed to you, I hereby transfer the same to you."

As a rule, this type of deed is more commonly used in special situations when it is intended to correct defects in title —e.g., when one spouse conveys property to another or if an owner, or parent or relative, gives property as a gift. Again, however, if your seller insists on giving you this type of deed and a title insurance company is willing to insure the title, then you need not worry. Take it.

[A sample copy of the Quitclaim Deed is reproduced on p. 140. Blank copies of the deed forms are obtainable from the Legal Publishers. See the Order Form on p. 191.]

viii) Catastrophe Clause

Catastrophes may not— but they may and do—happen. To protect yourself against the possibility of a catastrophe (flood, hurricane, earthquake, fire, who knows what!?) occurring between the date of the contract and the closing, prudence dictates that you see that a simple clause that reads like this is contained or inserted in the contract:

> "The seller assumes all liability for fire, storms, earthquake, flood, vandalism, or other disasters or damage
> prior to the closing."

ix) Time and Place of Closing

The date, time and place of closing will usually be specified in the contract. Generally, unless otherwise expressly provided for, the date specified therein is considered to be "on or about" the stated date, meaning that either side can ask for a reasonable postponement, say *for* 2 weeks or even up to 2 months. Nevertheless, it is also a wise practice, especially if you think you may possibly need more time, to have a clause added in the contract providing for an extention for a reasonable cause.

Watch out, though! There's one situation where the issue of timing has been found to be an explosive one in closings: when the contract contains the phrase *"time is of the essence."* In such situations, the courts have been known to interpret this rather harmless-looking phrase to mean that a given date means *exactly* that, and that any delay by one side may entitle the other to a penalty or cancellation of the deal with damages. If time happens to be critical for you and you need the house by a certain date, have this phrase included in the contract, and, alternatively, watch out whenever the contract contains this phrase or one like it and make sure that you yourself abide by all intermediate deadlines.   In line with this, if your situation requires that you occupy the house by a certain date, you should ensure that a clause is provided in the contract stipulating that the seller will bear the cost of your storage and lodging costs if the seller doesn't "vacate and broom-clean" the property by the time of the closing, or by the time you've moved out of your apartment or closed on the sale of your old home, whatever is your preference or situation.

x) "Subject to" Clauses

Most pre-printed forms and other contract forms provide that the premises are sold "subject to" any zoning regulations, encroachments, covenants, restrictions, and easements *of* record then existing. This provision is ordinarily not objectionable. However, for the buyer's maximum protection, the buyer should still seek to add this provision to that: "providing the same do not render title unmarketable or subject to forfeiture."

xi) Adjustments to Be Made At Closing

The general rule is that the seller is responsible for all assessments for sewers, roads, and the like, as well as for taxes, fuel, insurance, and the like, falling due up to the date of closing. Hence, the contract should provide an **"apportionment clause"**, apportioning any prepaid expenses accordingly (e.g., taxes already paid by the seller, fuel adjustments, "points" paid by seller or buyer). Something like:

> "Taxes, water charges, rents, if any, interest on mortgage, premiums on insurance policies being transferred,
> and fuel, will be apportioned at closing."

xii) The Contract Signing Event

Finally, when it comes time for the signing of the contract, here's how you approach it. First and foremost, don't rush to sign. <u>Don't</u> give in to pressure by anyone (the seller or his lawyer, your spouse or partner, the broker, etc.) that you sign "right now"—especially if you are not quite totally clear about or agreeable to even a single provision or clause in the contract.

Look the contract over. Take your time. If necessary, you could ask for a break, or even to take the contract home for a few days to go over it. *Read and re-read it over and over again. Make sure that everything you want is in it—you may not get another chance to correct your mistake.* If there's anything that's not perfectly clear to you, ask. Find out what it means, or ask the realtor or seller (or his attorney, if he has one) to explain it to your satisfaction.

When there's something in the contract that you don't agree with or didn't agree to, ask that it be deleted, or modified as may be your preference; don't be afraid or intimidated to speak up. Crossing out any unwanted language contained in the contract, or adding any phrases to it, is permissible, but everybody (the principals) on both sides should initial the changes as proof or confirmation that the parties consent to those changes. *Only then— after you shall have understood each and every detail and agreed to them—may you finally put your signature to the contract paper.*

If the seller is married, or the seller owns the property "jointly" or as "tenants in common" with a spouse or another person (you find this out by looking at the seller's existing deed or the title report), then require the signature of the seller as well as the signature of his spouse or mate on the purchase contract. In fact, in some states, even if one spouse alone owns the property, the other spouse still must sign the papers; so it wouldn't hurt to require *both* signatures, anyway, if and when at all possible.

The contract must be dated, and the date of the signing may not be on a Sunday or a legal holiday—contracts signed on either of those days are generally considered unenforceable under many states' laws.

FINALLY, MAKE SURE YOU GET YOUR OWN SIGNED COPY OF THE CONTRACT AND KEEP IT!

> <u>NOTE:</u> This suggested Sales/Purchase Contract form reproduced on pp. 43-6 (like the other forms reproduced in this manual, it's the type of form that can be used in all states), assumes that the home buyer is "assuming" (taking over) an old <u>existing</u> mortgage to finance the purchase. Purchasers who are, on the other hand, to refinance and/or make a totally new mortgage, may either modify this form accordingly (i.e., cross out Paragraph 4, and the relevant portions of Paragraphs 3 & 5), or use another form altogether.

CONTRACT OF SALE

M 337—Contract of sale of real estate,
plain English format, 11-78

© 1978 BY JULIUS BLUMBERG, INC.,

Contract of Sale

Date...... *[On the date of signing, enter that date here]* ....

[Seller/Sellers' names. If a corporation, enter business information, e.g.: BOA CORP., A NEW YORK CORPORATION HAVING ITS PRINCIPAL OFFICE AT...?]

Seller and Purchaser agree as follows:

Parties

Seller :Dow D. Dean and Mary M. Dean, his wife.
address: I27 Seller Street, Brooklyn, New York, II234

Purchaser (s) JOHN H. Johnson, and Diana A. Johnson, his wife;
address: I22 Purchase Street, Queens New York, II437   *[Buyer/buyers' address(es)]*

Purchase agreement

1. Seller shall sell and Purchaser shall buy the Property on the terms stated in this Contract.

Property

2. The Property is described as follows:

[The official description ("map designation") of the property] (Get this information from the old deed.]

BEGINNING at a point on the southwesterly side of I5th Street
distant Two Hundred Seventy-six feet ten inches southeasterly
from the corner formed by the intersection of the southwesterly
side of I5th Street with the southeasterly side of Third Avenue;
running thence southwesterly at right angles to I5th Street and
part of the distance through a party wall One Hundred Nine feet
eleven inches to land now or formerly of Deborah L. Carson ; thence
southeasterly along said land now or formerly of Deborah L. Carson,
Seventeen feet two and one-eighth inches, thence northeasterly
along the northwesterly side of Lot No. 26 on Map of Land of John
Dimon, et al., filed in Kings County June I7, I835, One Hundred
Ten feet seven inches to the southwesterly side of I5th Street,
thence northwesterly along the southwesterly side of I5th Street,
Nineteen feet six inches to the point or place of Beginning.

[The property's street address]

SAID premises is further known as: II2 I5th Street, Brooklyn, New
York.

[Use is made in this space to spell out the terms, as agreed (or agreeable) by the parties, for various matters, such as: the existing liens on the property, and who bears financial obligation for same; any special bills outstanding on the property and to whom it's chargeable or apportionable; any special provisions may deem necessary or wise in order to protect yourself, etc. etc.]

The Parties acknowledge the existence of a lien for $600 imposed by
the Emergency Service Division of the City of New York's Housing
Department. It is agreed that the Purchaser will purchase this
property subject to the existing lien but will be given credit for
same by the Seller, with the proper adjustment made accordingly at
closing.

Sellers acknowledge an outstanding Con Edison Bill for $I80. Sellers
will pay this item separately. This will remain the Seller's sole
obligation.

Purchasers(or, as the case may be, the Sellers) expressly state that
it is their choice and their preference to represent themselves,
and to close without an attorney.
Accordingly, where and whenever the term "attorney" or "lawyer" is
used in this contract, or in other papers pursuant to this transaction, it shall be presumed to mean the Purchasers (or, the Sellers?)
themselves also.

Additional to Paragraph I2 of this contract below, the Sellers represent that the heating, plumbing, and electrical systems are in good
working order, and will be in good working order at the time of closing, and that they have received no notice of any housing violations
within the past_??___ year(s).

Additional to Paragraphs 3 and 5 of the contract below, in the event
that Purchaser is unable, within_??___ days from the date of this
contract, to obtain a Purchase Money Mortgage for no less than $_??___
payable over _??___ years with interest at __??___percent or better
after having made a diligent and good faith effort to obtain one from
lending institutions, this contract shall be null and void and the
Purchaser shall be entitled to a return of his down payment.

Seller shall vacate the premises no later than _??__days from the closing, otherwise said seller shall pay $_??___ to Purchaser as rents,
which shall increase by $_??___ for every month thereafter which seller
remains in the premises.

—OVER—

[Use is made in this space to spell out the terms, as agreed (or agreeable) by the parties, for various matters, such as: the existing liens on the property, and who bears financial obligation for same; any special bills outstanding on the property and to whom it's chargeable or apportionable; any special provisions you may deem necessary or wise to make in order to protect yourself, etc. etc.]

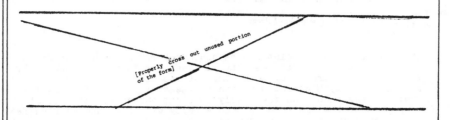

[Properly cross out unused portion of the form]

The sale includes:

(a) All buildings and improvements on the Property.

Buildings and improvements Streets, assignment of unpaid awards

(b) All right, title and interest, if any, of Seller in any land lying in the bed of any street or highway, opened or proposed, in front of or adjoining the Property to the center line thereof. It also includes any right of Seller to any unpaid award to which Seller may be entitled (1) due to taking by condemnation of any right, title or interest of Seller and (2) for any damage to the Property due to change of grade of any street or highway. Seller will deliver to Purchaser at Closing, or thereafter, on demand, proper instruments for the conveyance of title and the assignment and collection of the award and damages.

Fixtures, personal property

(c) All fixtures and articles of personal property attached to or used in connection with the Property, unless specifically excluded below. Seller represents that they are paid for and owned by Seller free and clear of any lien other than the Existing Mortgage(s). They include but are not limited to plumbing, heating, lighting and cooking fixtures, fire, smoke, and burglar alarms, radio and television aerials, blinds, shades, screens, awnings, storm windows, window boxes, storm doors, mail boxes, weather vanes, flagpoles, pumps, shrubbery, clothes washers, clothes dryers, garbage disposal units, ranges, refrigerators, freezers, air conditioning equipment and installations, and wall to wall carpeting.

Excluded from this sale are:

[If any of the items listed under paragraph (c) above, or any other special item(s), are not to be included in the sale, then list such items here]

→ Furniture and household furnishings; clothes washers and clothes dryers; drapes; barbeque grill; chandelier; and fireplace andirons.

Price

3. The purchase price is $100,000.00

payable as follows:

On the signing of this Contract, by check subject to collection: .... $ 4,000.00

By allowance for the principal amount still unpaid on the Existing Mortgage (applicable if buyer will assume $ 20,000.00 exist. mortg)

By a Purchase Money Note and Mortgage from Purchaser (or assigns) to Seller: .... $ 46,000.00

BALANCE AT CLOSING .... $ 30,000.00

The BALANCE AT CLOSING shall be paid in cash or good certified check, or official check of any bank, savings bank, trust company, or savings and loan association having a banking office in the State of New York. A check must be payable to the order of Seller, or to the order of Purchaser and duly endorsed by Purchaser (if other than a corporation) to the order of Seller in the presence of Seller or Seller's attorney.

Existing Mortgage

4. The Property will be conveyed subject to the continuing lien of the following mortgage ("Existing Mortgage"): Mortgage now in the unpaid principal amount of $20,000 and interest at the rate of 13 % per year, presently payable in monthly installments of $175.26 which includes principal, interest,

and with any balance of principal being due and payable on ??? 19 ??.

[Enter — applicable only if there's an existing mortg. and/or some kind of 'balloon' payment in the end]

Purchase money mortgage

5. If a purchase money note and mortgage is to be given it shall be drawn by the Seller or the attorney for the Seller. Purchaser shall pay for the mortgage recording tax, recording fees and the charge for drawing the note and mortgage.**

The purchase money note and mortgage shall provide that it will always be subject to the prior lien of any Existing Mortgage even though the Existing Mortgage is extended, consolidated or refinanced in good faith; and it shall be in the amount of $46,000.00 , for a term of ?? years, at an interest rate of ?.% per annum payable $?? monthly, for principal & interest. **Charge for drawing up mortg. papers shall in no wise exceed $???

—OVER—

Title transfer subject to

6. The Property is to be conveyed subject to:

    (a) Applicable zoning and governmental regulations that affect the use and maintenance of the Property provided that they are not violated by buildings and improvements on the Property.

    (b) Conditions, agreements, restrictions and easements of record.

    (c) Any state of facts an inspection or survey of the Property may show, *providing* it does not make the title to the Property unmarketable. *or subject to forfeiture.*

    (d) Existing tenancies.

    (e) Unpaid assessments payable after the date of the transfer of title.

[The type of DEED being employed?]

Use of purchase price to pay encumbrances

7. Seller may pay and discharge any liens and encumbrances not provided for in this Contract. Seller may make payment out of the balance of the Purchase Price paid by Purchaser on the transfer of title.

Deed and transfer taxes

8. At the Closing Seller shall deliver to Purchaser a *Bargain & Sale with covenants* deed so as to convey a fee simple title to the Property free and clear of all encumbrances except as stated in this Contract. The deed shall be prepared, signed and acknowledged by Seller and transfer tax stamps in the correct amount shall be affixed to the deed, all at Seller's expense. The deed shall contain a trust fund clause as required by Section 13 of the Lien Law.

Adjustments at closing

9. The following are to be apportioned pro-rata to the date of transfer:

    (a) Rents as and when collected.

    (b) Interest on the Existing Mortgage.

    (c) Taxes, water rates and sewer rents based on the fiscal period for which assessed.

    (d) Premiums on existing transferable insurance policies and renewals on those expiring prior to closing.

    (e) Fuel, if any.

    (f) Deposits in escrow held under Existing Mortgage.

[If possible, add this - just for the Buyer's added protection]

Water meter readings

10.- If there is a water meter on the Property, Seller shall furnish a reading to a date not more than thirty days prior to the time herein set for Closing. The unfixed meter charge and sewer rent, if any, shall be apportioned on the basis of this last reading. *(or, alternatively, does provide)*

Fire, other casualty

11. This Contract does not provide for what happens in the event of fire or casualty loss before the title closing. Unless different provision is made in this Contract, Section 5-1311 of the General Obligations Law will apply. *(Seller assumes all liability prior to closing)*

Condition of Property

12. Purchaser has inspected the buildings and improvements on the Property and the personal property included in this sale. Purchaser agrees to take title "as is" and in their present condition subject to reasonable use and natural deterioration between now and the time of closing.

Seller unable to convey, liability

13. If Seller is unable to convey title in accordance with this Contract, Seller's only liability is to refund all money paid on account of this Contract and pay charges made for examining title.

Closing date and place

14. The Closing will take place at the ~~office of~~ the home of the Seller, which is:___

    (address?) _____ at (time?) .M. on (date?) _____ 19___

Broker

15. Purchaser represents that Purchaser has not dealt with any broker in connection with this sale other than ___ *ABC REALTY CO 2 Water St. Brooklyn NY;* and Seller agrees to pay broker the commission earned (pursuant to separate agreement with broker).

[Enter business name of the applicable broker(s), if any was used, [If no broker was used, then enter NONE]

Purchaser's lien

16. All money paid on account of this Contract, and the reasonable expenses of examination of the title to the Property and of any survey and inspection charges are hereby made liens on the Property. The liens shall not continue after default by Purchaser.

Notice

17. Any notice or other communication from one party to the other shall be in writing and sent by registered or certified mail in a postpaid envelope addressed to the party at the address above. The address above may be changed by notice to the other party.

Entire Agreement

18. All prior understandings and agreements between Seller and Purchaser are merged in this Contract. This Contract completely expresses their full agreement and has been entered into after full investigation. Neither party is relying upon statements made by anyone that is not a party to this Contract.

No Oral Change

19. This Contract may not be changed or ended orally.

Successors

20. This Contract shall apply to and bind the distributees, executors, administrators, successors and assigns of the Seller and Purchaser.

Multiple Parties

21. If there are more than one Purchaser or Seller the words "Purchaser" and "Seller" used in this Contract includes them.

Signatures

Seller and Purchaser have signed this Contract as of the date at the top of the first page.

WITNESS *[Some Witnesses to the signing event, if any, will each sign here. Could be the Notary Public]*

X ---------------------------------

SELLER(S)

X ---------------------------------
[Seller(s) signs his/their full names here]

X ---------------------------------

PURCHASER(S)

X ---------------------------------
[Buyer(s) signs his/their full names here]

X ---------------------------------

—OVER—

STATE OF NEW YORK, COUNTY OF ???   ss.:
On _____ 19 before me personally came

Dow D. Dean and Mary M. Dean,

to me known to be the individual described in and who executed the foregoing instrument, and acknowledged that he/ she/they executed the same.

[A Notary Public signs and affixes his stamp here]

(NOTARY PUBLIC)

STATE OF NEW YORK, COUNTY OF _____ ss.:
On ?? 19 before me personally came

John H. Johnson and Diana A. Johnson,

to me known to be the individual described in and who executed the foregoing instrument, and acknowledged that they executed the same.

(NOTARY PUBLIC)

[Used when a corporation/a Partnership is involved]

STATE OF NEW YORK, COUNTY OF _____ ss.:
On 19 before me personally came
to me known, who, being by me duly sworn, did depose and say that he resides at No. _____

that he is the (Office held by this person of (Name of the corporation)
the corporation described in and which executed the foregoing instrument; that he knows the seal of said corporation; that the seal affixed to said instrument is such corporate seal; that it was so affixed by order of the board of directors of said corporation, and that he signed h name thereto by like order.

(Notary Public)

STATE OF NEW YORK, COUNTY OF _____ ss.:
On 19 before me personally came
to me known and known to me to be a partner in

(name of the partnership)
a partnership, and known to me to be the person described in and who executed the foregoing instrument in the partnership name, and said (name of the office holder) duly acknowledged that he executed the foregoing instrument for and on behalf of said partnership.

(Notary Public)

Adjournment
Closing of title under this Contract is adjourned to   19 , at   o'clock,
at
and all adjustments are to be made as of   19

Assignment
Date: 19
For value received, this Contract is assigned to

and Assignee assumes all obligations of the purchaser in the Contract.

....
Purchaser

....
Assignee of Purchaser

NOTE: As a rule, this page is often ignored and not generally filled in or employed in the vast majority of cases, since it's not customarily required (or a legal necessity) that the Sales Contract be notarized or officially recorded with the public registry's office. Use of this page (and the need to notarize the signatures of the parties to the contract) generally become relevant only when one party or the other wishes, for whatever his reasons, to record the contract publicly, or, alternatively, for an agreement on a postponement of the closing date, when applicable.

Dow D. Dean and Mary M. Dean   Seller
and
John H. Johnson and Diana A. Johnson   Purchaser

Contract of Sale of Real Estate

Date 19
Deed to pass on 19

STATE OF NEW YORK
County of

RECORDED ON THE
day of _____, 19
at _____ o'clock _____ M.
in Liber _____ of Deeds
at Page _____ and examined

CLERK

STEP ⑦: ARRANGE FOR A TITLE SEARCH AND SURVEY REPORT ON THE HOUSE

A. The Title Search

When you buy a house (or merely plan to buy one) from a given seller who comes along telling you that he or she owns the property, how do you get to make sure that the person is actually the legitimate owner of the property?   Furthermore, though the seller may have told you otherwise—and even honestly believed that to be so—do you know, for sure, that there may in fact not be some judgments, claims or liens (some that the seller may not even know about) existing against the house, or unpaid taxes or debts for which you'll have to be responsible as a new owner of the property? And can you be sure that there are no restrictions existing on the building, forbidding the owner from putting the property to certain uses? Well, uncovering answers to questions such as these is what a "title search" is all about.

Arranging for a title search to be run on the property you're buying is one thing you should do as soon as the contract is signed. *The purpose, of course, is to protect yourself.* It is a simple matter to arrange. As a practical matter, you may even elect to conduct the search yourself and save yourself the few hundred dollars it would otherwise cost you in title search fees to hire an outside professional to do it for you. You simply go to the local public records office in which deeds and liens are recorded for the area in which the house is located (e.g., the city's registry or county clerk's office) and ask to look through the records. [Or, if you happen to have a family or an inheritance situation—say, a situation where a trusted friend or family member is the transferring party, or where you are inheriting a house from a decedent family member—you could even decide, as many in such situations often do and with relatively little or no risk whatsoever, to do without a title search altogether!]

In any event, if you should find (as most of us probably do!) that having to take the time and trouble to rummage through official documents and public records is just a little too confusing and impractical for your taste, **there's another option for you:** Do exactly what practicing real estate professionals themselves (lawyers, realtors, developers, etc.) do in almost all such cases. Hire yourself a professional **"title searcher"** to do it for you! Aside from the fact of greater convenience and the element of greater professionalism involved when you use a professional title searcher (actually, a title insurance company or abstract company) to do the work, there's one further distinct advantage in using one: his work carries with it an insurance policy of his company guaranteeing his work—guaranteeing that the title company will for ever be financially liable to you for any damages you might suffer (to the extent of the policy coverage) for any defects in title the title searcher may have failed to discover.

To find a title insurance or abstract company, look in the Telephone Directory's Yellow Pages under "Title Insurance" or "Abstracts." The fee for a title search alone could run anywhere from $100 to $250, and, if coupled with insurance protection, you may add another $300 or $400, all depending on the value of the property and the location in the country.* According to many experts in the field, one way a buyer can often get a better price for this service than he would otherwise get, is to look up the company which provided that service for the property when the present owner bought it (ask the present seller, or his mortgage holder, or take a look at a copy of his title insurance policy or survey) and apply to the same company for your own title search and insurance. The reason this is so is that when the same company is used, it would often mean less work and greater speed of examination for it because, rather than start entirely from the scratch, all the title searcher will probably need to do is to pull out the old title search report from the company records and simply upgrade the existing information, thereby making for a reduced charge. Another potential way of reducing the cost of title insurance in a situation in which the buyer will be purchasing his property through a mortgage loan, is to wait, and then upon approval of the mortgage, apply to the same title company that is insuring the lending institution's mortgage and have the same company handle his own (the buyer's own) title insurance. As a rule, the title insurance companies generally charge a reduced combined rate for two policies when obtained simultaneously from the same company.

---

*A May 1984 report by the New York Times gave the following fees for New York metropolitan areas: in New Jersey $553 for a policy on a $100,000 house; $614 for the same policy in New York and Nassau County, and $633 for Suffolk and Westchester counties; and $390 as "allocable rate" on a $100,000 house, plus $200 for the actual search, in Connecticut.

NOTE: Buyers, especially those financing the purchase through a lending institution, should take note, however, of this fact: that there are TWO types of this title insurance policies—one type, the "lender's" title insurance policy which is often required by the mortgage institution, is one which insures the mortgage for the bank's or lender's benefit but not your own rights or interest in the property; while the second type is the "buyer's" title insurance in that such policy specifically insures the buyer's own separate rights and interest in the property. The two policies are distinctly different and should not be confused by buyers as being one and the same thing; they protect two completely different interests, one the lender, and the other, the home buyer.

What do you get from a title company's search? They'll issue you a title report—a report stating its findings as to the status of the title of the property, who holds legal title, which liens and encumbrances (e.g., mechanic's or contractor's lien, etc.) are presently outstanding on the property, what the taxes on the property are, and whether or not they are paid up to date, and so forth. The report will give the official description of the property, sometimes referring to a filed map, and giving a particular "section," "lot," "block," or "parcel," of land. For each parcel of land, there's a record in a book kept by the land registry's office that tells you where deeds, mortgages, easements, and restrictions are recorded for that particular parcel— in another book, or even on microfilm.

In the metropolitan New York area, for example, the method employed is for the title company to issue a title report to the applicant, which sets forth all objections to the title and defects disclosed by the record. The report may also list some special requirements or objections as preconditions to the title company's willingness to insure the title for the property buyer. Then, if those objections are cleared, the company will go ahead and insure the property buyer's title to the full extent of the property's gross purchase price. Or, alternatively, the title company may elect to insure the title "subject to" certain enumerated objections and exceptions—that is, excepting those objections or defects from its protection and coverage.

B. The Survey

As an additional way of protecting his best interests before hand, it may— just may—be advisable for a would-be home buyer to obtain and examine a survey print on the house being purchased. What is a "survey"? While the home inspection report (pp. 33-4) is concerned with finding out the actual condition of the *house* itself, a survey print is primarily concerned, on the other hand, with finding out the actual and exact status and dimensions of the *land* part of the property. A survey print—an architectural or engineering-type drawing of the property— will set forth the property's dimensions and boundaries in relation to the neighboring land, noting and accurately locating all structures, driveways, paths, major trees, improvements, and other such landmarks.

Is it absolutely necessary that you have this report? Unless otherwise required (say by the lender or title insurance company), you don't necessarily have to seek one, if you feel pretty comfortable about it. You may omit ordering a survey; and your purchase will be that much cheaper—some $350 to $600 in surveyor's fees, depending on the value of the property and the amount of advance research and preparation required. But here's the potential risk: although a deed may accurately describe a house on a parcel of land, only a survey can show exactly where it is located on the ground and, more important, the location of other structures (the fences tele-phone and electrical wires, roads and paths, etc.), and, as a rule, although a title insurance company will guarantee the ownership of the land (as set forth in the deed), without an up to date survey it normally excludes from coverage any additional facts that a survey may bring to light.   Hence, the obvious principal purpose (and benefit) of a survey to a home purchaser is to give the new buyer a better idea of the property, and to give him the oppor-tunity to uncover any potential encroachment of the neighboring buildings upon the land the buyer is buying, if any, or of the seller's building upon the neighboring land.   And, if such encroachment should happen to be timely uncovered, the buyer may then prevail upon the seller to remedy the defects (or to compensate him in kind for it)—before the sale is consummated, and thereby guarantee the future marketability of the property.

How do you obtain a survey print? Frequently, you may be able to obtain an old, existing one (at no cost to you) from the seller. Or, you might be able to get a copy (at a nominal or no cost to you) from the title company which insured the seller's title, or perhaps from the holder of a mortgage on the properties. Sometimes, though, especially with regard to older houses and parcels, no survey may exist or is available, and your only option in such instances   (after all searches and inquiries shall have been exhausted and none is found to exist), would be to order one afresh from an area Licensed Surveyor (ask for recommendations from area mortgage lenders or brokers, or look up some names in the Yellow Pages.)

If a survey is available, you should walk the property with it in hand, and make sure there have been no structural changes or significant encroachments, either by a neighboring property upon the seller's property, or vice versa. If changes have occurred, then contact the original surveyor or, if not available, another surveyor, for an updating to incorporate such changes and to issue a certified, new survey print to you or the title company.

STEP ⑧: FIND THE MEANS OF FINANCING

O.K. You've previewed, considered and decided on a house, negotiated and signed a sales contract with the seller, and in accordance with the terms of that contract, you made a down payment to the seller towards the purchase price, and set a date —the date of "closing"—by which you are to produce the agreed balance of the purchase price. The contract, among other things, requires the following of you and the seller: You are to pay the seller a certain sum in cash on or by such closing date, in return for which the seller is then to deliver a good and marketable title of ownership of the house to you.

THE NEXT ORDER OF BUSINESS, THEN, IS TO SET ABOUT TO FIND A SOURCE BY WHICH YOU ARE TO OBTAIN (OR OTHERWISE HAVE) THAT REMAINING SUM OF MONEY—by or before the date set for the closing.

BANKS, SAVING AND LOAN ASSOC'S. —OR YOUR LOADED (RICH) UNCLE!!

A. Sources of Financing

1. Self-Financing

The simplest way to purchase your new home would, of course, be for you to be independently and sufficiently wealthy and have all the money you'd need to make the purchase all by yourself, in which case you'll simply pay all cash for the house price — and save yourself much of the troubles, aggravations, and details involved in the whole business of financing a home purchase! Unfortunately, though, as a practical matter, only very few people can afford to do so. Consequently, if you are like the overwhelming majority of buyers, you'll probably have to resort to one type of "mortgage" loan or the other in order to be able to pay for the house you are buying.

2. Mortgage Loan Financing

Broadly speaking, there are two basic ways by which you can obtain a home mortgage loan; there are two basic types of mortgage assistance you can get. They are:

a) seller-assisted financing of the purchase; and

b) where the buyer applies for and gets a new (first) mortgage from a bank

We'll consider each type separately.

a) *The seller-assisted financing*

In the traditional house-purchase transaction, the usual process is for the buyer to use his own savings to pay for the down payment, normally about 20 percent of the purchase price, and the remainder of the purchase price, the 80 percent, is then obtained as a bank mortgage loan. This way, the seller receives full payment for the house at the closing — part (the 20 percent) from the buyer's own resources, and the rest (the 80 percent) from the bank.

Ideally, it would, of course, be nice to be always able to have buyers who would be able to have the 20 percent cash at hand, and also be able to qualify for a bank loan for the 80 percent balance. But what if, as is often the case, you have a situation where the seller finds a serious and desirable buyer, but who does not quite have the full 20 percent down payment? Or, who has the down payment but can only qualify for part of the balance, say 60 percent, rather than the 80 percent.

In such a case, the seller may elect to serve as a bank for the buyer, for part of the money he'd need to effectuate the purchase. In effect, the seller makes a conclusion that, to make the sale, he'll have to help the buyer with the financing.

THE 'SECOND MORTGAGE' OR SELLER TAKE-BACK

The most common form of seller-assisted financing is the "SECOND MORTGAGE" FINANCING. It's a form of seller-takeback because here, instead of the seller getting all cash, he takes back a mortgage for a part of the sale price. For example, let's say the buyer has only 10 percent cash to put down but can qualify only for an 80 percent bank mortgage. So, the seller will agree to carry the remaining balance for 10 percent.

80% mortgage from a bank	10% takeback or 2nd mortgage	10% cash

It's also a "second mortgage" because any such mortgage loan is a mortgage which will begin to be protected (with the property as collateral) *only after* a previous mortgage is first satisfied and retired. For this reason, a lender making a second mortgage will likely want a HIGHER interest rate, and usually does offer less money for a shorter period of time.

The need for a second mortgage arises usually when, as a purchaser, you find there's a gap between the amount of mortgage money the conventional lender (a bank) grants you, and what you actually need to fully meet the purchase price of the house (including the settlement costs). The seller, then, not wanting the deal to fall apart for want of a relatively small extra amount of money, may agree to become a source of a "second mortgage" money to you; he "lends" you (i.e., he lets you owe him) the shortfall amount you need, and gets you to sign a Promissory Note promising to pay him the amount over a period of time (usually a short period, such as a few months or years), and, as his security in the event that you don't, he'll also have you sign a "second" mortgage document for him (meaning merely that this mortgage is 'second' to or behind the first, original mortgage for the main purchase money). [See Appendix C at pp. 157-165 for more on seller-oriented types of mortgage loans].

EXAMPLE: The seller agrees to sell his house for $100,000. This total price will come from the following Sources:

Buyer's out-of-pocket cash	$ 10,000
Buyer's first mortgage (e.g., loan from bank)	$ 80,000
Second mortgage extended from seller to buyer	$ 10,000
Total house price	$100,000

This kind of second mortgage is also known as a "purchase money mortgage" because it is part of the total purchase price of the property. Sometimes brokers and sellers also refer to this arrangement as "taking back paper," in that the seller (the mortgagee) is accepting (taking back) "paper" (the mortgage note) from the buyer (the mortgagor) for a certain amount of money in lieu of actual cash, and will be paid back over a period of time at the agreed terms and conditions.

The second mortgage, although the most common form of seller financing, is not the only kind of this type of mortgage. If the seller owns the property free and clear with no mortgage outstanding on it, he can handle the whole financing himself by giving the buyer a FIRST MORTGAGE. In this method, known as THE INSTALL-MENT SALE OR LAND CONTRACT METHOD, the buyer will typically give the seller a down payment and make payments for the balance over a number of years.

There are certain advantages and disadvantages associated with seller-assisted financing. For the seller, the obvious advantage of the seller-assisted financing is that it would facilitate a sale, particularly in a soft real estate market environment. Furthermore, as a seller, you can often get a relatively higher interest rate for such a loan, as compared with putting the same money in the bank. The bank may, for example, pay only 4 percent, while the second mortgage might be set at an interest rate of say 9 or 10 percent — a far bigger return. On the other hand, the prime disadvantage for the seller is that, if the buyer should for any reason default on the mortgage and fail to make the payments, the seller's only recourse would be to foreclose on the second mortgage and take the property back — a move that would generally be economically practicable only in a robust real estate market where the value of the property shall have considerably appreciated over the original sale price to allow for the house to be disposed at a high profit, since the costs and time factor associated with foreclosure are themselves often horrendous.

b) Obtaining a Totally New Mortgage of Your Own From A Lending Institution

A second basic source by which a buyer can obtain a purchase loan financing, is to obtain a totally new financing in his own name from a regular home financing or lending institution, as differentiated from getting it from the seller as in the method described in the preceding section above.

There are two basic types of 'outside' mortgage loans:
i) The government-sponsored types; and
ii) the so-called "conventional" (non-government) types of mortgages.

i) *The FHA/VA Government-Sponsored Types/Sources of Mortgage Loans*

There are two main sources of government-sponsored mortgage loans—**the Federal Housing Administration (F.H.A.),** and **Veterans' Administration (V.A.)** types. These two federal agencies, it should be noted, do not themselves directly make the loans.   Rather, all they do is merely to provide the 'coventional' lending institution who wishes to lend under the F.H.A. or V.A. rules the "guarantee" or "assurance" that they will pay back the loan in the event that you (the private borrower) fail to do so—and thus, by so doing, to lessen the lender's risk factor and make it easier and more possible that the conventional lender will more readily extend loan to you than he would otherwise have.   By one account, in 1982, one-third of all mortgages originated in the United States were either an F.H.A. or V.A. mortgage.

If at all you can qualify for these federal programs, first try those sources before you seek the conventional sources. There are a few important advantages to having them: to date, they continue to grant 30-year fixed-interest rate loans, and graduated-payment payments are also offered; the cost of the loans are cheaper than conventional type loan rates as the interest rates are set by law, and any other charges to the borrower for making the loan are forbidden; the down payments required for such loans are smaller; and, just as importantly, the criteria used to judge how large a mortgage the borrower can afford are more liberal.

Government-sponsored loans are not without some difficulties, however. These loans are not always as easily obtainable: Many lenders and home sellers shy away from making these types of loans —the lenders, because it means a lower interest rate and lower profit margin for them, extra paperwork, and a longer delay (30-40 days in 1982); and the seller, because it takes too long to get the necessary government "approvals" required by the program, and he may often have to make expensive repairs to upgrade the condition of the house to the more demanding standards required for the F.H.A. and V.A. mortgage approval. One traditional result, therefore, has been that conventional lending institutions, in order for them to make an F.H.A. or V.A. loan, will generally **"discount the loan"** as a kind of compensation to them for the supposed inconveniences and the lower interest rate they're compelled to charge by law for such loans—that is, they will impose for such loans a higher one-time charge called **"points"** (a single point is equivalent to 1 percent of the mortgage value.) [This, of course, is in addition to other so-called **"origination" charges.]** However, since, by law, the home buyer involved in an F.H.A. or V.A.-sponsored mortgage is permitted to pay only 1 point (and no more than that), all the extra "points" charges over and above the 1 point will therefore have to be paid by the home seller. The practical effect of this is that the average seller will, on his part, make every effort either to avoid selling to an F.H.A. or V.A. buyer, or attempt to make up for the additional costs of doing so by inflating his asking price for the house in the first instance.

How do you qualify for an F.H.A. or V.A. loan? Anyone who has served 181 days or more in the military since 1940 is eligible for a lifetime for a V.A. loan, including current members of the military and spouses of deceased veterans who have not remarried. You need not put down any down payment to qualify, and you can often borrow the full purchase price of the house.

As for an F.H.A. loan, the only stipulation is that you be able to afford it, the generally applied criteria being that the borrower must spend <u>no more than</u> 38% of his monthly income on carrying the loan and paying fixed costs on the house, such as property taxes and home insurance.* In addition, you must be able to put down out of your own pocket a down payment of 4 or 5 percent of the mortgage value, and the house must be owner-occupied.

How do you apply? You'll normally begin the process by applying to the conventional lending institution you wish to deal with (and not to the F.H.A. or V.A. itself.) The financial institution will, in turn, have you fill out some detailed financial application forms. [See pp. 67 & 69 for sample F.H.A. and V.A. loan application forms.] The lending institutions will then arrange for an inspection of the property and, if you or the seller haven't already done so, a formal appraisal of the house will also be ordered.

---

*The criteria used for determining whether a V.A. loan applicant can afford a loan, on the other hand, vary by regions.   In Northern New Jersey in 1982, for example, a single veteran qualified for one if he or she had $440 left over per month after all debt payments were subtracted from the net monthly income. By contrast, the applicable requirement for a "conventional" type loan was that the applicant may not use up to 28% of his monthly income for those costs.

For more information on F.H.A. and V.A. mortgages, look in the Yellow Pages under "government," or contact a local mortgage banker or broker, or the regional Housing and Urban Development (H.U.D.) office nearest you as listed in Appendix F of this manual.

ii) The 'Conventional' Types/Sources of Mortgage Loans

The most common sources of mortgages you may have to turn to, used by the vast majority of home buyers, are the so-called **"Conventional" mortgage lenders**—regular commercial lending institutions, such as savings banks, savings and loan associations, commercial banks, mortgage companies, life insurance companies, credit unions, and the like. In general, conventional loans are usually the fastest to process, with less red tape than most others, and is often the easiest to obtain. By the same token, however, the interest rate for this type of loan, which is directly payable by the borrower himself is usually a few percentage points (3 to 5 percent) higher than for the F.H.A. or V.A. loans, and the down payment is almost always much higher, generally about 20% of the home purchase price on the average. The repayment period is customarily shorter, typically 15 to 25 years.

B. Follow the Following Guidelines to Seek Out a Conventional Loan:

- Make a list of possible mortgage lenders in your area. (You may be able to get some names from your real estate broker, the Yellow Pages under "MORTGAGES," and from local Homebuilders, Savings and Loan, or Mortgage Banking Associations).

- A good place to start, if you are a good customer there, is your own bank. Call your own bank first. If they are willing to give you the type of loan you need, then just check around with other lenders merely to compare the interest rates and other costs and charges.

- When calling lenders, the initial questions you should ask include:

    —Are you making mortgage loans now? At what interest rates—on fixed, and on variable rate loans?

    —How much down payment do you require?

    —What is the size of loan you will make? [Most lenders have a limit on the size of loan; it may be a total dollar amount above which they will not loan, or a certain percentage (say 75% or 80%) of the value of the property, as appraised by the lender.]

    —What is the loan-to-income ratio required to qualify?

    —How many years will the mortgage run? [The longer the term of repayment, the smaller the payment per month, but also the larger the overall total interest amount you shall have paid at the end of the loan term.]

    —Is the loan amount "discounted," and if so, by how many "points"? [If a lender makes you a $100,000 loan, but discounts it by 3 points (i.e., 3 percentage), then you had better be aware that all he'll physically hand over to you is $97,000 —i.e, $100,000 less the 3% 'discount'.]

    —What other one-time costs and how much will I have to pay for the processing of my application (such as legal fees, application fees, "origination" fees, appraisal fees, etc.)?

    —What documents will you need the borrower to provide? [May include items like: tax returns, W2 forms, gift letter from a would-be donor, summary of employment, history and salaries earned, social security number, account number and locations of your bank accounts; the particulars on your life insurance policies, retirement plans, automobiles owned; summary of all your credit accounts, etc.].

    —How long will it take to process my application?

- As an alternative to having to conduct an exhaustive search of the market place yourself for the best loan, you may consider simply contacting a **"mortgage broker,"** and letting him do it for you—that is, a professional who specializes in doing this for a living (he gets paid a commission, not by the borrower or the home seller, but by the lending institution, based on the loan amount he "places" with the lender.) A great many real estate brokers (though not all) either qualify as, or function as mortgage brokers as well.

Generally, a good and experienced mortgage broker will keep up with the ups and downs of the local mortgage market, and would have developed an ongoing working relationship with the loan officers and mortgage lending institutions. And, in light of his need to preserve his "professional credibility" with his loan sources and the fact that he'd lose out on his commission unless he can place the loan, you can be certain that the mortgage broker will usually not take you on or steer you to a source unless he's first certain that your loan application stands some chance. He will, if he is any good, instantly know the answers to the important basic questions: Where is mortgage money currently available? What lenders are making what different variations of loan? What size of loan? Is there a bargain loan—a certain loan variation or long-term loan, available at a smaller interest rate than others? Are there lenders whose approach towards property or credit analysis will tend to favor your own particular profile?

[The same criteria recommended in pp. 16-19 with respect to picking the right real estate broker, are equally applicable here, and should be followed in attempting to pick the right mortgage broker.]

- Check in your area for a new hybrid of real estate brokers who make a specialty of providing home buyers direct, broker-sponsored mortgage financing through their own agencies. Such **"direct mortgage access" brokers,** a relatively recent phenomenon in the industry around the country, pride themselves on being able to obtain a fast mortgage commitment at competitive terms, and on being able, in some cases, to even deliver the loan papers at the closing without the intervention of a banker, thereby eliminating the hassle of dealing separately with a lender. In the New York area, for example, the following agencies offer such services, among others: **Electronic Realty Associates,** a national franchise; **Merrill Lynch** real-estate brokerage chain; the offices of **Schlott Realty; Preferred Properties;** and other larger real-estate concerns and franchises connected to **Shelternet,** a direct mortgage-access service run by the **First Boston Capital Group;** and any of the 200 agencies connected to **Citibank's Mortgage Power Program.**

- Whatever method you use in finding your source of mortgage loans, however, and whoever you use for that, whether you made a direct personal application to the lending institution, or used a real estate broker, a mortgage broker, or a direct mortgage-access broker, as your source— *the one thing you still must always do in the end is to "comparison shop around" independently before making a final choice.* Many loan applicants are so thrilled at being able to find a lender willing to "give" them a loan, that they jump at the first loan offer they get just because it's available and look no further. This need not be the case. It would still pay to shop around, to call upon other lenders and compare costs and loan features— chances still are that another lender down the street will find you just as worthy of a loan, and perhaps even at a better term! And, in line with that, just because the realtor, or the seller, "refers" you to or "recommends" a particular bank or mortgage company, don't accept its offer blindly. You should still do some independent searching and checking on your own, regardless. [Such referral or recommendation may not always be the best deal for you. In some instances, the recommender may—just may—be getting a commission ("finder's fees") from that particular lender for steering your loan to him, and if so, BEWARE: you may not be getting the most competitive terms available; the type of loan that may best suit you could be the last thing in his mind!!]

- Read advertisements and promotional materials carefully. They don't always tell you all you need to know; in fact, they can't, or there won't be room for the ad! Get all the information you need, independently, before you make a decision.

- Don't be too tempted or automatically persuaded simply by an interest rate that may be way below the market. How long is the rate good for? (Mortgages, especially adjustable rate mortgages, can have "introductory" rates). Are there higher fees and/or points to make up for that low rate?

- There's one relatively uncomplicated and cheap method of "comparison-shopping" that you can almost always use: using the telephone to make a "phone poll" of lenders who advertise in the area's regional newspapers and to ask them all the right questions previously enumerated above. Secondly, you may also use a service provided by organizations who now specialize in comparing mortgage rates and terms on a regional basis. In New York-New Jersey area, for example, for a $20 fee, an organization called **HSH Associates** (1200 Route 23, Butler, NJ 07405, 1-800-UPDATES) will provide you a printout of lenders and their lending terms in the purchase area you specify; and the **Seldin Organization** in New Hyde Park, New York, which is paid by the participating bankers to offer the service, offers the same service free of charge to callers. Their telephone number is 1-516-775-2200.

- Finally, on what is probably one of the most important issues on this subject, namely the shopping process by which to make the choice of a lender, a recent report by the HSH Associates, one of the nation's largest publishers of mortgage information, sums up its advice on the matter to aspiring home buyers in these words:

> ...there are a lot of lenders [who would be] competing for your business...savings and loans, savings banks, and other thrift institutions...commercial banks...mortgage banks...credit unions...and mortgage brokers...all of these types of lenders are vying for your business...Rates and terms vary widely from lender to lender...
>
> Don't hesitate to shop—you never know who might have your 'best' mortgage! Everyone has his own system for mortgage shopping...In general, the more thoroughly you shop, the best chances of finding just the right program, with the right terms, and at *saving considerable amounts of money* on your mortgage. Many consumers use HSH Updates [which list mortgage bankers and institutions and their terms] to follow the market before applying. They watch for lenders who are consistently competitive with their chosen program, narrow down the choices to two or three lenders, and, when they are ready to apply, select the lender which best meets their needs.*

C. The Actual Process of Applying for the Mortgage Loan

How do you practically apply for a loan? Upon your finding the lending institution or institutions you want to borrow from, you will ask for their application form. And you'll complete them. [See a sample of conventional mortgage loan application form at p. 67]. The application form is basically a complete outline of who you are, the property you want to buy, the terms of the mortgage you want, and the assets and means of income you have to pay for it.

Shortly after you take the application forms, and often upon your returning the completed application to the lending institution, by Federal Law, you are at that point to be given a Truth-in-Lending Disclosure Statement document by the lending institution. *This document is a very important element in your mortgage borrowing process, in that it is specifically mandated by the Federal government to be given to every mortgage loan applicant as a way of providing applicants the essential information to better and more independently understand the home buying and financing process.*

The Truth-in-Lending Disclosure Statement (see sample copy on pp. 71-2) will tell you all the terms of the mortgage, how it works, an estimate of the costs, fees and charges you'll pay, your legal rights and obligations, and so on. It will, for example, tell you the annualized percentage rate (APR) of the loan you are contemplating — that is, what the total cost of the loan (interest, points, closing costs, etc.) is, as though you had a year to pay them off (on an "annualized" basis), which is then expressed as an interest rate, thus enabling you to compare "apples with apples."

---

*Another expert voice, by Richard F. Gabriel, the real estate sales specialist and author, makes a similar point: "Shopping for a mortgage, contrary to popular opinion, does not mean getting a quote from one, two, or three local lending sources, but requires extensive systematic search for the best possible deal." Gabriel advises loan seekers:

"Prepare a chart, and on the left side indicate all the items that you'd want to know concerning a possible mortgage being offered to you, such as interest rate, whether the rate is fixed or variable, the term of the mortgage, percentage of cash down required, the number of points required, any prepayment penalty conditions, and so on. Then visit as many banks or savings and loan associations...*Do not just talk to one, or two, or three possible lending sources and from that assume that all lending sources will have the same story to tell you. In order to get the best possible overall mortgage for yourself, you should contact, in person where possible, from five to ten lending sources.* Why so many? Because different lending sources have different changing needs at different times and there is no way that you can anticipate what kind of mortgage package and costs will be offered unless you make *direct contact*. What a lender was prepared to offer to do, mortgage-wise, 30 to 60 to 90 days ago, is different than what they're prepared to offer you today. Also, what a possible mortgage lender was willing to offer a friend, associate or acquaintance of yours, has little or nothing to do with what they might, or might not, be willing to offer you. Also, different lenders might perceive you differently as a security, risk and growth, etc...("How To Buy Your Own House When You Don't Have Enough Money!" pp. 87-8).

The important point to make about the disclosure statement is that this is a document you will want to study; it will familiarize you with all of the loan's features. And you should keep it handy for future reference.

NOTE: It's important that you press to be given the disclosure statement immediately at the time you pick up the application, and not a minute after. This way, you will be able to verify the terms of the mortgage even BEFORE you apply. Why? Because it may have been too late already after you applied.

CREDIT CHECK, SURVEY AND APPRAISAL, INSPECTION, LENDER'S TITLE SEARCH AND INSURANCE, ETC...

What happens next — after you've filed your loan application with the lending institution? Its mortgage loan officer will set about the task of collecting detailed information about you (and about the property), and analyzing such information in order to make a decision as to whether, in the loan officer's or loan committee's estimation, you fit the institution's "profile" for a borrower whose loan is likely to be both secure and trouble-free — whether you have, in other words, the ability and willingness to meet the monthly payments of the loan in the lender's opinion.

What is on the loan officer's (or committee's) mind as he considers your application? First and foremost, he wants to assure himself that if it ever happens that you can't keep up with your mortgage payments and they have to take the property back ("foreclosure"), that they will be able to resell the property for at least as much money as you'll owe them on it. So, even before they set up a meeting with you, the institution arranges for a survey of the property and gets the property officially appraised and sets its own "appraisal price" on the property to be sure that it is worth what you're paying for it. At the same time, the lender will arrange for inspection of the property to prove that it is structurally sound: independent inspectors will check the structure and its various systems (plumbing, septic, electric, etc...). Then he wants to know about your present financial status, your credit history, and all of the personal aspects of your life that will affect your ability to meet the monthly payments: Do you earn enough steady income in the household? Do you already owe other significant debts to others that will eat into your monthly income and, thus, make it more difficult for you to be able to make the mortgage payments? (See Figures 2.5 & 2.6 on pp. 11-12). What other property or assets (other than real estate, automobile, bank savings, jewelry, antiques, furs, stocks, bonds, other securities, etc...) do you have, if any, which you could tap or fall back on in the event of an emergency? Are you a "good credit risk," and is there a record of "willingness to pay" on your part — your credit rating? What reading can the lending officers make of your "character" — are you part of a growing, stable family, for example, and what is your relationship (your salary, length of stay, position, etc...) to your career or employer?

Still on the credit check, the lender's credit department will draw, usually at your expense, a full credit report on you from a professional credit information storage agency. (You have a legal right to ask for, and to see a summary of this report, though not the actual report itself, and to protest any contents of the report that you consider factually inaccurate). In deed, as a smart shopper, you should already have ordered your own credit report from a credit reporting agency so as to make sure that no problems should arise anyway. The lender will call your bank to verify your claimed balance, and probably check court records in counties where you live or have lived, to establish that you've left no trail of unpaid debts.

Meanwhile the lender is conducting a title search — a historical check of all the records showing the past ownerships of the property — so as to assure that if you were to buy the property, you will, in deed, own it with a free and clear title. [See p. 47 for details of the title search process]. The lender also arranges for title insurance, an insurance policy to protect the lender — not you, the buyer — against unforeseen problems that might affect your ownership. (Note that the policy is the lender's policy; it protects the **lender,** not you. Yet, it is paid for by you, however.)

LOAN APPROVAL & COMMITMENT

Once the application, appraisal, and survey are done, the mortgage banker will send the ream of documents, called the "credit package," to the underwriter. The underwriter will inspect it. And, if he approves it, you qualify for the mortgage, subject only to legal requirements, and completion of the required documentations.

The lender then sends you a loan commitment, or contract, to make you the loan under certain enumerated terms and conditions — the specific amount at a specific interest rate, the charges and fees you'll pay, the closing requirements and documents needed to close, etc.

The commitment may also list some specific conditions that are to be met before the loan can be made. For example, you may be required to pay off some outstanding bills in order to qualify, or that you meet other requirements.

The commitment is subject to negotiations and change by either party. The lender, for example, may alter the mortgage terms if they have changed since you submitted your application, and in that case you are welcome to check that over and make your "counter-offer." You can either sign and return the commitment, or you may make your own counter-offer by physically making changes on it. *Your counter offer becomes a contract, however, only when the lender accepts it with the changes and signs it.* In the end, after you review the commitment, and assuming you agree with the terms, you sign and return it. At that point you have a MORTGAGE CONTRACT with the lender. The mortgage lender issues you a note and mortgage.

D. A rule-of-thumb for estimating the likelihood of your getting the loan

Will you qualify for the mortgage loan? Will you get it? Who knows. Here's a simple rule-of-thumb to judge whether your means and resources probably stand you in the position of getting the loan you applied for. (It's only a rough, imprecise estimation). EVALUATE OR ACTUALLY COMPUTE THESE THREE BASIC FACTORS:

(i.) Your Effective Monthly Income

Include ONLY your take-home income, and the amount you can dependably count on now and in the future. If the income varies significantly from year to year, you must then average it out. If the purchase is contemplated by a married couple, include BOTH parties' incomes.

(ii.) Your Monthly Housing Expenses

What it will costs you, each and every month, to occupy the house (for maintenance, repairs and gardening, mortgage payments, real estate taxes, heat and utilities, home owner's insurance, any special fees, etc.)

(iii.) Your Monthly Debt Repayment Needs and Living Expenses

The amount you owe out, on a monthly repayment basis, to other persons or institutions (for instalment or charge card payments, other loans, car payments, life insurance, medical bills, and the like), and your everyday living expenses (food, clothing, education, transportation, other taxes not deducted from your paycheck, recreation, gifts, savings, children's tuition, and the like.)

Now, add up the totals of Items (ii) and (iii) above, and compare that figure against the total of Item (i) above. If Item (i) (your effective income) is at least equal to the combined totals of Items (ii) and (iii), then it is reasonable to assume that you'll get the mortgage you need.

[See Figures 2.5, 2.6 & 6.9, respectively, "Worksheet on Figuring Your Net Worth", "Worksheet on Figuring Your Liabilities", and the "Fact Sheet," for aid in itemizing and computing these figures.]

FOR MORE ON MORTGAGES AND THE VARYING TYPES OF 'CREATIVE FINANCING' ARRANGEMENTS AVAILABLE IN THE MODERN MARKET, SEE APPENDIX B AT PP. 150-8.

STEP ⑨: PREPARE FOR THE CLOSING; PREPARE THE SETTLEMENT DOCUMENTS & COSTS

As a rule, once the mortgage commitment is accepted by the buyer and the lender (the subject matter of STEP 8), it's almost time to get to the last step: "THE CLOSING."

There are two basic routes you may elect to follow in the handling of the closing of your purchase (or sale): a) you may hire an **"escrow agent"** to do it for you; or, (b) alternatively, you may elect to handle the matter completely by yourself.

A. Consider Having An Escrow Agent Handle The Closing For You

If you are buying under an F.H.A. or V.A.-sponsored mortgage (or buying under a sales contract that calls for use of an "escrow agent"), you may not have any other choice other than to use an escrow; the closing (also called 'settlement') transactions for houses financed by F.H.A. and V.A.-sponsored mortgages are, as a rule, required to be handled through an escrow agent, a neutral third party who is generally hired by the home buyer (he's usually a representative of the title insurance company or a bank or the lending institution, or an independent third party, such as an attorney) whose main specialty is the handling of closing and settlement transactions.

Some experts highly recommend the employment of escrow in the transaction of all matters pertaining to closings, holding that this mechanism affords the do-it-yourself home buyer or seller the safest, least cumbersome method, and a relatively inexpensive alternative. Indeed, in some states, particularly in those states where the use of attorneys in real estate transactions is uncommon, such as in the Western states, escrow officers who work in conjunction with title insurance companies and brokers (who are, as a rule, the parties who generally handle the paperwork in such states), are generally used for the closing work. But, in any event, where at all possible or reasonable, you should generally consider employing escrow; considering the relatively small fees they charge relative to the amount of work they render, and considering the assurance of having all the 'loose ends' of the closing process tied up for you by this acknowledged specialists in the field, it may well be worth it to have an escrow agent undertake the closing and settlement tasks for you in many instances, if not most.

Real estate affairs author, Harley Bjelland, who sold his own house several times himself without a broker, is all praise for the idea: "Although my total closing costs for my house were $700, only $150 of that was the escrow fee for handling all paperwork. It was one of the best bargains I've ever had in my life. I highly recommended using escrow. Actually I consider escrow a necessity."

To "open the escrow" (i.e., to employ one), the principals (usually the seller) simply takes the sales contract, upon its signing, to an escrow company and receives an escrow number from the company.

What does an escrow do?

When an escrow agent handles the settlement and closing process (as is the case, anyway, with F.H.A. and V.A.-mortgaged deals, as well as the custom in some areas of the country), the agent will handle much of the paperwork involved, make the necessary apportionments of cost between the buyer and seller, assemble all the required documents and signatures, and make sure that the monies go to the right places. He is the stakes holder who keeps the money in an "escrow account" during the closing transactions so as to make sure that the right parties (the buyer, the seller, the lender, the title insurance agent, the broker, and the like) get what they have each contracted for. Basically, what the escrow agent does is to take the signed Sales Contract, study its provisions and terms, and apply those terms and provisions to ensure that both the buyer and the seller (and others involved or having a stake in the home sale) live up to their agreements in the contract. He lists what charges are payable by the seller and which ones are payable by the buyer. If there are unpaid real estate taxes or utility bills, or what have you, he "prorates" (i.e., apportions) it to the seller—i.e., for the amount of the time of the year for which the seller owned the house. He makes sure that the lender pays the amount he is supposed to under the contract, and that the seller gets what he/she is entitled to under the contract (after the necessary deductions listed in the "Settlement Sheet" are made.) He may also withhold some money from the seller, and hold it in escrow until the seller has performed a promised obligation, say the painting of the house or the making of some repairs, as agreed in the contract.

The escrow agent's job, in short, is simply to aid you (the home buyer and/or seller) in seeing that the terms and provisions of the Sales Contract are properly and comprehensively carried out.

Usually, the escrow agent goes to work immediately AFTER the buyer and seller have signed the Sales/ Purchase Contract ("Step 6", at p 35 above). At the start, he will collect the deposit from the buyer and, with the buyer and seller present, he will prepare a document titled the **"ESCROW INSTRUCTIONS",** a written agenda of the sequence of details and of the requirements both sides are to meet, and provide each party with a copy. The escrow then orders from a title insurance company a title search to be made to make sure that the seller has a clear title to the property. The escrow company will prepare all the documents needed to complete the sales transaction (with the exception of the loan documents, which will usually come from the lender), including a Grant Deed document, for the seller to sign; and at the closing, the escrow will see to it that the buyer signs the necessary mortgage papers and the promissory papers for repayment of the loan.

The escrow receives the mortgage money from the lender, collects the remainder of the down payment from the buyer, allocates the "points," as necessary, and may also handle the paying of the money for inspection services and any special debts owed on the property. He'll make sure that all these debts are accounted for usually before the closing. After all the necessary documents are signed, and the money is paid directly into the escrow's account, the escrow then records the necessary documents, prorates the costs of taxes, insurance, etc., and, upon making sure that all the necessary conditions have been met, the escrow pays the money (or makes sure that they are otherwise paid) to the appropriate parties for inspection services, title insurance, points, recording fees, etc., and, finally, the seller will be given a check for the equity he has in the house.

Most of the escrow agent's work is done by mail, with the phone frequently used to track down and put the pieces of the process together. The escrow agent's fees are often split between the buyer and the seller, but remember that, as the H.U.D. Booklet reminds you, just about any fee or settlement service is open to negotiation as to the amount and who is to pay it.

B. Handling the Settlement or Closing Process Yourself

Whether you are handling it by yourself, or using the services of an escrow agent for it, it is nevertheless still necessary—and most useful to you—that you learn and know as much as you can about the procedures and costs involved in settlement of real estate deals. The term **"settlement"** is often used interchangeably with another term, **"closing"**, in real estate deals, and is used to refer to the final tasks in the purchasing of real estate. Technically speaking, it is that final act when the seller signs the deed and hands it over to you, the buyer, as the new owner. However, the process of real estate settlement (or closing) involves more—much more—than just the act of formally passing papers from seller to buyer and vice versa; for it involves being clear on not merely the cost of the home, or of the loan with which to buy it, but on the actual costs of the whole *process* of buying it —the process involved in having all the details, loose ends, and other additional services required to settle the deal, cleared up. *That's why it's of such great importance to you, the home buyer (as well as to the home seller), that you make some preparations for the closing—IN ADVANCE of its actual date.* For the do-it-yourself home buyer (or seller), the great value of making an elaborate and proper preparations in advance of the actual closing, lies not only in the fact that it makes you better able to get clearer on the details of the costs, and hence better able to arrange for the means of meeting those costs. But, even more importantly, its great value for you lies in the fact that the buyer (or seller) could thus better shop for better prices, and is better able to bargain for better prices with those who will provide him the 'settlement' services.

In this connection, **THIS IS WHAT YOU SHOULD ALWAYS REMEMBER AND NEVER FORGET:** the *respective terms and charges involved in settlement services are generally negotiable as to the amounts, and at times even as to who will be responsible for paying what item, and there's nothing, absolutely nothing, final or predetermined about them*.*

---

*This much clarifications should be made. Though sometimes negotiable, the matter of who will pay for what settlement cost item is dictated by local customs in most communities, and generally works out as follows: escrow costs and transfer taxes are generally divided equally between the buyer and the seller. The buyer is usually responsible for the costs of the appraisal necessary for obtaining the loan or to fulfill the local law, and for the loan "origination" charges and "points" (to the extent not prohibited by law) payable to the lender in making a new loan. The buyer is also responsible for his legal fees, where applicable, as well as the cost of obtaining a report on his credit rating; the cost for the document or revenue stamps necessary for the deed to be recorded in the county or state land registry, the notary fees for the signatures to the deed; and the transfer fee to the mortgage company. The expense of a survey is more often than not charged to the buyer, but the policy varies widely.

The seller is usally responsible for the brokers' commissions on the sale of the house, and for taxes, insurance, mortgage (or other) payments that are in arrears.

Ultimately, though, the key as to who gets to pay what costs in any given home buying/selling situation at a given time and locality, seems to hinge on one fundamental factor: the good, old, law of economic supply and demand! Its been widely observed that in areas where (and in times when) houses are plentiful and unsaleable (in so-called 'buyers market'), the seller can frequently be persuaded to pay all of the closing costs, even the costs and expenses involved in the buyer's new mortgage loan application; and, that in times and areas of home-for-sale scarcity, the so-called 'sellers market,' the opposite experience is the norm!!

BEGIN BY MASTERING THE GOVERNMENT'S SPECIAL INFORMATION BOOKLET*

If indeed you are using a mortgage loan to finance your home purchase, one of the papers you shall have probably received from the lending institution is a booklet titled *"SPECIAL INFORMATION BOOKLET"* **(SIB),** which you get at the time of your loan application. This is the requirement of a federal law, the Real Estate Settlement Procedures Act (RESPA)! Now, look in this booklet (if you haven't already done so earlier several times over on your own!). Look, particularly in the SIB section captioned, *"Settlement Costs Guide";* you'll find fully outlined here, every major item you are to encounter in the settlement process. Closely read and review, on an item-by-item basis, the detailed discussions and explanations provided therein on each item. In deed, a good grasp of the information provided there should be of tremendous help to you in being able to analyze and understand your own settlement statement and process. Read the advice given in that same section about how to shop effectively for the settlement services and how to evaluate the various services. But, more important, *you must go right out* and *actually use the advice* in going about your home settlement business.

The next most helpful thing to do (and which you should actually have already done by now!): carefully study and review the second document which, by virtue of the RESPA law, you are also required to have gotten from your mortgage lender just three days after your loan application, or earlier—a **GOOD FAITH ESTIMATE (GFE)** Statement . As the name implies, this statement is a tabulation by the mortgage lender of the settlement costs the home buyer should expect to have in his home purchase deal. *The information contained in this (Good Faith) Estimate sheet is of invaluable value. In deed, a good analysis—and grasp—of your lender-supplied settlement statement, and of the lender-supplied Special Information Booklet,* particularly the section dealing with the settlement costs, should take all of the surprises out of the final moves in the settlement process!* And the formulas given in the Booklet for calculating closing costs will enable you to know just what you will need for that final event. Furthermore, additionally, the federal RESPA law also requires that, <u>providing you request it</u> from them, your lenders must give you for your inspection at least 24 hours before the closing, a copy of the actual **"Uniform Settlement Statement" (USS),** the statement to be used at the closing to document and record all fees and costs you'll need for closing and settlement costs. [See Figure 5.4 at p. 73 for a sample of the Uniform Settlement Statement].

C. Summary Checklist of Questions You Ought to Have Had Answered <u>BEFORE</u> You Go to the Closing:

1. Have you thoroughly read and reviewed the *Special Information Booklet* given you by the mortgage lender, especially the section dealing with the settlement process?

2. Were these papers delivered to you in advance of closing, so that you can have time to examine them: The title insurance binder or abstract? (Look for any exceptions or liens, and ascertain that the title binder insures **"marketability"**). Survey and title search reports? (Clear up any objections, if any, with the seller). Copy of existing mortgage or mortgages and promissory note(s), if you are taking over an existing mortgage from seller? (Check for "balloon" payments). Copy of any restrictions or easements existing on the premises?

3. Are all the necessary inspections done? (Bring inspection reports with you to the closing).

4. Are all the required repairs complete? (Bring certificate of completion to the closing).

5. If you plan to move, did you give your old landlord notice?

6. Have you confirmed with the seller his firm move-out date?

7. Have you made a final personal inspection of the house just the previous day, or even a few hours before the closing? (Check physical condition, for any late changes. Make sure tenants, if any, are out).

---

*A 1980 Federal Government's Housing and Urban Development-sponsored study found that the overwhelming majority of consumers who take the trouble to actively study and use this Booklet in their home buying/selling deals, are substantially profited by it, and that most consumers and real estate professionals conside it a very useful tool to them. Among the study's findings are the following: most consumers receive the SIB (57%) and GPEs (83%); most consumers find the SIB to be adequate and the GPEs to be reasonably accurate estimates of actual settlement charges; most consumers (70%) and providers of real estate services (60%) view the uniform settlement statement (USS) as a reasonably adequate, understandable, and convenient document for displaying settlement charges; and the one day prior inspection of the HUD-1 form is made available to the home buyers, but few (20%) exercise the right of inspection.

8. Have you arranged with utility companies to start service after closing?

9 . Have you obtained from the lender (or, if more applicable, the escrow agent) the exact amount of money you will need for, and at the closing?* (Countercheck those amounts against your own using the formulas for calculating closing costs provided in the settlement section of the lender-supplied *Special Information Booklet*).

10. Have you arranged for the needed money in advance? [The custom is to bring to closing a "certified check" (or bank check or money order) for the major money items, such as the purchase price, and then bring along a personal check for use to pay the other remaining lesser bills and charges.]

11. Do you have additional cash (or merely your checkbook) with you "just in case"?

12. Have you, at least one week before, confirmed the time, date and place set for the closing with the seller, broker, lending institution, the title company (or escrow agent, where applicable), and all other relevant parties to the deal, to make sure that every one of significance will be available on the date and time scheduled?

13. Do you have the receipts for those items (e.g., earnest money" deposit, down payment, etc.) you have already paid for on the house?

14. Have you computed all adjustments—in advance of the closing (see sample below)? If possible, have your figures counterchecked for you by someone who knows closing customs, e.g., an escrow agent or your accountant. To save the time and trouble that might arise from a conflict in figures on the closing occasion, phone the other party (or, if applicable, his broker or attorney, if any) and compare figures in advance so as to be sure that your figures match each other's.]

FIGURE 5.2
SAMPLE ADJUSTMENTS AND ESCROWS
(Assuming a hypothetical closing date of July 31st)

CREDITS TO SELLER:

Hazard insurance premium ($240 per.
yr., apportionment for 2 months
remaining on prepaid policy to Sept. 30th)................................... $ 48.00

Real estate taxes ($950 per yr., 5 months re-
maining on policy prepaid to Dec. 31st)..395.83

Remaining oil in tank (500 gals. @ $1 per gal.)..............................500.00

Fire insurance premium ($144 per yr., 6 months
remaining on policy prepaid to Jan. 31st)..72.00

Adjustments for prepaid interest on mortgage
from date of the closing to date of first
mortgage payment (last 15 days of the month)..................................100.00

TOTAL CREDITS TO SELLER...1,115.83

---

*If you are taking out a mortgage loan for the deal, remember to factor in the fact about the "discounting" of the loan—as previously explained in the manual, your $100,000 loan discounted three "points," will only be fetching you a check for $97,000 (not $100,000!), from your lender! Furthermore, remember that the average cost of 'closing costs' often amount to a large chunk of money over and above the purchase price of the property—anywhere between 3% to 8% of the purchase price of the house.

CREDITS TO BUYER:

Water and sewer ($40 due next month for 4-month
period)..$30.00

TOTAL ADJUSTMENT IN FAVOR OF BUYER...................... **$30.00**

STEP ⑩: ATTEND THE HOME CLOSING; TAKE LEGAL TITLE TO HOME'S OWNERSHIP

Everything else has been done. And, at long last, now comes the grand finale of your efforts— **THE "CLOSING."** Briefly, this is that appointed day and occasion when and where the purchase will, at long last, be finalized, as you pay the balance of the home purchase price (and other closing and settlement costs), sign the necessary mortgages and notes, and finally receive the deed from the seller transferring the legal ownership of the house to you!

A typical closing (it is often referred to also as a "settlement" as well) is a meeting between the home buyer(s), sellers, representatives or agents of the lender (and of the title insurance company in some cases, and the real estate broker, if applicable.) THE CENTRAL PURPOSE OF THIS MEETING IS TO FORMALLY TRANSFER TITLE (OWNERSHIP) OF THE LANDED PROPERTY FROM THE SELLER TO YOU, THE BUYER.

A. How Does a Typical Closing Work?

Very briefly summarized, the sequence of activities at closings runs roughly this way:

- The lender's agent (or, in some states, the "escrow agent") will ask for your paid Insurance Policy (or binder) on the house.

- The agent will list the **"adjustments"** (What you owe the seller: remainder of the down payment, pre-paid taxes, etc.; and what the seller owes you: unpaid taxes, pre-paid rents, etc.)

- You (the payer) will sign for the lender the **mortgage** or **deed of trust** papers (the legal document which gives the lender the right to take back the property if you fail to meet your mortgage payments.) Then, you will also sign the **mortgage NOTE** (the promise to repay the loan in regular monthly payments of specified amounts.) [A sample copy of Mortgage is reproduced on pp. 76-9, and a Note or Bond is reproduced on pp. 74-5. Blank copies of these forms are obtainable from the Legal Publishers. See the Order Form on p. 191].

AT THE CLOSING?

- You will then be "loaned," by the lender's representative, the money to pay the seller for the house.

- The seller hands over to you the **TITLE** (proof of ownership of the property), in the form of a **DEED** (the document that legally transfers the title), and ownership thereby "passes" to you at that point by that act.

- The lender's agent will collect the "closing costs" from you, and give you a **Loan Disclosure Statement** (a list of all the items you have paid for.)

- You collect the keys to the premises from the seller and make plans about moving into your new home.

- You (or the lender's representative) will then promptly go and have the deed and the mortgage **"recorded"** (i.e., entered on the official public record) in the town's or county's office for the registry of deeds.

- Thereafter, the purchasing or selling transaction is, for all intents and purposes, done!

B. A Few Pointers for Going Through a Closing

BE FORWARNED: In a typical closing, the barrage of legal forms, and other papers piling up around the closing- room table can be intimidating, especially to the uninitiated, and frequently much of the paper shuffling is unnecessarily confusing. Hence, here are a few things you should know to be able to get through the heaps of paper and the frequently unnecessary shuffling of papers back and forth at closing sessions. [Actually, if you did your homework in advance of this occasion— if you already did what you are advised to do in "Step 9" above - (pp. 5 7-63)—the closing should be as easy as the proverbial eating of a piece of cake for you! In deed, as amply emphasized in "Step 9" above, an *adequate advance preparation is the one dominant KEY to you or to anybody else for having a relatively easy closing.]*

1. To begin with, as a practical matter, if you go into a typical closing ever expecting to go through (or to be able to go through) each of the papers in any details, forget that! It's a physical impossibility. You will have to be there for weeks, perhaps even up to a month, to be able to do that. So, what you do (and what the professionals in the business do) is this: mark and initial those forms and papers you have already read and reviewed previously, and on this particular occasion at the closing, merely concentrate mainly on going over those ones you have not read before or thoroughly read before.

2. If you happen to be financing the purchase through a mortgage loan from a commercial lending institution, as is often the case with most people, you don't even have to worry that much about the paperwork. You shall have had much of the work done for you by your lenders: their attorneys, escrow agents, or mortgage loan specialists, shall have already prepared the important and necessary papers—the note and mortgage and any affidavits or other papers you're to sign, and a list of the expenses and costs (the "closing statement") involved. The seller, or the seller's lawyer, when he's using one, would have generally prepared the deed document. However, many times the lending institution would prepare the deed for the seller to sign, and even when they don't, they'd be just as concerned as you are—perhaps even more so—to see that the deed is in proper form, inasmuch as the integrity of their mortgage is actually dependent on your getting good title to the property. **SO, HERE'S THE CLUE:** *if your lender's representative or lawyer says the deed is correct, you can be reasonably certain that it is!*

3. And, what of the Note and Mortgage documents, how do you handle those? You won't have to study in detail all the small print in them, either, (assuming that the lending concern you are dealing with is a reputable institution.)* As a rule, those documents follow a standard format, anyway. So, here again is the clue: just limit yourself to checking out any alterations, typed-in or penned-in entries in the form. Also, you'll need to check closely to make sure that the important details regarding the loan (the amount of the loan, the interest rate, the repayment schedule, any pre-payment penalty, and the like) are all entered in the form in the amounts agreed.

Be sure, also, to check the charges on the Closing Statement, to make sure that you understand the charges and that you don't pay anything the seller is supposed to pay or to adjust. Check, especially, all the expenses that are charged to you.

---

*If, however, you are not making a new loan, but are merely taking over an existing mortgage, then you ought to examine these papers much more closely.

C. Summary Checklist of Things to Do or to Expect

NOTE: If, of course, you are employing an escrow company to undertake the closing process for you, then you'll mostly have to turn over much of these tasks to the escrow employed. As fully expressed elsewhere in the manual, employing an escrow for the specific purpose of handling the closing and settlement process is frequently a decision far worth it and advisable for the money and relatively inexpensive. Turn to Section A of "STEP 9" (p. 58), for use and method of employing escrow.

A) ITEMS THAT SHOULD BE DELIVERED TO YOU AT THE CLOSING SESSION

i. Any releases required by the title insurance binder. [The title company should provide to you the actual title insurance policy you've purchased, or, if it is not yet ready, an "abstract" of the title, or a summary, or binder, as proof of the company's commitment to insure.]

ii. The Seller's copy of his hazard insurance policy, if applicable. [Or, if he's not willing to let you retain his, get a new one.]

iii. A Copy of the lender's new Mortgage (or, alternatively, Deed of Trust), and of the Note (Bond)—where a new loan is being made. [Check the loan amount, the interest rate, repayment schedule, pre-payment penalty term, etc.] (A sample copy of the Mortgage is reproduced on pp. 76-9; a copy of the Deed of Trust is at p. 80; and a copy of a Note or Bond is at pp. 74-5. To obtain blank copies of these forms, see the Order Form on p. 191)

iv. Last year's property tax receipt or other proof of up-to-date payment, paid utility receipts (where applicable).

v. The Seller's copy of any unexpired warranties or service contracts still in force (on extermination, on heating and cooling system, garbage, etc.); inspection reports, as applicable, relating to the house's condition (termite, plumbing, wiring, roof, heating, etc.)

vi. An up-to-date status letter or statement from the mortgage company as to the status of loan, and the mortgage payment book used by the seller. (Applicable only where you are taking over an existing old mortgage from the seller).

vii. A notice of change of ownership to mortgage company, signed by the seller.

vi. Death certificate from the seller showing death of a joint owner, if applicable.

ix. An Affidavit (a notarized or sworn statement) of the seller certifying that there are no liens on the property and that there are no other parties in possession of the property.

x. The Closing Statement. (Look over the charges contained therein).

xi. Current homestead exemption card or receipt, where homesteading applies.

xii. The seller's Bill of Sale for any personal property items that are to come with the house.

xiii. New DEED of the type agreed to by the parties (*"Warranty," "Bargain and Sale,"* or *"Quitclaim" type*), with the correct documentary stamps affixed on it (or appropriate credit given you for the cost of a stamp.) [See p. 39 of Chapter 5 and p. 134 of Chapter 6 for details about how the home seller should properly draft and prepare this very important document. Sample copies of the deed forms are in pp. 136, 138, & 140]*

Examine the deed, especially as to the correctness and completeness of the description of the property, and of all the necessary names and signatures. Names of ALL the sellers (and of their spouses, if married) are to be entered in the appropriate "sellers" spaces; and names of the purchasers (and their spouses, if applicable and so desired) are to be entered in the appropriate "buyers" spaces in the form in which the title is desired to be "held"

*To obtain blank copies of these forms, see the Order Form on p. 191.

**See Appendix E, "Glossary of Real Estate Terms," for definition.

by the buyer(s) i.e., whether as **'joint tenants (owners) with the right of survivorship,'** or as an **'estate by the entireties,'**** or as **"tenants (owners) in common,"**** or as a **'life estate'****]

xiv. If by any chance possession of the house will not be delivered at closing, get a letter from seller that he'd have to keep the house in safe condition and good repair and is to deliver possession by a date certain.

B) THINGS TO DO AT THE CLOSING SESSION

i. Make a complete, actual list and identification of everyone who is at the closing, the name, address, capacity for which there, etc. , of the buyer, seller, attorneys, bank representative, title company agent, broker, etc. This is an essential and important formality, often serving a vital purpose as a future reference in the event that questions arise in the future.

ii. If there are at this stage any newly discovered problems (say, from the title or survey search), or uncleared matters still remaining—unpaid mortgage, unsatisfied judgments, unpaid taxes or other liens, or what have you— have those matters cleared up by the seller, get written proof from the seller that they have been cleared up or get an appropriate credit for what it will take to clear the given matters up.

iii. Have the seller (or sellers), and their respective spouses, if applicable, properly sign (in their own real names) all the necessary papers, especially the DEED and any applicable affidavits of seller, and have them *notarize* and acknowledge their signatures to the deed before a Notary Public. [All the sellers are to sign the deed, and if married, their spouses also. Persons requested to witness the passing of title, if any, should also sign as witnesses and enter their addresses. If purchaser is taking over an existing old mortgage, he, too, may be required to sign the deed. The seller's or sellers' (and their spouses') signatures must then be notarized and acknowledged by any available Notary Public.]

iv. You (the buyer(s)) sign for the lender the mortgage Note, the Mortgage, and any other necessary and applicable papers, and then lender hands you the check for the mortgage loan.

v. You deliver the balance of the purchase price to seller.

vi. You clear up the many and different closing and settlement costs and pay up your own shares to the respective parties—the title insurance company, your lawyer, if any, the home inspector, the escrow agent, credit report and bank appraisal fee, fee for deed recording, and what have you, as applicable—on the amounts agreed upon. (See chart below for a sample of possible charges.)

FIGURE 5.3
AVERAGE CLOSING COSTS ON A $200,000 HOME (1990) [SOURCE: N.Y. TIMES]

vii. You obtain from seller your own copy (an original) of a properly signed and notarized deed; you obtain the keys to the property from seller.

C) THINGS TO DO AFTER THE CLOSING

i. You (the buyer (s)) record the deed. [You should <u>immediately</u> hurry to the county clerk's office, or the appropriate land recording department or registry of deeds for the property's locality—usually located in the courthouse—and have the deed recorded therein. ***Do this PROMPTLY! This is most important to protect yourself.*** In any event, if a commercial lender is involved in the deal, you can be almost certain that their representative will usually take it upon himself to record the deed, along with the mortgage, to make sure that it's timely done, and will usually send you your own copy of the recorded deed thereafter.]

ii. Give notice to the title insurance company to issue you your policy.

iii. Send notice of change of ownership to mortgage company, with the transfer fee, if an old mortgage applies.

iv. Notify hazard or fire insurance company to issue endorsement showing new ownership.

v. Notify the utility companies.

Paid all the closing costs and the Deed and Mortgage are recorded? Get the keys from seller—YOU NOW OWN THE HOME!

MORTGAGE LOAN APPLICATION (FOR CONVENTIONAL, FHA, OR VA-TYPE LOANS)

RESIDENTIAL LOAN APPLICATION

MORTGAGE APPLIED FOR ☛	Type ☐Conv. ☐FHA ☐VA	Amount $	Interest Rate %	No. of Months	Monthly Payment Principal & Interest $	Escrow/Impounds (to be collected monthly) ☐Taxes ☐Hazard Ins. ☐MI ☐

Prepayment Option

SUBJECT PROPERTY

Property Street Address		City		County	State	Zip	No. Units

Legal Description (Attach description if necessary)	Year Built	Property is ☐Fee ☐Leasehold ☐Condo ☐PUD ☐DeMinimis PUD

Purpose of Loan ☐Purchase ☐Construction-Perm ☐Construction ☐Refinance ☐Other (Explain)

Complete this line if Construction-Perm or Construction Loan	Lot Value Data Year Acquired $	Original Cost $	Present Value (a) $	Cost of Imps (b) $	Total (a+b)	ENTER TOTAL AS PURCHASE PRICE IN DETAILS OF PURCHASE

Complete this line if a Refinance Loan	Purpose of Refinance	Describe Improvement ☐made ☐to be made
Year Acquired	Original Cost	Amt. Existing Liens		Cost $

Title Will Vest in What Names?

How Will Title Be Held? (Tenancy)

Note Will Be Signed By?

Source of Down Payment and Settlement Charges?

BORROWER					CO-BORROWER*				
Name		Age	Sex**	School Yrs	Name		Age	Sex**	School Yrs

Present Address	No. Years	☐Own ☐Rent	Present Address	No. Years	☐Own ☐Rent
Street			Street		
City/State/Zip			City/State/Zip		

Former address if less than 2 years at present address	Former address if less than 2 years at present address
Street	Street
City/State/Zip	City/State/Zip
Years at former address ☐Own ☐Rent	Years at former address ☐Own ☐Rent

Marital Status ☐Married Yrs ☐Unmarried ☐Separated	(Check One)** ☐American Indian ☐Negro/Black ☐Oriental ☐Spanish American ☐Other Minority ☐White (Non-minority)	Marital Status ☐Married Yrs ☐Unmarried ☐Separated	(Check One)** ☐American Indian ☐Negro/Black ☐Oriental ☐Spanish American ☐Other Minority ☐White (Non-minority)
Dependents other than Co-Borrower		Dependents other than listed by Borrower	
Number	Ages	Number	Ages

Name and Address of Employer	Years employed in this line of work or profession? _____ years Years on this job _____ ☐Self Employed***	Name and Address of Employer	Years employed in this line of work or profession? _____ years Years on this job _____ ☐Self Employed***
Position/Title	Type of Business	Position/Title	Type of Business

GROSS MONTHLY INCOME				MONTHLY HOUSING EXPENSE			DETAILS OF PURCHASE	
Item	Borrower	Co Borrower	Total		PREVIOUS	PROPOSED		
Base Income	$	$	$	Rent			a Purchase Price	$
Overtime				First Mortgage (P&I)		$	b Total Closing Costs	
Bonuses				Other Financing (P&I)			c Pre Paid Escrows	
Commissions				Hazard Insurance			d Total (a + b + c)	$
Dividends/Interest				Taxes (Real Estate)			e Amt. This Mortgage	(
Net Rental Income				Assessments			f Other Financing	(
Other (see sched. below)				Mortgage Insurance			g Present Equity in Lot	(
				Homeowner Assn. Dues			h Amt. of Deposit	(
				Total Monthly Pmt	$	$	i Closing costs paid by Seller	(
				Utilities			j Cash required for closing	$
Total	$	$	$	Total	$	$		

DESCRIBE OTHER INCOME

◇ B – Borrower   C – Co-Borrower   NOTE: ALIMONY/CHILD SUPPORT PAYMENTS NEED NOT BE LISTED UNLESS THEIR CONSIDERATION IS DESIRED | Monthly Amt $

IF EMPLOYED IN CURRENT POSITION FOR LESS THAN TWO YEARS COMPLETE THE FOLLOWING

B/C	Previous Employer/School	City/State	Type of Business	Position/Title	Dates From/To	Monthly Salary $

QUESTIONS APPLY TO BOTH BORROWERS

If Yes, explain on attached sheet

	Borrower Yes or No	Co-Borrower Yes or No		Borrower Yes or No	Co-Borrower Yes or No
Have you any outstanding judgments, ever taken bankruptcy, had property foreclosed upon, or given deed in lieu thereof?			Do you have health and accident insurance?		
Co-Maker or endorser on any notes?			Do you have major medical coverage?		
Defendant/Participant in a Law Suit?			Do you intend to occupy property?		
Obligated for child support/alimony payments?			Will this property be your primary residence?		
Any portion of the down payment borrowed?			Have you previously owned a home?		
			Value of previously owned home	$	$

*Complete this section and all other co-borrower questions about spouse if the spouse will be jointly obligated with the borrower on the loan or if the borrower is relying on the spouse's income or on community property in obtaining the loan.
**This information is requested only for statistical purposes in accordance with the intent of fair housing law. Furnishing this information is voluntary, but borrowers are urged to do so. No lending decision will be made on the basis of this information or on whether or not it is furnished.
***FHLMC requires self employed to furnish signed copies of one or more most recent Federal Tax Returns or audited Profit and Loss Statements. FNMA requires business credit report, signed Federal Income Tax returns for last two years, and, if available, audited P/L plus balance sheet for same period.

FHLMC 65 Rev. 3/76   FNMA 1003 Rev. 3/76

68

This Statement and any applicable supporting schedules may be completed jointly by both married and unmarried co-borrowers if their assets and liabilities are sufficiently joined so that the Statement can be meaningfully and fairly presented on a combined basis; otherwise separate Statements and Schedules are required (FHLMC 65A/FNMA 1003A). If the co-borrower section was completed about spouse, complete this statement and supporting schedules about spouse also.

☐ Completed Jointly ☐ Not Completed Jointly

ASSETS			LIABILITIES AND PLEDGED ASSETS		
Description	Cash or Market Value		Owed To (Name, Address and Account Number)	Mo. Pmt. and Mos. left to pay	Unpaid Balance
Cash Toward Purchase held by			Indicate by (*) which will be satisfied upon sale or upon refinancing of subject property.		
			Installment Debt (include "revolving" charge accounts)	$ Pmt./Mos.	$
Checking and Savings Accounts (Indicate names of Institutions/Acct. Nos.)				/	
				/	
				/	
Stocks and Bonds (No./description)				/	
				/	
Life Insurance Net Cash Value Face Amount ($			Automobile Loan		
SUBTOTAL LIQUID ASSETS				/	
Real Estate Owned (Enter Total Market Value from Real Estate Schedule)			Real Estate Loans (Itemize and Identify Lender)		
Vested Interest in Retirement Fund					
Net Worth of Business Owned (ATTACH FINANCIAL STATEMENT)					
Auto (Make and Year)			Other Debt Including Stock Pledges (Itemize)		
Furniture and Personal Property			Alimony and Child Support Payments		
Other Assets (Itemize)				/	
			TOTAL MONTHLY PAYMENT	$	
TOTAL ASSETS	A. $		NET WORTH (A – d.) $	TOTAL LIABILITIES	B. $

SCHEDULE OF REAL ESTATE OWNED (If Additional Properties Owned Attach Separate Schedule)

Address of Property (Indicate S if Sold, PS if Pending Sale or R if Rental being held for income)	Type of Property	Present Market Value	Amount of Mortgages & Liens	Gross Rental Income	Mortgage Payments	Taxes, Ins. Maintenance and Misc.	Net Rental Income
TOTALS →							

LIST PREVIOUS CREDIT REFERENCES

B—Borrower C—Co-Borrower	Owed To (Name and Address)	Account Number	Purpose	Highest Balance	Date Paid
				$	

AGREEMENT The undersigned hereby applies for the loan described herein to be secured by a first mortgage or trust deed on the property described herein and represents that no part of said premises will be used for any purpose forbidden by law or restriction and that all statements made in this application are true and made for the purpose of obtaining the loan. Verification may be obtained from any source named herein. The original or a copy of this application will be retained by the lender even if the loan is not granted.

I fully understand that it is a federal crime punishable by fine or imprisonment or both to knowingly make any false statements concerning any of the above facts, as applicable under the provisions of Title 18, United States Code, Section 1014.

Signature (Borrower) _____ Date _____ Signature (Co-Borrower) _____ Date _____

Home Phone _____ Business Phone _____ Home Phone _____ Business Phone _____

The Federal Equal Credit Opportunity Act prohibits creditors from discriminating against credit applicants on the basis of sex or marital status. The Federal Agency which administers compliance with this law concerning this _____ is _____
(type of lender)   (regulatory agency and address)
Additionally the Federal Fair Housing Act also prohibits discrimination on the basis of race, color, religion, sex or national origin.

FOR LENDER'S USE ONLY

(FNMA REQUIREMENT ONLY) This application was taken by _____ , a full time employee of
Interviewer

_____ , in a face to face interview with the prospective borrower.
(Name of Lender)

FHLMC 65 Rev. 3/76   REVERSE   FNMA 1003 Rev. 3/76

MORTGAGE LOAN APPLICATION (GUARANTEE REQUIRED IN VA-TYPE LOANS)

VETERANS ADMINISTRATION
APPLICATION FOR HOME LOAN GUARANTY

1. VA LOAN NUMBER

2. LENDER'S LOAN NO.

3. NAME AND PRESENT ADDRESS OF VETERAN (Include ZIP Code)

5A. VETERAN: If you do not wish to complete Items 5B or 5C, please initial here ▶

INITIALS

5B. RACE/NATIONAL ORIGIN

☐ AMERICAN INDIAN ALASKAN NATIVE   ☐ ASIAN, PACIFIC ISLANDER
☐ BLACK   ☐ HISPANIC
☐ WHITE   ☐ OTHER (Specify)

5C. SEX
☐ FEMALE
☐ MALE

4. NAME AND ADDRESS OF LENDER (Include No., street or rural route, city, P.O., State and ZIP Code)

6A. SPOUSE OR OTHER CO-BORROWER: If you do not wish to complete Items 6B or 6C, please initial here ▶

INITIALS

6B. RACE/NATIONAL ORIGIN

☐ AMERICAN INDIAN ALASKAN NATIVE   ☐ ASIAN, PACIFIC ISLANDER
☐ BLACK   ☐ HISPANIC
☐ WHITE   ☐ OTHER (Specify)

6C. SEX
☐ FEMALE
☐ MALE

7. PROPERTY ADDRESS INCLUDING NAME OF SUBDIVISION, LOT AND BLOCK NO., AND ZIP CODE

8A. LOAN AMOUNT $

8B. INTEREST RATE %

8C. PROPOSED MATURITY YRS. MOS.

DISCOUNT: (Only if veteran to pay under 38 U.S.C. 1803 (c) (3) (C) or (D)) ▶

8D. PERCENT %

8E. AMOUNT $

The undersigned veteran and lender hereby apply to the Administrator of Veterans' Affairs for Guaranty of the loan described here under Section 1810, Chapter 37, Title 38, United States Code to the full extent permitted by the veteran's available entitlement and severally agree that the Regulations promulgated pursuant to Chapter 37, and in effect on the date of the loan shall govern the rights, duties, and liabilities of the parties.

SECTION I—PURPOSE, AMOUNT, TERMS OF AND SECURITY FOR PROPOSED LOAN

9. PURPOSE OF LOAN-TO:

☐ PURCHASE EXISTING HOME PREVIOUSLY OCCUPIED   ☐ CONSTRUCT A HOME-PROCEEDS TO BE PAID OUT DURING CONSTRUCTION   ☐ PURCHASE EXISTING HOME NOT PREVIOUSLY OCCUPIED   ☐ PURCHASE NEW CONDOMINIUM UNIT   ☐ PURCHASE EXISTING CONDOMINIUM UNIT

10. TITLE WILL BE VESTED IN:
☐ VETERAN   ☐ VETERAN AND SPOUSE   ☐ OTHER (Specify)

11. LIEN
☐ 1ST MORTGAGE   ☐ OTHER (Specify)

12. ESTATE WILL BE
☐ FEE SIMPLE   ☐ LEASEHOLD (Show expiration date)

13. IS THERE A MANDATORY HOMEOWNERS ASSOCIATION?
☐ YES   ☐ NO (If "YES", complete Item 14F)

14. ESTIMATED TAXES, INSURANCE AND ASSESSMENTS		15. ESTIMATED MONTHLY PAYMENT	
A. ANNUAL TAXES	$	A. PRINCIPAL AND INTEREST	$
B. AMOUNT OF HAZARD INSURANCE ON SECURITY		B. TAXES AND INSURANCE DEPOSITS	
C. ANNUAL HAZARD INSURANCE PREMIUMS		C. OTHER	
D. ANNUAL SPECIAL ASSESSMENT PAYMENT			
E. UNPAID SPECIAL ASSESSMENT BALANCE		D.	
F. ANNUAL MAINTENANCE ASSESSMENT		TOTAL	$

SECTION II—PERSONAL AND FINANCIAL STATUS OF VETERAN

16. PLEASE CHECK THE APPROPRIATE BOXES. IF ONE OR MORE ARE CHECKED, ITEMS 18B, 21, 22 AND 23 MUST INCLUDE INFORMATION CONCERNING THE VETERAN'S SPOUSE (OR FORMER SPOUSE IF BOX "D" IS CHECKED). IF NO BOXES ARE CHECKED, NO INFORMATION CONCERNING THE SPOUSE NEED BE FURNISHED.

☐ A. THE SPOUSE WILL BE JOINTLY OBLIGATED WITH THE VETERAN ON THE LOAN

☐ B. THE VETERAN IS RELYING ON THE SPOUSE'S INCOME AS A BASIS FOR REPAYMENT OF THE LOAN

☐ C. THE VETERAN IS MARRIED AND THE PROPERTY TO SECURE THE LOAN IS LOCATED IN A COMMUNITY PROPERTY STATE

☐ D. THE VETERAN IS RELYING ON ALIMONY, CHILD SUPPORT, OR SEPARATE MAINTENANCE PAYMENTS FROM A SPOUSE OR FORMER SPOUSE AS A BASIS FOR REPAYMENT OF THE LOAN

17A. MARITAL STATUS OF VETERAN	17B MARITAL STATUS OF CO-BORROWER OTHER THAN VETERAN'S SPOUSE	17C. MONTHLY CHILD SUPPORT OBLIGATION	17D MONTHLY ALIMONY OBLIGATION	18A. AGE OF VETERAN	18B. AGE OF SPOUSE	18C. AGE(S) OF DEPENDENT(S)
☐ MARRIED ☐ UNMARRIED ☐ SEPARATED	☐ MARRIED ☐ UNMARRIED ☐ SEPARATED	$	$			

19. NAME AND ADDRESS OF NEAREST LIVING RELATIVE (Include telephone number, if available)	20A. MONTHLY PAYMENT ON RENTED PREMISES VETERAN NOW OCCUPIES $	20B. UTILITIES INCLUDED? ☐ YES ☐ NO

21. ASSETS		22. LIABILITIES (Itemize all debts)		
		NAME OF CREDITOR	MO. PAYMENT	BALANCE
A. CASH (Including deposit on purchase)	$		$	$
B. SAVINGS BONDS-OTHER SECURITIES				
C. REAL ESTATE OWNED				
D. AUTO				
E. FURNITURE AND HOUSEHOLD GOODS				
F. OTHER (Use separate sheet, if necessary)				
G. TOTAL	$	JOB-RELATED EXPENSE (Specify)		
		TOTAL	$	$

23. INCOME AND OCCUPATIONAL STATUS			24. ESTIMATED TOTAL COST	
ITEM	VETERAN	SPOUSE	ITEM	AMOUNT
			A. PURCHASE EXISTING HOME	$
A. OCCUPATION			B. ALTERATIONS, IMPROVEMENTS, REPAIRS	
			C. CONSTRUCTION	
			D. LAND (If acquired separately)	
B. NAME OF EMPLOYER			E. PURCHASE OF CONDOMINIUM UNIT	
			F. PREPAID ITEMS	
C. NUMBER OF YEARS EMPLOYED			G. ESTIMATED CLOSING COST	
			H. DISCOUNT (Only if veteran permitted to pay)	
D. GROSS PAY	MONTHLY $ HOURLY $	MONTHLY $ HOURLY $	I. TOTAL COST (Add Items 24A through 24H)	
			J. LESS CASH FROM VETERAN	
E. OTHER INCOME (Disclosure of child support, alimony and separate maintenance income is optional) $		$	K. LESS OTHER CREDITS	
			L. AMOUNT OF LOAN	$

NOTE - IF LAND ACQUIRED BY SEPARATE TRANSACTION, COMPLETE ITEMS 25A AND 25B.

25A. DATE ACQUIRED

25B. UNPAID BALANCE $

READ CERTIFICATIONS ON REVERSE CAREFULLY

VA FORM JUN 1977 **26-1802a**

SUPERSEDES VA FORM 26-1802a, DEC 1975, WHICH WILL NOT BE USED

VA 2

70

SECTION III – LENDER'S CERTIFICATIONS (Must be signed by lender)

The undersigned lender makes the following certifications to induce the Veterans Administration to issue a certificate of commitment to guarantee the subject loan:

26A. The information furnished in Section I is true, accurate and complete.

26B. The information contained in Section II was obtained directly from the veteran by a full-time employee of the undersigned lender or its duly authorized agent and is true to the best of the lender's knowledge and belief.

26C. The credit report submitted on the subject veteran (and spouse, if any) was ordered by the undersigned lender or its duly authorized agent directly from the credit bureau which prepared the report and was received directly from said credit bureau.

26D. The verification of employment and verification of deposits were requested and received by the lender or its duly authorized agent without passing through the hands of any third persons and are true to the best of the lender's knowledge and belief.

26E. This application was signed by the veteran after Sections I, II and IV were completed.

26F. This proposed loan to the named veteran meets the income and credit requirements of the governing law in the judgment of the undersigned.

26G. The names and functions of any duly authorized agents who developed on behalf of the lender any of the information or supporting credit data submitted are as follows:

	NAME	ADDRESS	FUNCTION (e.g., obtained information in Sec. II; ordered credit report, verification of employment, verification of deposits, etc.)
(1)			
(2)			
(3)			

☐ (Check box if all information and supporting credit data were obtained directly by the lender.)

26H. The undersigned lender understands and agrees that it is responsible for the acts of agents identified in Item 26G as to the functions with which they are identified.

26I. The proposed loan conforms otherwise with the applicable provisions of Title 38, U.S. Code, and of the regulations concerning guaranty or insurance of loans to veterans.

27. DATE	28. NAME OF LENDER	29. TELEPHONE NO. (Include area code)	30. SIGNATURE AND TITLE OF OFFICER OF LENDER

PRIVACY ACT INFORMATION: No loan may be approved unless a complete application form is received (38 U.S.C. 1810). Failure to provide the information will deprive VA of data needed in reaching decisions which could affect you. Any disclosure of information outside VA will only be made as permitted by law.

SECTION IV – VETERAN'S CERTIFICATIONS (Must be signed by veteran)

31. As a GI home loan borrower you will be legally obligated to make the mortgage payments called for by your mortgage loan contract. The fact that you dispose of your property after the loan has been made WILL NOT RELIEVE YOU OF LIABILITY FOR MAKING THESE PAYMENTS.

Some GI home buyers have the mistaken impression that if they sell their homes when they move to another locality, or dispose of it for any other reason, they are no longer liable for the mortgage payments and that liability for these payments is solely that of the new owners. Even though the new owner may agree in writing to assume liability for your mortgage payments, this assumption agreement will not relieve you from liability to the holder of the note which you signed when you obtained the loan to buy the property. Also, unless you are able to sell the property to a credit-worthy obligor who is acceptable to the VA and who will assume the payment of your obligation to the lender and the Veterans Administration, you will not be relieved from liability to repay any guaranty claim which the VA may be required to pay your lender on account of default in your loan payments. The amount of any such claim payment will be a debt owed by you to the Federal Government. This debt will be the object of established collection procedures.

Payment of the loan in full ordinarily is the way in which continuing liability on a mortgage note is ended. Therefore, if you expect to move from the area in which you are now considering the purchase of a home and should you be unable to sell such home with the purchaser obtaining new financing to pay off your loan you should understand that you may continue to be liable to the holder of your mortgage and to the Veterans Administration.

I, THE UNDERSIGNED VETERAN, CERTIFY THAT:

a. I have read and understand the foregoing concerning my liability on the loan.

b. I now actually occupy the above-described property as my home or intend to move into and occupy said property as my home within a reasonable period of time.

c. I have been informed that $_____ is the reasonable value of the property as determined by the VA.

IF THE CONTRACT PRICE OR COST EXCEEDS THE VA REASONABLE VALUE, COMPLETE EITHER ITEM d. OR e., WHICHEVER IS APPLICABLE.

d. ☐ I was aware of this valuation when I signed my contract and I have paid or will pay in cash from my own resources at or prior to loan closing a sum equal to the difference between the contract purchase price or cost and the VA reasonable value. I do not and will not have outstanding after loan closing any unpaid contractual obligation on account of such cash payment.

e. ☐ I was not aware of this valuation when I signed my contract but have elected to complete the transaction at the contract purchase price or cost. I have paid or will pay in cash from my own resources at or prior to loan closing a sum equal to the difference between the contract purchase price or cost and the VA reasonable value. I do not and will not have outstanding after loan closing any unpaid contractual obligation on account of such cash payment.

f. Neither I, nor anyone authorized to act for me, will refuse to sell or rent, after the making of a bona fide offer, or refuse to negotiate for the sale or rental of, or otherwise make unavailable or deny the dwelling or property covered by this loan to any person because of race, color, religion, sex or national origin. I recognize that any restrictive covenant on this property relating to race, color, religion, sex or national origin is illegal and void and civil action for preventive relief may be brought by the Attorney General of the United States in any appropriate U.S. District Court against any person responsible for the violation of the applicable law.

g. The foregoing information contained in these certifications and in Section II of this application is true and complete to the best of my knowledge and belief.

READ CERTIFICATIONS CAREFULLY – DO NOT SIGN UNLESS APPLICATION IS FULLY COMPLETED

32. DATE	33. SIGNATURE OF VETERAN (Before signing, review accuracy of application and certifications.)

FEDERAL STATUTES PROVIDE SEVERE PENALTIES FOR ANY FRAUD, INTENTIONAL MISREPRESENTATION, OR CRIMINAL CONNIVANCE OR CONSPIRACY PURPOSED TO INFLUENCE THE ISSUANCE OF ANY GUARANTY OR INSURANCE BY THE ADMINISTRATOR.

TRUTH IN LENDING DISCLOSURE STATEMENT
(THIS IS NEITHER A CONTRACT NOR A COMMITMENT TO LEND)

LENDER: NATIONSBANC MORTGAGE CORPORATION
2059 NORTH   PARKWAY
TUCKER, GA 30084

DATE   05/24/64
LOAN NO.   0983144o
Type of Loan   CONVENTIONAL

BORROWERS

ONICA E. ANADU
USTINE I. ANADU

ADDRESS   290 ARROWHEAD DRIVE, APT. #G-3
CITY STATE / ZIP   AUGUSTA, GA 80909
PROPERTY   1113 RIVER RIDGE
AUGUSTA, GA 30907

ANNUAL PERCENTAGE RATE The cost of your credit as a yearly rate.	FINANCE CHARGE The dollar amount the credit will cost you.	Amount Financed The amount of credit provided to you or on your behalf.	Total of Payments The amount you will have paid after you have made all payments as scheduled.
8.66874 %E	$ 146,740.14 E	$ 82,387.06 E	$ 229,127.20 E

PAYMENT SCHEDULE: E

NUMBER OF PAYMENTS	AMOUNT OF PAYMENTS	PAYMENTS ARE DUE BEGINNING (MONTHLY)	NUMBER OF PAYMENTS	AMOUNT OF PAYMENTS	PAYMENTS ARE DUE BEGINNING (MONTHLY)
118	663.08	08/01/94			
240	623.81	06/01/04			
1	609.76	06/01/24			
1	607.60	07/01/24			

DEMAND FEATURE: [X] This loan does not have a Demand Feature.   [ ] This loan has a Demand Feature as follows:

VARIABLE RATE FEATURE:
[X] This Loan has a Variable Rate Feature. Variable Rate Disclosures have been provided to you earlier.

SECURITY: You are giving a security interest in the property located at: 1113 RIVER RIDGE
AUGUSTA, GA 30907

ASSUMPTION: Someone buying this property [X] cannot assume the remaining balance due under original mortgage terms
[ ] may assume, subject to lender's conditions, the remaining balance due under original mortgage terms.

FILING/RECORDING FEES: $ 25.00 E

PROPERTY INSURANCE: Homeowner's Insurance or fire and extended coverage is required as a condition of the loan. Also, if the property securing this loan is located in a flood hazard area, you will be required to obtain flood insurance. You may obtain property insurance from anyone you want, provided the insurer is acceptable to us.

LATE CHARGES: If your payment is more than   15   days late, you will be charged a late charge of   5.00   % of the overdue payment.

PREPAYMENT: If you pay off your loan early, you
[ ] may   [X] will not   have to pay a penalty.
[X] may   [ ] will not   be entitled to a refund of part of the finance charge.
See your contract documents for any additional information regarding non-payment, default, required repayment in full before scheduled date, and prepayment refunds and penalties.
e means estimate

I/We hereby acknowledge reading and receiving a complete copy of this disclosure.

_____ 6/10/94   _____
BORROWER / DATE   BORROWER / DATE

_____ 6-10-94   _____
BORROWER / DATE   BORROWER / DATE

01-ZZ-558-01 (1/93)

DEFINITIONS OF TRUTH-IN-LENDING TERMS

The following are definitions of some of the terms which are used in Truth-in-Lending disclosures which are required by federal law. The disclosures are provided to enable an applicant to compare the mortgage terms of various lenders.

PREPAID FINANCE CHARGES

PREPAID FINANCE CHARGES are those direct loan charges, paid by the borrower (not a third party), that are required by Truth-in-Lending regulations to be included in computing the Annual Percentage Rate. They include, but are not limited to: loan origination, discount and commitment fees; prepaid mortgage insurance premiums (PMI); prepaid FHA mortgage insurance premiums (MIP); VA funding fee; underwriting, processing, tax service, and messenger fees, if paid to the lender; buydown and shortfall funds; and prepaid interest.

ANNUAL PERCENTAGE RATE (APR)

The APR is not the same as the note interest rate, if there are any PREPAID FINANCE CHARGES or buydown fees paid by the borrower. The APR takes into account all of these charges and fees and gives the applicant(s) a way to measure and compare the effective annual interest cost of the loan.

FINANCE CHARGE

The total cost of credit as a dollar amount. It is the total PREPAID FINANCE CHARGES plus the total interest and mortgage insurance premiums, if any, which would be paid over the life of the loan, if paid according to the Payment Schedule. If the loan is based upon an adjustable rate of interest, the FINANCE CHARGE will be subject to change if the interest rate varies.

AMOUNT FINANCED

This is not the loan amount, it is the amount requested as a loan by the applicant (including any MIP which is to be financed), less applicable PREPAID FINANCE CHARGES paid at closing.

TOTAL OF PAYMENTS:

This amount is usually the total of the Finance Charge and the Amount Financed. It is the total of PREPAID FINANCE CHARGES, plus principal, interest and mortgage insurance premium, if any, which would be paid over the life of the loan, if paid according to the Payment Schedule. If the loan is an adjustable rate mortgage, the amount may be subject to change if the annual percentage rate changes.

PAYMENT SCHEDULE:

The payments indicated include only principal and interest (and if applicable, mortgage insurance premiums). The amounts do not include payments into escrow for homeowners insurance or property taxes. If the loan is a variable rate transaction in which the initial interest rate is not determined by the index of formula used to make later interest rate adjustments, the Payment Schedule must reflect a composite APR based on the initial rate for as long as it is charged and, for the remainder of the term, the rate that would have been applied using the index or formula at the time the loan closes. The effect of any rate or payment caps are reflected in the Payment Schedule. If the loan is a variable rate transaction in which the initial interest is determined by the same index or formula used to make later adjustments, then the Payment Schedule is prepared on the assumption that the rate used will not vary over the life of the loan.

The above definitions are intended to assist the applicant(s) in better understanding Truth-in-Lending disclosures. The definitions are only intended to be short summaries. Applicant(s) with legal questions should consult their own attorney for advice.

01-AA-743-00 (12/91)

Figure 5.4
Uniform Settlement Statement

HUD-1 Uniform Settlement Statement (Back)

L. Settlement Charges	Paid From Borrower's Funds at Settlement	Paid From Seller's Funds at Settlement
700. Total Sales/Broker's Commission based on price $ @ % =		
Division of Commission (line 700) as follows:		
701. $ to		
702. $ to		
703. Commission paid at Settlement		
704.		
800. Items Payable In Connection With Loan		
801. Loan Origination Fee %		
802. Loan Discount %		
803. Appraisal Fee to		
804. Credit Report to		
805. Lender's Inspection Fee		
806. Mortgage Insurance Application Fee to		
807. Assumption Fee		
808.		
809.		
810.		
811.		
900. Items Required By Lender To Be Paid In Advance		
901. Interest from to @ $		
902. Mortgage Insurance Premium for months to		
903. Hazard Insurance Premium for years to		
904. years to		
905.		
1000. Reserves Deposited With Lender		
1001. Hazard insurance months @ $ per month		
1002. Mortgage insurance months @ $ per month		
1003. City property taxes months @ $ per month		
1004. County property taxes months @ $ per month		
1005. Annual assessments months @ $ per month		
1006. months @ $ per month		
1007. months @ $ per month		
1008. months @ $ per month		
1100. Title Charges		
1101. Settlement or closing fee to		
1102. Abstract or title search to		
1103. Title examination to		
1104. Title insurance binder to		
1105. Document preparation to		
1106. Notary fees to		
1107. Attorney's fees to		
(includes above items numbers:)		
1108. Title insurance to		
(includes above items numbers:)		
1109. Lender's coverage $		
1110. Owner's coverage $		
1111.		
1112.		
1113.		
1200. Government Recording andd Transfer Charges		
1201. Recording fees: Deed $; Mortgage $; Releases $		
1202. City/county tax/stamps: Deed $; Mortgage $		
1203. State tax/stamps: Deed $; Mortgage $		
1204.		
1205.		
1300. Additional Settlement Charges		
1301. Survey to		
1302. Pest inspection to		
1303.		
1304.		
1305.		
1400. Total Settlement Charges (enter on lines 103, Section J and 502, Section K)		

I have carefully reviewed the HUD-1 Settlement Statement and to the best of my knowledge and belief, it is a true and accurate statement of all receipts and disbursements made on my account or by me in this transaction. I further certify that I have received a copy of HUD-1 Settlement Statement.

Borrowers   Sellers

The HUD-1 Settlement Statement which I have prepared is a true and accurate account of this transaction. I have caused or will cause the funds to be disbursed in accordance with this statement.

Settlement Agent   Date

WARNING: It is a crime to knowingly make false statements to the United States on this or any other similar form. Penalties upon conviction can include a fine or imprisonment. For details see: Title 18 U.S. Code Section 1001 and Section 1010

HUD-1 Uniform Settlement Statement (Front)

A. Settlement Statement

U.S. Department of Housing and Urban Development

OMB No. 2502-0265 (Exp. 12-31-86)

B. Type of Loan

1. ☐ FHA 2. ☐ FmHA 3. ☐ Conv. Unins. 4. ☐ VA 5. ☐ Conv. Ins.

6. File Number | 7. Loan Number | 8. Mortgage Insurance Case Number

C. Note: This form is furnished to give you a statement of actual settlement costs. Amounts paid to and by the settlement agent are shown. Items marked "(p.o.c.)" were paid outside the closing; they are shown here for informational purposes and are not included in the totals.

D. Name and Address of Borrower | E. Name and Address of Seller | F. Name and Address of Lender

G. Property Location | H. Settlement Agent | Place of Settlement | I. Settlement Date

J. Summary of Borrower's Transaction		K. Summary of Seller's Transaction	
100. Gross Amount Due From Borrower		400. Gross Amount Due To Seller	
101. Contract sales price		401. Contract sales price	
102. Personal property		402. Personal property	
103. Settlement charges to borrower (line 1400)		403.	
104.		404.	
105.		405.	
Adjustments for items paid by seller in advance		Adjustments for items paid by seller in advance	
106. City/town taxes to		406. City/town taxes to	
107. County taxes to		407. County taxes to	
108. Assessments to		408. Assessments to	
109.		409.	
110.		410.	
111.		411.	
112.		412.	
120. Gross Amount Due From Borrower		420. Gross Amount Due To Seller	
200. Amounts Paid By Or In Behalf Of Borrower		500. Reductions In Amount Due To Seller	
201. Deposit or earnest money		501. Exccess deposit (see instructions)	
202. Principal amount of new loan(s)		502. Settlement charges to seller (line 1400)	
203. Existing loan(s) taken subject to		503. Existing loan(s) taken subject to	
204.		504. Payoff of first mortgage loan	
205.		505. Payoff of second mortgage loan	
206.		506.	
207.		507.	
208.		508.	
209.		509.	
Adjustments for items unpaid by seller		Adjustment for items unpaid by seller	
210. City/town taxes to		510. City/town taxes to	
211. County taxes to		511. County taxes to	
212. Assessments to		512. Assessments to	
213.		513.	
214.		514.	
215.		515.	
216.		516.	
217.		517.	
218.		518.	
219.		519.	
220. Total Paid By/For Borrower		520. Total Reduction Amount Due Seller	
300. Cash At Settlement From/To Borrower		600. Cash At Settlement To/From Seller	
301. Gross Amount due from borrower (line 120)		601. Gross amount due to seller (line 420)	
302. Less amounts paid by/for borrower (line 220)	( )	602. Less reductions in amt. due seller (line 520)	( )
303. Cash ☐ From ☐ To Borrower		603. Cash ☐ To ☐ From Seller	

Principal & Interest: $
1/12 City Taxes:
1/12 County Taxes:
1/12 Hazard Insurance:
1/12 Mortgage Insurance:
1/12 Flood Insurance:
Adjustment:

Total Monthly Payment: $

We acknowledge that the tax prorations contained herein are made in accordance with the best information available at the time of closing and if the actual taxes differ, the parties hereto agree to adjust the prorations between themselves at the time of receipt of the actual bills.

Previous Edition Is Obsolete

HUD-1 (3-86)
RESPA, HB 4305.2

MORTGAGE NOTE
(PROMISSORY) NOTE/BOND

74

T 676—Mortgage note, financial institution, plain English format, 11-78

© 1978 BY JULIUS BLUMBERG.
PUBLISHER, NYC

-FORM-

CONSULT YOUR LAWYER BEFORE SIGNING THIS FORM. THIS FORM SHOULD BE USED BY LAW ONLY.

[NEVER MIND THIS — THE LAWYERS' IDEA!]

[Date when this note/bond is made or signed]

Mortgage Note
(PROMISSORY) MORTGAGE NOTE/BOND

$46,000.00 .... 19........

[Enter here the Lending Party's name/address]

Promise to pay

We, the Undersigned, promise to pay to:

DOW D. DEAN, and MARY M. DEAN, his wife,

(the "Lender")

to their or order the sum of:

principal amount

FOURTYSIX THOUSAND and OO/100 lawful United States Dollars ($46,000.00)

interest

with interest at the rate of ___??___ % per year from the above date until the debt is paid in full.

payments

[Get the facts from Paragraphs 3, 4 & 5 of Sales Contract (pp. 34-37) and, generally, from the Lending terms agreed to by the parties. If an existing mortg. is not applicable, then strike out the clause.]

I will pay the debt as follows:

MONTHLY, in monthly instalments of $_??___ each and every month, with the first installment to be paid on the _(1st. ?)_ day of _??_, 19 _??_, and a like installment to be paid by or on the same day of each succeeding month thereafter until the entire unpaid balance of principal and interest shall be fully paid. Each of the said monthly payments, as and when received by the mortgagee (the Lender), shall be applied first to pay the interest accruing from pay period to pay period, at the rate of _??___ per cent (____%) per annum, and the balance of each of the payments remaining shall thereafter be applied to pay and reduce the principal sum.

[Include clause, only as applicable in your given case!]

AFTER two (two) years from the date hereof, this Note/Bond may be prepaid without penalty.

THIS is a Second Mortgage, and any default in the terms of payment of the First Mortgage shall constitute a default hereunder.

[ENTER HERE ANY OTHER STIPULATIONS/ CONDITIONS YOU MIGHT PREFER]

payment address

Payment is to be made at [if required, then so specify the address] _____ or at whatever other address I am directed to pay.

application of payments

The Lender will apply each payment first to interest charges and then to repayment of the principal amount of the debt.

Escrow payments

If a box below is initialed, in addition to the monthly payments listed above, I will have to pay to the Lender (or whomever the Lender directs me to pay) each month, until the debt is fully paid, the following extra payments:

[ ] 1/12 of the estimated taxes, assessments, water rates and sewer rents for the following 12 months on the mortgaged property, and

[ ] 1/12 of the annual premium for the insurance which must be maintained in accordance with the mortgage.

[Both parties initial the appropriate boxes, it applicable. Other-wise, strike out clauses]

These payments will be held by the Lender in an escrow account (one held by the Lender for this purpose). The Lender will then pay the taxes, assessments, water rates and sewer rents, assessments and insurance premiums directly. If the Lender does not have enough money on deposit to pay these charges when due, I will pay the difference to the Lender within ten days after Lender requests payment. If requested, I will make larger monthly payments to the Lender based on the Lender's estimate of these charges.

The Lender will pay interest on the escrow funds on deposit only if the law requires it and at the rate required by law.

This is a mortgage note

This Note is secured by a Mortgage dated the same day as this note.

Default, when full amount due immediately

Lender may declare the full amount of this Note due immediately for any default. The following are defaults:

(a) failure to pay, when due, any amount payable on any of my obligations under this Note;

(b) Failure to do anything I am obligated to do under the Mortgage.

Anything that would be a default under the Mortgage will also be a default under this Note. This means that upon the Lender's demand, I will have to pay the full amount of this debt plus any other charges which the Lender is entitled to under the Mortgage.

—OVER—

Prepayment	I can repay the entire debt in advance whenever I want, ~~·~~ *after two (2) years from the date hereof,* or I can repay part of the debt in multiples of $100 in advance whenever a regular monthly payment is due. There will be no extra charge for this. If I pay ahead of time, I will have to pay interest on the payment prepaid only to the date of prepayment.
Notice not required	If the Note is not paid when due, the Lender does not have to notify me before the Lender can enforce rights to collect all amounts due. The Lender does not have to present this Note, demand payment or protest.
No waiver	Delay or failure of the Lender to take any action will not prevent the Lender from doing so later.
Applicable law	The laws of the State of __??__ shall apply to this Note.
No oral changes	This Note cannot be changed except in writing signed by the Lender.
Who is bound	"I", "me" and "my" refer to each signer of this Note. Each of us is liable to pay any amount due or which may become due separately and individually.

[Buyer(s) signs his/their full name(s) here]

X _____
Signature, print or type name beneath
(Borrower - Purchaser)

:[Name and address of [Buyer(s)]
_____
Address

X _____
Signature, print or type name beneath
(Borrower/Purchaser)

_____
Address

[Used when individuals are involved]

STATE OF NEW YORK, COUNTY OF _____ **ss:**

On the _____ day of _____ 19 ___ , before me personally came

[Names of the Borrower(s)/Buyer(s)]

to me known to be the individual described in and who executed the foregoing instrument, and acknowledged that **they** executed the same.

[A Notary Public signs and affixes his stamp here]

_____
(Notary Public)

STATE OF NEW YORK, COUNTY OF _____ **ss:**

On the _____ day of _____ 19 __ , before me personally came

[Names of the Borrower(s)/Buyers]

to me known to be the individual described in and who executed the foregoing instrument, and acknowledged that **they** executed the same.

[A Notary Public signs and affixes his stamp here]

_____
(Notary Public)

[Used when a corporation/a Partnership is involved]

STATE OF NEW YORK, COUNTY OF _____ **ss:**

On the _____ day of _____ 19 __ , before me personally came [corporate officer's name] to me known, who, being by me duly sworn, did depose and say that he resides at No. [officer's home add.] ; that he is the [officer's position, e.g. Pres.] of [name of the corporate borrower(s) e.g. ABC CORP.] , the corporation described in and which executed the foregoing instrument; that he knows the seal of said corporation; that the seal affixed to said instrument is such corporate seal; that it was so affixed by order of the board of directors of said corporation, and that he signed h name thereto by like order.

_____
(Notary Public)

[Some Witnesses to the closing and signing event, if any, will each sign here.]

STATE OF NEW YORK, COUNTY OF _____ **ss:**

On the _____ day of _____ 19 , before me personally came [names of witnesses present] the subscribing witness to the foregoing instrument, with whom I am personally acquainted, who, being by me duly sworn, did depose and say that he resides at No. [address-(es) of said witness/witnesses] ; that he knows

[Names of the Purchaser/Borrower(s)] to be the individual s described in and who executed the foregoing instrument; that he, said subscribing witness, was present and saw [their nm] execute the same; and that he, said witness, at the same time subscribed h name as witness thereto.

_____
(Notary Public)

John H. and Diana A. Johnson
(Borrowers)

TO

Dow D. Dean and
Mary M. Dean (Lenders)

Mortgage Note

Dated _____ , 19

A 367 | Standard N.Y.B.T.U. Form 8015
Mortgage (Subordinate) Individual or Corporation.

DATE CODE

JULIUS BLUMBERG

CONSULT YOUR LAWYER BEFORE SIGNING THIS INSTRUMENT—THIS INSTRUMENT SHOULD BE USED BY LAWYERS ONLY.

Mortgage

[Enter same date as that entered for the note/bond (p. 67)]

[NEVER MIND THIS THE LAWYERS' IDEA!]

THIS MORTGAGE, made the _____ day of _____, nineteen hundred and _____

BETWEEN

[Buyer/Buyers' names/address(es)]

JOHN H. JOHNSON and DIANA A. JOHNSON, his wife, both residing at 122 Purchase Street, Queens, New York, 11437,
the mortgagor,

[Enter here the Lending Party's name(s)/address — if a corporation, partnership, enter business information, e.g.: BOA CORP., A NEW YORK CORPORATION HAVING ITS PRINCIPAL OFFICE AT...?]

and DOW D. DEAN and MARY M. DEAN, his wife, both residing at 127 Seller Street, Brooklyn, New York, 11234,
the mortgagee,

[Transfer herein the same information as is set forth in the NOTE/BOND (p. 67 above)]

WITNESSETH, that to secure the payment of an indebtedness in the sum of FOURTYSIX THOUSAND ************* ****** ********* ($46,000.00) ***************** dollars, lawful money of the United States, to be paid in monthly installments of $?? each and every month, with the first installment to be paid on the (1st ?) day of ??, 19 ?, and a like installment to be paid on the same day of each succeeding month thereafter until the entire unpaid balance of principal and interest shall be fully paid. Each of the said monthly payments, as and when received by the mortgagee, shall be applied first to pay the interest accruing from pay period to pay period, at the rate of ?? per cent (? %) per annum, and the balance of each of the payments remaining shall

~~with interest thereon to be computed from the date hereof, at the rate of _____ per centum per annum, and to be paid on the _____ day of _____ 19 , next ensuing and thereafter,~~

cipal sum
thereafter be applied to pay and reduce the prin/ according to a certain bond, note or obligation bearing even date herewith, the mortgagor hereby mortgages to the mortgagee:

[Complete with the name of the locality, city, and state of the property's location.]

ALL that certain plot, piece or parcel of land, with the buildings and improvements thereon erected, situate, lying and being in the Borough of Brooklyn, County of _Kings_, city and State of _New York_, which property is described as follows:

[Enter here exactly the same description of the property, as set forth in the Sales/Purchase Contract. (See the first and second passages of Paragraph 2 on p. 23)]

BEGINNING at a point on the southwesterly side of 15th Street distant Two Hundred Seventysix feet ten inches southeasterly from the corner formed by the intersection of the southwesterly side of 15th Street with the southeasterly side of Third Avenue; running thence southwesterly at right angles to 15th Street and part of the distance through a party wall One Hundred Nine feet eleven inches to land now or formerly of Deborah L. Carson; thence southeasterly along said land now or formerly of Deborah L. Carson, Seventeen feet two and one-eighth inches, then northeasterly along the northwesterly side of Lot No. 26 on Map of Land of John Dimon, et al., filed in Kings County June 17, 1835, One Hundred Ten feet seven inches to the southwesterly side of 15th Street, thence northwesterly along the southwesterly side of 15th Street, Nineteen feet six inches to the point or place of Beginning.

SAID premises is further known as: 112 15th Street, Brooklyn, N.Y.

[Transfer herein the same information as is set forth in the NOTE/BOND (p. 67 above)]

AFTER two (2) years from the date hereof, this mortgage may be prepaid without without penalty

THIS is a Second Mortgage, and any default in the terms of payment of the First Mortgage shall constitute a default hereunder.

—OVER—

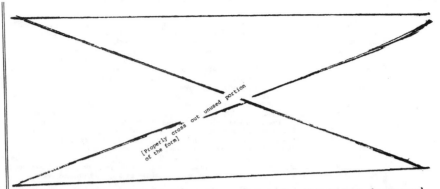

[Properly cross out unused portion of the form]

TOGETHER with all right, title and interest of the mortgagor in and to the land lying in the streets and roads in front of and adjoining said premises;

TOGETHER with all fixtures, chattels and articles of personal property now or hereafter attached to or used in connection with said premises, including but not limited to furnaces, boilers, oil burners, radiators and piping, coal stokers, plumbing and bathroom fixtures, refrigeration, air conditioning and sprinkler systems, wash-tubs, sinks, gas and electric fixtures, stoves, ranges, awnings, screens, window shades, elevators, motors, dynamos, refrigerators, kitchen cabinets, incinerators, plants and shrubbery and all other equipment and machinery, appliances, fittings, and fixtures of every kind in or used in the operation of the buildings standing on said premises, together with any and all replacements thereof and additions thereto;

TOGETHER with all awards heretofore and hereafter made to the mortgagor for taking by eminent domain the whole or any part of said premises or any easement therein, including any awards for changes of grade of streets, which said awards are hereby assigned to the mortgagee, who is hereby authorized to collect and receive the proceeds of such awards and to give proper receipts and acquittances therefor, and to apply the same toward the payment of the mortgage debt, notwithstanding the fact that the amount owing thereon may not then be due and payable; and the said mortgagor hereby agrees, upon request, to make, execute and deliver any and all assignments and other instruments sufficient for the purpose of assigning said awards to the mortgagee, free, clear and discharged of any encumbrances of any kind or nature whatsoever.

AND the mortgagor covenants with the mortgagee as follows:

1. That the mortgagor will pay the indebtedness as hereinbefore provided.

2. That the mortgagor will keep the buildings on the premises insured against loss by fire for the benefit of the mortgagee; that he will assign and deliver the policies to the mortgagee; and that he will reimburse the mortgagee for any premiums paid for insurance made by the mortgagee on the mortgagor's default in so insuring the buildings or in so assigning and delivering the policies.

3. That no building on the premises shall be altered, removed or demolished without the consent of the mortgagee.

4. That the whole of said principal sum and interest shall become due at the option of the mortgagee: after default in the payment of any instalment of principal or of interest for fifteen days; or after default in the payment of any tax, water rate, sewer rent or assessment for thirty days after notice and demand; or after default after notice and demand either in assigning and delivering the policies insuring the buildings against loss by fire or in reimbursing the mortgagee for premiums paid on such insurance, as hereinbefore provided; or after default upon request in furnishing a statement of the amount due on the mortgage and whether any off-sets or defenses exist against the mortgage debt, as hereinafter provided. An assessment which has been made payable in instalments at the application of the mortgagor or lessee of the premises shall nevertheless, for the purpose of this paragraph, be deemed due and payable in its entirety on the day the first instalment becomes due or payable or a lien.

5. That the holder of this mortgage, in any action to foreclose it, shall be entitled to the appointment of a receiver.

6. That the mortgagor will pay all taxes, assessments, sewer rents or water rates, and in default thereof, the mortgagee may pay the same.

7. That the mortgagor within five days upon request in person or within ten days upon request by mail will furnish a written statement duly acknowledged of the amount due on this mortgage and whether any off-sets or defenses exist against the mortgage debt.

8. That notice and demand or request may be in writing and may be served in person or by mail.

9. That the mortgagor warrants the title to the premises.

10. That the fire insurance policies required by paragraph No. 2 above shall contain the usual extended coverage endorsement; that in addition thereto the mortgagor, within thirty days after notice and demand, will keep the premises insured against war risk and any other hazard that may reasonably be required by the mortgagee. All of the provisions of paragraphs No. 2 and No. 4 above relating to fire insurance and the provisions of Section 254 of the Real Property Law construing the same shall apply to the additional insurance required by this paragraph.

11. That in case of a foreclosure sale, said premises, or so much thereof as may be affected by this mortgage, may be sold in one parcel.

12. That if any action or proceeding be commenced (except an action to foreclose this mortgage or to collect the debt secured thereby), to which action or proceeding the mortgagee is made a party, or in which it becomes necessary to defend or uphold the lien of this mortgage, all sums paid by the mortgagee for the expense of any litigation to prosecute or defend the rights and lien created by this mortgage (including reasonable counsel fees), shall be paid by the mortgagor, together with interest thereon at the rate of six per cent, per annum, and any such sum and the interest thereon shall be a lien on said premises, prior to any right, or title to, interest in or claim upon said premises attaching or accruing subsequent to the lien of this mortgage, and shall be deemed to be secured by this mortgage. In any action or proceeding to foreclose this mortgage, or to recover or collect the debt secured thereby, the provisions of law respecting the recovering of costs, disbursements and allowances shall prevail unaffected by this covenant.

—OVER—

13. That the mortgagor hereby assigns to the mortgagee the rents, issues and profits of the premises as further security for the payment of said indebtedness, and the mortgagor grants to the mortgagee the right to enter upon and to take possession of the premises for the purpose of collecting the same and to let the premises or any part thereof, and to apply the rents, issues and profits, after payment of all necessary charges and expenses, on account of said indebtedness. This assignment and grant shall continue in effect until this mortgage is paid. The mortgagee hereby waives the right to enter upon and to take possession of said premises for the purpose of collecting said rents, issues and profits, and the mortgagor shall be entitled to collect and receive said rents, issues and profits until default under any of the covenants, conditions or agreements contained in this mortgage, and agrees to use such rents, issues and profits in payment of principal and interest becoming due on this mortgage and in payment of taxes, assessments, sewer rents, water rates and carrying charges becoming due against said premises, but such right of the mortgagor may be revoked by the mortgagee upon any default, on five days' written notice. The mortgagor will not, without the written consent of the mortgagee, receive or collect rent from any tenant of said premises or any part thereof for a period of more than one month in advance, and in the event of any default under this mortgage will pay monthly in advance to the mortgagee, or to any receiver appointed to collect said rents, issues and profits, the fair and reasonable rental value for the use and occupation of said premises or of such part thereof as may be in the possession of the mortgagor, and upon default in any such payment will vacate and surrender the possession of said premises to the mortgagee or to such receiver, and in default thereof may be evicted by summary proceedings.

14. That the whole of said principal sum and the interest shall become due at the option of the mortgagee: (a) after failure to exhibit to the mortgagee, within ten days after demand, receipts showing payment of all taxes, water rates, sewer rents and assessments; or (b) after the actual or threatened alteration, demolition or removal of any building on the premises without the written consent of the mortgagee; or (c) after the assignment of the rents of the premises or any part thereof without the written consent of the mortgagee; or (d) if the buildings on said premises are not maintained in reasonably good repair; or (e) after failure to comply with any requirement or order or notice of violation of law or ordinance issued by any governmental department claiming jurisdiction over the premises within three months from the issuance thereof; or (f) if on application of the mortgagee two or more fire insurance companies lawfully doing business in the State of New York refuse to issue policies insuring the buildings on the premises; or (g) in the event of the removal, demolition or destruction in whole or in part of any of the fixtures, chattels or articles of personal property covered hereby, unless the same are promptly replaced by similar fixtures, chattels and articles of personal property at least equal in quality and condition to those replaced, free from chattel mortgages or other encumbrances thereon and free from any reservation of title thereto; or (h) after thirty days' notice to the mortgagor, in the event of the passage of any law deducting from the value of land for the purposes of taxation any lien thereon, or changing in any way the taxation of mortgages or debts secured thereby for state or local purposes; or (i) if the mortgagor fails to keep, observe and perform any of the other covenants, conditions or agreements contained in this mortgage; or (j) if the mortgagor fails to keep, observe and perform any of the covenants, conditions or agreements contained in any prior mortgage or fails to repay to the mortgagee the amount of any instalment of principal or interest which the mortgagee may have paid on such mortgage with interest thereon as provided in paragraph 16 of this mortgage.

15. That the mortgagor will, in compliance with Section 13 of the Lien Law, receive the advances secured hereby and will hold the right to receive such advances as a trust fund to be applied first for the purpose of paying the cost of the improvement and will apply the same first to the payment of the cost of the improvement before using any part of the total of the same for any other purpose.

16. If the mortgagor fails to pay any instalment of principal or interest on any prior mortgage when the same becomes due, the mortgagee may pay the same, and the mortgagor on demand will repay the amount so paid with interest thereon at the legal rate and the same shall be added to the mortgage indebtedness and be secured by this mortgage.

Strike out clause 17 if inapplicable. 17. That the execution of this mortgage has been duly authorized by the board of directors of the mortgagor.

18. This mortgage is subject and subordinate to an Existing First Mortgage in the amount of $20,000.00 (TWENTY THOUSAND DOLLARS), which is recorded on the ?? day of ?? 19 ?? , in Liber ?? of Deeds at Page ?? , and the interest at the rate of (13%) per year, presently payable in monthly installments of ($175.26) which includes principal, interest, and with any balance of principal being due any payable on ?? 19 ?? .

This mortgage may not be changed or terminated orally. The covenants contained in this mortgage shall run with the land and bind the mortgagor, the heirs, personal representatives, successors and assigns of the mortgagor and all subsequent owners, encumbrancers, tenants and subtenants of the premises, and shall enure to the benefit of the mortgagee, the personal representatives, successors and assigns of the mortgagee and all subsequent holders of this mortgage. The word "mortgagor" shall be construed as if it read "mortgagors" and the word "mortgagee" shall be construed as if it read "mortgagees" whenever the sense of this mortgage so requires.

IN WITNESS WHEREOF, this mortgage has been duly executed by the mortgagor

IN PRESENCE OF:

1. _____

2. _____

X John H. Johnson (Purchaser)

X Diana A. Johnson (Purchaser)

—OVER—

STATE OF NEW YORK, COUNTY OF _____ ss:

On the _____ day of _____ 19 ___ , before me
personally came·

    John H. Johnson and Diana A. Johnson
      (name of the Purchaser/borrower)
to me known to be the individual S described in and who
executed the foregoing instrument, and acknowledged that
they   executed the same.

[Used when individuals are involved]

[A Notary Public signs and affixes
hi stamp here]
_____
     (Notary Public)

STATE OF NEW YORK, COUNTY OF _____ ss:

On the _____ day of _____ 19 ___ , before me
personally came

  (name(s) of the Purchaser/borrower)

to me known to be the individual   described in and who
executed the foregoing instrument, and acknowledged that
_____ executed the same.

[A Notary Public signs and affixes
his stamp here]
_____
     (Notary Public)

[Used when a corporation/a Partnership is involved]

STATE OF NEW YORK, COUNTY OF _____ ss:

On the _____ day of _____ 19 ___ , before me
personally came (nm. of the corporate offcr)
to me known, who, being by me duly sworn, did depose and
say that he resides at No.(his home address)   ;

that he is the(the office person holds)
of [name of the corporation - borrower]
         , the corporation described
in and which executed the foregoing instrument; that he
knows the seal of said corporation; that the seal affixed
to said instrument is such corporate seal; that it was so
affixed by order of the board of directors of said corporation, and that he signed h name thereto by like order.

_____
     (Notary Public)

STATE OF NEW YORK, COUNTY OF _____ ss:

On the _____ day of _____ 19 ___ , before me
personally came [name(s) of witness(es) prese-
the subscribing witness to the foregoing instrument, with nt]
whom I am personally acquainted, who, being by me duly
sworn, did depose and say that he resides at No. [address
of said witness/witnesses]   ;
that he knows

    [nms of the Purchaser/Borrower]
            to be the individual
described in and who executed the foregoing instrument;
that he, said subscribing witness, was present and saw
(nms of borrower) execute the same; and that he, said witness,
at the same time subscribed his name as witness thereto.

_____
     (Notary Public)

Mortgage
    (SUBORDINATE)
TITLE No. _____

   John H. and Diana A. Johnson
     (Borrowers)
        TO

   Dow D. Dean and Mary M. Dean
     (Lenders)

SECTION 4
BLOCK IO46
LOT 24
COUNTY OR TOWN Kings

[Enter here the Lending Party's
name/address by which this Mortg./
Note is to be returned to them after
it's been officially recorded.]

        RETURN BY MAIL TO:

    Dow D. and Mary M. Dean
    I27 Seller Street,
    Brooklyn N.Y. II234
            Zip No.

Reserve this space for use of Recording Office.

[Leave everything below this line
blank]

STATE OF COLORADO
FHA FORM NO. 2105M
January 1977

DEED OF TRUST

This form is used in connection with deeds of trust insured under the one- to four-family provisions of the National Housing Act.

THIS INDENTURE, made this   day of   in the year of our Lord one thousand nine hundred and   , between   , whose address is   , County of   , State of Colorado, hereinafter referred to as the grantor, and the Public Trustee of   , County of   , State of Colorado, hereinafter referred to as the trustee, Witnesseth:

THAT, WHEREAS, the grantor has executed his certain promissory note, bearing even date herewith, payable to the order of

, hereinafter referred to as the beneficiary, in for the principal sum of   Dollars ($), with interest at the rate of   per centum (%) per annum until paid, and payable as follows, namely: In monthly installments of   Dollars ($), commencing on the first day of   , 19   , and on the first day of each month thereafter until the principal and interest are fully paid, except that the final payment of principal and interest, if not sooner paid, shall be due and payable on the first day of   , Said principal sum, together with interest thereon, and other payments provided to be made under the terms of this indenture, are hereinafter referred to as the indebtedness;

AND WHEREAS, the grantor is desirous not only of securing the prompt payment of the indebtedness, but also of effectually securing and indemnifying the beneficiary for and/or on account of any assignment, endorsement, or guarantee of the indebtedness;

NOW, THEREFORE, the grantor, in consideration of the premises, and for the purposes aforesaid, has granted, bargained, sold, and conveyed, and does hereby grant, bargain, sell, and convey unto the trustee, in trust forever, all those certain premises and property situate in the   County of   , and State of Colorado, known and described as follows, to wit:

TO HAVE AND TO HOLD the same, together with all and singular the privileges and appurtenances thereunto belonging: In Trust Nevertheless, That in case of default in the payment of the indebtedness, or any part thereof, as the same shall become due, or in the payment of any prior encumbrance, principal or interest, if any, or in case default shall be made in, or in case of violation or breach of any of the terms, conditions, covenants or agreements herein contained, then upon notice and demand in writing filed with the trustee as provided by law, it shall and may be lawful for the trustee to foreclose this deed of trust, and to sell and dispose of said premises en masse or in separate parcels (as the trustee may think best) and all the right, title, and interest of the grantor, therein, at public auction at the front door of the Courthouse, in the   , County of   , State of Colorado, or on said premises, or any part thereof, as may be specified in the notice of such sale, for the highest and best price the same will bring in cash, four weeks' public notice having been previously given of the time and place of such sale, by advertisement, weekly, in some newspaper of general circulation then published in the county aforesaid or by such other notice as may then be required by law and to issue, execute and deliver his certificate of purchase, Trustee's Deed and/or certificate of redemption all as then may be provided by law; and the trustee shall, out of the proceeds or avails of such sale, after first paying and retaining all fees, charges, the costs of making said sale and advertising said premises, and attorney's fees as herein provided, pay to the beneficiary hereunder, or the legal holder of the indebtedness, the amount of such indebtedness, and all moneys advanced by the beneficiary or legal holder of the indebtedness for insurance, repairs, and taxes and assessments, with interest thereon at the rate set forth in the note secured hereby, rendering the overplus, if any, unto the grantor; which sale or sales and said deed or deeds so made shall be a perpetual bar, both in law and equity, against the grantor and all other persons claiming the premises aforesaid, or any part thereof by, from, through or under the grantor. The legal holder of the indebtedness may purchase said property or any part thereof; and it shall not be obligatory upon the purchaser or purchasers at any such sale to see to the application of the purchase money. If a release deed is required, the grantor hereby agrees to pay all the expenses thereof.

And the grantor covenants and agrees to and with the trustee, that at the time of the ensealing of and delivery of these presents he is well seized of the said premises in fee simple, and has good right, full power and lawful authority to grant, bargain, sell and convey the same in manner and form aforesaid; hereby fully and absolutely

—OVER—

waiving and releasing all rights and claims he may have in or to said premises as a homestead exemption, under and by virtue of any act of the General Assembly of the State of Colorado now existing or which may hereafter be passed in relation thereto; and that the same are free and clear of all liens and encumbrances whatever, and the above bargained premises in the quiet and peaceable possession of the trustee, against all and every person or persons lawfully claiming or to claim the whole or any part thereof, the grantor shall and will Warrant and Forever Defend.

And the grantor, in order more fully to protect the security of this Deed of Trust, does hereby covenant and agree as follows:

1. That he will promptly pay the principal of and interest on the indebtedness evidenced by the said note, at the times and in the manner therein provided. Privilege is reserved to pay the debt in whole, or in an amount equal to one or more monthly payments on the principal that are next due on the note, on the first day of any month prior to maturity; provided, however, that written notice of an intention to exercise such privilege is given at least thirty (30) days prior to prepayment.

2. That, together with and in addition to the monthly payments of principal and interest payable under the terms of the note secured hereby, he will pay to the beneficiary, on the first day of each month until the said note is fully paid, the following sums:

(a) An amount sufficient to provide the holder hereof with funds to pay the next mortgage insurance premium if this instrument and the note secured hereby are insured, or a monthly charge (in lieu of a mortgage insurance premium) if they are held by the Secretary of Housing and Urban Development as follows:

(I) If and so long as said note of even date and this instrument are insured or are reinsured under the provisions of the National Housing Act, an amount sufficient to accumulate in the hands of the holder one (1) month prior to its due date the annual mortgage insurance premium, in order to provide such holder with funds to pay such premium to the Secretary of Housing and Urban Development pursuant to the National Housing Act, as amended, and applicable Regulations thereunder; or

(II) If and so long as said note of even date and this instrument are held by the Secretary of Housing and Urban Development, a monthly charge (in lieu of a mortgage insurance premium) which shall be in an amount equal to one-twelfth (1/12) of one-half (½) per centum of the average outstanding balance due on the note computed without taking into account delinquencies or prepayments;

(b) A sum equal to the ground rents, if any, next due, plus the premiums that will next become due and payable on policies of fire and other hazard insurance on the premises covered hereby, plus taxes and assessments next due on these premises (all as estimated by the beneficiary) less all sums already paid therefor divided by the number of months to elapse before one month prior to the date when such ground rents, premiums, taxes, and assessments will become delinquent, such sums to be held by the beneficiary in trust to pay said ground rents, premiums, taxes, and special assessments; and

(c) All payments mentioned in the two preceding subsections of this paragraph and all payments to be made under the note secured hereby shall be added together and the aggregate amount thereof shall be paid by the grantor each month in a single payment to be applied by the beneficiary to the following items in the order set forth:

(I) premium charges under the contract of insurance with the Secretary of Housing and Urban Development, or monthly charge (in lieu of mortgage insurance premium), as the case may be;
(II) taxes, special assessments, fire and other hazard insurance premiums;
(III) interest on the note secured hereby; and
(IV) amortization of the principal of said note.

Any deficiency in the amount of such aggregate monthly payment shall, unless made good by the grantor prior to the due date of the next such payment, constitute an event of default under this Deed of Trust. The grantee may collect a "late charge" not to exceed four cents (4¢) for each dollar ($1) of each payment more than fifteen (15) days in arrears to cover the extra expense involved in handling delinquent payments.

3. That if the total of the payments made by the grantor under (b) paragraph 2 preceding shall exceed the amount of payments actually made by the beneficiary for taxes or assessments or insurance premiums, as the case may be, such excess, if the loan is current, at the option of the grantor shall be credited by the beneficiary on subsequent payments to be made by the grantor, or refunded to the grantor. If, however, the monthly payments made by the grantor under (b) of paragraph 2 preceding shall not be sufficient to pay taxes and assessments and insurance premiums as the case may be, when the same shall become due and payable, then the grantor shall pay to the beneficiary any amount necessary to make up the deficiency, on or before the date when payment of such taxes, assessments, or insurance premiums shall be due. If at any time the grantor shall tender to the beneficiary, in accordance with the provisions of the note secured hereby, full payment of the entire indebtedness represented thereby, the beneficiary shall, in computing the amount of such indebtedness, credit to the account of the grantor all payments made under the provisions of (a) of paragraph 2 hereof, which the holder of said note has not become obligated to pay to the Secretary of Housing and Urban Development, and any balance remaining in the funds accumulated under the provisions of (b) of paragraph 2 hereof. If there shall be a default under any of the provisions of this Deed of Trust resulting in a public sale by the trustee or trustees of the premises covered hereby, or if the beneficiary acquires the property otherwise after default, the beneficiary shall apply, at the time of the commencement of such proceedings, or at the time the property is otherwise acquired, the balance then remaining in the funds accumulated under (b) of paragraph 2 preceding, as a credit against the amount of principal then remaining unpaid under said note, and shall properly adjust any payments which shall have been made under (a) of paragraph 2.

4. That he will pay all taxes, assessments, water rates, and other governmental or municipal charges, fines, or impositions, for which provision has not been made hereinbefore, and in default thereof the beneficiary may pay the same; and that he will promptly deliver the official receipts therefor to the beneficiary.

5. That he will keep the improvements now existing or hereafter erected on the said premises, insured as may be required from time to time by the beneficiary against loss by fire and other hazards, casualties, and contingencies in such amounts and for such periods as may be required by the beneficiary and will pay promptly, when due, any premiums on such insurance provisions for payment of which has not been made hereinbefore. All insurance shall be carried in companies approved by the beneficiary and the policies and renewals thereof shall be held by the beneficiary and have attached thereto loss payable clauses in favor of and in form acceptable to the beneficiary. In event of loss the grantor will give immediate notice by mail to the beneficiary, who may make proof of loss if not made promptly by the grantor, and each insurance company concerned is hereby authorized and directed to make payment for such loss directly to the beneficiary instead of to the grantor and the beneficiary jointly, and the insurance proceeds, or any part thereof, may be applied by the beneficiary at its option either to the reduction of the indebtedness hereby secured or to the restoration or repair of the property damaged. In event of foreclosure of this Deed of Trust or other transfer of title to the said premises in extinguishment of the indebtedness secured hereby, all right, title, and interest of the grantor in and to any insurance policies then in force shall pass to the purchaser or grantee.

—OVER—

82

6. That he will keep the said premises in as good order and condition as they are now and will not commit or permit any waste of the said premises, reasonable wear and tear excepted.

7. That if the premises, or any part thereof, be condemned under any power of eminent domain, or acquired for a public use, the damages, proceeds, and the consideration for such acquisition, to the extent of the full amount of indebtedness upon this Deed of Trust, and the note secured hereby remaining unpaid, are hereby assigned by the grantor to the beneficiary and shall be paid forthwith the beneficiary to be applied by it on account of the indebtedness secured hereby, whether due or not.

8. The grantor further agrees that should this Deed of Trust and the note secured hereby not be eligible for insurance under the National Housing Act within   from the date hereof (written statement of any officer of the Department of Housing and Urban Development or authorized agent of the Secretary of Housing and Urban Development dated subsequent to the   time from the date of this Deed of Trust, declining to insure said note and this Deed of Trust, being deemed conclusive proof of such ineligibility), the beneficiary or the holder of the note may, at its option, declare all sums secured hereby immediately due and payable.

9. That in the event of default in the payment of the indebtedness or any part thereof, or of a breach or violation of any of the covenants or agreements herein, then, and in that event, the whole of the indebtedness and the interest thereon to the time of sale, may at once, at the option of the beneficiary or the legal holder of the indebtedness, be declared due and payable, and the said premises to be sold in the manner and with the same effect as if the indebtedness had matured, and that if foreclosure is made by the trustee, the grantor agrees to pay the sum of   Dollars ($), as attorney's fees for services in connection with said foreclosure proceedings, and said attorney's fee shall be allowed and added by the trustee to the cost of foreclosure; and if foreclosure be made through the courts, a reasonable attorney's fee shall be taxed by the court as a part of the cost of such foreclosure proceedings, and any and all such attorney's fees shall be and become a part of the indebtedness secured hereby.

10. That in case of default, whereby the right of foreclosure occurs hereunder, the beneficiary or the holder of the indebtedness or certificate of sale shall at once become entitled to the possession, use and enjoyment of the property aforesaid, and to the rents, issues and profits thereof, from the accruing of such right and during the pendency of foreclosure proceedings and the period of redemption, if any there be; and such possession, use, enjoyment, rents, issues and profits shall at once be delivered to the beneficiary or the holder of the indebtedness or certificate of sale on request, and on refusal, the delivery of such possession may be enforced by the beneficiary or the holder of the indebtedness or certificate of purchase shall be entitled to a Receiver for said property, and of the rents, issues and profits thereof, after any such default, including the time covered by foreclosure proceedings and the period of redemption, if any there be, and shall be entitled thereto as a matter of right without regard to the solvency or insolvency of the grantor or of the then owner of said property and without regard to the value of the property, and such Receiver may be appointed by any court of competent jurisdiction upon ex parte application, and without notice, notice being hereby expressly waived, and the appointment of any such Receiver, on any such application without notice, being hereby consented to by the grantor for and on his own behalf of his heirs, assigns and legal representatives, and all persons claiming by, through or under him, and all rents, issues and profits, income and revenue of said property shall be applied by such Receiver according to law and the orders and directions of the court.

Notice of the exercise of any option granted herein, or in the note secured hereby, to the beneficiary is not required to be given, the grantor hereby waiving any such notice.

The covenants herein contained shall bind, and the benefits and advantages shall inure to, the respective heirs, executors, administrators, successors and assigns of the parties hereto. Whenever used, the singular number shall include the plural, the plural the singular, and the use of any gender shall be applicable to all genders.

IN WITNESS WHEREOF, the grantor has hereunto set his hand and seal on the day and year first hereinbefore written.

Signed, sealed and delivered in the presence of

_____ [SEAL]

_____ [SEAL]

_____ [SEAL]

_____ [SEAL]

STATE OF COLORADO   } ss:

COUNTY OF

The foregoing instrument was acknowledged before me this   day of   19   , by

WITNESS my hand and official seal.

My commission expires

[SEAL]

_____
Notary Public

STATE OF COLORADO   } ss.

COUNTY OF

I hereby certify that this instrument was filed for record in my office at   o'clock   M., 19   , and is duly recorded in book   page

_____
Clerk and Recorder

Fees, $_____

By _____
Deputy

GPO 918-292

Chapter 6

ARE YOU SELLING? HERE ARE THE COMPLETE STEP-BY-STEP PROCEDURES, FROM START TO FINISH

A. Different Categories of Home Sellers; Reasons Why Homeowners Would Want To Sell Their Homes Themselves

Certainly, you have a legal right, if that is your preference, to sell your home yourself, without using a broker (or a lawyer). And, in deed, the evidence is that in recent times the number of homes sold by the owners without brokers has been on a steady increase throughout the country, as can be imagined even by the common sights of FSBO (For Sale By Owner) signs which abound around the country among houses up for sale. In deed, the informed estimate is that in recent times the number of homes sold directly by the sellers, range from 20 percent of all home sales, in some states, to more than 30 percent in some areas.*

But why would home sellers wish to sell through the FSBO (For Sale By Owner, pronounced "Fizbo") method? There are many reasons for which selling by oneself might make sound practical and economic sense to a given homeowner, among which are the following:

• By selling yourself, you acquire invaluable knowledge of what's involved in selling (and buying) a home and, in the process, you open to yourself a new method of investing through real estate, since the successful selling of real estate by oneself is the greatest builder of knowledge and confidence in one. In deed, in addition, even if you're a casual seller who doesn't want, to spend a lot of time, or have a lot of time to spend on the sale, or even if in the end, you are unsuccessful in selling the property, you can still benefit from the mere act of trying to sell your property by yourself. As one expert, a 20-year veteran as a real estate broker and consultant in real estate investment, put it: "I've always advised those who are going to sell their home to at least try to sell it by owner first...If you are successful, of course, you stand to save a great deal of money and perhaps get a quick sale. But even if you don't sell by owner, you will at least find out what's involved in selling a home and be better able to pick a [real estate sales] agent who will work hard for you.."**

• If you sell by yourself, you can save yourself the whopping broker's commission (as high as 7 percent of the selling price) you would otherwise have to pay out to the broker. This factor becomes particularly relevant in a stagnant or declining real estate market, where the value of the house may have remained the same or gone down. For, in such a situation, the broker's commission represents an even greater portion of your equity—what is left for you after you shall have subtracted the mortgage still left on the house, the taxes, sales expenses, etc., on the house.

Let's say, for an example, that you wish to sell your home today which you had bought for $100,000 some 5 years ago and had put a down payment of $20,000, and that the house is still worth $100,000 today. If you list the property with a broker and pay, say 6 percent, you would be paying $6,000, or what amounts to 30 percent of your equity (30% of your $20,000 down payment)! Now, as you can see, when you subtract the $6,000 broker's commission from your $20,000 equity, all you would be getting out of it is $14,000 at most! And it would be even worse if the property had actually gone down in value!!

---

*Figures cited in Robert Irwin, *The For Sale By Owner Kit*, p. 1.

**R. Irwin, *The For Sale By Owner Kit*, p. 3.

• Finally, there's another important reason why one may want to sell one's home himself: selling your property yourself can help get you a sale when you otherwise may not have been able to make a sale. For example, by simply lowering the asking price of the property by an amount, or a portion thereof, that you would otherwise pay in commission, you can correspondingly make your property more competitive in the market place and thereby attract more owners and substantially enhance your chances of making a sale.

In light of the above reasons and considerations as to why people choose to sell their own homes by themselves, it is probably not too surprising that analysts have found that *frustrated sellers in bad markets who previously had listed their homes with brokers and had no success selling their homes through brokers, make up a sizable portion of those who sell by owner.* And this group is followed by another, possibly larger, group made up of first-time sellers who are just now putting their homes on the market for the first time.

B. Do You Have What It Takes, Though, The Human Qualities, To Be Able To Do It Yourself?

There is, though, a more fundamental question than the above issues and considerations we have so far addressed, in determining whether to go ahead and handle the selling of your property by yourself. Sure, there are great advantages in doing it yourself, and with a relatively little coaching and knowledge you can successfully sell your own home. And, certainly, with this guidebook, any remaining mystery or intimidation about the selling of your home shall have been amply dispelled. All of that notwithstanding, however, a primary question before you may finally undertake that task, is: *can you do it, DO YOU HAVE THE PERSONALITY, THE TEMPERAMENT, AND THE RELEVANT HUMAN ATTRIBUTES TO BE ABLE TO DO IT?*

In reality, quite apart from all the positive reasons which abound for which it's advisable to sell by owner, it should be strongly pointed out that not every person can—or should—sell the FSBO way. Robert Irwin, a real estate expert, author, and consultant of over 30 years experience, who had professionally coached lenders, sellers and brokers, in the technique of successfully selling property, explains it this way: "I've owned dozens of properties. Some I've sold through [real estate sales] agents. Others I've sold myself. The truth...is that some people can sell their own homes by themselves, and some can't. And some properties need [real estate sales] agent, and some don'ts."

According to Irwin, as well as other experts in the field, that determination ultimately turns on a number of extraneous factors—factors which range from a person's personality, to his level of confidence and competence, the market conditions, the home's location, its state of repair, the price at which the house is set for sale, and the like. Hence, a fair knowledge and consideration of such factors by a would-be owner-seller, is called for in helping him/her decide whether he should sell by the FSBO way at all, or not.

Do you possess the human attributes required for you to sell as a FSBO seller? For the purposes of simplification, here's the CHECKLIST (Figure 6.1 on p. 85) for you to use in determining if you have the temperament and personal attributes to sell your property by yourself, and not have a broker do it for you.

FIGURE 6.1

Checklist For Determining If You Have The Temperament To Sell By FSBO Method

1. Are you willing to give up evenings and weekends for the next three months? Yes _____ No _____

2. Will you be willing to let strangers into your home? Yes _____ No _____

3. Can you be ready to show your home day or night on a moment's notice? Yes _____ No _____

4. Are you a risk taker? Yes _____ No _____

5. Are you willing to learn how to do new and different things? Yes _____ No _____

6. Are you determined to save money on the sale of your home? Yes _____ No _____

7. Do you want a quick sale? Yes _____ No _____

8. Are you willing to handle the paperwork yourself? Yes _____ No _____

9. Are you willing to negotiate face-to-face with a buyer? Yes _____ No _____

10. Are you a patient person? Yes _____ No _____

ANSWERS

1. You have to be ready to show the house when the buyers want to see it. Remember, there's no agent to show it for you.

2. You also have to screen the buyers yourself and then let perfect strangers into your house. If you're concerned about security, you're not a good candidate to be a FSBO seller.

3. Spontaneity is needed. A potential buyer who calls wants to see your place *now*. Tell the caller to come back later and you could lose a deal.

4. It's riskier to venture into the unknown and sell FSBO rather than list. But it's also frequently quicker and more profitable.

5. You'll have to work with attorneys, escrow and loan officers, inspectors and others. You'll have to learn about sales agreements and other documents. It's not hard, but it does require determination to succeed.

6.& 7. Proper motivation is essential here. If you don't want to save money and sell quickly, why bother going FSBO?

8. You'll need to do some of it.

9. There's no intermediary to blunt the buyer's criticism, anger or frustration. You have to deal with it all and turn it into something positive.

10. You'll need lots of patience to succeed.

SCORE

9 to 10 = Yes. You're a natural FSBO.

7 to 8 = Yes. You need to dwell a little longer on how much money a 5 to 7 percent commission really is.

5 to 6 = Yes. Borderline—try it for a while to see if you like it.

1 to 4 = Yes. Don't waste time. List your house now.

This chart is reproduced courtesy of Deaborn Financial Corporation, from *The For Sale By Owner Kit*, by Robert Irwin, pp. 6-7.

```
┌─────────────────────────────────────────────────────────────────────┐
│                            NOTE                                       │
│  Outlined in the remainder of this chapter, is a systematic, sure-fire, 10-Step, step-by-step proce-  │
│  dure for successfully getting your house sold, from start to finish.  The system works.  It can work  │
│  for you.  But for it to work for you with all ease and simplicity, you've got to closely follow the   │
│  instructions outlined under each "STEP" in the system, and employ some God-given common    │
│  sense and intelligence.  And, more particularly: YOU MUST FOLLOW AND DO THE PROCE-   │
│  DURES STEP-BY-STEP—IN EXACTLY THE SAME ORDER THEY ARE LISTED BELOW    │
│  IN THE REST OF THIS CHAPTER.  Don't (REPEAT, Don't) SKIP OR JUMP AROUND!    │
└─────────────────────────────────────────────────────────────────────┘
```

C. Step-By-Step Procedures For Selling Your Own Home

To sell your real property, simply follow these STEPS in the EXACT order they are listed below:

STEP ❶: DO A LITTLE TAX PLANNING HOMEWORK

One of the very first important and, many experts say, indispensable determinations for any intending home seller to make, even before embarking on the actual selling efforts, is to assess what tax breaks might be available to him (her) from the sale of his (or her) personal residence, and how to take advantage of that. This is so because, under the personal tax rules, the very best tax advantages available to the average person relate to the sale of a person's personal residence.

Of necessity, our treatment of this subject here cannot be detailed nor cover the ramifications of the tax rules involved. We can only look at the issue from the perspective of a brief, limited overview. But, strictly speaking, providing you meet certain strict requirements, the tax rules relating to the sale of one's *personal residence* allows you to "defer" paying any taxes on your profits from the sale of your home, and, at age 55, even allow you to exclude forever up to $125,000 in taxable gain. By "deferral," is meant that you won't have to pay the tax due on any taxable gain immediately, but rather the payment of the tax you owe is pushed into the future.

Basically, to qualify for such deferral of the gain, the main requirements to meet are as follows: First, the house must be, or qualify as, your (the seller's) *personal residence.* (If you had to move and had rented out your per- sonal home, say because you relocated or were transferred to another location and couldn't sell the house, the house may still qualify as a personal residence subject to gain-deferral, providing it is ultimately sold in no more than 2 years. But to be absolutely certain , you should always consult with your tax advisor or accountant in each situation). The second requirement is that you must buy another personal residence within 2 years of the sale of the first house for an equal or greater dollar amount, and you must occupy that property within the 2-year term. In other words, you must replace the existing personal residence you sell with a new one within two years from the date of the sale, and actually occupy the new property.

Then, to be legitimately able to defer all of the gain on the sale of your old personal residence, the price of your new residence must be greater than the adjusted sales price of your old one. (If, on the other hand, you were to buy a cheaper home than your old personal residence, you may still be able to defer some but not all of the gain.)

You can have only one personal residence at a time. Under the rules, you cannot have frequent replacements or roll-overs; rather, generally you can apply the deferral rule only once every two years, and if you do it sooner than that, you will be liable for capital gains taxes on one or more of your transactions.

Finally, under the over-55 rules of exclusion, providing you meet certain strict qualifications,* upon your reaching the age of 55 you qualify for a once-in-a-lifetime $125,000 exclusion when you sell your personal residence—that is, up to $125,000 of any gain you make on such a sale can be permanently excluded from your

---

*Basically, the qualifications are: you must be 55 or older as of the date of the sale; you must have lived in the home and owned it for at least the past 3 out of 5 years ending with the date of sale; and neither you nor your spouse, if any, may have previously taken the exemption.

taxes and you won't have to pay taxes on it, ever. This provision is designed especially for the benefit of taxpayers who are nearing retirement age and who have most of their assets invested in their equity in their home . The idea is to provide such persons with an avenue by which they could sell, then buy a cheaper home and keep up to $125,000 out for their other needs , without paying taxes on it. (For a good planning idea, you can combine this exclusion with the deferral plan described above. Assuming, for example, you sell your home at a gain of, say, $250,000, you can exclude $125,000 of the gain under the over-55 "exclusion" rule, and then buy a lower-priced house and defer the remaining gain under the "deferral" rule, thereby totally avoiding taxes on your whole gain, at least for now!)

By way of summarizing, the important point to be made in this section, is *the need and advisability for planning ahead of time on the tax issue before you decide to sell, so that you can make the right moves at the right time, and not lose the tax advantages that should otherwise accrue to you.* Consequently, the essence of this section for you to bear in mind is this: before you embark on selling your house, hire a competent tax accountant or consultant first ,to advise you on whether your situation qualifies; and, furthermore, since the rules on this subject are often extremely complex and arcane, or often involves a gray area of the tax law, this may be one area you may also be well advised to hire a competent tax advisor to wade through the rules and procedures for you before you undertake a sale so as to avoid costly mistakes or the loss of valuable tax breaks.*

STEP ❷: CLEAN UP, FIX UP, GET THE HOUSE READY FOR SHOWING TO BUYERS

Let's just say that you've sufficiently thought it over. You've now decided, for whatever your needs or reasons may be, that it is worth it and that the timing is good: YOU WANT TO SELL YOUR HOUSE. Now, Where do you begin? It should be rather obvious: *You should first put the house in a good and "presentable" enough shape—a condition where it's good for presentation to the buying public.*

---

*For example, because of the 2-year replacement time rule, one should actually plan on buying or building another personal residence within 2 years of sale of a home. Yet, a common mistake some people make, is to think that because they can defer money in the year they sell their old personal residence, they don't have to do anything more. They forget that they have to replace the old home, with a new one (within 2 years); they spend the money and awaken years later to find a huge tax bill plus interest penalties.

As is true with the selling of anything of any kind, whatsoever, unless the prospective buyer can "see" the beauty, the attractiveness and the worth of your piece of real property, he wouldn't buy it — which means, in other words, you wouldn't be able to sell it! An unattractive, or a neglected or untidy house not only fetches less dollars, but fewer and less substantial prospective buyers, or even no prospects at all. According to experienced salesmen and expert brokers who make a living selling real property on a regular basis, *it's a common mistake, but a costly and deadly one, among uninitiated home sellers, to neglect the necessity of tidying up and fixing up the property BEFORE ever putting it on the market.* Nevertheless, say these experts, often all it will take is no more than just a few hours of labor time and a few hundred dollars worth of materials, to give your property the kind of "face-lift" sufficient to bring about a substantially faster sale as well as the top price for the property. It's an open secret among real estate sales experts that one central business philosophy common among them is that *even purely "cosmetic" improvements costing just a few hundred dollars tangibly adds several thousand dollars to the home sale value on the average. And the need for prior home improvements is just as applicable, whether you sell your home by yourself, or employ a broker to help you with it.*

One real estate sales expert *and author, summed up the crucial significance of making the house presentable in successfully selling a house, this way:

> "People make surface judgements on a house just as they make surface judgements about people. If we like what we see on the surface, our first impression is to like what's underneath. So, let's make sure the surface look of your house is pleasing to the eye…Remind yourself that *50 percent of the job of selling a house is to make the buyers [who come to see the house] get out of their cars. If your house doesn't make a good first impression, they'll simply shrug and drive by."* [Emphasis added by the writer]

And another expert,** a veteran real estate sales consultant, offers a more graphic but brutally frank and instructive piece of professional wisdom and perspective on the centrality of making the house presentable for 'showing' purposes:

> *"When it comes to buyers…they absolutely believe in what they see and have no imagination…* Your home may boast an absolutely smashing entry with tile floors, wood trime, solid oak doors, marble columns and more. But, if the floor, walls and doors have been painted over with a dull ugly paint, that's what the buyer will see — the dull paint, not the quality beneath. *Ninety-nine percent of buyers won't pay any attention to it [to what is beneath].* All they'll see and remember is an ugly painted entry, and they'll probably dismiss your home from their minds as a contender for purchase.
>
> Even worse, let's say that you've got a [really] wonderful home inside…But you didn't get around to taking good care of your lawn this year and the shrubs out front are wild because they weren't trimmed and the paint has weathered and has peeling patches. *Many buyers won't even bother to stop and look inside! Never mind that the inside of your house is beautiful…they'll drive on."* [Emphasis added by the writer]

THE MESSAGE: You MUST "dress up" and "spruce up" your for-sale home to catch the prospective buyer's attention; you should leave nothing to the buyer's imagination (remember, they don't have any!); but, instead, give them something tangible and direct to physically "see"—a glamorous, exciting, splendid, even "sexy" display, capable of making that all-important first impression on the viewer!

POINTERS FOR MAKING THE HOUSE PRESENTABLE FOR SHOWING

Here are a few pointers for improving the general looks of your house in readiness for putting it up for sale:

1. Undertake the task with common sense and a sense of perspective. Don't go on a wild, expensive spending or "remodeling" spree at this late hour (such as installing a new generator or converting to gas from oil or adding a new swimming pool). Just improve what you already have; concentrate on fixing up and repairing the existing fixtures on the house so that they are in good working order and are functioning well.

---

*Harley Bjelland, in *How To Sell Your House Without A Broker* (Cornerstone Library: 1979, pp. 12-13).

**Robert Irwin, in *The For Sale By The Owner Kit.*

2. Soap, hot water, sponge, scrubbing tools, and paint, are widely recommended as the cheapest but most effective, and, often times, the only tools you'll require. With these, get down to work. Clean, scrub, paint, "spruce up" and "face-lift" the entire house and its surroundings inside and out, including the built-in fixtures and appliances that go with the house. Eliminate toilet, bathtub and sink stains; repair light fixtures, plumbing leaks, drips and clogs; shampoo the rugs or vacuum clean them (or, for a few dollars, rent a cleaning machine, or, better still, hire a professional carpet cleaning service to do it); wash the window glasses, and the drapes and curtains; clean the household accessories and the appliances and plumbing (e.g., the counters, the closets, stove, oven, refrigerator, sink, etc.); empty out the garbage to eliminate odors. Keep the house well-lit during showing, and put away exotic materials and weird objects of art.

3. On painting—which is one of the primary aspects of the fix-up undertaking—you should first do the front of the house, and the entry room and the front door. Then continue with the rest of the house — the kitchen, the guest bathroom, the master bedroom, then all the other rooms, in that order. Paint them from the floor to ceiling.

What color do you choose? Experts suggest the "neutral" colors —a beige, white or light color of some different sorts — since most people, probably by a ratio of as much as 50 to 1, are said to be offended by stronger colors, such as blues, greens and yellows.

4. Look at and around your house *objectively, unemotionally,* and, above all, *with a critical eye* — just the way a prospective buyer would. Does your backyard lawn, for example, need weeding or trimming? Do you have a lot of junk lying around the house — in the backyard, the basement, garage, or what have you? They should be thrown out and cleared out of the premises. Throw out what you can't use, for those things you can still use (the out-of-season clothing or Christmas decorations), neatly store them away in the basement or garage. In deed, some real estate sales experts even recommend "moving out half of the furniture," contending that as a particular homeowner the household items you have in your premises reflect your own individual likes and tastes, what you can afford and feel comfortable with as an individual, but which a total stranger with totally different likes and dislikes who comes as a prospective home buyer to view the house may possibly see as something out of "a den, as in animal," rather than a presentation. *(Home owners, you should remember, are after all different individuals with different tastes and likes from you, who generally are visualizing how <u>THEIR own</u> furniture, and <u>not yours</u>, will look and fit in the home, hence what they really need is to get an impression that <u>their own</u> furniture will fit!)*

5. Remember this: As a rule, home buyers like to have the feeling of large spaces and spaciousness and are discouraged, on the other hand, by tight (or tight looking) quarters and cluttered or crowded rooms. Lesson: Do all that is necessary to create and maximize the impression of spaciousness in the eye of the prospective buyer — keep things near walls rather than in the center of rooms; clear the rooms (and house surroundings) of garbage and unused or discarded items; generally retain a clean, uncluttered look.

Perhaps the most significant negative effect of the cluttered house, is not just that it makes the house look small, or that buyers, as a rule, want a spacious house. Rather, it is that *cluttering diverts attention and shifts attention away from the house. Instead of focusing on and remembering how spacious your home is, the prospective buyer will largely recall it as a jumble of crowded, unmatched and uncoordinated furniture!*

6. Is the kitchen and the pantry sparklingly clean, free of dirt, and uncluttered, with all the cooking appliances which go with the house in good working order? [Nothing, it is said, would turn a female prospect away more than a dirty, odor-filled kitchen and eating area!]

7. Are the door knobs, hinges, etc., firmly fixed in place and smooth running — to the rooms, the cabinets, cupboards, closets, etc.? Make sure, especially, that the main front door leading directly into the house is particularly flawless: well painted with attractive colors, no scratches, free of squeaking. [According to real estate sales experts, the front door to the house creates a powerful, extraordinary "first impression" on the prospect, and such first impression carries over into how he views the rest of the property at a home showing!]

Indeed, say experienced sales experts, if at all you can find the means to do it, you should even install a totally new front door, for, they contend, at a cost of around $300 to $500 that's not a lot of money "when you think of the impression it makes" on prospective buyers.*

8. Follow this general principle and its logical implication: as a general rule, for a successful home selling, the home should appeal to the basic senses of those looking at it — especially the sense of <u>sight</u>. A prospective buyer's impression, good or bad, is all too likely to come through his/her eyes. [Lesson: everything about the house should — must— look good to the prospective buyer who comes looking at the house.]

9. Note that smart house shoppers who are knowledgeable in how to go about it, would often insist on doing their inspection of the property from the basement first. And what they see in the basement alone — say it's damp or smelly, or the furnace and hot water heater are old, or the wrapping on the pipes show signs of deteriorating asbestos — may persuade them not to proceed further in the inspection endeavor, as they'll conclude that whatever else they may find upstairs are merely cosmetics. So, be sure to give as much attention to your basement as any other parts of your house; keep it clean, dry, and brightly lit with a modern furnace that is in good working order, and clear of clutter with a lot of space and plenty of storage room, among other things.

STEP ❸: SET THE RIGHT SELLING PRICE FOR THE HOUSE AND DETERMINE OTHER PRELIMINARY MATTERS RELATED TO FINANCES

A. The Critical Importance Of Setting the Right Selling Price

The next major order of business, after you've gotten the house in a ready-to-show-and-sell condition, is to SET THE RIGHT PRICE at which the house is to be sold. ***This, by most accounts, is probably the most important single step in one being able to sell a house***—the single most crucial 'make or break' issue in determining whether you sell your property, and how quickly you do so.

One analyst, with more than three decades of practical experience in real estate sales and consultancy, summed up the pivotal importance of the proper pricing of property or being able to make a successful sale, this way:

"The hardest thing of all is to be realistic about price. If you price your house low enough it almost doesn't make any difference what the market is like. You will get a sale today…you want to sell? Price your house realistically. You will sell it right away." **

Indeed, many experts will tell you that few decisions concerning the selling of a house cause more anxiety and uncertainty to the home seller than the setting of a asking price! And it's easy to see why: The price set must be set at a level that is <u>precisely</u> "right"—right, both for the seller and for the buyer. If the price were to be set at a level that is above what could be perceived as reasonable, the house may be condemned to sit on the market for months without takers; you're liable to lose most of your potential buyers, and to incur on-going out-of-pocket costs in continuing mortgage and tax payments and home maintenance expenses. And if, on the other hand, the price were to be set at a level that is substantially below the home's "reasonable" price, you'll in effect be throwing away a few thousands of dollars in the deal. Besides, a low price could provoke a sense of suspicion on the part of the prospec-

---

*"A great looking front door will knock the socks off potential buyers. I believe it returns far more than it costs in your ability to resell quicker and at a higher cost." (Irwin, The For Sale By Owner Kit, p. 63).

**Irwin, The For Sale By Owner Kit, p. 22.

tive buyers, making them wonder whether there's a "catch to it"—some serious, undisclosed defects in the property. Remember: Chances are that a potential buyer who comes knocking on your door has probably looked at many other homes besides yours and is well aware of the prevailing home values in the community!]

What, then, is the most effective way of arriving at a asking price that is just right—one that will fetch a quick enough sale and at the best price possible? One thing on which virtually every real estate professional is agreed upon,   is that, whatever the technique used or whoever may be the person setting the price, the *key element* for *arriving at the right price determination is knowledge:* a solid grasp of what is going on in the local housing market, and an ability and facility to make a careful market analysis of that data.

B. The Three Basic Methods of Establishing a Price

Basically, these are among the three basic methods by which you may attempt to establish the right price for your house:

i. *Method #1:* Make up a **"Comparative Sales analysis," by yourself,** of recent sales of houses of similar size, construction, and features, in the area of your property's location. (See Fig. 6.2 below for a sample) The basic comparison is on $ value per square foot of living area. For example, if a 1600 square foot house in your area recently sold for $100,000, that's a market value of $100,000 divided by 1600 square feet or $62.50 per square foot. (See Figure 6.2 for a sample).

ii. *Method #2: Use a Realtor's Evaulation*—get separate value estimates from at least two (perhaps more) experienced and respected licensed brokers or realtors in the immediate area of the home in question. (See Figure 6.3 for a sample).

iii. *Method #3:* Hire a **professional appraiser** to appraise the value of the house.

FIGURE 6.2

*Comparative Sales Analysis (A Sample Illustration)**

House No.	Square Footage	Bdrms.	Extras	Listed Price (Dollars)	Selling Price (Dollars)	Selling Dollars per sq. ft.	Month Listed	Month Sold	Days to Sell	Dollars below asking price	Percen below asking price
1	1600	3	Family Room	89,000	86,000	54	Nov	Feb	105	3,000	3.5
2	1810	4	View	99,900	95,000	52	Feb	Feb	3	4,900	5
3	1800	3		89,400	89,400	50	Feb	Feb	4	0	0
4	1370	3		81,990	81,990	60	Feb	Feb	3	0	0
5	1500	3		85,000	78,000	52	Dec	Mar	103	7,000	9
6	1390	3		83,800	80,000	58	Dec	Mar	90	3,800	4.8
7	1650	4		89,000	87,000	53	Jan	Mar	46	2,000	2.3
8	1650	4	Pool	97,000	96,000	58	Feb	Mar	18	2,000	2
9	1370	3		81,900	80,000	58	Mar	Mar	3	1,900	2.4
10	1800	4		93,800	90,000	50	Mar	Apr	22	3,800	4.2
11	1700	3	View	90,000	90,000	53	Apr	Apr	6	0	0
12	1700	4		91,000	90,000	53	Apr	Apr	5	1,000	1
13	1650	4		95,800	94,500	57	Apr	May	16	1,300	1.4
14	1390	3		81,900	80,000	58	Apr	May	20	1,900	2.4
15	2000	3	Pool	105,800	104,000	52	Apr	May	17	1,800	1.7
16	1990	5		97,800	94,000	47	Apr	June	63	3,800	4
17	1620	3	View & Pool	98,000	92,000	57	Mar	Jul	126	6,000	6.5
18	1390	3		91,000	88,600	64	May	Jul	52	2,400	2.7
19	1440	3		85,800	82,000	57	May	Jul	40	3,800	4.6
20	1450	3		87,900	85,000	59	Jun	Jul	27	2,900	3.4
21	1400	3		79,800	76,000	54	Jun	Jul	25	3,800	5
22	1930	4	View & pool	105,800	104,500	54	Jun	Jul	5	800	1
23	1630	3		93,800	93,800	58	Jun	Jul	6	0	0
24	2100	4	View & Pool	129,900	127,000	60	Jun	Jul	13	2,900	2.3
25	1440	3		85,800	82,000	57	Jun	Jul	40	3,800	4.6
26	1300	3		97,600	87,000	67	Jun	Jul	27	10,600	12
27	1650	4	View	93,800	93,000	56	Jul	Jul	10	800	1
28	1300	3		85,800	83,400	64	Jul	Jul	11	2,400	2.9
29	1490	3		87,900	85,000	57	Jun	Aug	55	2,900	3.4
30	1390	3		87,000	84,000	60	Jul	Sept	61	3,000	3.6
31	1980	3		105,000	102,000	52	Aug	Sept	26	3,000	2.9
32	1650	4	View	95,000	94,000	57	Aug	Sept	20	1,000	1
33	1660	3	View	103,000	99,800	60	Sept	Sept	1	3,200	3.2
34	1630	3		103,800	101,800	62	Sept	Oct	6	2,000	2
35	1540	3	View	105,800	103,800	67	Sept	Oct	13	2,000	2
36	1650	4		97,900	97,000	59	Oct	Oct	15	2,900	1
37	1400	3		95,900	93,000	66	Oct	Oct	17	2,900	3
38	1390	3	View	89,800	88,000	63	Oct	Nov	5	1,800	2
39	1390	3		93,900	92,000	66	Nov	Nov	6	1,900	2

Pertinent Interpretation (Fig. 6.2): There are 39 houses listed in this chart, ranging in selling price from $76,0000 to $127,000. The price per square foot ranges from $47 to $67. The average house in the list has about 1600 square feet and sold for $91,000. The average time to sell a house was 29 days. The average house sold for $2640 less than the asking price, which is three percent below the asked price. The average 3 bedroom house sold in 33 days, the average 4 bedroom in less than half the time, 16 days; 4 bedrooms are generally more sought after. The average house with a pool sold faster, in 13 days, and the same is true with the average house with a view (sold in under 10 days), but in either case the owner won't get back the money he invested in the pool and view.

FIGURE 6.3

Realtor's Comparison Analysis (A Sample Illustration*

HOUSES FOR SALE

	Bedrooms	Baths	Listed Price	Square Footage	Dollars per sq. ft.
A	4	1¾	$113,800	1,650	69
B	4	1½	$109,000	1,650	66
				(Average)	67.5

HOUSES RECENTLY SOLD

	Bedrooms	Baths	Listed Price	Square Footage	Dollars per sq. ft.	Month Sold
C	4	1½	$103,000	1,650	62	April
D	3	1¾	$105,000	1,650	64	May
E	3	1¾	$109,000	1,650	66	June
F	3	1¾	$106,000	1,650	64	June
				(Average)	64	

Figures 6.2 & 6.3, used for illustrations in this manual, are reproduced from, and by the courtesy of Harley Bjelland's *"How To Sell Your House Without A Broker,"* to whom the Publishers are greatly greatful.

A New, Innovative, Electronic Alternative

In deed, what is probåbly the most innovative alternative to have come on the scene for getting comparative home sales prices, is a brand new approach that is available in some areas of the country. The system is to get prices of homes through what is called the **Home Sales Lines,** an interactive computer system you can access by phone and fax. The service, praised by the Money Magazine, as the "best real estate idea of 1995," gives you (the caller) the sales price of a specific house, prices for homes on a specific street, or addresses of houses that sold for a specific price. As of this research in mid-1996, the service is available only in California, Massachusetts, New York, New Jersey, Rhode Island, metropoitan Washington D.C., southern Florida, metropolitan Detroit, and parts of Ohio and Colorado. It's rapidly expanding to more and more areas, however.

To search for home prices through the Home Sales Line, all you do is simply call 800-487-6534. For a fee of just $5 (add another $2 if you want a fax transcript of it), a price search will be made for you, and the information given you over the phone right away.

Given below is an ad, as shown in a New Jersey newspaper announcing the service for the area's home buyers and sellers.

Which pricing and evaluation method should you (a seller) use for your specific property?

For our purposes here, it is advised that you simply forget about doing the evaluation yourself (the Method #1 listed above). Rather, hire, or merely consult with, outside professional evaluators under either Method #2 or Method #3 listed above, and have them appraise for you what "fair market price" a house like yours ought to be going for. Having a "directly interested party" himself (i.e., either the seller or the buyer) set the price, is advised against for this primary reason: it is a common occurrence that when it comes to the selling or buying of a home, even the most sophisticated seller or buyer tends to be emotional rather than objective—that, on the one hand, buyers, because they often lack intimate knowledge of the local market, frequently err on the side of offering much too little, prompting sellers to not even respond or take them seriously; and that sellers, on the other hand, tend to overprice their homes for a variety of reasons (a tendency to overvalue improvements they made to the property, a belief that their neighbors underpriced their own homes, or, simply, a hope that they, too, can make a "killing" in a rising market.)*

---

*In an allusion that could apply just as much to the buyer or the seller, one expert, Norman Kailo, a past president of the New Jersey Association of Realtors and the then owner of the Soldoveri Agency in Wayne, N.J., summed it up this way: "They always think their home is special because they live there. It's such a danger that even after 22 years in real estate, I would not try to set a price on my own house. I would make sure someone else made the decision for me." (As cited in The N.Y. Times, Section 8, May 8, 1983, p. 1).

A) PRICE FORMULATION METHOD #2: USING A REALTOR'S EVALUATION

Of the two price formulation methods recommended above, one method, the use of some two or more experienced real estate brokers or realtors to make separate evaluations of the house, has the advantage of being the quicker and least costly one. And actually, this is the method mortgage appraisers, sales agents, and others involved in real estate, use more often in determining the value of a home. [Normally, the brokers will provide an evaluation free of charge, in the hope of obtaining the right to market the property.]

This method is really quite simple. Basically, this is all you do: find four or five houses that are "comparable" to yours in your residential area, which sold over the past 6 months; determine what they sold for, then average it out, and that's what your house is worth.

There are a number of ways you can get the comparables, but here's the simple way to do it. Wait until after you shall have finished fixing up and putting your house in a ready-to-show condition. Then, check with a few realtors and brokers located in the area where your property is situated, or invite them to look over your home, and request them to give you an estimate of what is should sell for. Just make sure, though, that the realtors you pick are actively selling homes in the area in question, since property values vary considerably from one section of the city to the other. Invite only one realtor over at a time. Be frank with the realtors, tell each you're going to try to sell your home by yourself for about 2 months, but that if the property doesn't sell you'll hire the realtor. (But don't make any tentative selection or commitment in writing or otherwise to any realtor at this time). Ask each realtor (individually and independently) to give you a "Comparison Chart" similar to that shown in Figure 6.3 on p. 92. Using the computer system now available to most real estate sales offices, realtors can quickly punch up a list of comparable sales in your area—houses of similar size and similar style and design, similar area of town and age, similar number of rooms, baths, car garages, and square footage, and roughly the same amenities, that are sold no longer than 6 months ago.

To keep their analysis honest and sincere, insist from each realtor on a comparison analysis report IN WRITING. And, secondly, be sure to get more than one (preferably three or more) analysis charts from different realtors and then compare them to see how the realtors estimates compare. This way, you shall have guarded against the possibility that some realtors may overstate or understate their estimates. By this chart, each of the realtors shall have compared recent sales in your neighborhood, of houses of rough similarity (in size and construction), based on the dollar vallue per square foot of living area. From such a written comparison analysis report from some 3 to 5 different realtors, you can then easily calculate a price per square foot at which you can list your property.

For example, say a 2400 square foot house in your area recently sold for $100,000, that would mean a market value of $100,000 divided by 2400 square foot, or $41.67 per square foot. And from this data you can easily calculate a price "per square foot" at which to list your house, by merely taking an average or middle ground figure of all 3, 4 or 5 realtors estimates. If one of their estimates is way out of line, totally discard it. Typically, you will advertise your house at a price of sale based on the "listed" price per square foot (upper part of Figure 6.3 Chart on p. 92), but you'll be prepared to negotiate down to the price listed under the "selling price" per square foot (lower part of chart on p. 92).

B) PRICE FORMULATION METHOD #3: USING A PROFESSIONAL APPRAISER

Finally, depending on your particular preference, another alternative method of determining the right selling price for your home, would be to hire a skilled, independent, professional appraiser and have him appraise the value of the property. The main advantage of using a professional appraiser is that, at least in theory, his judgment is more likely to be independent, objective and unbiased, inasmuch as his practice is limited to appraisals and he does not get involved in sales. For one thing, the cost of hiring an appraiser is relatively nominal ($2-$4 per $2,000 value of the house or anywhere from $200-$400 for a $200,000 home). And the appraiser's fee is tax-deductible from any profits you make from the sale.

An important factor worth considering in this connection, is that the professional appraiser's evaluation report is one thing you can use to your advantage in the whole selling process—as a powerful and influential selling "ploy" to impress your prospects about the true worth of your property, and, hence, about the apparent reasonableness of the selling price you are quoting them.

Since setting the price exactly right is one of the most important tasks in making a timely sale, the investment of a few hundred dollars to get an independent, unbiased, professional evaluation of the true market worth of your property may well be a wise investment worth being made.

To locate an appraiser, look in your local "Yellow Pages" under the headings "Real Estate Appraiser," or ask for recommendations from a savings bank in the area. There's one way (among others) of ensuring hiring a competent appraiser with at least a minimum professional ability: Look for those appraisers who are certified current members of at least one of the four major national residential home appraisal organizations.

THE ORGANIZATIONS ARE:

Society of Real Estate Appraisers
Chicago, Ill. (Headquarters)

American Institute of Real Estate Appraisers
430 North Michigan Ave.
Chicago, Ill. 60011 (Headquarters)
(312) 329-8559

American Society of Appraisers
P.O. Box 17265
Washington, DC 20041 (Headquarters)
(703) 620-3838

National Assoc. of Independent Fee Appraisers, Inc.
7501 Murdoch
St. Louis, MO. 63119 (Headquarters)

C. And Now, Here's The Right Price At Which You Should Sell As A FSBO Seller

Now, let's assume you've done the normal data-gathering and price comparison calculations of the kind outlined in Section B above, and that, based on either one (or both) of the two popular evaluation methods, you arrive at a particular price at which homes that are just like yours have recently been sold. Does that then mean that, as an FSBO (For Sale By Owner) seller, you should simply adopt that price and automatically list (or sell) your property at that price?

The answer is, ABSOLUTELY NO! *Actually, as a FSBO seller, if you are to make a successful and quick sale of your property, there is a "special" way you are to price the property—slightly different from the way a broker-assisted house would ordinarily be priced!* What is this "special" pricing strategy you should employ as a FSBO seller? We shall get to that in a moment. But before that, let's discuss for a moment the reasons for which such a special pricing strategy is imperative for the FSBO seller, according to knowledgeable real estate marketing experts with vast practical experience in the sales field.

DICTUM: First, here are two fundamental operative truths of real estate sales you've got to work with: First, most FSBO-sold houses are unrealistically priced, they are typically put on the market at a higher price than the houses that are listed with real estate agents and brokers. And second: as a rule, buyers have a resistance to, even a dislike for, a FSBO-sold house, and given equal conditions (identical houses, same location, identical price etc.), they'd flock to buy the house listed with a real estate agent rather than the one being sold by an FSBO.

How and why is it that the average homebuyer would likely have the above-stated attitude of lesser preference towards the FSBO-sponsored property? Essentially, it stems from the first stated "operative truth": that, for most buyers, a FSBO-sponsored house is, from a practical standpoint, a less desirable home on which to make an offer than an agency-listed property, precisely because they (the buyers) are aware, intuitively at least, that the FSBO-sold house is typically priced higher than comparable homes in the same area, and because buyers generally feel more comfortable dealing with the broker in that they can better tell the broker "their mind," and it is far less confrontational for them, among other reasons. Experts contend that owner-sellers tend to price their property too high because they are usually too sentimental, rather than objective, about the value of their house and tend to overvalue improvements they made to the property. Every homeowner, it is said, thinks of his or her house as being "special" and having unique qualities, and hence figures that his or her home is worth more.

"They [homeowner-sellers] always think their home is special because they live there," said one expert, Norman Kailo of Wayne, NJ, a past president of the New Jersey Association of Realtors. "It [the emotional aspect of it] is such a danger that even after 22 years in real estate, I would not try to set a price on my own house. I would [rather] make sure someone else made the decision for me."

Another real estate veteran and sales expert, Robert Irwin, explains the same point this way: "what often happens is that the homeowner...begins focusing on two different things: how much he or she wants for the property and how much he or she can save by not paying an agent's commission; hence, more money in the bank. The real end result is [unrealistic expections], a house that's priced too high."*

Irwin explains that, initially, buyers are attracted to homes that are being offered for sale by the homeowner. But, he says, there's however a specific pragmatic reason on the part of the prospective home-buyer for their attraction to the FSBO seller. "The reason, quite simply, is that they are looking for a bargain," he explains. "They also realize that you're not paying a commission to an agent. Hence, they anticipate that you'd pass the savings on to them." However, the moment they call or stop by and realize that your house isn't any cheaper, or that in fact it may even be more expensive than others they've looked at, they will "drop you like a hot potato," says Irwin. "Furthermore, they'll assume that the real reason you listed is to save the commission an agent would charge for yourself. In short, buyers won't want to deal with you."**

THE POINT, THEN, IS THAT IF YOU WISH TO SUCCESSFULLY SELL YOUR PROPERTY AS A HOMEOWNER-SELLER, YOU MUST BE SURE TO ADOPT A SPECIAL PRICING STRATEGY.

DICTUM: HERE'S THE SPECIAL RULE OF PRICING TO FOLLOW: As an FSBO seller, to be able to sell your home successfully, you've got to generously give back to your buyer a share of the savings you'll make on the broker's commission; use that savings to discount your selling price for the property and make the listing price of your property more competitively attractive to buyers, and you'll find that you will sell your house quickly and surely.

And now, we come to the central point of what should be the right price of sale to set for your home when it's being sold the FSBO method? To illustrate, let's assume the following:

 i) you've made your normal price comparison calculations and analysis either by a realtor comparison analysis or a professional appraiser's report set forth above (pp. 94-5), and you have found that comparable homes to your own should reasonably be listed for, say, around $250,000.

 ii) the broker's commission typically charged in your area is, say, 6 percent, (the rate charged by individual brokers is always negotiable, but most run from 5 to 7 percent), meaning that the commission would amount to $15,000 on a $250,000 sale. Thus, if you were to make the sale of your house through a broker , it would actually net you just $235,000 ($250,000 minus $15,000).

HOW MUCH DO YOU ASK FOR FOR YOUR PROPERTY IN THIS CASE? It's simple. Avoid being greedy. Simply split the "savings" you would presumably make on the commission down the middle, assign one-half of that to yourself, and one-half to the customer by discounting your asking price by that amount. Thus, the figures will work out this way: The asking price for the property would be $250,000 minus the $7,500 discount (one-half of the $15,000 commission amount), or an amount of $242,500. So, there you have it.! You'll list your house for sale (in this specific case) for $242,500. If you sell at that price, you'd still net $7,5000 more than comparable sellers who had sold at $250,000 through a broker and paid a commission. And your house would have sold quicker.

---

*Irwin, Ibid., p. 28.

**Irwin, Ibid., p. 29.

Listed/asking price $250,000
Less: probable broker's commission @ 6%   -15,000
Net to you in sale through a broker $235,000

Savings accruing to you if sale is made by FSBO method.............................$15,000
Savings on commission divisible between you & buyer: $7,500 to each party

FIGURE 6.4
Comparable Estimating Sheet

Address_____
Square footage _____
Style _____
Condition _____

Bedrooms?	Number _____	
Baths?	Number _____	
Family room?	Yes _____	No _____
Garage?	Yes _____	No _____
2 car?	Yes _____	No _____
3 car?	Yes _____	No _____
Pool?	Yes _____	No _____
Spa?	Yes _____	No _____
Fireplace?	Yes _____	No _____
Hardwood floors?	Yes _____	No _____
Air conditioning?	Yes _____	No _____
Good front yard?	Yes _____	No _____
Heavily traveled street?	Yes _____	No _____
General		
Same neighborhood?	Yes _____	No _____
Same style?	Yes _____	No _____
Same size?	Yes _____	No _____
Same amenities?	Yes _____	No _____

List Price $_____
Sales Price $_____

FIGURE 6.5
Master Comparable Evaluation Sheet

	SALES PRICE	ADD/ SUBTRACT	COMP PRICE
House #1	$_____	$_____	$_____
House #2	_____	_____	_____
House #3	_____	_____	_____
House #4	_____	_____	_____
House #5	_____	_____	_____
House #6	_____	_____	_____
House #7	_____	_____	_____

Average Sales Price $_____
Average Comp Price $_____

STEP ❹: DECIDE ON A FEW PRELIMINARY FINANCIAL ISSUES

A. How Much "Earnest Money" Deposit Are You To Accept?

There's no set figure on the amount of "earnest money" deposit (also called **"good faith" deposit**) a buyer may give, or a seller accept. It's all a matter of negotiations and agreement in each situation—what your prospect will let you get away with. But if you are a seller, you would want to get as much "earnest money" deposit from the prospective buyer as you can possibly get from him. [From the buyer's perspective, on the other hand, you would as a buyer, want to do exactly the opposite—to pay as little "earnest money" deposit as possible!] *As a seller, you want as high a deposit as possible for a rather obvious reason:* the higher the deposit left you by the buyer, the greater the loss he'd incur in forfeiting it, if he were to back out of the deal without a legitimate reason, and hence the greater the inducement the prospective buyer will have to take the binder agreement more seriously (more 'earnestly'). And a second reason, a *practical* one, why, as a seller, you would want to get as big a deposit as possible, is that in a typical sale, between the time of the signing of the contract and the final closing, you, the seller, will have to incur certain expenses along the way—e.g., title insurance or abstract fee, expenses for a survey or a termite extermination service, and the like. So, you want to make sure that if the buyer backs out without a just reason, you will at least have enough of his money to cover your out-of-pocket expenses.

[Earnest money and binder agreement principles, in general, are more elaborately treated in "Step 4" of Chapter 5 (pp. 29-30) and those sections are no less useful for a seller than for a buyer.]

Keep in mind, though, that what you're after is not the deposit. Your primary goal is not to get the deposit; rather, it is to sell your house. *Hence, in the final analysis, therefore, the reasonable measure for determination of the right deposit to accept, is that the amount should be large enough, relative to the price of the property, to convince the seller that the buyer is really serious.* Robert Irwin, an expert realtor, gives the following schedule of how big a deposit he usually asks for from a buyer: For a

Asking Price of House	Deposit Asked for
Up to $50,000	$1,000 minimum up to 5% (of asking price)
$50,000 to $100,000	$2,000 minimum up to 3%
$100,000 to $300,000	$3,000 minimum up to 3%
over $300,000	$5,000 minimum up to 3%

B. Will You Accept an F.H.A. or V.A.-Loan Buyer

The workings of, and the principles involved in government-sponsored Federal Housing Administration (F.H.A.) and the Veterans' Administration (V.A.) mortgage loans, have been fully elaborated in the preceding Chapter 5. And readers, buyers and sellers alike, should review the material contained therein for additional knowledge. [See "Step 8" of Chapter 5 especially pp. 52-4].

From your standpoint as a seller, the most relevant question in regard to the issue at hand is: will you consider selling your home to an F.H.A. or V.A.-sponsored buyer? If your answer to this question is 'yes," then consider the main 'disadvantages' and 'inconveniences' (from the seller's point of view) of selling to such a buyer, and consider whether you are prepared to "live with" them.

Consider the fact that it'll generally take much longer, in comparison to a regular or 'conventional' loan, for the government to o.k. your buyer's loan application. Consider the fact that frequently you may probably have to make extensive (and, oftentimes quite expensive) repairs in the house to upgrade its condition to the relatively higher standards required for getting the F.H.A.'s and V.A.'s mortgage approval. Also, the F.H.A. (the same for the V.A.) generally has restrictions against a seller accepting a second mortgage, or deferred payments, from the buyer. [In other words, if, for example, your house is selling for $100,000 and the buyer will be getting an F.H.A. mortgage of $99,000, then the buyer himself will still have to come up with the remaining balance of

$1,000 in cash—at once. You are not allowed to offer him a credit term to pay that $1,000 over a period of time by installment, and if you do, you'll be breaking the law.]

Another common 'problem' with which F.H.A. and V.A. mortgages are often associated, involves the tendency by the agencies' appraisers to appraise the house at values below, and often even dramatically below, the agreed selling price, thereby significantly lowering the actual loan amount the buyer would wind up getting from such a loan inasmuch as the loan value is necessarily based on the value assessed to the purchase house.

But, perhaps most significantly, consider the "extra" costs you will almost certainly have to bear, as a seller, when you sell to an F.H.A. or V.A. mortgage loan buyer —the several extra "points" in lender's charges the seller is obligated to pay on behalf of the borrower by mandate of a federal law. (See p. 52 for elaboration).

Finally, take note of the fact that the closing costs on an F.H.A. or V.A. loan can also be high.   At the very least, you should get an estimate from the lending institution in advance of your making a decision, of how much such costs will be, and determine how much of that you'll be required to pay.

C. What Share of the Selling/Buying Costs Are You to Pay

[See "Step 9" of the chapter on home buying (Chapter 5), especially Section B therein, at p. 59 (including the footnotes.)]

D. Would You Take a 'Second' Mortgage

A second mortgage can be a valuable tool in speeding up or making possible the sale of your property.   [See discussion on the buyer's use of this option to finance a purchase deal in "Step 8" of Chapter 5 at p. 50.] However, for a seller, there's still a need to determine in each instance whether the seller's own situation warrants it in a given case.

Here's how it works. Let's assume that your house is worth $100,000, and that your mortgage that's still outstanding on the house (i.e., the money you still owe on the house) now stands at only $20,000. This means, in other words, that your **"equity"** (that part of the worth of the house that is really yours) is $80,000—i.e., $100,000 minus the $20,000 you still owe on the house.

Naturally, you'll love to have a buyer come along and give you your $80,000 equity in the house, and have him "assume" (take over) the $20,000 mortgage balance.

But now, let's say you couldn't find anybody with that kind of cash ($80,000) and that the most that the only serious prospect you could find could come up with is $60,000 in cash. Now, you could have the prospect keep the existing old ("first") mortgage of $20,000 on the house and accept the $60,000 from this prospect as his down payment, and then allow him to pay you the remaining balance of $20,000 over a period of time in agreed upon monthly installments. As evidence of his debt to you and his promise to repay you, you'll have the buyer sign a "promissory note" for the $20,000, and as security in the event that he doesn't, you'll have him sign a mortgage on the house, which, because it is behind the original first mortgage, is called a "second" mortgage.

Pointers On What to Watch Out For Concerning a 2nd Mortgage

1. You must decide on how much the buyer should—and can—pay you each month (the amounts shouldn't be too little as to stretch out for more than a few months or years).

2. Interest, at the prevailing market rate, should be charged on the mortgage (ask your bank for the current rate).

3. Note that if the "first" mortgage loan on the house were to go into default, you yourself (the holder of the second mortgage) will either have to be able to catch up with the payments on that on your own, or pay off the entire remaining balance. Otherwise, the first mortgage can be foreclosed, and in such an event, your own second mortgage will be wiped out. *So, you had better be sure to keep an eye on the first mortgage and see that the payments are always current.*

4. Most second mortgage forms are standard printed forms, and contain provisions to protect the home seller against the common problems associated with giving second mortgages. Forms reproduced on pp. 74 & 76 fall under this category and may be adapted for use by readers.* Letter on p. 142 could also be necessary for your further protection. [Blank copies of the proper forms are obtainable from the Do-It-Yourself Legal Publishers. See the Order Form on p. 191]

E. Decide On Whether You May Give a 'First' Mortgage To Buyer

But, what if the mortgage on your house is already fully paid off, and you owe no money on the house? Then, in such a case, the kind of mortgage loan you can possibly extend to your buyer, if any (say, as a way of expediting or making a sale possible), will be called a "first" mortgage. Here's the way it'll work: Let's say your selling price for the house is $100,000, and that what the buyer could come up with in cash is $80,000, meaning that what he needs to borrow is $20,000. To avoid all the delays, uncertainties, and costs involved in the purchaser applying for a regular commercial loan, you may simply elect to finance the sale yourself; you'll carry the $20,000 mortgage yourself, made repayable to you over a period of time in monthly installments at the appropriate rate of interest.

POINTERS: Thoroughly check out the buyer and ensure that he's a good credit risk before undertaking this, exactly the same way as a regular financial institution would do. (See, "Rule-of-Thumb for Estimating the Likelihood of Your Getting The Loan," p. 57; and pp. 6-9). You may adapt the specimen forms of the note and mortgage on pp. 74 & 76, for use in extending a first mortgage, with the references to a second mortgage changed -accordingly.** [For a supply of blank forms, see Order Form on p. 191.]

STEP ❺: PICK AN APPROPRIATE MONTH IN WHICH TO SELL

According to real estate experts, the slowest selling period for houses all around the country, from sunny California to wintry Maine, is usually December thru February, and is said to be the vacation months for the real estate people. The biggest selling real estate season, on the other hand, is said to be the spring and the summer, with the month of July being the best month of all. A common explanation for this is that house-hunting parties with school age children often find it most convenient to make a purchase in July, giving them just enough time to make repairs and move in by August or September, before the school starts.

So, as a preparing home seller, a wise selling strategy on your part would be to schedule your sales advertising campaign for early or mid June, with the hope of being able to sell the property by July or thereabout.

STEP ❻: TO KICK OFF THE ACTUAL SELLING, GET THE WORD OUT: ADVERTISE THE HOUSE TO THE BUYING MARKET

Having fixed up your house and brought it up to the level where it's ready to show to prospective buyers, (STEP 2 above), and having had an idea of how much money you'll ask for the house (STEP 3 above) and decided on other essential preliminary matters (STEP 4 at pp. 98-100 above), your next order of business is rather crystal clear: PUT THE HOUSE UP FOR SALE AND FIND THE CUSTOMERS. How do you go about this? Where do you start?

---

*NOTE: The specimen form of a Note/Bond and Mortgage used for illustration in this manual (pp. 74 & 76, respectively), assumes that a <u>second</u> mortgage applies. When only a <u>first</u> mortgage applies, you may use the same forms, but carefully delete the references therein to a second mortgage; or, alternatively, you may use other forms altogether that are specific to First Mortgages. NOTE, ALSO, that, for the lender's protection, the note and the mortgage forms should be witnessed and notarized, and that the mortgage needs to be <u>promptly</u> filed with the local recording department.

**See, also, the above footnote.

A. Using a Real Estate Broker For It

One obvious avenue that immediately comes to most minds would be, of course, the use of a real estate broker for this purpose. The use of a broker (or a realtor) for this purpose will be alright (and perhaps, inevitable) if, for example, you decide you don't have—and can't possibly have—the time, energy, inclination, human temperament or know-how, to undertake the things needed to put a house up for sale. And, more importantly, if you decide you don't care much about passing up some 6 percent or 7 percent of the price of your house in brokers' commission! *If you happen to decide that this is the case with you and you must employ the services of a broker or realtor, then that's just fine. It's your decision. But, at least, understand how a real estate broker works, and at what costs to you.* The various uses and purposes served by a good, knowledgeable, and conscientious real estate broker in the buying or selling of real property, and the merits and demerits involved in employing the services of a broker, have been amply outlined in a previous section elsewhere in this manual. And readers, home buyers and sellers alike, should review and familiarize themselves with the facts and information outlined therein. [See Chapter 1, "Must You Necessarily Buy/Sell A House Through A Lawyer or a Broker," (pp. 1-5), and Section B of Chapter 3, captioned "Now Search For That Proper House To Buy," (pp. 13-20).]

In this instance, as far as you are concerned, from the standpoint of a home seller (as differentiated from a buyer), it should be noted that there are many advantages that working with a broker can bring you, even as you operate as an FSBO (for-sale-by-owner) seller. *A broker is obviously more knowledgable and experienced at the intricacies of home selling, and has certain resources that are not available to you as a for-sale-by-owner (FSBO) seller, including ways and means of finding potential buyers. Depending on the specific details of the arrangement you make with the broker, the broker can be particularly good at handling the advertising of the house, its showing to customers and prospective buyers, and, in many parts of the country, the preparation and drafting of the sales contract, and even the drawing up of the deed document transferring ownership. And, not the least of all, a broker can always be valuable in performing the most primary function for which he is often engaged by a seller—the use of the resources, knowledge and facilities possessed by him and his organization, to produce a buyer that is "ready, willing and able" to buy your property, in return for which you'll need to pay him a set fee or commission.*

So, the real question for you—as is usually the case for most sellers in your situation—should not really be whether you should use the services of a broker under any circumstances. But, under what financial terms you may do so. In brief, you can arrange to work with a broker for a flat-fee that is less than a full commission, on the understanding that you'll do some of the selling work while the broker does some.

In deed, in the last few years, a whole new group of brokers has developed who would readily share the sales tasks with you for lower commission. One such national franchise is **Help-U-Sell.** Others are springing up in many communities across the country. They would let you do some of the work, such as the fixing up of the property, and the showing of the property to prospects, while they do some, such as the advertising, promoting, negotiating and selling.

B. Pointers For Getting The Most Out Of The Broker's Services

1. In the first place, as a FSBO (for sale-by-owner) seller, the best approach for you to follow, is for you to set a time limit at the very beginning as to how long you will try to sell the house yourself. Keep that time limit confidential to yourself. It could be a month, three or six months, or one year. Or, whatever length of time you choose. But what is important is that you resolve in your own mind that if such a pre-determined time should elapse and you still haven't made a sale, you will then try a different method of making a sale—such as handing it to a local broker.

So, we shall assume here that that is the situation with you. And, assuming that that is the case, that you have first exhausted your best efforts and that for whatever the reasons (say, the house is not well fixed up, or is just poorly located or too highly priced, or the current market is terrible, or you're simply not the greatest salesman in the world, or whatever), you were not able to find a buyer and the deadline is up, this point in time may well be the right time for you to stop trying to sell the property entirely by yourself and seek the help, the expertise and collaboration of a professional—a broker. Your goal, after all, is to make a sale.

2. The important question, then, becomes: HOW DO YOU GET A BROKER THAT WILL DO A GOOD JOB OF GETTING YOU A SALE for your house, and yet give you the best possible commission that is lower than a full commission? So, what you are looking for is some sort of a "shared listing" arrangement with a broker—where you do some of the work and the broker does some. The breakdown of the duties between the homeowner/seller and the broker will vary with different agents (check around with various brokers) but a typical arrangement may look like the depiction in Figure 6.6 below.

FIGURE 6.6: SHARED LISTING RESPONSIBILITIES

> **Your duties and responsibilities:**
> •Fix up/clean up the property.
> •Pay for part of the advertising.
> •Show the property.
>
> **The Broker's duties and responsibilities:**
> •Put a sign on your property.
> •Pay for part of the advertising.
> •Design, create and run the advertising.
> •Find buyers.
> •Handle the major technical negotiations
>   with the buyers.
> •Handle the paperwork

3. Go over Chapter 3 (pp. 13-18) of the manual carefully; follow the same broker evaluation and broker-selection principles outlined therein to pick out the brokers to list your house with. Pick some two or three big, experienced and reputable firms in the area wherein the property is located (follow the same criteria and particulars as outlined on pp. 16-18).

4. In attempting to engage the broker to work for you, one thing you'll probably discover is that most (if not all) of them will quickly present you with a written **"listing" contract** which they'll want you to sign, officially "listing" the house (that is, putting it in their hands) for sale. Just remember that this document is a CONTRACT like any other; do not allow yourself to be rushed into signing it—until and unless you've studied it carefully and made the necessary changes, and until and unless you are ready and agree with the contents. [Follow the same contract-signing procedures outlined in "Step 6" of Chapter 5, especially at p. 42.]

5. You'll probably find that you'll be quoted an almost identical commission rate by most brokers you'll talk to—generally about 6 percent or 7 percent of the selling price of the house, especially when the deal is for **"multiple listing"** (meaning that the principal broker lists the house with several other 'cooperating' brokers who will then lend a hand in selling the property) . Don't be fooled into thinking, by this, that the commission rate is "fixed" or meant to be uniform with every broker.* The truth is that this is absolutely not so; no law says it should be so. Quite to the contrary, ***brokers' commissions are absolutely negotiable; you are totally at liberty to negotiate with the brokers the commission rate you'd rather pay,*** and if you both can't agree on a rate, you can look for another, and yet another and another broker, until you can finally find one with a rate structure acceptable to you.

---

*According to one expert, Peter G. Miller, a Washington, D.C. real estate broker and author of "How to Save Money When You Hire A Real Estate Broker," studies show that one-third of the people who hire brokers do not even know that brokers' commissions are negotiable! Miller's point was borne out by a later, staff study report released in May 1984 by the Federal Trade Commission (Los Angeles office), which found that not only are home sellers not aware that full-service brokers are frequently willing to negotiate and accept lower brokerage prices, but that they are also largely unaware that there are alternative or discount brokers who charge less than the standard industry commission of 6 or 7 percent.

6. But, even more importantly, you should remember, though, that what you actually want is not a **"full service"** broker; but, rather, a **"discount"** type or **"flat-fee"** type broker—(a "discounter") which performs only the basic service of selling the property and, in turn, charges a considerably lower rate of commission (about 3-4 percentage points lower. (A flat-fee broker charges a set amount which is not tied to the price the house is sold. For example, you pay a flat fee up front, say 1 percent of the asking price of the house, and then pay an additional amount, say, another 2 or 3 percent, later on if the broker produces a buyer. If no buyer is found, or if you eventually sell the property yourself, then your up-front fee is all you pay.) A discount or flat-fee type of broker is the same type of broker we have in mind in Item 2 above when we speak of a broker that engages in a "shared" listing arrangement as in Fig 6.6.

7. As elaborated in Chapter 3 at pp. 16-19 of the manual, all other things being equal, list your house with a broker or brokerage company connected to a national network, and one with a proven record of ready access to mortgage facilities and sources. Especially for a seller, you want to look for an agent whose office phone number has voice mail, a home phone, and a car phone or beeper. You need to work with someone who can be reached quickly once you can find a buyer who is interested.

8. How do you know that a real estate agent (or a couple of them you may have to use) is the "right" one to use? Much of that ground has been thoroughly gone over in Chapter 3. [Please refer to pp. 13-19]. But, just for a brief summation here, as a seller probably your best evidence are references by satisfied customers—neighbors and other homeowners who sold a house priced like yours. Call several and ask how well the agent they used kept in touch, how long their homes were on the market, what kind of listing arrangement and split in commission they had with their agent, whether the deals went smoothly, and, above all, whether they will engage the agent again, etc.?

You want someone with the professional credentials, proven home sales job knowledge and experience, and character and integrity. Off the bat, look, for example, for evidence that the agent knows what he's talking about, evidence that he has done his (her) homework. For example, has he looked up the price you paid for your property and what you now pay in property taxes and other housing expenses that you pay? Has he given you (or can he, in an instant, do so) a list of recent sales prices and of comparable or competing properties on the market, plus information about your comparables?

Does he seem knowledgeable about what's affecting values in your property's neighborhood—e.g., a new road or recent layoffs by a key employer, increased rates in property tax, location of prison or large facility like a stadium, etc.?

As one analyst puts it, summing it up, "If you know more about your neighborhood than the agent seems to, keep looking!"

9. Preferably, the "listing" contract with the broker should not run indefinitely, but should specify how long the arrangement is to remain in effect (say 90 days or 180 days), so that if the house hasn't been sold within the specified time you'll at least have the legal option to turn to another broker or to try another method of sale.

10. The discounted, shared listing type of arrangement that we have so far discussed above, could be one of three basic types. It could be either: **i)** an exclusive right-to-sell shared listing agreement, or **ii)** an exclusive agency shared listing agreement; or **iii)** an open agency shared listing agreement.

As a rule, most brokers will probably want you to sign with them an *"exclusive right to sell"* contract. Or, alternatively, they may want you to sign with them an *"exclusive listing"* contract . Before you enter into such a contract—if at all you are to do so—make sure you understand its full implication and meaning.* The *"exclusive right to sell"* contract requires, in effect, that you pay a commission to the listing broker even if another broker, or even the home owner himself, sells the property. And in the *"exclusive listing"* contract situation, on the other hand, the listing broker is entitled to collect the commission even if sold by another broker, but no commission is collectable by him if the home owner sells the property himself.

The third type of shared listing arrangement, the **"open"** *listing,* gives a homeowner a <u>non-exclusive</u> listing to any broker who wants it. Basically, this arrangement says that the commission payable is open to whoever finds a buyer for you; that if the buyer you sell the house to is one that is brought in by a particular broker with whom you had

---

*One related situation to watch out for in this connection, is what is known as "oral" listing. In many states, even without a written listing contract, the courts may find that you have an "implied contract," if the real estate salesman or broker acts with your consent in getting a buyer; or if he introduces you to somebody and you eventually sell to that person, the court may decide he is the "procuring cause," and that he is entitled to collect a broker's commission.

T 486—Real Estate Listing Agreement: Non-exclusive. 11-78

JULIUS BLUMBERG, INC.
PUBLISHER, NYC 101?

-FORM-

REAL ESTATE LISTING AGREEMENT

BROKER:	OWNER:	PREMISES:
Address	Address	
Telephone No.		
Broker is Licensed in the State of	Telephone No.	Date:
Commission:		

NOTE: To complete this form, simply enter the details above, then clearly strike out the clauses below to conform to the wishes and agreement of the both sides.

Owner hereby lists the above Premises with Broker for sale in accordance with the information, terms and conditions set forth above and following:

Licensed broker 1. Broker is a licensed real estate broker under the laws of the state set forth above.

When Commissions earned 2. Broker shall not earn the Commission unless:

  a) a contract of sale has been signed by the Owner and a purchaser upon terms acceptable to the Owner in the Owner's sole judgment

  b) the contract was brought about through the Broker's efforts

  c) the deed conveying title is delivered in accordance with the contract and the full purchase price is paid.

Failure to close title 3. If a contract of sale has been signed by Owner and a purchaser and title does not close,

  a) because owner does not have good title conveyable in accordance with the contract, broker is not entitled to the Commission.

  b) Broker is not entitled to the Commission unless Owner intentionally defaulted.

  c) because purchaser defaults, Owner is not required to enforce purchaser's obligations and Broker is not entitled to the Commission.

Price change 4. The purchase price at which the Premises are listed with Broker may be changed by Owner without liability to Broker. Owner is not liable to Broker for any expenses, fees or disbursements paid or incurred by Broker in connection with Broker's efforts to sell the Premises.

Commission Payable 5. If earned, the Commission payable to Broker, shall be paid upon the delivery of the deed.

Termination, withdrawal 6. Owner may terminate this agreement or withdraw the Premises from sale at any time by either oral or written notice to Broker without liability.

Non-exclusive 7. Owner may list Premises with other Brokers

Margin headings 8. The margin headings are for convenience only.

This agreement contains all the terms and conditions of the listing and shall not be changed except by a written agreement signed by both Owner and Broker.

This agreement has been signed by Broker and Owner on the date set forth above.

Broker: (the business name) .... Owner: ....

By X (name of its personal representative) X ....

.... X ....

signed an open listing agreement (let's call him Broker A), you will pay that broker a commission, but that if you sell to someone you find or to someone brought in by another broker, you don't have to pay Broker A a commission.

(NOTE: To avoid potential problem with determination of who brought whom to see the property, it is advisable that you keep a complete list of the prospective buyers and by what method they are attracted to the house).

The reason you gain in this kind of arrangement, though, is because in this kind of situation the commission is split between the FSBO seller and the broker. A common split in open listing arrangements is 50/50 between the selling party (you) and the listing party (the broker).

True, often you may not be able to get an agreement to an open listing arrangement with most brokers. But you should always try for one. And, *in any case, in any kind of deal with a broker, always ask (and be sure it's entered in the written listing agreement) that you retain the right to independently find a buyer and sell your house yourself without having to pay commission to anyone.* To accomplish this, seek to have a *"private sale"* clause in your listing contract with the chosen broker, something like this: "In the event that the owner sells the house privately to someone not specifically introduced by the broker, then no commission shall be paid the broker."

11. Finally, regarding getting the most out of the broker's services whenever you enlist the broker's expertise in your sales efforts, here's one more tactic for you. Find out how the brokers' commissions are split among brokers in your area, and always use that knowledge to negotiate with your broker to your advantage. Here's how it works. Suppose, for example, you list your house with a broker with an agreement to pay him a commission of 6 percent of the selling price. If another broker (a co-broker) were to be the one that finds the buyer, the broker you hired will split the commission—usually on a 50-50 basis—with the broker who provided the buyer. That is, each broker will end up getting 3 percent. Now, you could use this knowledge of the brokers' fee-splitting system to negotiate with your broker in a number of ways. You might, for example, contract with your listing broker (the one you hired) to the effect that if the house is sold on a 'cooperative' basis with another broker, you will pay a 6 percent commission, but that if, however, the listing broker finds the buyer and makes a "direct" sale himself, you will pay a commission of 4 percent.

You save money with a "direct" sale and your listing broker has a financial incentive to strive to make such a sale. Why? Because he gets a full 4 percent by making a direct sale himself instead of the 3 percent he would get if he has to split the commission with another broker.

> **NOTE:** It ís an open secret that real estate brokers and agents generally view every
> FSBO seller as a potential source of listing. And it is not uncommon for some
> agents (the unethical ones among them) to call pretending they have a buyer when
> they don't, primarily as a ruse to solicit a listing of any kind, open or otherwise,
> from you. The idea is to first impress you into giving them an open listing, at least.
> They may then trot anyone, even their relatives or office colleagues, through the
> property in order to impress you further and come closer to you to the point of
> winning your confidence into giving them a more traditional and lucrative listing,
> such as an exclusive deal.
>
> Consequently, partly because of this, and because many FSBO sellers are
> frequently so pestered by real estate agents, unfortunately many FSBO sellers
> would not even talk to agents, let alone agree to give them an open listing. In
> deed, some will even add a line on their for-sale signs expressing that sentiment,
> such as "Principals Only" or "No Agents."
>
> Experts suggest, however, that *a better approach would be to welcome the
> broker's cooperation in the sales endeavor in that the more people one has
> working on the sales effort the better the chances of making a sale.* The better
> policy, it is said, is to have a smaller sign on the property welcoming broker
> assistance, such as a sign that reads "will cooperate with serious brokers", but to
> put any brokers you deal with on notice that while you are willing to "co-broke"
> (cooperate with brokers) on selling your property, and will split the sales efforts
> as well as the commission with them, that does not mean you are willing to give
> the brokers a traditional listing or traditional listing's full commission.

C. Use Of Other Methods By Which To Reach Prospective Buyers Directly

There are three basic and more inexpensive ways open to you as a seller by which you could advertise your property most effectively and reach your customers directly, without going through a broker:

1. Using Newspaper classified ads
2. Using For Sale By Owner Signs
3. Miscellaneous methods—e.g., word of mouth, bulletin board notices or company newspaper ads, and the like.

USE OF FOR-SALE-BY-OWNER SIGNS

Of the above three designated basic methods of getting the word out and advertising a for-sale property, the most powerful and dominant one is the use of newspaper classified ads. We shall soon address that method. But here, we shall first examine the use of the FOR-SALE-BY-OWNER SIGN METHOD.

Judged in terms of the dollar-for-dollar returns relative to the expenditure involved, the use of signs placed *on (or near) the property, is probably the cheapest, single most effective advertising tool at a home seller's command.* In deed, some home sale experts see the for-sale-by-owner sign as the most cost-effective and powerful advertising tool available to the house seller. Harley Bjelland, the real estate sales specialist and author who has made a career out of selling his houses himself, calls that medium the "inexpensive and highly effective method," and adds that "about 30 to 40 percent of the people we showed through our house did so as a result of the *For Sale By Owner* sign I'd planted on our front lawn. Many people looking for houses to buy first decide on the location they want to live in, then they drive around the neighborhood looking for just such a sign or an *Open House* sign."

Its obvious but often very effective function, is that it lets everyone in the area, and those who drive or pass by the property, know that a property is for sale. And even for prospects who seek to get to the property, the for-sale sign could be an excellent source of direction that brings them directly to the home.

Space for your message (make it short)

The important element for you to know concerning the use of signs, is that *for the method to be effective, though, there are definite dos and don'ts you must follow.* According to skilled real estate professionals and expert salespersons, you should not just simply buy a cheap, ready-made sign that reads "For Sale By Owner" and has a phone number, and place it anywhere or anyhow on the property. *Rather, both the quality of the sign, and where and how you place it on the property, are all very important factors in determining the effectiveness of this as an advertising tool.*

First, you should spend more money to secure a more decent, professionally made sign that stands out—such a sign conveys a certain image and message to prospective buyers, it immediately tells them that you're a serious seller who is committed to actually selling the property and knows what you're doing. What type of sign? In a word, bypass completely the cheap, ordinary looking hardware store's offerings, and go for the more expensive but superior custom sign shop—a difference in price of, say, paying $60 as against $24! The sign should, in short, be one that looks professional, one that looks just like a sales agent's or broker's sign—one that is attractive and immediately catches attention. It should be large (should measure roughly 2 feet by 3 feet) and the contents bold and readable, with the lettering clear and in color; it should be a color that is readily seen, such as red, on a black background. The sign should be well designed and not look amateurish. And, very importantly, the sign should contain certain key information written in short, large, legible letters, such as the following:

- FOR SALE BY OWNER. Design and contents of the sign must be so well done that they will be prominently distinguished from other signs that are frequently placed in yards—signs by builders, landscapers, political campaigners, etc—and show passers-by that, in this case, it's the house that is on sale. And it must clearly indicate that this sale is being made by the owner. [Clue: The words 'For Sale By Owner' should be printed in giant letters]. The letters should be large and easily read from the street.

- BEDROOMS/BATHROOMS. Give an idea of the size and usable housing space, such as how many bedrooms and bathrooms the house has.

- ONE SPECIAL FEATURE. Include either on the main sign or attach a smaller separate part thereof, one special feature possessed by the property. For example: a "pool," or "two-car garage" or "Large Yard."

- SHOWN BY APPOINTMENT. To minimize having to be constantly pestered by prospects and to also give you a chance to pre-screen prospects before they show up at your door, it's important that you include a "by appointment only" notation in the sign.

- PHONE NUMBER. Include in the sign a phone number by which you can be reached at all times, day and night.

Where and how do you place the sign? In general, the sign should be placed at a conspicuous place atop or near the house, and/or nearby. It should be placed in such a way that it is clearly visible—and easily readable— from cars and by persons going in both directions on the street. [To make sure, walk and/or drive out to the opposite side of the street and see if you can readily read the message as well as write the phone number down without getting out of your car]. Preferably, particularly for corner lots, you should post separate signs, one at each end of the property, and, often, it may also be advisable to post two signs back-to-back, placed perpendicular to the house in front of the house and each facing the direction of oncoming traffic. This way, the signs can be read easily by people in the car going in each direction as they drive by. (Check with the local zoning department of your city to see if there are any restrictions on the size or kind of sign you may put on a property). Furthermore, seriously consider buying *more than one* sign—signs with different messages. One set of signs with one message should be placed at and near the property; another set of signs should have an identical message, but include a direction to the house. For example: *3 bedrooms—view, 2929 Ben Drive, Right → 3 blocks*

Include An Information Box & Leaflet

The whole idea behind your putting up the for-sale sign is, of course, hopefully to attract potential buyers. And the greater hope is to make any such potential buyers who may become attracted to the property look harder at the home, and to jot down the phone number and call you later. But, what if a potential buyer who comes by your for-sale sign has no pen or piece of paper with him to write with? Or doesn't feel like doing any writing at the time?

To make it as easy as possible for the potential buyer who comes by the sign to contact you, as well as to get more information to such persons, one more related measure has been found to be helpful by modern real estate agents: namely, providing an information box (a small wood or metal box) just below the "For Sale" sign wherein you'll leave additional follow-up information for the potential buyer. In the box, you will leave more detailed information about the property. Potential buyers who stop by, may simply get out of their cars (or walk to the box) and pick up a leaflet containing more detailed information about the house. Such information, which should simply be put in a concise, typed one-page "Information Leaflet", or "Fact Sheet," such as Figures 6.8 & 6.9 below, must be painstakingly drafted with two vital objectives in mind. Firstly, to answer the potential buyers' more immediate questions and provide them much of the information they may need to decide that your

FIGURE 6.7
FACT SHEET/LEAFLET INFORMATION BOX

home may be worth taking a look at; and secondly, to whet their appetites well enough for them to want to actually see the house. Consequently, such a leaflet, if done properly and competently, could be a great marketing tool in selling your property. The Information Leaflet (see Figures 6.8 and 6.9 for a sample form of that) could also contain a photo of the house.

In deed, the more clever of the real estate sales agents, have in recent times taken the use of this information package still one step farther. They have, in addition, taken to providing a photo of the house as an integral part of the information leaflet. Agents fervently contend that the old adage that "a picture is worth a thousand words" fully applies in their trade. (For an excellent photo, be sure to take the picture on a day that is overcast, and not in bright sunlight, so as to avoid ending up with too many shadows (4 x 5 is the ideal size). You can either make up these flyers and leaflets yourself if you can do a decent job of it, or pay a desktop publishing outfit some reasonable fee to produce a professional-looking material for you!

Finally, you should recognize that once you've taken the trouble to draft and produce the Information Leaflet, there should be nothing stopping you from reproducing it in large quantities and then going ahead, also, to distribute the leaflets far and wide in a variety of other places having potential buyers—schools, offices, bulletin boards, supermarket stores, libraries, your church, shopping centers, civic centers, etc. And in those places where you hang copies of the leaflet up, just keep in mind to go back every few days or so to make sure they are still hanging there. When a broker holds an open house near your house, nothing should stop you from placing one of your 'For Sale By Owner' signs (with you address included) a discreet distance near the broker's open house sign! Be sure, however, to obtain a property owner's permission before you may place your sign on his property.

FIGURE 6.8
INFORMATION LEAFLET

Buyer's guide to (address goes here) _____
Price _____
Seller's name _____
Grammar school _____
Intermediate school _____
High school _____
# of Bedrooms _____
# of Baths _____
Size of garage (1, 2 or 3 car) _____
Air conditioned? _____
Pool or spa? _____
Lot size _____ × _____
Age _____
Special features: _____

Photo (in color, if possible) of your house

Seller's phone number (large) goes here _____

FIGURE 6.9
FACT SHEET

FACT SHEET

Sample

Address: _____ County: _____

City: _____ State: _____ Zip: _____

Square Footage: _____ Lot Size: _____

No. Bedrooms: _____ No. Baths: _____ Age of House: _____

_____ Car Garage: _____ Basement: _____

Total Rooms: _____

Room Dimensions:

    Kitchen: _____ Bedroom: _____

    Dining Room: _____ Bedroom: _____

    Living Room: _____ Bedroom: _____

    Family Room: _____ Bedroom: _____

Financial Information:

Current Mortgage(s): _____

_____

Monthly Mortgage Payments: _____

_____

Taxes Per Year: _____ Insurance Per Year: _____

Major Improvements Added: _____

_____

_____

Special Features: _____

_____

_____

Items Included in Purchase Price: _____

_____

_____

Legal Description: _____

_____

_____

Zoning/Building Restrictions: _____

_____

Selling Price: _____

Terms: _____

_____

Owners: _____ Tel.: Home: _____

    Bus.: _____

Utilities—Average Per Month:

Electricity: _____ Fuel: _____ Gas: _____

Trash: _____ Water: _____ Other: _____

General Data:

Air Conditioning: _____ Heating: _____

Antenna: _____ Hot Water Tank: _____

Appliances: _____ Insulation: _____

    Elec.: _____ Landscaping: _____

    Gas: _____ Lawn Sprinklers: _____

Built-ins: _____ Patio: _____

    Plumbing: _____

Carpeting: _____ Roofing: _____

Drapes: _____ Sewer: _____

Elec. System (Cap.): _____ Walls: _____

    220 V Avail.: _____ Water: _____

Exterior Const.: _____

Fencing: _____

Fireplace: _____

Schools:

Elementary—Name: _____ Location: _____ Grades: __

Secondary—Name: _____ Location: _____ Grades: __

High School—Name: _____ Location: _____ Grades: __

Jr. College—Name: _____ Location: _____

4-Yr. College—Name: _____ Location: _____

_____

_____

Shopping Centers: _____

_____

Public Transportation: _____

Facilities:

Churches: _____

Hospital(s): _____

Fire Station: _____ Police Station: _____

Post Office: _____

Distances to Important Points: _____

_____

_____

_____

Deliveries:

Bottled Water: _____ Milk: _____

Newspapers: _____

Trash Pickup: _____ times per week.

D. Using Newspaper Classified Advertising To Find Prospective Buyers

As stated above, of the THREE basic methods of advertising the house for sale and reaching customers mentioned herein, the use of newspaper classified ads is clearly the most powerful and dominant method used. *And, most experts consider it the most cost-effective method. By one informed estimate, about one-third of all home sales in the United States are initiated through such newspaper ads, and, what is even more relevant and gratifying—for you, as a do-it-yourself home seller—is that it is estimated that private ads placed by non-professional home sellers get 4 times more customer response than similar-sized ads placed by brokers and other professionals, according to a New York Times survey!*

In any event, suffice it simply to say that so important is newspaper advertising viewed in the eyes of real estate sales professionals, that they generally consider it indispensable as an advertising and sales tool. As one such expert real estate sales agent put it, "[though] the trouble with newspaper ads is that they are so expensive... Nevertheless, to get the word out, you can't afford to miss this important medium."*

Where, How Much, And When To Advertise

Among the initial, major, relevant questions are the following: what newspapers should you advertise in? What days of the week are you to advertise, and how do you write your ad? The answers to these questions are actually simple: Do what experienced marketing experts and advertisers have always done and recommended—namely, make a personal survey and inspection of the area's newspapers,** and look to see in which papers your main competition, the major real estate brokers and big professional home sellers, advertise their for-sale homes on a regular basis for your location; see what they say and use in their ads (the popular code words and phrases they use, the graphics and the artworks or pictures); see what days of the week they advertise most heavily in. THEN, SIMPLY IMITATE THEM: *do the same things they do!*

Firstly, as a general rule, when looking for the right newspaper to advertise in, generally look for the "big dailies," the large metropolitan newspapers with large readerships, which have special real estate sections (e.g., the NY Times, LA Times, Washington Post, Chicago Sun Times, Wall Street Journal, and the like). Such newspapers are popular with real estate professionals. So, you too, can't go wrong advertising in them. Secondly, consider placing the bulk of your ads in the weekends (Fridays, Saturdays and Sundays) and weekend editions of the papers—it's on weekends that most people look at or for homes. Thirdly, consider supplementing your advertising with a separate set of ads placed in a local type of newspaper which covers mainly the property's locality. In other words, try two kinds of newspaper ads, one ad, a smaller and inexpensive one, and another, the bigger and more descriptive ads in which you elaborate on the home . You should alternate the bigger and smaller ads on different weeks. But, remember this: NEVER RUN THE SAME AD FOR MORE THAN ONE OR TWO WEEKS. Certainly, don't run the same one all the time. Rather, be sure to change your ads periodically. Why? Because when potential buyers keep seeing the same ad over and over again, they begin to recognize it and tend to get weary and wary; they may conclude that no one else seems to want the house, and so why should they want it? The point is that you want your potential buyers to think of your house as fresh on the market! Furthermore, with different ads, you will be able to focus on different selling points and emphasize different things. One ad might say how numerous or spacious the rooms are or how suitable the area is for raising a family, or for a single parent; another might emphasize the "creative financing" aspects and that you'll help with a mortgage; and a third might dwell on how close the house is to public transportation or a major metropolitan area. Hence, the better approach is that you come up with many different ads, about two to four good ones, and rotate them from time to time.

What The Ad Should Say

How do you "write" your ad? Again, study the real estate ads in your metropolitan and local newspapers. Note which ads caught or held your attention. Did any one ad assault your eyes and mind, and enticed you to read on? The ads will probably use lively, colorful, language that are "grabby"—terms like "elegant," "executive," "roomy," "immaculate," "sparkling." They'll have pleasant information about the location and amenities—"3-car garage,"

---

*Irwin, The For Sale By Owner Kit, p. 79.

**Simply go to any major local newsstand, or go to a local library having a periodical section, and browse through the local and regional newspapers, to see which ones carry big or sizable real estate sales advertising. Or, call up a local library and ask the readers' guide librarian for suggestions and recommendations.

"2 fireplaces," "lighted tennis court," "pool with spa," "oak floors," "secluded," "full acre." Make a note. Jot down the key words and phrases in the ads that grab you the most, and the key features they emphasize. Then write your own ad (write and re-write it over and over again until you finally have a finished product), patterned after the most impressionable key words, phrases and art work and graphics gathered from those of your competition. In deed, this is one important reason, among others, why it's advised that you first check other ads from your local newspapers and take a clue from them: buyers in different areas of the country are interested in different things, and words used in ads may have different meanings in different parts of the country, and by studying the real estate ads in local newspapers you will be able to spot the things that are applicable, important, and acceptable in your particular locality.

Figure 6.10, which is some three to five lines, is a typical example of a short, yet effective classified ad. Yet, even with an average larger (and therefore more expensive) ad where you can presumably expand on the features and benefits of the house, you're simply not going to be able to get a whole lot into it—something like 8 or 9 lines [see Figure 6.11 below]. Hence, in the average ad, if you can include the basics but effectively phrase your message, you've done all that can be done.

At a base minimum, your ad should include information on the basic facts concerning the house: for sale-by-owner, the location, the type of house (ranch-style, colonial, town house, brownstone, 1-family or multi-family, condominium, co-op, etc.), number of bedrooms, square footage of the house, selling price, and your phone number. But, ideally, the ad should contain more than the base minimum. The ad should further be "jazzed up," highlighted with some prominent and attention getting "selling points" possessed by your property: phrases like —"BY OWNER—SPLIT BROKER'S COMMISSION $$$," or "SAVE $$$ ON NO BROKER'S FEES AND NO REDTAPE;" "QUIET, TREE-LINED NEIGHBORHOOD," "5 LARGE BEDROOMS, LARGE KITCHEN," "MINUTES TO SCHOOLS, WALK TO BEACH," "ULTRA MODERN," "8 PERCENT LOAN, OWNER WILLING TO GIVE MORTGAGE."

The final part of the ad should give the square footage of the house and the selling price (make it exact), and conclude with the "call to action" phrase, such as: PROMPT SHOWING, BY APPOINTMENT ONLY, PHONE...

FIGURE 6.10
Sample Short, Yet Effective Ad

BY OWNER
$250,000 on 1 acre, Middletown,
12 large rooms, greenhouse,
anxious, make offer (201) 555-1234

FIGURE 6.11
Sample Larger Feature Ad

Elegant Mansion
Huge 5 + 4 with 2-storey view of Mt.
Milgo, 2 marble fireplaces, terrazzo flooring.
Secluded, one-of-a-kind.
Desirable Westtake area. $300k
BY OWNER —(201) 555-5656

Martin Shenkman and Warren Boroson, long time New York area attorney and reporter, respectively, and specialists in real estate sales, aptly summed up the proper ad-writing process and what should go into a good newspaper ad, this way:*

> "Be specific, not vague. Instead of "large yard." say "full acre"; instead of "bright," mention "skylights" or "floor/ceiling windows"; instead of "your dream house becomes reality," use "garage, Elk, frplc, 4 bdrms."... When you write an ad, have your Fact Sheet in front of you, to help you recall all of your house's key selling points. If yours is a small, inexpensive house, you can play up whatever apartment dwellers would love— even an attached garage, or a family room. Higher-priced houses should mention important extras—like a sauna, exercise room, greenhouse, three-car garage.
>
> The headline should, ideally, be arresting "JUST LISTED" is powerful. So is "PRICE REDUCED." "FOR SALE BY OWNER" will attract bargain-hunters along with buyers who don't like dealing with agents. Don't be timid about swiping someone else's clever headline. But don't be timid about creating your own, such as, "WE HAVE TO LEAVE THIS CREAMPUFF," or "$100,000—AND WORTH MUCH MORE."
>
> Keep in mind that you want your ad not only to attract the largest number of buyers but also to ward off buyers who wouldn't be interested. If your house has only two bedrooms, say so. Otherwise, you may get a host of callers who want three or more bedrooms. On the other hand, don't write "Needs work" or "Handyman's special" or "Needs TLC," unless the place is on the verge of being condemned. The low price will indicate that the house needs work.
>
> Don't try to tell everything about a house in an ad—that could be expensive. State the most important features, and for the rest, "Many extras" should do.
>
> The conventional wisdom is that you shouldn't say "Asking $100,000," which indicates that you'll lower the price drastically. Or even "$100,000 firm," because some buyers might believe it—even if you'll gladly accept $98,000.
>
> Don't use the word "desperate" unless you're looking for bargain hunters. Buying a house should be a happy occasion, and buyers may be turned off by a sad situation."

How do you actually place the ad? Assuming you've selected the newspapers in which to advertise, and have made up your ads, call up the "classified ad section" of the selected newspapers and get their rates for various sizes of ads to know what your budget can withstand. Do not go wild. The best way to do it is to set a total budget— something like 0.25 percent of the asking price of the house ($250 for a $100,000 home)—and go by that.

How do you know when an ad is doing well, and which one(s) may not be doing so well and may need to be discontinued? One suburban Chicago woman who in 1994 sold her home FSBO, Ms. Sandra Bauman, used this excellent method. To promote her first open house, she had spent $200 on four days ad in the Chicago Tribune and suburban weeklies covering eight nearby towns. But then, something clicked: 90 people came to the first open house. When the prospective buyers came in, she routinely asked them to write down their names, addresses, and phone numbers, and to enter how they learned about the house. Her examination of the responses immediately told her that the suburban weeklies weren't working. So the next week she advertised only in the Tribune!

STEP ⑦: WHAT TO DO WITH PROSPECTS WHEN THEY FIRST CONTACT YOU

Now, let's say you've fully fixed up your property and fixed the right selling price for it, as described in Steps 2 and 3 above, and have put out the word on the selling of your property (Step 6 above). And your advertisements are now beginning to have an effect. And that, assuming you are not using a broker in the sales effort, you are beginning to get some calls from prospects. (If you are using a broker, presumably in some kind of commission splitting discount arrangement, your broker will usually be the one doing the talking, since brokers fear that home owners having unsupervised contacts with prospective buyers are prone to unthinkingly saying the wrong things to them). The next important step, then, is: WHAT DO YOU DO WITH AND ABOUT THESE INITIAL CALLS AND CONTACTS WITH PROSPECTIVE BUYERS? Just how do you properly deal with prospective buyers at first contact, which usually means the initial phone call?

---

*Shenkman & Boroson, *How To Sell Your House In A Buyer's Market*, pp. 109-110.

Install an Answering Machine

First of all, unless you did run the ads with a broker's number, in which case then the phone calls should be coming in on the broker's line, you should immediately make sure you have an answering machine installed in your home. This way, you won't miss calls when you are out of the house. For, *if you are to play well the part of a good salesperson in your role as an FSBO seller,* **it is critically essential that you get one fundamental principle unmistakably straight: the customer is NUMBER ONE, not you; your selling of the home is at your customer's convenience, not yours!** Consequently, as a good salesperson, you must recognize, at the very onset, that it should not be the buyer's responsibility to keep calling you repeatedly until he or she finally finds you at home, but rather, that it is YOUR responsibility to facilitate every customer's efforts in reaching you, and that you must promptly respond to the customer or answer his/her call.

What this means, is that promptly after you put your house up for sale and have taken out the ads and other measures to publicize that move, your phone should never be left unattended thereafter and should always be answered. The ideal thing, of course, would be for you to be home 24 hours a day starting from the day your ads hit the papers and the streets. But that, obviously, is unlikely to happen. Hence, you should have an answering machine as the second best alternative. In fact, even still better from the standpoint of greater effectiveness with prospective buyers, would be for you to put in a separate phone line in your home just for that duration when your home is on sale, set apart solely for the business of the house sale. This way, when that phone line rings, you know right away that it has to do with the business of the house on sale, and accordingly, you (or anybody answering the phone) will respond professionally.

Figure 6.12

A Sample Answering Machine Message

"You've reached the Jackson home. Yes, it's for sale, and yes, we'll be happy to show it to you. The price is $196,000. Great Westchester location overlooking the hill. We'll offer excellent financing for the right buyer. Please leave your name and phone number, and we'll call you back as soon as possible to make an appointment to show it."

How To Properly Answer Prospects' Phone Calls

OF FAR GREATER IMPORTANCE, THOUGH, IS HOW TO ANSWER THE PHONE CALLS, what you are to say and how you are to compose yourself with the prospects upon their initial contacts with you?

In regard to this, you should know that what you really want to be able to do, in the end, is primarily this: *to determine what the buyers' real NEEDS and REASONS are in wanting to buy a home, their real motivations.* This is of importance because, ultimately, it is on such motives, both emotional and rational, that buyers would base their buying decisions. And, ideally, the more and earlier you can uncover this, the better for you in being able to close a sale. However, here's the critical trick: *when a potential buyer makes his initial calls to inquire about the house, you absolutely don't begin the conversation by asking any questions that would immediately suggest what you are after. Rather, your primary attitude at this stage should be purely informational; you want to give him or her information, and to answer any questions about the house — description of the house, how it looks, how big it is, how good the location is, it's special features, and the like.*

BUT BE VERY CAREFULLY! This does not mean that you jabber on and on, or pepper the caller with one question after another. Listen. Listen carefully. Not only are you simply to give the "right" answers, or even to ask the right questions, but *you should also be careful to stop long enough to really listen to what the caller says, and to get his/her true response and interest. And then you can try to answer the questions — honestly and completely.* As a rule, for the buyer, typically the very preliminary conversation is always a matter of attempting to get a rough idea as to whether the house in question is even remotely close to what they are looking for and can afford. Hence, typically, a first time caller will ask about matters having to do with the price, size, special terms, and, most important, location.

But here's the critical stage. Keep your fingers crossed! If the conversation goes on for a while and the caller seems interested, only then should you ask him whether he would like to be shown the house. And then, if he or she agrees to that, then that's when you may rightly ask for personal information about him, initially starting with the more routine matters —his(her) name, phone number, home address, etc. [See Figure 6.13 for the kinds of questions you may ask, progressing from the more routine and straightforward, to the trickier.] Then, depending on the degree of cooperation and interest exhibited by the caller, you can advance to the more sensitive questions down the line.

The questions should be asked informally in the course of a conversation, as if you're just curious (which you are), and not as if you are an interrogator. The later set of questions in Figure 6.13 involve more probing questions that will help you determine if this is a potentially real buyer whom you give a lot of time, or just a curiosity seeker or a dreamer. For example, if the caller already owns and lives in a home and hasn't sold or even put it up for sale, that should indicate to you that this person is probably not ready or able to buy as of today. The questions about income and down payment funds, will give you a clue as to whether or not the person can qualify for a mortgage loan.

FIGURE 6.13
SAMPLE INFORMATION-GATHERING QUESTIONS

1. Who referred you to me?
2. What is your name?
3. What is your phone number?
4. What is your work phone number in case I can't catch you at home?
5. Do you and your wife both work?
6. Are you a local resident?
7. Where do you live? (What part of town?)
8. Are you an out-of-towner?
9. Where are you staying locally?
10. What is the main reason you are moving?
11. What is the one requirement you must have in your new home?
12. Do you currently own your own home, or do you rent?
13. Is your current house sold? Recent changes in your life?
14. Is it listed or being sold by FSBO?
15. When do you plan to sell and move?
16. How many are there in your family?
17. Ages of your children?
18. What is your monthly or annual income?
19. How important is it for you to have a pool? View?
20. What is the price range of the kind of house you are looking for?
21. What kind of down payment are you looking to put down?
22. And do you have this money at hand right now?

However, as you get to the more sensitive questions, you must thread the ground very skillfully. Most people, for example, will be a bit wary to disclose information about their finances on the initial call, particularly to a stranger, and particularly to the FSBO seller, the very one they are going to negotiate with if they wish to go for the house. For this reason, experts say, the best approach is to withhold entirely asking questions concerning finances at this stage, unless you've by now established a good rapport with the caller. And, even then, you should ask it only if a financial subject and being able to qualify to purchase the house comes up in the normal course of conversation.

Robert Irwin, an experienced house sales instructor and expert, explains: "For example, the caller might say something such as 'Your price seems rather high. I don't know if we can afford that much.' To which you might reply, 'Well, how much do you make? I can quickly tell you if it's enough for a loan.' "

The point is that at this stage in your dealings with a caller, in his first contacts with you, you can probe and push a little bit, with skill and sensibility. But not too hard. If the caller should hesitate and doesn't want to give such information, let it go. Let it go for now — until you get to the appointments and actual negotiations stage. Just make sure, for now, that you get the essential information you absolutely must have for security reasons and to be able to call back and confirm an appointment before allowing a stranger into your home — the caller's name, address, phone number and dates of availability.

NOTE: The next important order of business you'll get into after this, is the showing of the property to prospective buyers [STEP 8 below]. You should note, in this connection, that the "showing" of your house should even start *before* the buyers arrive. For example, when the potential buyers call for an appointment or ask for directions, give them the scenic route that leads through a path that will give them a good impression of the kind of rich neighborhood you live in — not simply a major highway. Have them drive pass the best houses in the area, on their way to your house, the most impressive playgrounds, public buildings, stores, etc.

STEP ⑧: SHOW THE HOUSE TO INQUIRERS

The next order of business, after you shall have gotten your calls from prospects and made up appointments with them, is to begin to show the house to prospects. But, it's not nearly as simple as that. To be fruitful and productive, *the house showing has to be done in a PROPER and PARTICULAR way.*

HOW TO SHOW THE HOUSE TO INQUIRERS: POINTERS FOR EFFECTIVE HOUSE SHOWING

1. Before you even start taking calls from prospects (not to speak of having the first prospect into your house for a showing!), *there's one important thing you must first make sure of: know your house very well, and know the main selling points and features it possesses.* One way of doing this is to work up a **"Data Sheet" of facts** about your house. [See a sample Data (Fact) Sheet, Fig. 6.9, on p. 110]. Review and master the facts in your data sheet by heart, and keep a copy handy by the telephone. This way, you'll be prepared to talk knowledgeably about your house with prospects and be able to answer their questions and, on occasion, even "dazzle" and charm them with facts on certain impressive features possessed by your house.

2. According to one survey cited by a real estate sales expert,* here are some relevant facts that relate to the issue at hand:

> i) *95 percent of those who go so far as to take the trouble to come to see your house won't like it* (meaning that 19 out of 20 people who go through your house are outrightly not likely to have a favorable impression of it, anyway); ii) people do not visit a house once, but many, many times before they actually make up their minds to buy (the range was from 40% of the people who made 5 or more trips for a new house, to 50% of the people who made 2 trips for a used house); and iii) prospects look at many, many houses before they decide on a particular house (for new houses, it was an average of 10 or more different houses per buyer, looked at over a period of 3 months; and for old houses, it was an average of 5 houses per buyer, looked at over a period of 2 months).

Therefore, you had better conditioned yourself before hand to the basic realities of home selling and home showing, and be prepared not to take offense at any criticism or fault-finding from your prospects, and prepare yourself to be patient and to wait for as long as may be necessary to make a sale—at a good price.

3. You should try (through stipulating 'By Principals Only' and 'By Appointment Only' in your ads, and through your initial phone conversations) to *weed out the non-genuine callers beforehand.* Nevertheless, bear in mind that no matter how hard you might try, you'll in all likelihood still have plenty of so-called **"lookers"** rather than **"prospects"**—i.e., people who make a habit of perpetually going from house to house to look, and are either

---

*Harley Bjelland in *"How To Sell Your House Without A Broker,"* p. 71.

merely "dreamers" who lack the financial resources to buy, or sightseers who enjoy looking at houses as a kind of recreation or hobby. This is so because, as a rule, lookers are much more numerous than prospects, and are virtually impossible to separate from the serious prospects. Furthermore, serious prospects cruise neighborhoods in which they are interested in search of a house, and may not have time to come again to view your home if you were to schedule an appointment at a later date.

So, ONE OF THE SIGNIFICANT GENERAL RULES OF SHOWING YOUR HOUSE IS THIS: be nice to everyone; be polite, courteous and patient with everyone who comes. You never know when the guy at the door might be the guy who eventually turns out to be the true buyer!

So, if someone calls and wants to see the house right away or shows up at the door, and you are not quite sure whether he or she is a serious buyer, show the house to him or her anyway, providing the house is in a presentable showing condition at the time, and it is physically safe for you to do so. The customer is always the boss, remember? The point is that you must bend over backwards to accomodate prospective buyers and make time for them to see the house.

But, on the other hand, be forewarned, though: a few of your prospects will be rude, inconsiderate, intrusive, demanding, and downright insulting and disrespectful, either on the phone or when they are being shown the house. So, again, be prepared not to be unnecessarily offended or discouraged.

4. Before letting people in on a house showing, especially when such persons are drop-ins who show up without prior appointments, but preferably in all cases, get them to write down their names, addresses and phone number, the source of their information about the house, and the date of their visit. This serves as a good security purpose. Furthermore, for your further protection, never let any drop-in into your home after dark, and never show the property when you are alone. Simply explain that the time is inconvenient for you and your family and offer to set up an appointment during the daytime. Furthermore, by tabulating and analyzing the responses of the visitors as to how they came to know about the house for sale, you will be able to quickly determine which ones of your advertising media are effective and which ones may need to be continued or discontinued to save on your advertising expenses.

5. One thing you should consider is to hold an *OPEN HOUSE* one weekend, preferably the second or third one after the house has been on sale. This way, you can get most of the "lookers" out of the way.

6. Consider showing your house *on 'by appointment only' basis.* Not only is this a way of weeding out many of the lookers, it's also a way of letting you and your family live a halfway normal life in your home while you're trying to sell it. As explained elsewhere in this manual (see pp. 87-8), a most important point in selling a prospective buyer on a house, are the FIRST impressions the prospect gets of the house. Hence, by showing your house on an 'by appointment only' arrangement, you are better able to remain in control of things than you would otherwise on a shorter notice, and be better able to keep the premises in a clean and 'showing' condition for the benefit of customers.

7. Schedule the *showing appointments one at a time* for each customer, and make the time specific, always remembering to allow sufficiently for the 30 minutes or so the home showing will take you as well as some reasonable extra time thereafter before another appointment could be entertained. Respect each customer's appointment, do not let one person's appointment overlap into somebody else's as this could be a source of annoyance to prospects.

8. *Keep your house, both the inside and the surroundings, sparklingly clean,* tidy, odor-free, and organized when showing. [See pp. 87-90]. Send your kids, if applicable, over to the neighbors, or to a movie, or what have you, and keep them out of the way. Keep your pets out of sight and out of the way. Put some quiet background music on your radio or stereo. Turn off all appliances, and shut off the TV set. In short, remove from the way, anything that might detract from the house and divert the prospects from concentrating one hundred percent of their attention to the business of viewing the house!

---

*Danielle Kennedy, *Double Your Income In Real Estate Sales*, pp. 219 & 223.

9. Just like the house you are selling, **you too** *should also be prepared to make yourself neat,* well dressed (preferably in tie or dress), and presentable when you're getting ready to escort customers through the house. Introduce yourself and get the customers' names.

10. Your first step, upon meeting the prospects, is to get acquainted with them. You greet the prospective buyers (each one of them) warmly and ask friendly questions. "Did you have trouble finding this place?" (Or, if they never called before showing up, how did they hear about the house?) "Are you familiar with the area?" "Do you have a house now?" "Have you ever purchased a home from a self-seller?" "Do you have any children?" "Do you both work?" "Where?" "What are your hobbies?" "Are you handy with tools?" "Do you like football or soccer (or whatever other sports?)"

By knowing something about the buyers, you'll know what will appeal to them, and hence, how to start up a conversation and what to emphasize as you escort them through the premises. For example, if they have young children, you would play up the quality and reputation of the local school systems, or how close the house is to the school or public transportation. One particularly good starting theme, according to home sales experts, is the question relating to whether the potential buyer has ever purchased a home from a self-seller. Why? Chances are, said one expert, that the buyer never did, and so that will give you an "entry point" to start up a conversation that immediately puts you in a favorable light while not making your "sales pitch" appear so obvious or contrived. You can say something like: "Well, I'm selling my house myself to get a sale. And, for you, one of the big benefits you'd get from my not having to pay a full commission to some broker, is a lower sales price. You get to pay far less buying direct from me." *[But be sure that that's going to be actually the case, though!]*

11. Once the buyers get into the house and you've established preliminary rapport with them and put them at ease, what you want to do is to win the buyer's trust and confidence so he can "open up" to you. The aim—and hope— is that the buyer will get to the point where he trusts you enough that he can feel free to voice his true feelings to you about the house, without worrying about not hurting your feelings. The benefit of such a feedback for you is tremendous. If a prospect can honestly bring up objections and reservations, that's a very valuable feedback showing you his *"areas of resistance,"* and this is another opportunity to get to know the prospect better, to get to find out what is going on inside the prospect's head.

So, you start by telling the buyers right up front how you like to work with prospects, and that their own interest (and not yours) is paramount with you, and that they should feel free to speak up to you. Something like: "Before we begin our tour of the premises, I have an urgent request: GIVE ME A FEEDBACK. If you like the house, or there are some features or elements about the house or the neighborhood that you don't like, tell me. If you don't like or approve of the house, or the way I'm conducting the tour, or whatever, tell me as soon as you get the first indication this is not what you have in mind. I assure you, whatever your opinion, favorable or unfavorable, my feelings will not be hurt. I'd request it as a favor."

Add this to your communication with prospective buyers:

"You, of course, do not know me, and I know that it is only natural that you probably have some preconceived notion being that I'm trying to sell you something that the only thing on my mind is selling you a house and getting the money. Don't get me wrong. I am looking to make a sale because I know I have an excellent piece of property for any family to enjoy. But the last thing I want to do is to sell this house to anybody at all costs. What I want the most with you is to know your situation so that I can do the assessment. So, please tell me the precise facts. First of all, I need to know this—do you know what price range you are in, or do you feel you need financial counseling or a lending consultant?"

12. Once the home showing starts, on your own part as a seller and home showing guide, stop the talking completely or at least drastically. Curtail it. Escort the customers. Don't let them go through the home unescorted; they can only recognize and appreciate the features that each room or part of the house has if you are with them to point them out. Escort the parties, but be very careful: GET OUT OF THEIR WAY. And, as stated above, don't talk too much; that often gives the impression of "pushy" salesmanship to the buyer and most buyers just despise that passionately. What you don't do is to be pointing out every darling little nook and cranny, every precious little thing that is in your house. You can, though, point out things appealing that you feel the buyers might miss. In other words, avoid pointing out or dwelling on the obvious.

For example, you don't have to say, "This is the living room." (That should be obvious to anybody!) But you can say such things as: "You can see the lake, over there on the far left."

"This is a double-insulated glass-window—we don't need storm windows."

"It's somewhat hidden but notice that we have all hardwood oak floors under the carpet." "There's one other fireplace like this in the other bedroom."

"The fireplace works perfectly—here's the damper. And there's a cleanout pit in the room."

"The pipe opening in the basement floor is in case there's a flood from the washing machine—you can get rid of the water easily."

"That's an electrostatic precipitator, to help keep the air clean."

"The attic is cold because we keep the bent open—to get rid of moisture from the rest of the house."

13. *In a word, your whole objective here is to get the buyers to feel at ease, relaxed and comfortable. They need to begin feeling that <u>THEY</u> (as differentiated from you) could live in the house that had been yours for so long and make it <u>THEIR</u> own. To put it another way, you need to take any pressures off the buyers, and have them feeling in control and in the driver's seat in viewing and deciding on the property.* So, your main task is simply to give the information on items about the house you feel the buyer may have missed, or that may not be readily apparent. In this regard, you may say something like this to your prospects: "You and I are partners in the sale. Please, I want you to do most of the talking. I urge you, frankly and freely voice your opinion so that I can understand your point of view and your real needs, and help determine whether this place is at all suitable for you or if there's any way I can be of help."

14. In what order do you show the property? Sales experts recommend that, given the power of first impressions, *the tour guide should always start the tour in whatever is the "best part" of the premises*—whether it be a room in the house, the modernized kitchen, the recreation room in the basement, the beautiful landscaping in the backyard, or what have you. Better still, select for showing especially those rooms you know you'll have something special to say about them, or something to demonstrate. And as for the other rooms that are not so impressive, you may simply stand in the doorway and just let the prospects peer in. Do not rush it. Show your premises at a leisurely pace. Let the customers open the closets and ask questions. If the grounds are impressive— let's say it has a few car garages or a lot of trees and gardens , or an animal farm—you may take the buyers outside for a stroll, but if it's not all that impressive, give them just a brief look.

15. *Be active,* though. There are many ways you can do this. Point out one (or two) interesting highlights of every room you enter, even if it's "There are extra outlets built into the room because of all the electronic equipment in it." Open the closet and say something like: "This closet is especially large, the largest in this house." Show how large a room is: "We've had a party for sixty people in this room." Turn on and off the lights, run water, press buttons, open and close the doors or the windows, the refrigerator doors and so forth. Why do this? You're trying to show that everything is in good working order; but also trying to attract and keep the buyers' attention—to keep them awake and alert.

16. *Find out the prospect's motivations and "point of contact"—his or her main concerns, needs, interests, and desires*—and tailor your presentation to appeal to such needs. More preferably, if you can subtly put some "showmanship" into your presentation—a demonstration that will make the home showing more graphic and vivid and to "come alive" to the prospect. For example, in this age of amateur video photography, you can make a short-subject videotape about life in the community, summarizing all the features and benefits offered in the community, and either have the serious prospects take it home to review, or review it at the time of the showing of the property.

Another kind of subtle shomanship suggested by the noted realtor and author, Danielle Kennedy,* is the written presentation worksheet format, and will be just as effective, and probably simpler. It is one that can be more fittingly used with a prospect who is returning to the property for yet another or closer look. Essentially, what you do is to make out a written worksheet in which you match out each major desired feature specified by the prospect against the benefits, and give what type of "action" activity the home seller should demonstrate with each set of features and benefits. Here are some examples of this below.

---

*Kennedy, ibid pp. 223-4.

PRESENTATION WORKSHEET

Desired Feature	_Benefit Statement_	_Action_
Neighborhood with children	"On his block alone, there are six families with children under the age of 10. Here comes Mrs. Pearcy now. Let me introduce you…Lynn, this is Betty and Jack Peters. They are looking at homes in the area, and I promised them this one was full of children."	Slow down the car (as you drive the prospect through the area).
Large, fully equipped modern kitchen	"Four gourmet cooks like yourselves who both work, but want first class meals in the privacy of your home every night, look what this kitchen offers."	Pull out warming drawer. Serve hot snacks prepared by seller. Demonstrate gas range. Convection cooking oven.

"Realtors need more action and less talk," says Kennedy. "Go over your client file, and then rehearse your demonstration in your head and on paper, using the presentation worksheet format. Once you get the hang of it, you will find yourself naming corresponding benefits with every feature you point out."

17. *"Show," Not Talk The Features; Alas, Be A Good Listener.*

Whether in your showing of the property, or your subsequent discussions and negotiations with the prospect, always "show" the <u>features</u> possessed by the property, but "sell" the <u>benefits</u>; that is, tie in the special benefits to the buyers as they apply to each buyer, as in the demonstration in the *Presentation Worksheet* in Item 16 above. To put it another way, you do not only have to inform the prospects, but you have to keep a balance between "showing" and "telling"; you have to pace each demonstration as well as clarify the issues. This way, you do not confuse the prospect. Cover just ONE idea at a time and be very careful in your observations, making sure that the prospect understands each point you cover. Do not continually press on in your presentation. Rather, you must slow down and get a confirmation of understanding from the prospect each time a new issue or point is introduced, an agreement from the prospect that what you just explained is completely understood. Ask questions like, "Am I losing you?" "Does it make sense to you?" "Do you agree?" "Do you see the point?"

Then, *having asked the questions, you also have to do something else: you have to LISTEN, you have to stop long enough to really listen and get a true response, a feedback. **In other words, YOU HAVE TO BE A GOOD LISTENER.***

Real estate sales expert, Danielle Kennedy, reports that when she surveyed managers across the United States and asked them what all their top sellers did differently than the rest of their team, the majority of them responded with "They just listen more." Kennedy notes that her own observation of her own "brightest and best" sales agents in action during interviews, strongly confirm this. "As I walk by their desks, the prospects are very animated and are doing most of the talking. The pro has blocked out the rest of the world and seems completely enthralled with every word that comes out of the prospect's mouth."*

Why is being a good listener so critically essential? Because, to be an effective seller, you primarily need to be able to find out what the buyer's buying motives and needs are. And what better way to do so than, first, to listen and be able to grasp what the buyer really <u>means</u>!

And how, exactly, does one "listen" well? It's simple. According to sales experts, the best way to listen is to find out what the other person, the speaker, <u>means</u>, to take interest in the other party's expressed needs and problems. Then send back to the speaker an acknowledgment to let him (or her) know that you completely

---
*Kennedy, p. 220.

understand what he means. The approach is to repeat in your own words what you understand the speaker to have said, what you undertand him to <u>mean</u>; to verbalize the speaker's viewpoints and acknowledge his concerns. This way, you ensure that there was understanding during all parts of the communication process. In other words, you don't simply have to "hear" the speaker. Listening is different from, and far more than, hearing. You have to <u>understand</u> the other person. [When you argue with someone, for example, words are flying through the air alright, but the only thing in the non-speaking party's mind is getting things off his or her own chest by interrupting the other person, so you can hear each other out but neither party really listens to each other.]

18. In general, in a house showing just observe the buyers themselves and take the clues from them. Does your pace seem too slow, or too fast, for them? Do they seem to want a lot of comments or explantations, or less? Do they just glance, or do they spend time and study? And from that, you'll know what you should do more of, or less. You not only should not talk too much, but you also must <u>listen</u> to them and get what they really mean and feel. Listen carefully to their questions and comments; you could often get a lot of clues from them. One very important clue you could get from them, is whether they have an interest, or none at all. As one expert put it, *"If they start asking detailed questions like the size of the hot-water tank, room sizes, etc, they 're probably more than just lookers."*

19. One important point. Bear in mind that time is your friend here. The longer the buyers hang around viewing the premises, talking to you and wanting to see more, the more they have invested in the house, in terms of their own time, emotions, interest. And that would be a very good sign for you as a seller. One expert salesman boasted: "If you can get potential buyers to stick around for an hour, you may get yourself a sale."*

Another major source of important clues, the experts say, is the faces of the customers. Watch their faces as they go from room to room, as expressions written on their faces will often give you a truer picture than words concerning what they really think about the house.

20. *But in all of these, the one fundamental constant should be YOU: whatever the goings on, you must keep your spirits and enthusiasm high, and your excitement for the house undiminished and unambiguous.* As the tour goes on, don't just keep chattering to keep a converstation going. Give your prospects time to look and think and, as stated before, in the meantime make mention of details which are not readily obvious to the prospect as you show them around—the new dishwasher or new tile in the bathroom that was only recently installed, the schools or the parks or public libraries in the neighorhhood and how far they are; the churches, the shopping centers, the transportation systems, etc., in the neighborhood, etc.

21. Avoid ever conveying an air of desperation, even if the house has been on the market for too long. Buyers can easily pick up on this and tend to be scared away by that. Rather, try to be relaxed and confident, always displaying an attitude that suggests the house has just gone on the market and that the buyers at the moment are the first viewing visitor. Such an attitude boosts not only you, but even the buyer's confidence as well.

22. In your dealings with buyers, don't lie. Be honest, absolutely level with them. But don't necessarily tell the entire truth. What is meant by this? Well, let's say a buyer asks, why you are selling your house or moving. You don't have to reply, "The house is too cold in the winter and too hot in the summer." A more appropriate response would be something like: "We want to move to a warmer climate." Or, "The house has gotten too small (or too big) for our family now." Or a more innocuous answer like that.

Don't actively hide or disguise any defects the house has—a leaky roof, an environmental hazard, high taxes, swampy grounds, or whatever—especially defects that prospective buyers can't readily notice, such as radon contamination. That's the easiest way to guarantee losing a sale if a customer should stumble into the defects on his or her own.

23. Be alert and watchful. Watch your guests closely; after they shall have spent a reasonable amount of time walking through the premises, looking around and asking questions, you'll sense when they're about to conclude their inspection—you can tell when they begin to look at their watches or begin to stand around or to come out. At this point, that's when to jump in with a move to try to sound out the buyers for an idea about what they feel so

---

*Irwin, p. 113.

far about their inspection. One effective way to do this, is to hand them at the point the FACT SHEET* on the house (which you shall have prepared beforehand), and say something like, "By the way, taking a look at this Fact Sheet we've prepared for you, there are still a few great features you've got to see before you go. Please, if you don't mind?" Then you can briefly describe the features or areas of the house you have in mind, lead the buyers to them (or simply read from the sheet along the way as you quickly lead the buyers to the areas.)

Or, you can simply hand the buyers the Fact Sheet and say something like, "As you take a look at this Fact Sheet we have prepared for you to get a more complete picture of all the great features we have to offer in this house, would you like to see the attic now?" [Or, the basement, the grounds, the pools, the garage, or whatever, as the case for you may be.]

NOW, HERE'S THE IMPORTANT POINT: As you ask these questions or raise these issues, you must be sure to do so with a pleasant smile and attitude—be sure not to give the impression that you're either pressuring them, or that you're really saying that you are tired already and they should leave! Furthermore, be vigilant. If they should give the slightest indication that they would rather end the tour and go home, let them. Let them—with a smile and a cheerful attitude. In such a case, you could just add something like, "Thank you for coming. If you have any questions on anything about the house or from this Fact Sheet, whatever, I'll be glad to answer them for you."

> **NOTE:** Whatever you do, don't ever try to close (to finalize) a sale on the first showing. It will be totally naive and unrealistic on your part to try to do that; buyers feel unduly pressured in such a tactic, and that frequently backfires with loss of the sale. In any event, the overwhelming evidence is that buyers hardly ever make an offer, let alone a purchase, on the first viewing, and that a more general scenario is for a serious buyer to see the house many more times before actually deciding on a particular house.

24. In any event, whichever way the tour of the premises is concluded, whether it is concluded with the buyers cheerfully agreeing to a second round of inspection or otherwise, when it finally comes time to end the tour, end it on a positive note, leaving your prospect with a "last" impression that should be just as pleasant as the "first" impression. End it in your second "best" room, with your second best feature. Leave the parties with a copy of your Data or Fact Sheet (if you haven''t already done so), and make sure you get their names and telephone number.

Don't worry, if they're really interested, they'll probably call a number of times before long with some questions (or an offer), or ask to come back pretty soon for another look at the house, maybe twice or more times.

Summary

By way of summary, this analysis by the team of real estate experts, Martin U. Shenkman and Warren Boroson, offers an excellent description of the ideal manner for conducting a home showing by a FSBO home seller:

> "In dealing with buyers, in fact, the seller should behave like the ideal salesperson. When you show your house, you're a salesperson. Think of the ideal salesperson: someone pleasant and helpful. Not someone nervous, who hovers over you, who yaps away like a lunatic, who eyes you as if you're a notorious shoplifter just itching to sneak something into your pocket when nobody's watching.
>
> Here's what you want for service when you go into a store: you browse around by yourself for a while, and then, just when you start feeling the need for help, a smiling salesperson comes up and says, 'May I help you?' The salesperson gives you a clear and concise answer to your questions. He or she volunteers important information—the suit you want doesn't come in navy blue, or you can get a discount by buying a particular brand of VCR.
>
> If you mention that the VCR you're looking at is flawed because it doesn't automatically record 30 different programs, the salesperson may say, 'You pay $2,000 extra for such a VCR. Would you want to spring for that much?' Or: 'That's a limitation of this model, but it's very inexpensive, and it has a one-year warranty.' Not: 'What kind of nut would want to record 30 different programs?'"

---

*Experts are divided on this point. Some contend that the Fact Sheet should be handed out to the viewing buyers at the earliest opportunity—as soon as they walk into the house, contending that it would help them as a guide in viewing the house. Others, however, including the present writer, are of the opinion that as a sales tool the Fact Sheet serves a better purpose if given to the potential buyer <u>after</u> (not before) they've pretty much completed the house tour. In this writer's studied assessment, seeing and reading are two different things altogether. True, one reinforces the other. But, by handing the sheet to the buyer after he shall have essentially seen the house, you avoid having a divided attention, you ensure total concentration on the house during the inspection tour. The buyer can then use the sheet at that stage to determine if there are elements of the home he shall have missed or overlooked, or for a follow up or greater study later.

STEP ❾: HOW TO HANDLE PROSPECTIVE BUYERS' PRELIMINARY OBJECTIONS AND RESISTANCE

A. Make call-back to buyers

We are, of course, assuming here that this is a situation involving the use of no broker, for if actually you are using a broker, it would, by and large, be far more advisable and advantageous in such a case, that you let the realtor do all the talking and most of the negotiations. For one thing, they are professionals and obviously better trained, more skilled and smarter at this, plus the well known reality that many buyers are plainly uncomfortable dealing directly with FSBO (for-sale-by-owner) sellers, and if given the choice would rather negotiate or delve into their more personal, sensitive, or confidential matters with the sales agent.

As has been previously exphazised several times above, it's extremely unlikely that a buyer will walk into your house, take a look and a walk through it , and immediately make you an offer to purchase it. Rarely does that ever happen! House buyers, as a group, tend to be nervous. And, for obvious reason, too: they're making probably the biggest financial decision and investment of their lives, and they're rightly careful not to make the wrong decision. Consequently, what usually happens—and what is more likely to happen in your case — is that, far from making an offer to purchase on the first showing of the house, the interested buyer or buyers will probably call back (or you yourself will call them) a number of times, and probably want to see the house again and again before they finally settle on your house.

The most important thing, therefore, is that you fully educate and prepare yourself for the all-important "CALLBACK" from, or to, prospects following the initial showing of the house. *The callback has been called* ***"the most important call one will make [or receive] with regard to selling a property,"****** in that, unless a call is forthcoming following an initial showing of a house, the sale would never materialize, even if a deal could very well have been made. In fact, say some experts with vast practical experience in home sales, *so critical is the callback move, that you, the seller, should always make it a duty to pick up the phone yourself and make the callback — and not wait for the prospective buyers to call you.* "The point is," says Robert Irwin, a 30-year veteran of real estate sales and author echoing a widely shared view among professionals, "don't wait around for potential buyers to call you. After one day or two [of the house showing], call back. It could make you a deal."**

You shouldn't wait around for the buyers to call you, analysts explain, because by and large many buyers, even those who like the house and would actually like to make an offer on it, would frequently not summon the nerve to make the callback, and would often thank you for helping them avert losing out on the purchase when you do call them. Why? "That comes about," says Irwin, the real estate sales expert, "because they feel [that] if they call you back, you'll think that they surely want it, will pay full price, will give you cash …They may simply be afraid to call you for fear of giving you the wrong impression [that they are desperate to buy]."

In this author's assessment, one slight modification, though, is called for to this rule. It has to do with the proper timing of the follow-up call. The point of departure is that you should not just call back, automatically, every prospect after one or two days of the home visit; a premature call, or any seeming application of sales pressure, could destroy the chances of making a sale. Rather, a better approach would be to treat your prospects on a case-by-case basis. Study your prospects, their moods and level of enthusiasm, know each prospect well enough that you can instinctively slip into his or her shoes and imagine whether he or she will be pleased or displeased to receive a follow-up call so soon, or somewhat later. For those prospects about which your "sixth sense" tells you they will not be displeased, you may make the follow-up call shortly after the previewing. But for those about whom you're not quite sure, you may consider dropping them a quick postcard, first. The card may say something like this: "I am curious. What did you and your wife think of the home I showed you on ___? Your feedback, favorable or not, is important to me. If I don't hear from you in a few days, I will give you a call. I really enjoy working with you."

---

*Irwin, op. cit. p. 116.

**Irwin, p. 116.

B. How To Talk to the buyers upon the callback

O.K., so you (the seller), and not the prospective buyer, are the one who should take the initiative and make the follow-up callback following the prospective buyer's viewing (unless, of course, the buyer is so taken by the property that he or she beats you to it and calls you back first, which would be a more pleasant scenario). Now, what happens when you make this callback, how do you deal with the buyer?

A good starting point in a callback situation , would be for you to say something like this (after you shall have of course adequately indentified your house and who you are and introduced yourself): "I figure you've had ample time to reflect on the house. Your feedback, favorable or unfavorable, is important to me. I am curious, do you and your wife have any further thoughts on the house?" Or, "...I am curious, are there anything more about the house you'll like to see or know?"

Thereafter, the direction the conversation takes will largely depend on the reaction you get from the prospective buyer. If the prospect reacts favorably, you are on the proper path to a potential eventual sale. Better still, if the reaction is enthusiastic. More likely than not, however, the reaction will be something less than enthusiastic; the prospect will likely be restrained, noncommittal, and not particularly encouraging. *Nevertheless, even if the prospect you get does not quite give an unqualified "yes" right off the bat and immediately make an offer, that does not mean that you're getting a "no," either. It simply means, rather, that you have slightly more work to do regarding that particular prospect.*

C. Pointers for dealing with a potential buyer in follow-up contacts

1. At the preliminary stages, as soon as necessary in the follow-up call or contact, focus on attaining two basic elements: i) uncovering the true buying needs and motives of the prospect in wanting to buy; and ii) determining the buyer's main objections, reservations, and points of resistance to the property, if any.

Don't forget this: that you are being led by the buyers. The home you are seeking to sell them should be (or appear to them to be) the one most appropriate to their needs, otherwise they'll go elsewhere.

2. You can only determine what would be appropriate to the prospect's needs basically by asking the right questions of the prospect about his or her wishes, desires and requirements, and listening carefully to the prospect. In deed, realtors and analysts who have themselves been largely successful at real estate sales, have determined that *"the majority of lost sales result from the agent not discovering the buyer's point of contact,"* adding that *"This is the most important step in the sales process — gathering information and determining the truth about your prospect."**

3. The issue of being able to uncover and determine a prospective buyer's main objections and points of resistance to your property, will immediately begin to be particularly important right from the follow-up calls or other contacts following the previewing of the property. For, assuming that, as suggested earlier above, the response to your follow-up calls or other contacts with prospects would probably be unenthusiastic and not particularly encouraging, it then becomes necessary that you be able to counter that. (Even beyond that, even in a situation where you have prompt, positive reaction from a prospect, there still will remain a lot of negotiations to be done with the prospect regarding particular problems that may be causing him to resist your call for action — issues of price, terms of payments, terms of purchase, etc. etc.)

How do you uncover the prospect's objections and areas of resistance? As stated earlier, mainly by asking the right questions — and listening carefully. The underlying objective is to try to determine what the buyer sees as a problem, to get a feedback as to what is going on inside his or her head. In other words, you want to find out what the buyer's main "objections" to your property are, if any, what problems he (or she) has with it, why he's reluctant to buy it? Then, once you find out these points of objection, you can suggest plans by which to resolve the problems for the prospect. And if they are acceptable to the prospect, at that point you're well on your way to closing the sale!

---

*Danielle Kennedy, *Double Your Income in Real Estate Sales*, pp. 219 & 223.

You might ask a question such as:

"Do you like the house?," or "Do you think the property will suit your needs?," or "What about the property does not appeal to you?," or "Is there something about the property that you don't like?"

Or, you can start off with this question: "Do me this favor. On a scale of 1 through 10, how do you rate the house? Be absolutely honest with me!" [By the way, according to one hugely successful realtor who uses this same question in his own work, if a customer's rating on a property is 7 or above, you can estimate that the property has a very good chance of being among the final choices made by the customer].

4. In any relationship with the prospects, if you can do a good job of getting them to pour out their hearts to you and give you their true feelings, especially concerning their objections about the house, you are way ahead of the game. That's because, say sales professionals, once you are armed with that kind of information, unless it's something that is humanly impossible or totally unreasonable to do anything about (such as the location of the house), all you have to do is turn that "negative" (the feedback on the buyer's objections) into a "positive" and you've got a sale — that is, all that's left for you to do is use that information to know exactly what problems you have to focus on with the buyer, and the problems which, if remedied, you would likely win the sale with the buyer. For example, if it becomes clear to you that the buyer's main problem is really price or terms, then you can ask for negotiations and try to see how you can arrange financing and to structure the payment terms to fit the buyer's pockets. If the buyer's main problem or his complaint is something to the effect that the taxes are too high, you can counter that by pointing out other advantages and payback a homeowner in your locality gets in return, such as a good school system, or reasons why that negative point, though a negative, can be seen in a different, positive light. If the buyer points out actual flaws in the house (e.g., that the bathrooms are few or closet is small), you can offer some practical remedies or suggestions to remedy them. And so forth.

The following are the common objections raised by buyers in a home buying situation:
  • Not the right location
  • Bedrooms and/or bathrooms are either not enough in number or are too many
  • Bedrooms and/or bathrooms are too big/small
  • House is too expensive to buy or to live in (e.g., because of high taxes)
  • Poor financial terms and other terms of purchase
  • Property lacks features and amenities (garage, air conditioning, good heating system, big yard, etc.)
  • House is in poor condition

D. Preliminary negotiation methods in meeting buyers' objections and resistance

Somewhere along the line, pretty soon, if at all a potential buyer is interested in the property, preliminary negotiations would start back and forth with the prospect, going down the road from the raising of objections. HERE IS A FUNDAMENTAL REQUIREMENT: In this phase of the sales effort (as in all phases involving any negotiation of terms) the more you shall have known already about your prospect — his desired features, wishes, motive, needs, etc. — the more you will be in the position to "customize" your negotiation presentations to win over a prospect and convert him to a buyer. Most ideally, therefore, *you shall have, by now, gathered sufficient information (before and after the first meeting with the prospect, during the viewing of the house and after) about your prospect. You shall have, by now, uncovered much about the prospects' opinions, perceptions, viewpoint, needs, and motives, that you may now use to delve deeper into their minds and hearts and find out what really is bothering them or holding them back, what is motivating them to make a decision. You shall have had a pretty good idea of the answers to questions such as these: What is the main reason the prospect is moving? What are the main requirements and features he (she) must have in his ideal house? Will he need some creative financing arrangement? How much money does he want to spend? Where is the money coming from for the down payment? If married, do both the husband and wife work, what are their jobs, and how much do they make? How many are there in their family? Ages of the children? And so forth.*

In deed, experienced realtors strongly advise that sellers shall have formally drawn up a set of preplanned questions that are carefully designed to elicit the required information, and which they shall have posed to the prospects and gotten the answers to in ascertaining the truth about the needs of the prospects. [See Figure 6.12 for a fuller sample of such questions].

126

But, quite importantly, these questions would have to have been asked, and the answers to them acquired, with one major distinction: not through some sort of formal questions-and-answers scheme, not through a kind of interrogation. But, rather, in the normal course of ordinary, two-way communication and routine interviews and conversations between you and the prospects. As Danielle Kennedy, a skilled realtor with a vast experience in such practices, properly summed it up, "I do not sit down [with the prospective buyers] and ask them ten questions in a row. These answers [to the needed information about the buyers] come up during a conversation over a cup of coffee."*

The following presentation by a team of real estate sales experts, fairly well describes a typical conduct of the parties and the typical exchanges between a seller and prospective buyer and the of handling of the initial buyer's objections:**

"Keep in mind the example of the ideal salesperson when you talk to buyers. If the buyers aren't right for your house, you'll want to spare them as well as yourself wasted time. If they have objections, courteously counter them by mentioning advantages. Do they complain that there are no walk-in closets, or that there are too few bathrooms? Do they say the third bedroom is tiny? Do they point out that the plaster on the living room ceiling is cracked?

You can say, 'That's true. We wish we had bigger closets, and that's one of the reasons we've priced the house so reasonably. Especially considering how large the master bedroom is.' Or: 'It's true the third bedroom is small, but it's for a baby.' Or: 'Plaster always gets small cracks.'

If they say,'The taxes are too high,' you can say, 'That's why we have such a fine school system—our teachers are well paid,' (Just don't be clever, the way some sellers try to be: The buyers say, 'There's no living room.' The seller says,'One less room for you to clean.')

Gently remind buyers not only about the house's good points, but also the community's: 'The supermarket's only two blocks away and the elementary school's also within walking distance. There's a bus to downtown on the corner. This is a very convenient location.' "

The experts continue:

"If they point out true flaws or limitations of the house, say [to them] you can remedy them — if you get an offer. Here are a few possible exchanges:

Buyer: 'The kitchen could use more cabinets.'
You: 'Another cabinet could be installed right over here, and if I had a good offer, I'd have the cabinet installed myself.'
Buyer: 'The wallpaper in the living room doesn't go with my rugs.'
You: 'For the right offer, I'd pay for new wallpaper.'
Buyer: 'I've been thinking of having a new one put in. If someone wanted to buy the house, I'd take care of it before the sale.'

If the response to that is: 'Would you put it in writing?' Your answer should be: 'Of course...Would you want to put a deposit on the house now?'

Be prepared at any time to start negotiating seriously. Be prepared both to receive an offer and, if your prospective buyers are hanging back, to encourage them. Remember our ideal salesperson? In a case when buyers are hesitating, but seen very interested in a product, the salesperson who is alert may volunteer, "Should I write up the order?"

If the person is positive ("Nice house" will do), then you can ask the direct question: "Would you like to put down a deposit?"

[TIP: It's better to ask, "Would you like to put down a deposit?" than "Would you like to make an offer?" The latter is inviting the prospects to knock some money off your asking price.]

At this point, you may want to add, "Should I leave you alone a few minutes to discuss it? I can make some phone calls." You can also talk more about the house, reviewing what's on your fact sheet, while they use the time to think. Ask them if they would like a cup of coffee or tea. Ask them what they're looking for in a house.

Don't ask "Would you like to put down a deposit?" indiscriminately. You may frighten away some buyers by appearing overeager. But often there's a pregnant pause in the conversation. Husband is waiting for wife to say something; wife is waiting for husband; both may be waiting for the agent or seller to say something. That's the perfect time to put in, "Would you like to put down a deposit?"

Now you're at the point of negotiation. If the next question is, 'Would you consider taking back a mortgage?' you should proceed to [negotiate that]. If the offer is enough lower than your asking price for you to make a counteroffer, proceed to [negotiate that]. "

*Danielle Kennedy, ibid p. 237

*Shenkman and Boroson, op. cit. pp. 132-4.

STEP ⑩: HOW TO HANDLE BUYERS' OFFERS

O.K. You've made all the right preparations to sell the house, from cleaning and fixing up the house, to advertising and showing the house to prospects, and handling the initial objections of prospects. And, finally, let's say you've now come to the stage where you find you have one or more prospects who clearly stand out as serious prospects about buying your house, and are just on the verge of making an actual offer on the property. What do you do now—how do you, in a word, now transform one serious prospect into an actual final purchaser?

A. SEEK TO 'CLOSE THE BUYER' & GET AN OFFER FROM THE PROSPECTIVE BUYER—AND IN WRITING

What you want to do is, in the language of real estate salespersons, to "close the buyer"—that is, to preliminarily lock him or her into a deal. [Notice that this is not at all the same thing as closing the <u>house</u>, the subject matter of Steps 14 & 15 of this chapter].

In order to close the buyer at this stage in the selling process, there are basically three elements you wish to achieve: you want to get an agreement on a selling price, to get from the prospect a deposit towards the purchase, and to get a written preliminary contract signed by the prospect. And how do you do this?

Under the laws of just about every state, *a real estate transaction is legally binding ONLY IF it is in writing. In practical terms, therefore, no prospect really begins to qualify as a "serious" bidder unless and until he makes you an offer to buy—in writing.* And if you should get just a verbal offer you consider reasonable from a prospect, then it's strictly advisable not to waster your precious time discussing it, but to quickly counter with a suggestion such as this: "why don't you put it in writing and I'll give it serious consideration as soon as I get it." This way, then, you force the prospect to "commit herself" more concretely—and legally. Plus, by his putting his offer in writing, you'll be in a better position to see what and what conditions the prospect is actually attaching.

B. PRINCIPLES OF NEGOTIATION OF TERMS RELATED TO OFFERS

In the process of making an offer (or, more accurately stated, a series of offers), though, there will be a lot of little and big negotiations back and forth between you and the prospective buyers, a lot of bargaining and haggling, deal making and brokering.

What and what do you negotiate and bargain on? They are basically on the same issues and items as those outlined on pp. 21-2, matters ranging from move-in date, to what items of house fixtures or personal property are includable in the sale, and the financing. [Refer to pp. 21-2, 30-1, for a fuller listing of these]. Much of the general principles governing negotiations between home buyers and sellers have been amply detailed elsewhere in this manual, and you should refer to that section even as a seller. [See Chapter 4]. However, in this section, we shall only add some further rules and principles of negotiation that are more directly applicable to the home seller, as differentiated from the buyer.

The following are some helpful general rules and principles of negotiations to follow in dealing with a serious prospect:

1. As the seller, ask yourself this important question: is this a buyer's market or seller's market? In a buyer's market, be particularly careful; the first rule is, don't be so determined to win the bargaining contest at all costs. Rather, focus on winning the war—selling your house! You need not stubbornly insist, for example, on getting every last nickel on your sales price, or refuse to throw in, say, a washing machine or an old furniture that the buyer insists on, and risk losing the entire sale. If the prospective buyer offers to pay $99,000 on a house you want to sell for $100,000, sure that's $1,000 or 1 percent less than you want. A substantial amount for you, maybe. But remind yourself: ***don't let a whole 99 percent of the deal slip away from you because of 1 percent!***

In short, be prepared to give up a little, or to receive a little less than you would want to, in order to accomplish the ultimate goal—the selling of your house at a reasonable price.

2. Keep in mind that the house price is by no means the only thing you and the buyers can negotiate on or make a deal with. Quite to the contrary, you can just as importantly negotiate over the ***"conditions of sale" issues***—

issues like the move-in date, the down payment amount of money to lower the buyer's mortgage interest rate, whether the seller will pay for a variety of small improvements (e.g., having new wallpaper or new kitchen appliances put in), whether the seller will permit certain contingencies (e.g., the buyer to go ahead with the buying of the house only if he can obtain a mortgage for needed amount at a specified desirable rate within, say, 30 days), and so forth. Such CONDITION-OF-SALE ITEMS can be skillfully employed during the negotiating process as "negotiating trade-off tools" to lower the price of the property, or to raise it, as the case may be.

In deed, many seasoned real estate investors contend that, generally, conditions of sale are even more important than the price of the property. How? To put it simply, because as a seller you can often make out better selling on "my terms and your price," than on "my price and your terms."

Here's a somewhat exaggerated illustration of this concept. Say you want $100,000 for your house, and the buyer is insisting on paying $94,000. That would mean that, in terms of the traditional down payment of 20% of the sales price, the buyer would have to put down $20,000 as down payment (on $100,000 price). In addition, the buyer would have to come up with the closing costs —approximately another $5,000. Meaning that to purchase your house in the traditional way, the buyer would have to have some $25,000 cash at hand. Now, as a seller, you could make this offer, instead: the buyer pays 10% down on the same $100,000 (rather than 20%); this way, then, he'll have to worry about coming up with only a down payment of $10,000 (instead of $20,000), plus the $5,000 for the closing—total cash payment of $15,000, instead of $25,000. And so on. [See p. 50 for more detailed analysis of the mechanics of seller-assisted financing].

The point here, simply, is that both price and a number of conditions of sale are equally important variables that can be just as equally employed as "negotiation tools" by you [as well as by a knowledgable buyer, of course] to achieve a sale.

3. When you shall have uncovered what the buyer's needs, desires, and motivations are, present your offers precisely in terms of those needs. [See p. 24].

4. *If at all you engaged a broker who you are using in some aspects (or all) of the sales effort, this dimension (negotiations) will be one area where you had better used him. Leave the negotiations all to him; he will serve you better on that.* As Richard F. Gabriel, the real estate sales specialist and negotiator, sums it up, "the broker can play a valuable role on your behalf in the negotiation process because negotiating through him, rather than directly with a seller [or buyer, as the case may be], avoids any possible emotional outbursts, or rash statements by either side. A seasoned real estate broker who's experienced in negotiation can make or break a transaction and that is to your advantage too. He will know how to handle a seller [or buyer] in order to get the desired result. After all, he wants the sale as much as the seller wants to sell and the buyer [wants] to buy."*

5. As much as is humanly possible for you, make every effort not to appear nervous, worried or under pressure to make a quick sale. In short, even if you are really pressed and actually need a quick sale, try all you can to disguise your true motivation from the buyers. *The worse thing you can do as a seller is to give away your weaknesses and vulnerabilities to a buyer—to show that you're actually in a desperate need-to-sell situation!* [Important: see pp. 24-6 for detailed exposition of the so-called 'need-to-sell' seller syndrome, which you must endeavor to minimize as a seller].

6. Become as knowledgeable, educated, and well informed, as you can on your area's current real estate market conditions. Is the current real estate market soft or on the upswing, for example? What about the house prices, or mortgage interest rates? [If the market is on the upswing, that tells you the interest rates must be going down, and the inventory of houses for sale is shrinking, and home prices are going up!] In particular, what about the type of house you're selling—are they a growing or shrinking number on the market, and what are the possible reasons? [See pp. 23-4].

In this connection, as one added way of making an impression on the prospect, it will be a big plus for you if you can come up with some documentations to show to the buyer—something written, especially in printed form. Any articles in newspapers, magazines, newsletters or similar printed matter, suggesting that buying a home in such a wonderful and appreciating neighborhood as yours, or in such an appreciating real estate market, for example, will help bring lucrative credibility to your selling position in the eyes of the buyer.

---

* Gabriel, op. cit. p. 108.

7. An area in which you must especially be knowledgeable and informed, is in matters concerning CREATIVE FINANCING, and ways by which a buyer can get a good financial arrangement to be able to make the purchase. *"Today's consumer,"* said one analyst of the current real estate scene, *"is extremely price-conscious and value-driven. You must establish with your buyers that they will not lose if they buy now. So many buyers are afraid that they will pay too much for a home and then have to sell the house for less in 5 years. You must be knowledgeable and continuously prove value to the prospect."** *

Another analyst, a realtor, adds, making essentially the same point:

> "Buyers are not falling in love with a house anymore. They have become very practical. The cost of living, housing, the conditions of our economy, are such that people have taken off the rose-colored glasses.
>
> They look for an agent they can trust, but also an agent that will find them a good deal. 'Deal' was a word I thought I would never use in this business, but buyers think getting a good deal is a good thing, and I am now in complete agreement with them.
>
> In the beginning of the relationship, the buyer asks me if I can get him a good buy. Even a wife who does not work and has very little to do with the financial side of the family business wants a good deal now. She doesn't start out asking me about the color scheme of the home or if there are other little children in the neighborhood. *The only question is 'Can you get us a good deal?' "** * [Emphasis added by the writer]

8. Recognize that, according to expert salesmen, the first prospect to take an offer is often the person with the best offer. Why? According to experts, this is because when the house first comes on the market that's when the pool of buyers that's available is the largest. And hence, that's precisely the time when the chances of there being a "perfect" buyer for the house (one for whom your house is almost perfectly suitable) is usually at its highest. So, be careful not to unreasonably reject the first set of offers outrightly, purely in the belief and gamble that subsequent offers are bound to be better. The point is that *you should treat every prospect seriously,* and above all, use your God-given simple common sense.

9. If you make concessions with some cash substitutes or other trade-offs, invoke the notion of FAIRNESS to win concessions from the buyer as well, in exchange. "Look, we're only $3,000 apart. I've given your whole position on this a great deal of thought. I don't want to be the reason this deal falls through. Tell you what: I'm prepared to split that difference 50/50 with you. What do you say to that?" Or, "I'm prepared to throw in the fireplace equipment and the Ride'Em Mower and snow blower that are sitting in the garage. What do you say to that?"

[If the buyer, by the way, should first come up with the same ploy with you for mutual concessions, how do you respond to that? You can say something like, "I'd love to. But I can't. I simply can't afford to. I've made too many concessions to you already. That price is the very least amount I must have to buy the house I need."]

10. In regard to pricing the house, there are, to be sure, many theories on how to make price offers and concessions.. But one common axiom among experts about negotiations is that *whichever side makes the biggest concessions (the buyer, by raising the amount he'll pay, or the seller, by lowering the amount he'll accept), and makes them faster, loses.* Why? Because, experts say, making the bigger concessions and so quickly, immediately feeds the other side the idea that they can get you to make still more and more concessions. It only wets the other side's appetite and expectations for more. Hence, the prescribed strategy is to *make your concessions progressively smaller so as to dampen, rather than wet, the buyer's (the other side's) expectations.*

The common procedure in house sales upon the seller submitting his asking price, is for the buyer to come back with an initial written offer that's 5 to 10 percent below the seller's asking price. (They could, at times, be anything all the way up to 15 to 25 percent off the seller's price, however, depending on the overall condition of the property and the real estate market, how long the property has been on the market, and the buyer's sense of how pressured the seller is to sell). The seller would presumably reject the initial offer, and then make a counter-offer that is, say, 3 to 5 percent below the asking price. The buyer returns with an offer 5 percent or so below the asking price — and, after a series of offers and counteroffers, the deal is finalized.

---

*Danielle Kennedy, *Double Your Income In Real Estate Sales*, p. 239.

**Ibid, quoting another realtor.

As a seller (or buyer, as the case may be), the proper strategy is that, even before you put forth your asking price (or, for the buyer, the initial offer), you should have a definite "game plan" as to how low (or, for the buyer, how high) you'll be willing to go. The gameplan? Basically, you should have the initial asking price in mind, as well as a *"target price range"* (a range within which you'd be most satisfied to sell), and a *"lowest price range"* (the lowest price you can possibly accept). [For a buyer, the equivalent categories would be: the initial price offer, the target price range, and the top price range]. Among those three categories, the final price you receive will likely be somewhere between the lower end of the "target price range" and the top end of the "lowest price range."

EXAMPLE: Property is offered at $101,000. The initial offer by the buying prospect is $90,000 (approximately 10% less than the asking price). Your target price range is $96,000 to $97,000, and the lowest price range is $94,000 to $95,000. Hence, in all likelihood, the final price you'll get for the house will be anything between $95,000 to $96,000, and, following the prescribed "game plan" and the principle of making progressively smaller concessions to the buyer, about three concessions on your own part—$3,000, $1,500 and $500—will get you there.

Here is the basic sequence roughly involved in the whole matter of handling offers from prospective buyers:

1. The buyer makes you a <u>written</u> PURCHASE OFFER, outlining what he's willing to pay for the house, when and how, and any other preliminary conditions he may want to attach.

2. If you like the offer, you sign or otherwise "accept it" (in writing, of course); or, if you don't like the offer, you may either reject it outrightly or make a counteroffer. [See samples of Purchase Offer and Counter Offer letters at p. 31. A preprinted standard form used for this purpose is the "Offer to Purchase" form reproduced on p. 32. Blank copies of the pre-printed form are obtainable from the Legal Publishers. See the Order Form on p. 191].

To "accept" this offer, what the seller will need to do is to sign the back of the form captioned "ACCEP-TANCE," at which point the document now becomes a "BINDER" (agreement).

3. At this point when the buyer's interest seems to be genuine and heated, you may get on the phone, or physically get together, with the buyer and verbally negotiate the basic details back and forth (on the price as well as other details, such as those covered in the PURCHASE OFFER on p. 32). And after a series of offers and counter offers with some give and take by both sides, the parties will come to terms.

4. Assuming that the terms of the buyer's written Purchase Offer (pp. 31 or 32) are now acceptable to you, the buyer leaves you a "good faith" deposit money; you'll sign to accept the Purchase Offer (the lower part of pp. 31 or 32), and at that point, that accord becomes a so-called "BINDER" — a binding agreement between you and the buyer. [Relevant details on offer making procedures from a buyer's standpoint, are outlined in "Step 4" of Chapter 5, at pp. 29.]

At that time, you may leave the buyer with a copy of a *Property Disclosure Statement* (see Figure B.1 on p. 151 for a sample copy) as a way of living up to your fiduciary obligations to disclose the full condition of the house to the buyer, to legally protect yourself against future possible litigation and claims of being deceived by the buyers. (See Appendix B on Disclosure procedures).

You will, as a matter of good policy, want to put the buyer's deposit money into an "escrow," since the buyer will likely want to be reassured that his deposit is in good hands and secure. Basically, you do this by having the check written out to the name of an escrow you employ, an independent third party, such as an escrow company or a reputable broker. The escrow retains the deposit in a separate escrow account pending the closing [See p. 58 for the appointment and the workings of an escrow].

5. The buyer takes a short time out, for the length of time that's usually provided in the Binder Agreement (say 3 to 7 days) to make a closer inspection of the house and evaluate the property's physical condition. The buyer may probably have a professional home inspector conduct a formal inspection of the property to search for any possible defects in the property. (See Appendix A at pp. 143-5, and "Step 5" of Chapter 5, at p. 33 on home inspections and evaluation procedures).

Be prepared for some new demands by your prospective buyer or even re-negotiation of terms—if his inspection should uncover some really significant flaws or defects.

6. We should emphatically point out, though, *that at this point in the selling process, you should watch out!* Keep your fingers crossed!! Even at this stage in the game, when your prospect has said yes and even put down a deposit and is preparing for the signing of the contract, you're not out of the woods yet. The prospects may develop a case of the jitters—sudden nervousness and a feeling of fright or uneasiness about going through with the purchase. They may suddenly see flaws and defects they never complained about before, and develop cold feet. They may come up with a few array of demands — whether you will knock a little something off the price, whether you'll reduce the down payment amount, or whether you'll throw in one appliance or the other in the deal, and so forth. They may, in short, become nervous and scared and start to have second thoughts about going through with the purchase.*

How do you deal with such a situation? Simply be reassuring to them. Experienced realtors recommend statements like the following to prospects with the jitters: "Years from now, you'd be thanking me for helping you buy this house." Or, "This house has been good to us, and I'm sure it will be good for you. We've raised a healthy family in a great neighborhood, and I'm sure you will too. We've also made a decent profit on the place — not a big profit, mind you, but a decent one. And so will you. And if you ever have any problems, just call us. But as we've said, the basement's dry as a bone, the appliances are new, and the neighborhood's the best in town. We know you'll be as happy living here as we have been." Or , use just one sentence of reassurance: "You're getting a good house at a good price, and you'll never have any regrets."

You can tell the buyer who calls back sounding reluctant something like this: "Come over. Let's take one more look at the house and really imagine what it would be like if you were living there. I will get out of the way, so you and your wife can really get the feel of the place.

"Ask yourselves: 'Would we really be happy here?' If the answer keeps coming up yea, do not let $50 more a month stand in your way."

"When you two are sitting there thinking about owning that house, ask yourselves how important that extra $50 a month is going to be in the next five years?"

7. After the buyer's closer inspection of the property, assuming all is well and that the deal is still on, the next major step is for you and your prospective buyer to draw up and sign a PURCHASE (could also be called SALES) CONTRACT — the subject matter of "STEP 12" below.

STEP ⑪: PRE-QUALIFY THE BUYER YOURSELF TO BE SURE HE'LL BE ABLE TO OBTAIN A MORTGAGE LOAN

Experts contend that only 1 out of every 3 prospects who come looking for a house-purchase can really afford to buy it. Consequently, even after a serious prospect has committed to buy your house — and before you get into the elaborate matter of actually drawing up the contract — it is highly advisable that you "pre-qualify" the prospect to determine that he (or she) can really afford to pay you for the property, that he can get the necessary bank mortgage or other financing to make the purchase. *This way, if it should turn out that the prospects are not at all likely to qualify for a mortgage (or to have other resources) to be able to make the purchase, you'll spare yourself the troubles and expense of delving into the contract paperwork, or even proceeding further with the particular prospects.*

The point of this pre-qualification, is not that this will constitute the final or actual determination of who can and who can't ultimately obtain a mortgage. But, rather, the point is to get a rough idea of the prospect's likelihood to qualify for the needed mortgage, before you may get into spending any money or time on drafting the

---

*Realtor Danielle Kennedy explain the phenomenon this way: "Today's consumer is extremely price-conscious and value-driven. You must establish with your buyers *that they will not lose if they buy now.* So many buyers are afraid that they will pay too much for a home and then have to sell the home for less in 5 years. You must be very knowledgeable and continuously prove value to the prospect." (Kennedy, *Double Your Income in Real Estate Sales,* p. 239).

sales contract. As a seller, having this knowledge as to whether the buyer will probably qualify, is important to you because, among other things, once you and a prospective buyer sign a sales contract, you'd be taking your house off the market and tying up the property during the period between the signing of the contract of sale and going to closing, a period which often lasts for months. Hence, if you can determine earlier that the prospect cannot possibly qualify for a mortgage, you'll save yourself all that time — and trouble. You'll then be in a position to drop the deal with that prospect at this point and not proceed to the next step, the contract drafting and signing stage, knowing that the prospect just won't have the financial ability to follow through with a deal anyway.

How do you prequalify a buyer yourself? Turn to Chapter 2 (pp. 6-12) as well as Section D of "Step 8" in Chapter 5 (pp. 49-55, & 57), and follow the same guidelines outlined therein in making a rough determination of a buyer's qualification.

What should you do if you were to find that a prospective buyer has a serious credit problem, but not bad enough as to make it totally condemning? You should, of course, express your doubts to the prospects about their ability to qualify for a mortgage. However, since you are not quite the lender and can't really say for sure how the borrowers will fare at the hands of the actual lenders, you should have your prospects make an application with some two or three banks or mortgage brokers, anyway (see pp. 49-55 for the range of lender options). But, don't take the house off the market, however, and don't sign a sales contract with the buyers yet. Wait! Who knows, if they could come back with a preliminary qualification letter from a lender within a reasonable period, say 7 days, you can then enter into a sales contract with them at that point. If they can't obtain that and get turned down by the lenders, all bets are obviously off with such prospects about the house at that point.

STEP ⑫: SIGN THE SALES/PURCHASE CONTRACT WITH BUYER

Following the acceptance of a prospect's offer and your preliminary financial qualification of the buyer, the next major step, from the seller's perspective, is the drawing up and signing of the SALES CONTRACT with the prospective buyer.

THIS DOCUMENT IS THE SINGLE MOST IMPORTANT DOCUMENT FOR YOU (AND FOR THE BUYER, AS WELL) IN THE ENTIRE REAL ESTATE TRANSFER DEAL. And, customarily, it is YOU, the seller (or the seller's attorney, where he's using one), that prepares the initial draft of this document. In many regions of the country (notably in parts of the West, among them, states like Arizona, Arkansas, Michigan, Missouri, Minnesota, New Mexico, Wisconsin, and many others), it's not even a lawyer, but principally the real estate broker (if and where the buyer is using one), that handles the drawing up of the contract—using, as the lawyers themselves generally do, as well, a pre-printed standard form obtainable from the area title insurance company or a legal stationery store.

In any event, however, no matter who it is that specifically draws up this contract in a given instance, what is important for you to bear in mind, here, is one guiding principle: *that all that the document's preparer (whether he or she be you, or a lawyer, a broker, or whomever), must do is simply draw up (or modify) the provisions of the contract to reflect the terms and conform to the conditions that are previously discussed and agreed to by the buyer's and seller's sides.* In this regard, you may delete, add to, or alter any clauses in the pre-printed form to meet the needs of the parties, as applicable and mutually agreeable.

An illustrative sample copy of the printed Sales/Purchase Contract or Agreement is on p. 43. Your area's pre-printed form is obtainable from your area title insurance company or real estate agent, or a local legal stationery store. [Blank copies of the form are obtainable from The Legal Publishers, see the Order Form on p. 191]. Turn to "STEP 6" of Chapter 5 (p. 35), for an elaborate discussion of the contract and contract-drafting and signing procedures.

STEP ⓭: EFFECTUATE THE SALE BY HELPING YOUR BUYER GET A PURCHASE LOAN

As has been abundantly emphasized in earlier sections of this chapter, after all is said and done, except for a tiny few number of people who can afford to pay all cash for a home purchase, even the most "serious" prospective buyer in the world will ultimately do you no good whatsoever unless he can qualify for a mortgage loan! Hence, by common agreement among experienced real estate professionals, *one important way by which a home seller can ultimately bring about the sale of his house, or speed up its materialization, is by helping the buyer to get and qualify for a loan.*

In the preceding STEP 11 above, the focus is on the seller prequalifying the buyer primarily for the purpose of determining whether the buyer has a chance of getting financing from lenders on the property. In contrast, here the emphasis is on providing <u>active assistance</u> to the buyer to enable or assist him to apply for and obtain the loan. True, it's not yours, but the buyer's responsibilty to arrange for financing. But, as a practical matter, most buyers are lost when it comes to matters having to do with finances and financing, most simply don't have the foggiest idea as to how to go about it. Hence, if you want to translate the sale of your property into reality, you had better done what experienced real estate brokers and sales professionals often do in such instances: NOT ONLY SPEND SOME TIME TO LEARN THE BASICS OF MORTGAGE LOANS AND HOME FINANCING YOURSELF, BUT EDUCATE AND INFORM YOUR BUYERS ABOUT THIS, AND STEER THEM TO SUITABLE LENDERS.

In deed, if you have done your homework well, as you are actually supposed to have done before now, you shall have, yourself, by now made your own preliminary check with banks and mortgage companies and area brokers, and you'd have by now all the information you need to properly educate the prospect on what and what he's required to have to be able to meet the eligibility requirements to qualify for a mortgage. *You shall have readily had, already, at your finger tips, answers to questions such as these:* how much is the minimum down payment you must have, how much the monthly payments will be, the current loan rates, bank "point" charges, and loan application "origination" fees, whether you will possibly give a second or a first mortgage, whether you will possibly accept an F.H.A. or a V.A.-insured mortgage buyer, etc.?   And, furthermore, armed with such advance preparation and information, you can—and should have, yourself done—a preliminary financial qualification of the buyer by now and ensure not only that he can qualify for a loan, but that he can generally afford your house (its maintenance, the keeping up with the monthly mortgage payments, etc.) if he were to buy it.

[See details of the procedures for the various home mortgage financing categories and sources outlined in "Step 8" of Chapter 5, at p. 49. Additional financing considerations of particular relevance to a home seller, are further outlined in "Steps 3 & 4" of' the present Chapter, pp. 90 & 98, respectively). Appendix C (pp. 157-165) further outlines the basic characteristics of varying types of mortgages generally.]

Most importantly, at this stage in the home selling process when the next major step is the closing and when almost everything rides on the buyer being able to get a mortgage approval or a deal will not be had, *you've got to take a more active role in making sure that the buyer follows through seriously in seeking out the mortgage loan.* For example, while you await the closing date, check by phone with the buyers to find out which lenders they applied to and actively inquire to see how the application is progressing. Did your buyer get the preliminary letter of loan qualification from the lending institution within the designated period? And if not, what is the reason or explanation from the buyers, and from the lenders?

IMPORTANT: According to experts, in 99 cases out of 100, what makes a real estate deal go through is simply having buyers who can get the necessary mortgage. Hence, it is of the utmost importance—and entirely proper— here, that you be strict in pursuing this matter.

STEP ⑭: PREPARE FOR THE CLOSING, AND THE SETTLEMENT DOCUMENTS & COSTS

[Simply follow here, the same instructions and procedures outlined for the home buyer situation, in "Step 9" of Chapter 5, pp. 57-62].

IMPORTANT: DRAFTING/PREPARATION OF THE TRANSFER DEED DOCUMENT BY SELLER

Additional to the pertinent information set forth elsewhere regarding the home transfer process (see especially Step 10 of Chapter 5, and pp. xxx on deed making), we summarize here for the benefit of the reader, the essential paperwork procedure involved in transferring title (the ownership) in real estate.

Strictly speaking, the process of transferring any piece of real property basically boils down to this: you (the home-owner) will need to complete, sign and *notarize* a new DEED, bearing the home buyer's (or buyer's) name(s) in place of yours. And you (or, more commonly, the new owner) must then have the new deed recorded in the public record with the County Recorder of Deed's Office for the location.

The process is quite simple:

* Locate the original DEED (the present owner's existing deed) bearing their name(s) as the property's owner(s). (If unable to readily locate this, you can always acquire a "certified" copy of that document from the local land registry's or County Recorder's Office.)

* Purchase a blank transfer deed form (a "Warranty," or "Bargain and Sale," or "Quitclaim" type, depending on the type agreed upon) from a real estate agent or local legal stationery store in the state where the property is located (see the sample forms on pp. 136-141; and see the Order Form on p. 191 for an order of the blank copies of the form).

* Complete the blank form, by essentially entering the new buyers' name or names as the property's owner(s) to whom the property is now "deeded to" or "granted to," in place of yours. Be sure to enter on the new deed form the description of the property, etc., EXACTLY as they're shown on the original deed. (If, for example, the original deed says "See Exhibit A attached," then you must be sure to also provide the attached exhibit for the new deed, since it is considered to be part of the deed.)

* If married and the property in question is held in both spouse's names, you must have your spouse sign and *notarize* the deed documents and include it among the papers to be recorded in the county land and record's office.

* You (the present owner or owners, as applicable) sign the deed in the presence of a Notary Public and have it *notarized.*

* Attach thereto a covering letter of request, requesting the Recorder of Deed's office to change the property's ownership and designate the named parties as the new owners.

* The new owners (buyers) must hurry and take the Deed and the cover letter, to the County Recorder of Deed's office in the country where the real property is located, and have the Deed officially "recorded"— registered.

STEP ⑮: ATTEND THE HOME CLOSING, SETTLE THE SALES DEAL, AND TRANSFER LEGAL TITLE OF OWNERSHIP TO BUYER

[Follow here, the same instructions and procedures outlined for the home buyer situation, in "Step 10" of Chapter 5, pp. 62-66].

IMPORTANT: From the standpoint of a seller, if you must offer your buyer a seller-assisted financing (a "second mortgage") to enable him make the purchase (p. 50), the important thing is that you decide whether the risk (primarily the risk that the buyer may become unable to regularly make the payment and thereby force a foreclosure proceeding to recover the property, which is something often time-consuming and expensive), is worthwhile to you. If you are getting a high price for your house, of you are desperate to sell, you may go along with such a seller-assisted financing if you determine that the buyer is a person of honor and that the risk is worthwhile, all things considered.

However, if you offer a seller-assisted financing—purchase money mortgage, taking back paper, or whatever—just be sure to go through the same lending procedures that a normal lender (a banking institution) would. First, insist on a credit report, verify the buyers' income and normal expense, and get the buyers to put down in cash at least 10 percent of the asking price, plus the closing costs. And, secondly, you should use the standard mortgage documents and standard terms that an ordinary bank will use in such a situation—the "Note and Mortgage," the "Deed" (or "Deed or Trust"), and the "Guarantee." (See samples of these forms on pp. 74, 76, 136, 80, and 69, respectively). These forms can be readily purchased from your local legal stationery store, or obtained from a mortgage bank, and must be signed and *notarized* by the principles, usually at the closing. [See also the Order Form on p. 191 for obtaining blank copies of the forms from the Legal Publishers].

M 290—Warranty deed: basic covenants: ind. or corp.

[A WARRANTY DEED] [On the date of signing, -FORM-
(Closing) enter that date here]

This Indenture made JANUARY 17th _____ 19___

Between (Seller(s) full names here)
DOW D. DEAN and MARY M. DEAN, his wife, both residing at
I27 Seller Street, Brooklyn, New York, II234,
party of the First Part,

AND

[Buyer/Buyers' names & address(es)]
JOHN H. JOHNSON and DIANA A. JOHNSON, his wife, both residing at I22 Purchase Street, Queens, New York, II437,
party of the Second Part,

[NOTE:] Under the law of almost every state, some "consideration" (a thing of value) of any size is required to make a contract legal and binding. Hence, as a rule, it is customary to recite a consideration of $10, or even $1.00, in warranty deeds (and other like documents)]

Witnesseth that the party of the first part, in consideration of
* TEN Dollars ($ IO.00)
lawful money of the United States,
paid by the party of the second part, does hereby grant and release unto the party of the second part,
the heirs or successors and assigns of the party of the second part forever, all

[Complete with the name of the locality, county, city and state of property's location]

that piece of real property situated in the Borough of <u>Brooklyn</u>, County of <u>Kings</u>, city and State of <u>New York</u>, which is described as follows:

[Enter here exactly the same description of the Property as set forth in the Sales/Purchase Contract. (See the first and second Passages of Paragraph 2 on p. 33)]

BEGINNING at a point on the southwesterly side of I5th Street distant Two Hundred Seventysix feet ten inches southeasterly from the corner formed by the intersection of the southwesterly side of I5th Street with the southeasterly side of Third Avenue; running thence southwesterly at right angles to I5th Street and part of the distance through a party wall One Hundred Nine feet eve..en inches to land now or formerly of Deborah L. Carson; thence southeasterly along said land now or formerly of Deborah L. Carson, Seventeen feet two and one-eighth inches, then northeasterly along the northwesterly side of Lot No. 26 on Map of Land of John Dimon, et al., filed in Kings County June I7, I835, One Hundred Ten feet seven inches to the southwesterly side of I5th Street, thence northwesterly along the southwesterly side of I5th Street, Nineteen feet six inches to the point or place of Beginning.

SAID premises is further known as: II2 I5th Street, Brooklyn, N.Y.

[Get this information (these numbers) from the old deed]

[Get the facts from Paragraphs 3, 4, 5 of Sales Contract (pp. 34, 35) and, generally, from the parties. If an existing mortg. is agreed to by the lending terms then strike out the clause.]

SUBJECT TO an Existing First Mortgage in the amount of $20,000.00, which is recorded on the ____ day of _____ 19___, in Liber ____ of Deeds at Page _____; and further subject to Purchase Money Second Mortgage in the sum of $6,000, which mortgage is to be recorded with this deed.

Together with the appurtenances and all the estate and rights of the party of the first part in and to said premises,

To have and to hold the premises herein granted unto the party of the second part, the heirs or successors and assigns of the party of the second part forever.

And the party of the first part covenants as follows:

First, That the party of the second part shall quietly enjoy the said premises;

Second, That the party of the first part will forever **Warrant** the title to said premises.

Third, the party of the first part, in compliance with Section 13 of the Lien Law, covenants that the party of the first part will receive the consideration for this conveyance and will hold the right to receive such consideration as a trust fund to be applied first for the purpose of paying the cost of the improvement and will apply the same first to the payment of the cost of the improvement before using any part of the total of the same for any other purpose.

The word "party" shall be construed as if it read "parties" whenever the sense of this indenture so requires.

In Witness Whereof, the party of the first part has duly executed this deed the day and year first above written.

In Presence of:

1._____

2._____

X Dow D. Dean (Seller)   L.S.

X Mary M. Dean (Seller - Wife)   L.S.

_____   L.S.

_____   L.S.

[Used when individuals are involved]

STATE OF NEW YORK, COUNTY OF_____ ss.:
On_____ _____ 19__, before me personally came
Dow D. Dean and Mary M. Dean
to me known to be the individualS described in, and who executed the foregoing instrument, and acknowledged that they executed the same.

STATE OF NEW YORK, COUNTY OF_____ ss.:
On_____ _____ 19__ before me personally came
Dow D. Dean and Mary M. Dean
to me known to be the individualS described in, and who executed the foregoing instrument, and acknowledged that they executed the same.

[A Notary Public signs and affixes his stamp here]

_____(Notary Public)   _____(Notary Public)

[Used when a corporation/a partnership is involved]

STATE OF NEW YORK, COUNTY OF_____ ss.:
On_____ _____ 19__, before me personally came (corp. officer's nm) to me known, who, being by me duly sworn, did depose and say that deponent resides at No. (where corp. officer lives) deponent is (office?) of (nm of corp.) the corporation described in and which executed, the foregoing instrument; deponent knows the seal of said corporation; that the seal affixed to said instrument is such corporate seal; that it was so affixed by order of the Board of Directors of said corporation; deponent signed deponent's name thereto by like order.

STATE OF NEW YORK, COUNTY OF_____ ss.:
On_____ 19__, before me personally came (name of a witness at event) the subscribing witness to the foregoing instrument, with whom I am personally acquainted, who, being by me duly sworn, did depose and say that he resides at No. (witness's address) that he knows DOW D. DEAN and MARY M. Dean, to be the individualS described in and who executed the foregoing instrument; that he, said subscribing witness, was present and saw Dow D. & Mary M. Dean execute the same; and that he, said witness, at the same time subscribed his name as witness thereto.

_____(NOTARY PUBLIC)   _____(NOTARY PUBLIC)

[rotated text, left side:]
Deed
WARRANTY — BASIC COVENANTS

DOW D. DEAN and MARY M. DEAN

TO

JOHN H. JOHNSON and DIANA A. JOHNSON.

Dated,   19

STATE OF NEW YORK
County of Kings [Leave everything below this line blank] ss.

RECORDED ON THE
____day of____, 19__
at____o'clock____M.
____of Deeds
in Liber____
at Page____and examined

CLERK

PLEASE RECORD AND RETURN TO:

John H. and Diana A. Johnson
122 Purchase Street,
P.O. Box IB,
Queens N.Y. II437

[Enter here the purchasers' name/address by which this deed is to be returned to them after it's been officially recorded]

138 [A BARGAIN AND SALE DEED]

T 691 Standard N.Y.B.T.U. Form 8002: Bargain & sale deed, with covenant against grantor's acts—Ind. or Corp.: single sheet

DATE CODE

JULIUS BLUMBERG, INC., LAW BLANK PUBLISHERS

-FORM-

[A BARGAIN AND SALE DEED]

NEVER MIND THIS THE LAWYERS' IDEA!

CONSULT YOUR LAWYER BEFORE SIGNING THIS INSTRUMENT — THIS INSTRUMENT

[on the date of signing, enter that date here]

[Closing]

THIS INDENTURE, made the __17ᵗʰ__ day of __JAN__ , nineteen hundred and _____

[Name and address of Seller]

BETWEEN
DOW D. DEAN and MARY M. DEAN, his wife, both residing at I27 Seller Street, Brooklyn, New York ;

[Name and address of Buyer]

party of the first part, and JOHN H. JOHNSON and DIANA A. JOHNSON, his wife, both residing at I22 Purchase Street, Queens, New York, II437;

party of the second part,

WITNESSETH, that the party of the first part, in consideration of Ten Dollars and other valuable consideration paid by the party of the second part, does hereby grant and release unto the party of the second part, the heirs or successors and assigns of the party of the second part forever,

ALL that certain plot, piece or parcel of land, with the buildings and improvements thereon erected, situate, lying and being in the Borough of Brooklyn, County of Kings, city and State of New York, which property is described as follows:

BEGINNING at a point on the southwesterly side of I5th Street dist- ant Two Hundred Seventysix feet ten inches southeasterly from the corner formed by the intersection of the southwesterly side of I5th Street with the southeasterly side of Third Avenue; running thence southwesterly at right angles to I5th Street and part of the dista- nce through a party wall One Hundred Nine feet eve.en inches to land now or formerly of Deborah L. Carson; thence southeasterly along said land now or formerly of Deborah L. Carson, Seventeen feet two and one-eighth inches, then northeasterly along the north- westerly side of Lot No. 26 on Map of Land of John Dimon, et al., filed in Kings County June I7, I835, One Hundred Ten feet seven inches to the southwesterly side of I5th Street, thence northwest- erly along the southwesterly side of I5th Street, Nineteen feet six inches to the point or place of Beginning.

SAID premises is further known as: II2 I5th Street, Brooklyn, N.Y.

[Get this information (these num- bers) from the old deed]

SUBJECT TO an Existing First Mortgage in the amount of $20,000.00, which is recorded on the _____ day of _____ 19___ , in Liber _____ of Deeds at Page _____ ; and further subject to Purchase Money Second Mortgage in the sum of $+6,000, which mortgage is to be recorded with this deed.

[Note: Under the law of almost every state, some "consid- eration" (a thing of value) of any size is required to make a contract legal and binding. Hence, is a rule, it is customary to recite a consideration of $10, or even $1.00, in warranty deeds (and other like docu- ments)]

[Complete with the name of the locality, county, city and State. Enter here exactly the same de- scription of the property, as set forth in the Sales/Purchase Con- tract. (See the first and second passages of Paragraph 2 on p.33)]

[Get the facts from Paragraphs 3, 4 & 5 of Sales Contract (pp.33-35) and terms generally, from the lending. If an existing mortg. is agreed to by the parties. If an then strike out the clause.]

TOGETHER with all right, title and interest, if any, of the party of the first part in and to any streets and roads abutting the above described premises to the center lines thereof; TOGETHER with the appurtenances and all the estate and rights of the party of the first part in and to said premises; TO HAVE AND TO HOLD the premises herein granted unto the party of the second part, the heirs or successors and assigns of the party of the second part forever.

AND the party of the first part covenants that the party of the first part has not done or suffered anything whereby the said premises have been encumbered in any way whatever, except as aforesaid.

AND the party of the first part, in compliance with Section 13 of the Lien Law, covenants that the party of the first part will receive the consideration for this conveyance and will hold the right to receive such consideration as a trust fund to be applied first for the purpose of paying the cost of the improvement and will apply the same first to the payment of the cost of the improvement before using any part of the total of the same for any other purpose. The word "party" shall be construed as if it read "parties" whenever the sense of this indenture so requires.

IN WITNESS WHEREOF, the party of the first part has duly executed this deed the day and year first above written.

SIGNED : X _____

IN PRESENCE OF:

[Some Witnesses to the closing and signing event, if any, sign here. Could be each will the Notary Pub- lic]

1. _____

2. _____

X Dow D. Dean (Seller)

X Mary M. Dean (Seller - wife)

—OVER—

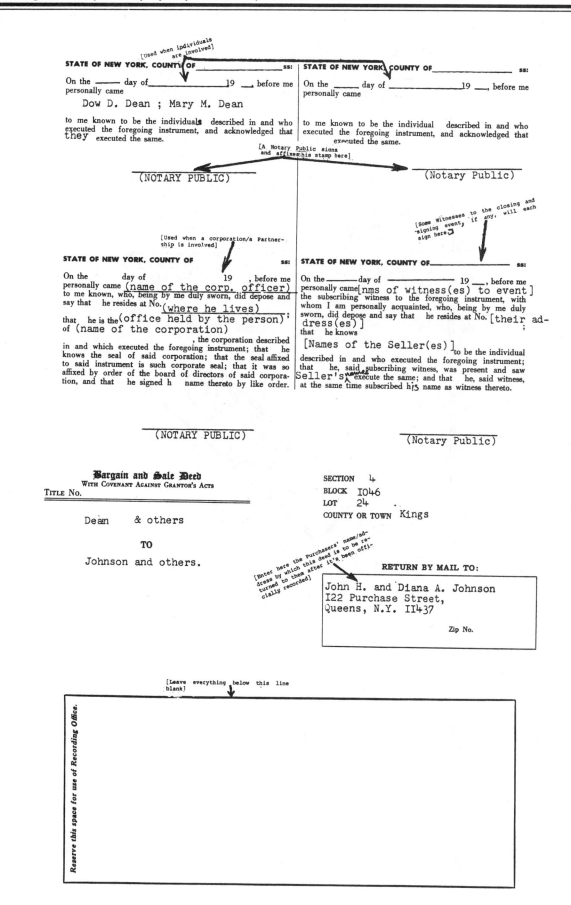

[Used when individuals are involved]

STATE OF NEW YORK, COUNTY OF _____ ss:

On the _____ day of _____ 19 __, before me
personally came
    Dow D. Dean ; Mary M. Dean
to me known to be the individuals described in and who
executed the foregoing instrument, and acknowledged that
they executed the same.

[A Notary Public signs
and affixes his stamp here]

_____
(NOTARY PUBLIC)

STATE OF NEW YORK, COUNTY OF _____ ss:

On the _____ day of _____ 19 __, before me
personally came
to me known to be the individual described in and who
executed the foregoing instrument, and acknowledged that
executed the same.

_____
(Notary Public)

[Some Witnesses to the closing and signing event, if any, will each sign here]

[Used when a corporation/a Partnership is involved]

STATE OF NEW YORK, COUNTY OF _____ ss:

On the _____ day of _____ 19 __, before me
personally came (name of the corp. officer)
to me known, who, being by me duly sworn, did depose and
say that   he resides at No. (where he lives)
that   he is the (office held by the person) ;
of (name of the corporation)
_____, the corporation described
in and which executed the foregoing instrument; that   he
knows the seal of said corporation; that the seal affixed
to said instrument is such corporate seal; that it was so
affixed by order of the board of directors of said corporation, and that   he signed h   name thereto by like order.

_____
(NOTARY PUBLIC)

STATE OF NEW YORK, COUNTY OF _____ ss:

On the _____ day of _____ 19 __, before me
personally came [nms of witness(es) to event]
the subscribing witness to the foregoing instrument, with
whom I am personally acquainted, who, being by me duly
sworn, did depose and say that   he resides at No. [their ad-
dress(es)] ;
that   he knows
[Names of the Seller(es)] to be the individual
described in and who executed the foregoing instrument;
that   he, said subscribing witness, was present and saw
Seller's execute the same; and that   he, said witness,
at the same time subscribed his name as witness thereto.

_____
(Notary Public)

Bargain and Sale Deed
WITH COVENANT AGAINST GRANTOR'S ACTS
TITLE No. _____

    Dean   & others

        TO

Johnson and others.

SECTION 4
BLOCK I046
LOT 24
COUNTY OR TOWN Kings

[Enter here the Purchasers' name/ad-
dress by which this deed is to be returned to them after it's been officially recorded]

RETURN BY MAIL TO:

John H. and Diana A. Johnson
I22 Purchase Street,
Queens, N.Y. II437

                    Zip No.

[Leave everything below this line
blank]

Reserve this space for use of Recording Office.

P 694—Quitclaim deed: ind. or corp. **[A QUITCLAIM DEED]** JULIUS BLUMBERG, INC., LAW BLANK PUBLISHERS

𝕿𝖍𝖎𝖘 𝕴𝖓𝖉𝖊𝖓𝖙𝖚𝖗𝖊 *made___ _____ 19 __*

𝕭𝖊𝖙𝖜𝖊𝖊𝖓

DOW D. DEAN and MARY M. DEAN, his wife, both residing at
I27 Seller Street, Brooklyn, New York, II234,

party of the first part, and

JOHN H. JOHNSON and DIANA A. JOHNSON, his wife, both residing
at I22 Purchase Street, Queens, New York, II437,

party of the second part,

𝖂𝖎𝖙𝖓𝖊𝖘𝖘𝖊𝖙𝖍 *that the party of the first part, in consideration of* ✱✱✱✱✱✱✱✱✱✱✱✱✱✱✱✱✱✱✱
✱✱**TEN** *Dollars* (**$** IO.00✱✱✱✱✱✱)
lawful money of the United States,
paid by the party of the second part, does hereby remise, release and quitclaim unto the party of the
second part, the heirs or successors and assigns of the party of the second part forever, all
that piece of real property situated in the Borough of [Brooklyn] ,
County of [Kings] , city and State of [New York] , which is described as follows:

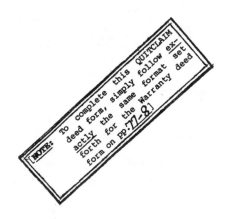

NOTE: To complete this QUITCLAIM
deed form, simply follow exactly the same format set
forth for the Warranty deed
form on pp. 77-8I.

-OVER-

𝕿𝖔𝖌𝖊𝖙𝖍𝖊𝖗 with the appurtenances and all the estate and rights of the party of the first part in and to said premises,

𝕿𝖔 𝖍𝖆𝖛𝖊 𝖆𝖓𝖉 𝖙𝖔 𝖍𝖔𝖑𝖉 the premises herein granted unto the party of the second part, the heirs or successors and assigns of the party of the second part forever.

𝕬𝖓𝖉, the party of the first part, in compliance with Section 13 of the Lien Law, covenants that the party of the first part will receive the consideration for this conveyance and will hold the right to receive such consideration as a trust fund to be applied first for the purpose of paying the cost of the improvement and will apply the same first to the payment of the cost of the improvement before using any part of the total of the same for any other purpose.

The word "party" shall be construed as if it read "parties" whenever the sense of this indenture so requires.

𝕴𝖓 𝖂𝖎𝖙𝖓𝖊𝖘𝖘 𝖂𝖍𝖊𝖗𝖊𝖔𝖋, the party of the first part has duly executed this deed the day and year first above written.

In Presence of

SIGNED: X
Dow D. Dean (Seller)   [L. S.]

X
Mary M. Dean (Seller - Wife)   [L. S.]

.... [L. S.]

.... [L. S.]

STATE OF NEW YORK, COUNTY OF_____ ss.:
On _____ 19 —, before me personally came (nm. of corp. officer) to me known, who, being by me duly sworn, did depose and say that deponent resides at No. deponent is (office?) of (nm. of corporation?) the corporation described in and which executed the foregoing instrument; deponent knows the seal of said corporation; that the seal affixed to said instrument is such corporate seal; that it was so affixed by order of the Board of Directors of said corporation; deponent signed deponent's name thereto by like order.

(Notary Public)

STATE OF NEW YORK, COUNTY OF_____ ss.:
On _____ 19___, before me personally came

DOW D. DEAN and MARY M. Dean

to me known to be the individual described in, and who executed the foregoing instrument, and acknowledged that he executed the same.

(Notary Public)

𝕯𝖊𝖊𝖉
QUITCLAIM WITH LIEN COVENANT

DOW D. DEAN and MARY M. DEAN
(Sellers)

TO

JOHN H. JOHNSON and
DIANA A. JOHNSON (Purchaser)

Dated, _____ 19___

STATE OF NEW YORK
County of _____ ss.

RECORDED ON THE
_____ day of _____, 19___
at _____ o'clock _____ M.
in Liber _____ of Deeds
at Page _____ and examined

CLERK

PLEASE RECORD AND RETURN TO:

John H. and Diana A. Johnson
122 Purchase Street,
P.O. Box IB
Queens, N.Y. II437

NOTICE TO HOLDER OF FIRST MORTGAGE

To: ABC Mortgage Company   My Address:
     200 Fifth Avenue   Date:
     N.Y., N.Y. 10011

Gentlemen:

     Reference your mortgage on this building: (give address), of which the buyer is Mr./Mrs. (name?), I wish to notify you that I am currently holding a second mortgage (or third, or fourth mortgage, as the case may be) on the said property, which mortgage was made by _____, who also has (have) a mortgage with your company.

     Please promptly notify me if and whenever payment is not made to you on time, or if and whenever there should be any default in the mortgage.

     Thank you.

                         Yours truly,
                           etc.

NOTE: This letter would be necessary and applicable only when a second mortgage (or more) applies.

Appendix A
INSPECTING AND EVALUATING
THE CONDITION OF A HOUSE: A PRIMER

A. Inspecting the Outside of the House
Use the inspection checklist on pp. 147 & 148.

MAKE SURE TO CHECK THE FOLLOWING ITEMS (the numbers refer to Figure A-1, the diagram on page 142):

1. *Foundation:* Check for holes, cracks, unevenness.

2. *Brickwork:* Look for cracks; loose or missing mortar.

3. *Siding (clapboards, shingles, etc.):* Look for loose or 'missing pieces, lifting or warping.

4. *Paint:* Look for peeling, chipping, blistering, etc.

5. *Entrance Porch:* Examine steps, handrails, posts, etc. , for loose or unsafe features.

6. *Windows/Screens:* Look for cracked or broken glass; holes in screens.

7. *Storm windows (northern climates):* Are they complete? Are they secure and properly caulked?

8. *Roof:* Look for worn or bald spots; ask how old and if under warranty or not.

9. *Gutters and Downspouts:* Check for missing sections; gaps or holes in joints; are there signs of leaks?

10. *Chimney:* Look for tilting; loose or missing bricks.

11. *Walls and Fences:* Look for holes, loose or missing sections, rotted posts.

12. *Garage (if separate from house):* Check doors, roof, siding, windows.

13. *Driveway and Sidewalks:* Look for holes and cracks.

14. *Grounds/Landscaping:* Locate property line; are trees, shrubbery and grass in good shape?

15. *Proper drainage:* Will rain (or snow) flow away from the house? Are there any problems with leaching fields or septic tanks?

FIGURE A-1
STRUCTURAL AREAS OF INTEREST FOR HOME INSPECTION

B. Inspecting the Inside of the House, [Check the Major "Systems" of the House (Plumbing, Electrical, Etc.), and All the Rooms]

THE NUMBERS REFER TO FIGURE A-2, THE DIAGRAM ON P. 146):

1. *Structure of the house:* Does the house feel solid? (Jump up and down on the floors). Check support posts and floor supports in basement; look for looseness, bending, rot or termites.

2. *Floors:* Check for levelness, bowing, movement when you walk on them.

3. *Stairs:* Look for loose treads; loose handrails.

4. *Plumbing System:* Check water pipes and sewer lines for leaking or rusting; flush all toilets; turn on faucets to test the water pressure; look for clogged or sluggish drains; dripping faucets.

5. *Heating System:* Find out what type of heat (warm air, hot water, electrical or steam); what type of fuel is used? How much does it cost to heat? (get last year's fuel bills); find out when system was last serviced.

6. *Hot Water Heater:* Check for signs of leaking or rusting. What is the capacity or "recovery rate"? (should be a minimum of 30 gallons for family of 4; more for larger families). How old is it?

7. *Electrical System:* Look at the "service box"—are there fuses or circuit breakers? Is it old or new? Look for exposed wires and signs of wear.

8. *Cooling/Air Conditioning:* What kind of cooling is there? What is the age and condition? Is the unit under warranty? How much did it cost to use last year?

9. *General Layout:* Are the rooms conveniently located? What are the "traffic patterns"?

10. *Kitchen:* What appliances are included (stove, refrigerator, dishwasher, garbage disposal)? Check for age, workability. Are there enough shelves and counter space? Are there enough electrical outlets? Are there leaks under the sink?

11. *Bathrooms:* Are there enough for your family? Check for cracks in tiles; signs of leaks; how long it takes to get hot water,, proper ventilation (window or fan?)

12. *Living Room/Dining Room:* Are they large enough? Is there a fireplace? If so, does the damper work; has the chimney been cleaned out recently?

13. *Bedrooms:* Are there enough for your family? Are they large enough? Does each have a window to the outside? Does each have a closet large enough for your needs?

14. *Storage Space:* Are there enough closets in the house? Are there other rooms you can use to store things?

15. *Windows:* Check for broken sash cords; loose frames; locks.

16. *Doors:* Do they close properly? Are there good locks?

17. *Walls/Ceilings:* Check for major cracks; loose or falling plaster; signs of leaks or stains.

18. *Basements (if present):* Check for signs of leaks, dampness or flooding; make sure there's enough lighting.

19. *Attic (if accessible):* Look for signs of roof leaks; check insulation (how much? what type?); are there signs of squirrels or other rodents?

FIGURE A-2
"SYSTEMS" NEEDING INSPECTION IN HOME INSPECTION

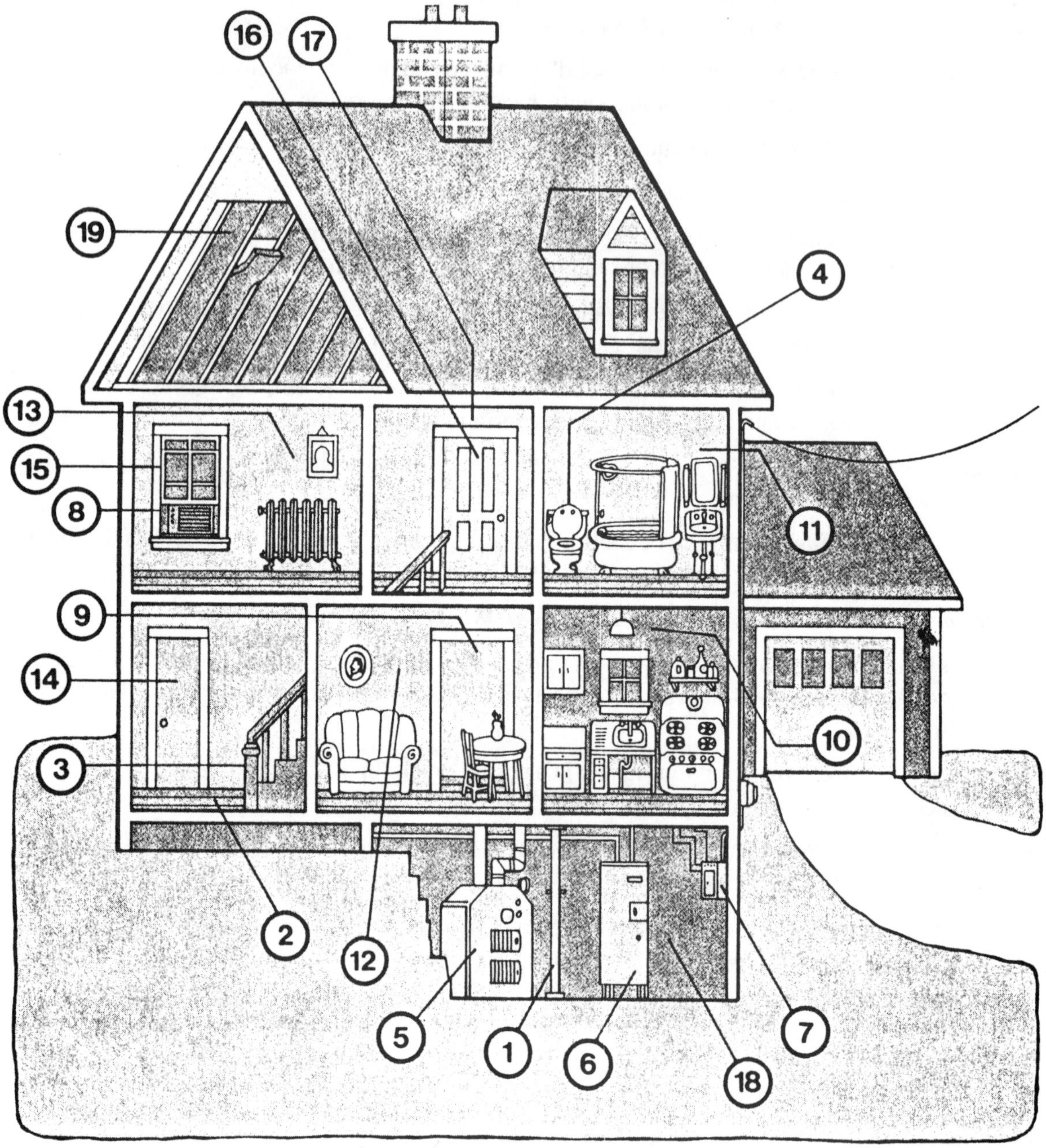

Whenever you look at a house, don't forget to...

- Bring a flashlight to look into those dark corners...
- Ask if you will need a termite inspection. This may be required by the lender, the F.H.A., the V.A. or your local building department.
- Ask about other inspections that may be required by state or local laws (in some cases sellers may have to pay for these). The broker or the lender can tell you which ones are required and who should pay for them.
- Ask about warranties on any items (such as roof, new appliances, hot water heater, furnace, air conditioning).
- Ask about builders' warranties on new homes (what is covered and for how long?)
- Get a professional inspection if you have any doubts.

- ASK AS MANY QUESTIONS AS YOU CAN THINK OF AND USE THE INSPECTION CHECKLIST ON PP. 147-8.

Figure A-3
HOME INSPECTION CHECKLIST

OUTSIDE THE HOUSE--STRUCTURE & GROUNDS--

[The numbers refer to the diagram on p.144]

INSPECTION ITEM	CONDITION		ITEM UNDER WARRANTY?	ADDITIONAL COMMENTS
	Adequate - Not a Problem	Inadequate - Needs Repair or Replacement		
1. FOUNDATION				
2. BRICKWORK				
3. SIDING				
4. EXTERIOR PAINT				
5. PORCH(ES)				
6. WINDOWS/SCREENS				
7. STORM WINDOWS				
8. ROOF				
9. GUTTERS & DOWNSPOUTS				
10. CHIMNEY(S)				
11. WALLS/FENCES				
12. GARAGE				
13. DRIVEWAY/WALKS				
14. GROUNDS/LANDSCAPING				
15. DRAINAGE/ SEPTIC SYSTEMS				
16. OTHER ITEMS OUTSIDE THE HOUSE				

FIGURE A-4

INSIDE THE HOUSE--STRUCTURE AND SYSTEMS--

[The numbers refer to the diagram on p.146]

INSPECTION ITEM	CONDITION		ITEM UNDER WARRANTY?	ADDITIONAL COMMENTS
	Adequate - Not a Problem	Inadequate - Needs Repair or Replacement		
1. STRUCTURE OF HOUSE • support posts (basement) • floor beams (basement)				
2. FLOORS				
3. STAIRS (treads, handrails)				
4. PLUMBING SYSTEM • water pipes ok? • sewer pipes ok? • water pressure ok? • toilets work? • sinks & faucets? • drains work?				Cost of water bills last year? $_____
5. HEATING SYSTEM • what type? • how old? • kind of fuel? • when serviced last?				Cost of heat last year $_____
6. HOT WATER HEATER? • how old? • capacity or recovery rate?				
7. ELECTRICAL SYSTEM • how old? • fuses or circuit breaker? • # volts/amps?				Cost of electricity last year $_____
8. COOLING/AIR CONDI-TIONING? • evaporative or cooling?				Cost to use last year $_____

[The numbers refer to the diagram on p. 116]

| INSPECTION ITEM | CONDITION | | ITEM UNDER WARRANTY? | ADDITIONAL COMMENTS |
	Adequate - Not a Problem	Inadequate - Needs Repair or Replacement		
9. GENERAL ROOM LAYOUT (traffic patterns)				
10. KITCHEN • size of kitchen • stove/oven • refrigerator • dishwasher • disposal/sink • counter space • cabinets/shelves • electrical outlets • floor condition • windows/ventilation				
11. BATHROOMS • no. of bathrooms • toilets, showers/ tubs ok? • tiles & floors? • lighting/ventilation?				
12. LIVING ROOM/DINING ROOM • size ok? • fireplace?				
13. BEDROOMS • no. & size • closets adequate? • windows?				
14. STORAGE SPACE				
15. WINDOWS IN HOUSE				
16. DOORS IN HOUSE				
17. WALLS/CEILINGS OK?				
18. BASEMENT • leaks/dampness? • lighting ok?				
19. ATTIC • signs of leaks? • insulation? • signs of rodents?				How much insulation?

Appendix B
MAKE FULL DISCLOSURE OF THE CONDITIONS OF & DEFECTS IN THE PROPERTY, IF ANY

In recent times, one of the biggest changes occurring in the field of real estate transfers is in the area of the seller's liability for any defects that may be found in the property. No more is the rule the "Buyer Beware." Rather, the current rule is "Seller Beware"; litigation brought about by protesting home buyers in many states has led to *a new concept that holds that the seller has the duty to disclose to buyers any known defects in the property, or any that the seller should reasonably have forreseen or be expected to have known.**

To be sure, no such dire results may actually come about in your case. They only happen very sparingly. Nevertheless, prudence dictates that you protect yourself now, just in case the buyer were to come back later on and claim to have been deceived. For, if that happens, the buyer could sue you for damages and, even for rescission (cancellation) of the sale.

In deed, in consequence of the growing concern about disclosure, more than half of the states in the nation (and the list is growing) have passed compulsory disclosure laws in recent years, requiring the seller, upon sale, to disclose defects in the property to the buyer. And nearly close to that number of states have expressed interest in adopting such a law. *The point is that as a seller, it's highly advisable and to your advantage, that you disclose all the defects you know about to your buyers.* As long as you have done that, and the buyer goes ahead with the purchase knowing that the defects exist, you would be free of any potential liability. The more extensive and detailed you can make your disclosures, the better for you in the long run as a seller.

One analyst, a realtor who himself is widely noted in the trade as "one who provides incredible disclosure statements" to his home buyers, makes the case for full disclosure very strongly:**

> "The moral here is that I believe it's best to disclose everything. ...And why not? Most sellers erroneously fear that disclosing defects will cause the buyer to shy away. I have found that not to be the case. Most buyers who are sincerely interested in the property will accept defects or will negotiate the price to compensate for them or will work with the seller to correct them. And, more to the point, the property is what it is. If it has defect, it's better that you get it out in the open than that the buyer discover it a few months later."

A. Methods of disclosure.

A good way to go about this is, first, to have a home inspector check over the house. This would be sufficient proof of a good effort on your part to determine any problems. Note, however, that you (the seller) won't usually have to pay for the inspection, since most buyers feeling they need an inspection to uncover any hidden defects the house may have, are often anxious and more than willing to pay for the inspection. All you have to do is recommend it and buyers are usually ready to pay for it. Then, secondly, tell the buyers about any problems or defects as you walk them through the house and show them the property. As you walk by the fireplace, for example, you'll note that it has a crack in the flue. You can add that the estimated cost of its repair is $1,000, and that you've already taken that into account in the pricing of the house. (Or, ask that if the buyer will add the extra

---

*See, for example, "An Appellate Ruling Rekindles Disclosure Debate," N.Y. Times, Sunday, April 24, 1994, Section D, p. 9

**Robert Irwin, *The For Sale By Owner Kit*, p. 143.

$1,000 to the price, you'd be prepared to fix the defect). ***Thirdly, and most importantly, you must thoroughly document such disclosures;*** have a good disclosure statement made up describing the entire condition of the property and any problems thereof, and have the buyers sign it for you acknowledging receipt of a copy.

DISCLOSURE STATEMENT

The actual written disclosure statement will vary greatly from locality to locality. In some localities there are recommended official disclosure statement forms, while in others there are none and the seller will have to devise his or her own statement. Figure B-1 set forth below is only one example of a typical disclosure statement.

B. What to do if defects are uncovered

What happens when defects are revealed, either by your own disclosure or in an inspection, and to which the buyer raises an objection? It's simple. On issues that involve health and safety, you should promptly move to fix those. For example, say the inspection shows that you don't have ground fault interrupter (GFI) plugs in your bathroom, plugs which help to prevent electric shock. You should immediately replace the plugs. On the other hand, if it concerns issues that do not involve health and safety, but that are negotiable, you can discuss the matter with the buyer and try to come to a compromise. You can, for example, offer the buyer a reduction in price of a certain amount in exchange for acceptance of the condition "as is." Or, offer to throw in some extra fixtures or house furniture or equipment in exchange for acceptance of the condition as is.

FIGURE B-1
Seller's Property Disclosure Statement — A Sample

THE FOLLOWING STATEMENT IS INTENDED TO BE AN ILLUSTRATIVE SAMPLE ONLY. CHECK WITH AN AREA REALTOR OR BROKER TO SEE IF YOUR STATE AND LOCALE USES A SPECIFIC OFFICIAL FORM FOR THIS PURPOSE.

(To be filled out by seller and given to buyer. Seller, use a separate page to detail/explain any defects or problems with property.)

WATER
Any leaks (now or before) in the roof? Yes____ No____ Not Sure____
Any leaks around a skylight or at a chimney? Yes____ No____ Not Sure____
Any leaks at sinks, toilets, tubs, showers or elsewhere in house? Yes____ No____ Not sure____
Does the house have rain gutters? Yes____ No____
 Their condition?_____
Does the house have any downspouts? Yes____ No____ Not sure____
 Their condition?_____
Does property have any drainage problems? Yes____ No____
 Explain_____
Water directed away from house? Yes____ No____
Any flooding or grading problems? Yes____ No____
 Explain_____
Is there presently flood insurance coverage on the house? Yes____ No____
Any settling, slipping, sliding or other kinds of soil problems? Yes____ No____
Public water?_____ Or well?_____
Date well pump installed?_____
Low water pressure? Yes____ No____
Any driveway cracks? Yes____ No____
Any problems with fences? Yes____ No____
Is house insulated? Yes____ No____
 Attic?_____ Walls?_____ Floor?_____
Double-paned glass windows? Yes____ No____

Moisture barrier in areas below ground level? Yes____ No____

Does property have sump pump? Yes____ No____

Where? _____

Why? _____

Does property have septic tank? Yes____ No____

 Active?_____ Abandoned?_____ Filled?_____

Connected to sewer? Yes____ No____

Were any improvements made to the property within the last 6 months? Yes____ No____

 What improvements? _____

Has a death occurred on the property? Yes____ No____

 Explain _____

EQUIPMENT

Central furnace? Yes____ No____

 Forced air?_____ Radiant/water?_____

 Radiant/electric? _____ Other?_____

Room heaters? Yes____ No____

 Type? _____

 Location? _____

Central air conditioning? Yes____ No____

Room air conditioning? Yes____ No____

 Location? _____

Furnace room vented? Yes____ No____

Temperature relief valve on water heater? Yes____ No____

Spa? Yes____ No____

Pool? Yes____ No____

 Pool heated? Yes____ No____

 Cracks, leaks or other problems with pool? Yes____ No____

 Explain _____

Any aluminum wiring? Yes____ No____

TITLE

Are you or have you been involved in a bankruptcy in the last 5 years? Yes____ No____

Does the property have any bond liens? Yes____ No____

Are there any boundary disputes? Yes____ No____

Any enroachments or easements? Yes____ No____

Any shared walls, fences or other such areas? Yes____ No____

Any areas held in common, such as pools, tennis courts, walkways, greenbelts or other? Yes____ No____

Are there any lawsuits against the seller and/or property that will affect title? Yes____ No____

Is property member of a Homeowners' Association to which you must belong? Yes____ No____

Any current lawsuits involving the Homeowners' Association? Yes____ No____

Any Conditions, Covenants and Restrictions (CC&Rs) in deed affecting property? Yes____ No____

Any easements or rights-of-way over property to public utilities or others? Yes____ No____

Have there been notices of reassessment of the property for
 real estate tax purposes during the last 6 months? Yes____ No____

STRUCTURE

Any cracks in slab? Yes____ No____

Any cracks in interior walls? Yes____ No____

Any cracks in ceilings? Yes____ No____

Any cracks in exterior walls? Yes____ No____

Any cracks or water leaks or shifting in foundation? Yes____ No____

Any retaining walls? Yes____ No____

      Cracked?____ Leaning?____ Broken?____

HAZARDS AND VIOLATIONS

Any accumulated asbestos? Yes____ No____

Any environmental hazards including, but not limited to, radon gas, lead-based paint, PCBs, storage tanks for
      diesel or other fuel, contaminants in soil or water, urea-formaldehyde (UFFI)? Yes____ No____

Any landfill on or near property? Yes____ No____

Is property in earthquake zone? Yes____ No____

Is property in wetlands areas? Yes____ No____

Is property in flood-hazard zone? Yes____ No____

Is property located in landslide area? Yes____ No____

Is property in high fire hazard area as described on a Federal Emergency Management Agency Flood insurance
      Rate Map or Flood Hazard Boundary Map? Yes____ No____

Is property in any special study zone that indicates a hazard or requires permission to
      add to or alter existing structure? Yes____ No____

Are there any zoning violations pertaining to propety? *(Expalin separately)* Yes____ No____

Were any room additions made without property permits required? *(Explain separately)* Yes____ No____

Was any work done to electrical, plumbing, gas or other home systems without proper permit?
      (Explain Separately) Yes____ No____

Does the property have an energy conservation retrofit? Yes____ No____

Does the property have a public sewer system, private sewer system, septic tank, or cesspool?
      (Explain Separately) Yes____ No____

Any odors caused by gas, toxic waste, agriculture or other? Yes____ No____

Were pets kept on the property? Yes____ No____

      Type?____ Inside?____

Are there any pet odor problems? Yes____ No____

Are there any active springs on property? Yes____ No____

Any sinkholes on property? Yes____ No____

Is property adjacent to or near any existing or planned mining sites, toxic waste sites or other environmental
hazards? Yes____ No____

Is there any real estate development planned or pending in immediate area such as commercial, industrial or
      residential development that could affect property values? Yes____ No____

Any abandoned septic tank? Yes____ No____

Is a Home Protection Plan available to the buyer? Yes____ No____

If common areas are part of shared ownership on this property, are there any defects or
      problems that could affect the desirability of this property? Yes____ No____

Is there an existing condition that could result in an increase assessments or fees? Yes____ No____

Are there any nearby property that is or has been used for manufacturing or automobile purposes? Yes___
No___

  If Yes, explain:_____

Are there any nearby property that is or has been used as schools, cleaning plants, military facilities, dumps or
truck lines? Yes____ No____

  If Yes, explain:_____

Is the property equipped with smoke detectors? Yes____ No____

REPORTS THAT HAVE BEEN MADE

The seller notes that the following reports, if any, have been made and are available to the buyer:

Structural Yes_____ No_____
Geological Study Yes_____ No_____
Roof Yes_____ No_____
Soil Yes_____ No_____
Sewer/septic Yes_____ No_____
Heating/air conditioning Yes_____ No_____
Electrical/plumbing Yes_____ No_____
Termite Yes_____ No_____
Pool/spa Yes_____ No_____
General home inspection Yes_____ No_____
Energy audit Yes_____ No_____
Radon test Yes_____ No_____
City inspection Yes_____ No_____
Spa equipment Yes_____ No_____
Pool heaters Yes_____ No_____
Central heating Yes_____ No_____
Central air Yes_____ No_____
Central evaporative cooler Yes_____ No_____
Water softener Yes_____ No_____
Space heaters Yes_____ No_____
Solar heating Yes_____ No_____
Window air conditioners Yes_____ No_____
Lawn sprinklers Yes_____ No_____
Security gates Yes_____ No_____
Television antenna Yes_____ No_____
TV cable connections Yes_____ No_____
TV satellite dish Yes_____ No_____
Attached garage Yes_____ No_____
Water heater Yes_____ No_____ Gas_____Electric_____
City water supply Yes_____ No_____
Public utility gas Yes_____ No_____
Propane gas Yes_____ No_____
Screens on windows Yes_____ No_____
Sump pump Yes_____ No_____
Built-in barbecue Yes_____ No_____
Garage door opener Yes_____ No_____
         Number of remote controls_____

ITEMS THAT GO WITH THE PROPERTY, IF APPLICABLE
Window coverings Yes_____ No_____
Floor coverings Yes_____ No_____
Range Yes_____ No_____
Stove/Oven Yes_____ No_____
Microwave Oven Yes_____ No_____
Dishwasher Yes_____ No_____
Trash compactor Yes_____ No_____
Garbage disposal Yes_____ No_____
Bottled water Yes_____ No_____

Burglar alarm system Yes____ No____
Swimming pools (if they are not permanently in the ground) Yes____ No____
Ceiling fans Yes____ No____
Storm windows and window screens Yes____ No____Gutters Yes____ No____
Fire alarm Yes____ No____
Intercom Yes____ No____
Electric washer/dryer hookups Yes____ No____
Sauna Yes____ No____
Hot tub equipment Yes____ No____
Lighting fixtures Yes____ No____
Smoke detectors Yes____ No____
Refrigerators Yes____ No____

SELLER IS FURTHER AWARE OF THE FOLLOWING DEFECTS AND/OR MALFUNCTIONS AND SPECIFICALLY INFORMED AND DRAWS BUYER'S ATTENTION TO THEM:

BUYER IS EXPRESSLY ADVISED TO PERSONALLY MAKE A PHYSICAL INSPECTION OF THE PROPERTY, AND TO EMPLOY THE SERVICES OF A COMPETENT INSPECTION COMPANY TO OBTAIN AN INDEPENDENT VERBAL AND WRITTEN REPORT OF THE PROPERTY'S CONDITION IN ALL RESPECTS.

Receipt and study of a copy of this *Property Disclosure Statement* is hereby acknowledged before the signing by each party.

Signed by Buyer   Seller:
X_____   X_____

Name(print)_____   Date:_____

FIGURE B-2
AREAS OF ENVIRONMENTAL CONCERN

Environmental Issues

Asbestos ceiling tiles

Urea Formaldehyde insulation

Radon gas

Lead paint

Contaminated ground water from nearby landfill

Underground storage tanks

Appendix C
SOME MODERN-DAY TYPES OF "CREATIVE FINANCING" MORTGAGES AND HOME FINANCING PLANS: A PRIMER

As already explained in several sections elsewhere in this manual (see especially p. 50), the vast majority of people who seek to buy a house cannot usually afford to personally finance the purchase, but must, of necessity, have to seek its financing through a mortgage loan. Consequently, the home mortgage industry is a key, pivotal integral part of the home buying and selling process for any interested party.

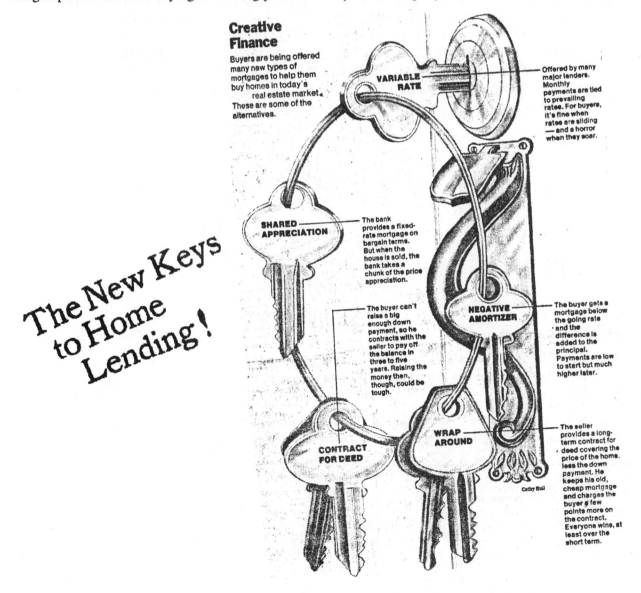

Creative Finance

Buyers are being offered many new types of mortgages to help them buy homes in today's real estate market. These are some of the alternatives.

The New Keys to Home Lending!

VARIABLE RATE — Offered by many major lenders. Monthly payments are tied to prevailing rates. For buyers, it's fine when rates are sliding — and a horror when they soar.

SHARED APPRECIATION — The bank provides a fixed-rate mortgage on bargain terms. But when the house is sold, the bank takes a chunk of the price appreciation.

NEGATIVE AMORTIZER — The buyer gets a mortgage below the going rate and the difference is added to the principal. Payments are low to start but much higher later.

CONTRACT FOR DEED — The buyer can't raise a big enough down payment, so he contracts with the seller to pay off the balance in three to five years. Raising the money then, though, could be tough.

WRAP AROUND — The seller provides a long-term contract for deed covering the price of the home, less the down payment. He keeps his old, cheap mortgage and charges the buyer a few points more on the contract. Everyone wins, at least over the short term.

Cathy Bull

In deed, by almost all accounts, home financing has become the single most overriding concern of the home buyer, seller, and real estate professional of the recent times, and the dominant determinant of whether or not a given home transfer deal is consummated.* As a rule, for the average home buyer, the search for the mortgage money would begin quite early in the game, directly after a home has been found and the contract signed, and continue indefinitely thereafter. In the process, the aspiring home buyer must necessarily go through the financial maze of the arcane world of the "mortgage industry," and while doing so, a whole range of questions must often be asked and decisions made, all of which will ultimately determine not only whether the aspiring home buyer succeeds in buying a house, but also whether he can do so under the best possible financial and legal terms. This, then, to our mind, makes it needful to devote a separate chapter on the basic facts and broad essentials, though by no means an exhaustive or even detailed exposition, of the modern-day mortgage world as they exist as of this writing.

Until recently, traditional mortgage features were a relatively uncomplicated and predictable matter—they generally had a fixed interest rate and a full amortization (or transfer of equity) over a relatively fixed period of 20 to 30 years. But, much of that has changed dramatically in recent times. Today, interest rates and purchase prices of homes have become dramatically fluctuating and unpredictable, making it increasingly or, at least, relatively less popular to go for traditional mortgages with fixed interest rates and long terms, and resulting in the emergence of a whole new variety of mortgage plans—the so-called *"creative financing" mortgages.* SUCH RECENT DEVELOPMENT IS ONE FURTHER REASON WHY IT IS INCREASINGLY IMPERATIVE THAT THE HOME BUYER (AS WELL AS THE HOME SELLER) SUFFICIENTLY EDUCATE HIMSELF IN THE BASIC CONCEPTS AND TECHNIQUES OF MODERN HOME MORTGAGE FINANCING: *IT CAN SAVE YOU TIME AND MONEY; IT CAN PREVENT YOU FROM GETTING A MORTGAGE THAT IS ILL-SUITED TO YOUR NEEDS AND BEST INTERESTS; AND, ABOVE ALL, IT CAN MAKE THE DIFFERENCE BETWEEN YOUR ULTIMATELY BEING ABLE TO PURCHASE THAT DREAM HOUSE OR NOT BEING ABLE TO!*

A. What Is a Mortgage?

A mortgage is a loan contract; it's a special loan given especially for the purpose of buying real property. The term is also used to mean a lien on real property given by a homeowner or buyer (borrower) to his lender as security for the borrowed money.

Here's how it works. A lender agrees to provide you the money you need to buy a specific home or piece of real property. You, in turn, promise to repay the money based on terms set forth in the mortgage (loan) contract.

*Thomas L. Friedman of the New York Times, not long ago summed it up this way: "The costs and complications involved in financing a home in today's world of 19 percent mortgages have become so great that they are supplanting the house itself as the most important aspect of any purchase. People in America no longer shop for homes; they shop for financing…Financing has always been a serious concern in the selection of any home, but it has become the overriding concern now that most Americans can no longer qualify for the simple, low-cost, fixed-rate, 30-year bank mortgage that sustained their parents and grandparents since the 1930's." (N.Y. Times, Sunday, Oct. 4, 1983, Section 3, pp. 1 & 17, "The New Keys to Home Lending.")

Under the *Federal Truth in Lending Law,* the contract should state the amount of the loan, the annual percentage rate (which, when computed, includes the mortgage interest rate, the premium paid for insurance, the mortgage, and "discount points"), the size of the repayment, and the frequency of payments.

As a borrower, you pledge your home as security.   It remains pledged until the loan is paid off. If you fail to meet the terms of the contract, the lender has the right to "foreclose", that is, obtain possession of the property, but he must follow the prescribed formalities of law to exercise the right of foreclosure.

Under the laws of most states in the East, the mortgagor (the borrower) retains title to the property, and the mortgage document does not give the mortgagee (the lender) title to the property, but merely gives him a lien (a claim) against the property. For most states west of the Mississippi, however, the mortgage arrangement is slightly different. Here, instead of the buyer receiving the actual title of ownership directly from the seller at the time of the purchase deal, a document is created, known as a *TRUST DEED* (also called *"Deed of Trust," "Mortgage Deed,"* or *"Deed to Secure Debt,"* depending on which state) for "holding the title during the mortgage period. This way, the power to carry out a foreclosure, should need be, is, in effect, vested in a third party and thereby makes it even easier for the lender to force a sale of the property if the borrower defaults on his mortgage payments as the lender would not have to go through many of the legal formalities and complications involved in formal foreclosures. In such western and other states (Alabama, Arkansas, Connecticut, Illinois, Maine, Maryland, Massachusetts, Missouri, New Hampshire, New Jersey, North Carolina, Ohio, Pennsylvania, Rhode Island, Tennessee, Vermont, and W. Virginia), the mortgage is, in fact, the deed, and the lender is legally regarded as the virtual owner of the property—until the mortgage loan has been repaid.

B. Some Major Financing Plans in Today's Market*

Given below, are some 13 home financing plans and techniques, representing the more basic variants of "creative home financing" on the market as of this writing. It's not attempted to outline every new or currently existing financing technique on the market since new financing alternatives are frequently being introduced while many of the existing ones frequently grow obsolete or disappear from the scene just as fast.

1. Fixed Rate Mortgage

Fixed rate mortgage is one having an interest rate and monthly payments that remain constant over the life of the loan. For example, suppose you borrow $50,000 at 10% interest for 30 years. Your monthly payments on this loan would be $632.22 and will never exceed that fixed predetermined amount.

Under the current market conditions, fixed rate mortgages are no more as readily available as they once were in the years past. Many lenders are reluctant to grant such mortgages nowadays, as they fear that a fixed rate would, in effect, lock them in a rate structure and they would not be able to adapt to new conditions in a market that is changeable.

2. Flexible Rate Mortgage

Flexible Rate Mortgage (also called "rollover," "adjustable," "variable" interest mortgage) is a mortgage with an interest rate which increases or decreases over the period of the loan according to pre-determined market conditions. The interest rate (the "price" of the loan) is not fixed, but is recomputed from time to time according to a certain financial index. One financial index commonly used, is the so-called "prime rate", the rate banks charge their most creditworthy customers to lend them money. However, the mortgage rate could be tied to one of the other financial indices less frequently used —e.g. , say the 3 to 5 year U.S. Treasury bill rate, or the Federal Home Loan Bank Board's interest rate, or some other price index.

The object for which the lender desires flexible-rate type of mortgages, is to protect himself against inflation and higher interest rates for his money, as he will be constantly able to keep his mortgage charges up as the market rates change (upwards) from time to time.

---

*Much of the rest of this appendix is excerpted from "The Mortgage Money Guide," an excellent booklet prepared and published under the auspices of the Federal Trade Commission by its staff members as a public service to home buyers. The present author is indebted to the FTC and its staff for this material.

There are many *variations* within the flexible-rate mortgage category.

To build predictability into your flexible rate loan, some lenders include provisions for "caps" that limit the amount your interest rate may change—a so-called "rate cap". Then, there is the "periodic cap", which

---

Rollover Mortgages: An Example

Tables show mortgage rates and monthly payments on a $75,000, 30-year rollover mortgage with an initial rate of 12.5 percent that is renegotiated (or "rolled over") every three years. The rate may rise or fall by a maximum of 5 percentage points over the life of the mortgage, and that the rate can fluctuate by no more than 1.5 percentage points during each renegotiation. Assume the rate rises or falls by the maximum allowed at each renegotiation.

If Rates Go UP:

	MORTGAGE RATE	MONTHLY PAYMENT
Year 1	12.5%	$ 800.44
Year 4	14.0%	$ 885.95
Year 7	15.5%	$ 970.21
Year 10	17.0%	$1,052.57
Year 13	17.5%	$1,078.92

If Rates Go DOWN:

	MORTGAGE RATE	MONTHLY PAYMENT
Year 1	12.5%	$800.44
Year 4	11.0%	$717.16
Year 7	9.5%	$640.76
Year 10	8.0%	$573.01
Year 13	7.5%	$553.37

Source: Federal Home Loan Bank Board

The New York Times/May 31, 1980

---

limits the amount the rate can increase at any one time [for example, a provision in the mortgage that even if the index increases by 2% in one year, the borrower's rate can only go up 1%]; and there's the "aggregate cap", which limits the amount the rate can increase over the life of the loan [e.g., a provision that even if the index increases by, say 2% every year, the borrower's rate cannot increase more than 5% over the life of the loan.]

Another variation of the flexible-rate mortgage is to fix the interest rate for a period of time— 3 to 5 years, for example — with the understanding that the interest rate will then be renegotiated. Loans with periodically renegotiated rates are also called *rollover mortgages;* and because the interest rate is fixed for at least a reasonable length of time, such loans make monthly payments more predictable. And, a final variation of the flexible rate mortgage we shall take note of here, is the *pledged account buy-down mortgage* with a flexible rate. Under this plan, the buyer (or it could be the builder, or anyone else willing to subsidize the loan) makes a large initial payment to the lender at the time the loan is made. The payment is placed in an interest-earning account with the lender, thereby offsetting the mortgage rate you pay and helping lower your interest rate for at least the first few years.

3. Balloon Mortgage

A balloon mortgage is one in which only the interest due is paid during the term of the mortgage, with the entire loan principal due and payable at the end of the term (which is usually a short one, commonly 3 to 5 years). Notwithstanding that the equal monthly payments to be paid in balloon mortgage plans are for the interest charge only, nevertheless that interest rate is a fixed rate thoughout the life of the loan.

Here's how a typical balloon plan works. Suppose you borrow $30,000 for a 5 year term at a 15% interest rate. And suppose your payments per month are only $375. In this example, payments of $375 per month for a 5-year period only amounts to a sum just equal to the interest charge on the loan, which means that the $30,000 principal becomes due at maturity—at the end of the 5 year period. That means, in other words, that after you shall have made 59 monthly payments of $375 each, you will then have to make one final, big ("balloon") payment of $30,375. And what if you can't make that final payment? Then you'll have to refinance the property, if that is available, or sell the property.

Some (not all) lenders guarantee refinancing when the balloon payment is due, though no guarantee is usually made on the associated interest rate. When no such guarantee on refinancing exists, the borrower (home buyer) could be forced to start the whole business of shopping for housing money once again, as well as paying closing costs and front-end charges all over again.

4. Graduated Payment Mortgage

Graduated Payment Mortgages (GPM) are designed for home buyers who expect to be able to make larger monthly payments in the near future. During the early years of the loan, the borrower makes lower monthly payments. The payments are structured to rise at a set rate over a set period, say 5 or 10 years. Then they remain constant for the remaining duration of the loan.

Even though the payments change, the interest rate is usually fixed. So, during the early years, the borrower's payments are lower than the amount that would have been warranted by the interest rate. During the later years, the difference is made up by higher payments. At the end of the loan period, the borrower would have paid off his entire debt.

5. Growing Equity Mortgage (Rapid Payoff Mortgage)

The "Growing Equity Mortgage" (GEM) and the "Rapid Payoff Mortgage" are among the more recent of mortgage plans on the market. These mortgages combine a fixed interest rate with a changing monthly payment. The interest rate is usually a few percentage points below the market rate. Although the mortgage term may run for 30 years, the loan will frequently be paid off in less than 15 years because payment increases are applied entirely to the principal.

Monthly payment changes are based on agreed-upon schedule of increases or on an index. For example, the plan might use the U.S. Commerce Department index that measures after-tax per capita income, and your payments might increase at a specified portion of the change in this index, say 75%.

Suppose you're paying $500 per month. In this example, if the index increases by 8%, you will have to pay 75% of the 8%, i.e., 6%, additional. Your payment increase, then, is to $530, and the additional $30 you pay will be used to reduce your principal.

To be able to use this mortgage plan, you have to have an income that is rising rapidly enough to keep pace with the increased payments. The chief advantage of this plan is that it can often permit the borrower to pay off his loan and acquire equity in the property rapidly.

6. Shared Appreciation Mortgage

In Shared Appreciation Mortgage (SAM), you make monthly payments at a relatively low interest rate. You also agree to share with the lender a sizable percentage (usually 30% to 50%) of whatever appreciation comes about in your house's value after a specified number of years, or when you sell or transfer the home.

The principal advantage of this plan to a borrower (which, it is to be recognized, comes about because of the shared appreciation feature), is that he gets to enjoy monthly payments which are lower than is available with many other regular plans. However, he's subject to some potential risks associated with the plan. For example, he may still be liable for the dollar amount of the property's appreciation even if he does not wish to sell the property at the agreed-upon date. Also, if property values do not increase as anticipated, the borrower may still be liable for an additional amount of interest agreed upon.

Here is how one variation of this idea, called *shared equity mortgage plans,* works, for an example. Let's suppose you've found a home for $100,000 in a neighborhood where property values are rising, and that the local bank is charging 18% on home mortgages. Assuming you paid $20,000 down and chose a 30-year mortgage term on the $80,000 balance, your monthly payments would have to be $1,205.67—which, let's say, you'd find to be about twice what you can afford. But, along comes a friend who offers to help. He offers to pay half of each monthly payment, or roughly $600, for 5 years. At the end of that time, you both assume the house will be worth at least $125,000. You can sell it, and your friend can recover the share of the monthly payments he had made to date (i.e., $36,000), plus half of the home's appreciation, or $12,500, for a total of $48,500 to him. Or, you can at the time pay your friend the same sum of money out of your pocket and gain increased equity in the house.

Shared appreciation and shared equity mortgages were inspired partly by rising interest rates and partly by the notion that housing values would continue to grow and grow over the foreseeable future. It should always be realized therefore, that if property values fall, or don't rise as high or rapidly as anticipated, these plans may not be as available or advisable.

7. Assumable Mortgage

An assumable mortgage is a mortgage that can be passed on to a new owner at the previous owner's interest rate. For example, suppose you're interested in a $75,000 home. You make a down payment of $25,000, and you still owe $50,000. The owner of the home has paid off $20,000 of a $30,000, 10% mortgage. You assume the present owner's old mortgage, which has $10,000 outstanding. You also make additional financing arrangements for the remaining $40,000, by, for example, borrowing that amount from a mortgage company at the prevailing market rate of 16%. Your overall interest rate is lower than the market rate because part of the money you owe is being repaid at 10%.

It should be noted that, as a practical matter, during periods of high rates, most lending institutions are reluctant to permit assumptions, preferring to write a new mortgage at the prevailing market rate. In such times this results in many lenders calling in the loans under *"due on sale"* clauses (see Appendix E). Because these clauses have increasingly been upheld in court, many mortgages are no longer legally assumable. Be especially careful, therefore, if you are considering a mortgage represented as "assumable." Read the contract carefully and consider having an expert or professional check to determine if the lender has the right to raise your rate in those mortgages.

8. Seller Take-back

This mortgage, provided by the seller, is frequently a *"second trust"* and is combined with an assumed mortgage. The second trust (or *"second mortgage"*) provides financing in addition to the first assumed mortgage, using the same property as collateral. (In the event of default, the second mortgage is satisfied only after the first). Seller take-backs frequently involve payments for interest only, with the principal due at maturity.

For example, suppose you want to buy a $150,000 home, that the seller owes $70,000 on the house on a 10% mortgage, and that you assume this mortgage and make a $30,000 down payment. You still need $50,000. So the seller gives you a second mortgage, or take-back, for $50,000 for 5 years at 14% (well below the market rate) with payments of $583.33. However, your payments are for interest only, and in 5 years you will have to pay the $50,000 principal The seller take-back, in other words, may have enabled you to buy the home. But it may also have left you with a sizable "balloon" payment that must be paid off in the near future.

Some private sellers are also offering first trusts as take-backs. In this approach, the seller finances the major portion of the loan and takes back a mortgage on the property.

9. Wraparound

Another variation on the second mortgage is the **wraparound.** Suppose you'd like to buy a $75,000 condominium and can make a $25,000 down payment, but can't afford the payments at the current rate (let's say it's 18%) on the remaining $50,000. The present owners have a $30,000, 10% mortgage. They offer you a $50,000 "wraparound" mortgage at 14%. The new loan "wraps around" the existing $30,000 mortgage, adding $20,000 to it. You make all your payments to the second lender or the seller, who then forwards payments for the first mortgage. You'll, in effect, be paying the equivalent of 10% on the $30,000 to the first lender, plus an additional 4% on this amount to the second lender, plus 14% on the remaining $20,000. Your total loan costs using this approach will be lower than if you obtained a loan for the full amount at the current rate (for example, 18%).

Wraparounds may cause problems if the original lender or the holder of the original mortgage is not aware of the new mortgage. Upon discovering this arrangement, some lenders or holders may have the right to insist that the old mortgage be paid off immediately.

10. Land Contract

Borrowed from commercial real estate, this plan enables you to pay below-market interest rates. The installment land contract permits the seller to hold onto his or her original below-market rate mortgage while "selling" the home on an installment basis. The installment payments are for a short term and may be for interest only. At the end of the contract the unpaid balance, frequently the full purchase price, must still be paid.

The seller continues to hold title to the property until all payments are made. Thus, you, the buyer, acquire no equity until the contract ends. If you fail to make a payment on time, you could lose a major investment.

These loans are popular because they offer lower payments than market rate loans. Land contracts are also being used to avoid the *due-on-sale clause* (see Appendix E). The buyer and seller may assert to the lender who provided the original mortgage that the due on sale clause does not apply because the property will not be sold until the end of the contract. Therefore, the low interest rate continues. However, the lender may assert that the contract in fact represents a sale of the property. Consequently, the lender may have the right to accelerate the loan, or call it due, and raise the interest rate to current market levels.

11. Buy-down

A buy-down is a subsidy of the mortgage interest rate that helps you meet the payments during the first few years of the loan. Suppose a new house sells for $150,000, that after a down payment of $75,000, you still need to finance $75,000, and that a 30-year first mortgage is available for 17%, which would make your monthly payments $1,069.26, or beyond your budget. However, a buy-down is available: for the first three years, the developer will subsidize your payments, bringing down the interest rate to 14%. This means your payments are only $888.65, which you can afford.

There are several things to think about in buy-downs. First, consider what your payments will be after the first few years. If this is a fixed rate loan, the payments in the above example will jump to the rate at which the loan was originally made —17%—and total more than $1,000. If this is a flexible rate loan, and the index to which your rate is tied has risen since you took out the loan, your payments could go up even higher.

Second, check to see whether the subsidy is part of your contract with the lender or with the builder. If it's provided separately by the builder, the lender can still hold you liable for the full interest rate (17% in the above example), even if the builder backs out of the deal or goes out of business.

Finally, that $150,000 sales price may have been increased to cover the builder's interest subsidy. A comparable home may be selling around the corner for less. At the same time it may well be the case that competition encouraged the builder to offer you a genuine savings. It pays to check around.

There are also plans called *consumer buy-downs.* In these loans, the buyer makes a sizable down payment, and the interest rate granted is below market. In other words, in exchange for a large payment at the beginning of the loan, you may qualify for a lower rate on the amount borrowed. Frequently, this type of mortgage has a shorter term than those written at current market rates.

12. Rent With Option to Buy

In a climate of changing interest rates, some buyers and sellers are attracted to a *rent-with-option* arrangement. In this plan, you rent property and pay a premium for the right to purchase the property within a limited time period at a specific price. In some arrangements, you may apply part of the rental payments to the purchase price.

This approach enables you to lock in the purchase price. You can also use this method to "buy time" in the hope that interest rates will decrease. From the seller's perspective, this plan may provide the buyer time to obtain sufficient cash or acceptable financing to proceed with a purchase that may not be possible otherwise.

13. Zero Rate and Low Rate Mortgage

These mortgages are unique in that they appear to be completely or almost interest free. The buyer makes a large down payment, usually one-third of the sales price, and pays the remainder in installments over a short term.

Suppose you want to buy a $90,000 home but you find the market interest rate unacceptable. You opt to use your savings to make the down payment, say $30,000, on a "zero rate" (or no-interest) mortgage. Then you pay a front-end finance charge—for example, 12% of the money you need to borrow, or about $8,400. You then agree to repay the principal ($60,000) in 84 monthly installments of $714.29. In 7 years, the loan will be paid off.

In these mortgages, the sales price may be increased to reflect the loan costs. Thus, you could be exchanging lower interest costs for a higher purchase price. Partly because of this, you may be able to deduct the prepaid finance charge and a percentage (for example, 10%) of your payments from your taxes as if it were interest.

14. Reverse Annuity Mortgage

If you already own your home and need to obtain cash, you might consider the reverse annuity mortgage (RAM) or *"equity conversion."* In this plan, you obtain a loan in the form of monthly payments over an extended period of time, using your property as collateral. When the loan comes due, you repay both the principal and interest.

A RAM is not a mortgage in the conventional sense. You can't obtain a RAM until you have paid off your original mortgage. Suppose you own your home and you need a source of money, you could draw up a contract with a lender that enables you to borrow a given amount each month until you've reached a maximum of, for example, $10,000. At the end of the term, you must repay the loan. But remember, if you do not have the cash available to repay the loan plus interest, you will have to sell the property or take out a new loan.

FIGURE C-1   HIGHLIGHTING THE ESSENTIALS OF CREATIVE FINANCING PLANS

Type	Description	Considerations
Fixed Rate Mortgage	Fixed interest rate, usually long-term; equal monthly payments of principal and interest until debt is paid in full.	Offers stability and long-term tax advantages; limited availability. Interest rates may be higher than other types of financing. New fixed rates are rarely assumable.
Flexible Rate Mortgage	Interest rate changes are based on a financial index, resulting in possible changes in your monthly payments, loan term, and/or principal. Some plans have rate or payment caps.	Readily available. Starting interest rate is slightly below market, but payments can increase sharply and frequently if index increases. Payment caps prevent wide fluctuations in payments but may cause negative amortization (see box, page 15). Rate caps, while rare, limit amount total debt can expand.
Renegotiable Rate Mortgage (Rollover)	Interest rate and monthly payments are constant for several years; changes possible thereafter. Long-term mortgage.	Less frequent changes in interest rate offer some stability.
Balloon Mortgage	Monthly payments based on fixed interest rate; usually short-term; payments may cover interest only with principal due in full at term end.	Offers low monthly payments but possibly no equity until loan is fully paid. When due, loan must be paid off or refinanced. Refinancing poses high risk if rates climb.
Graduated Payment Mortgage	Lower monthly payments rise gradually (usually over 5-10 years), then level off for duration of term. With flexible interest rate, additional payment changes possible if index changes.	Easier to qualify for. Buyer's income must be able to keep pace with scheduled payment increases. With a flexible rate, payment increases beyond the graduated payments can result in additional negative amortization (see box, page 15).
Shared Appreciation Mortgage	Below-market interest rate and lower monthly payments, in exchange for a share of profits when property is sold or on a specified date. Many variations.	If home appreciates greatly, total cost of loan jumps. If home fails to appreciate, projected increase in value may still be due, requiring refinancing at possibly higher rates.
Assumable Mortgage	Buyer takes over seller's original, below-market rate mortgage.	Lowers monthly payments. May be prohibited if "due on sale" clause is in original mortgage (see box, page 12). Not permitted on most new fixed rate mortgages.
Seller Take-back	Seller provides all or part of financing with a first or second mortgage.	May offer a below-market interest rate; may have a balloon payment requiring full payment in a few years or refinancing at market rates, which could sharply increase debt.
Wraparound	Seller keeps original low rate mortgage. Buyer makes payments to seller who forwards a portion to the lender holding original mortgage. Offers lower effective interest rate on total transaction.	Lender may call in old mortgage and require higher rate. If buyer defaults, seller must take legal action to collect debt.
Growing Equity Mortgage (Rapid Payoff Mortgage)	Fixed interest rate but monthly payments may vary according to agreed-upon schedule or index.	Permits rapid payoff of debt because payment increases reduce principal. Buyer's income must be able to keep up with payment increases.
Land Contract	Seller retains original mortgage. No transfer of title until loan is fully paid. Equal monthly payments based on below-market interest rate with unpaid principal due at loan end.	May offer no equity until loan is fully paid. Buyer has few protections if conflict arises during loan.
Buy-down	Developer (or third party) provides an interest subsidy which lowers monthly payments during the first few years of the loan. Can have fixed or flexible interest rate.	Offers a break from higher payments during early years. Enables buyer with lower income to qualify. With flexible rate mortgage, payments may jump substantially at end of subsidy. Developer may increase selling price.
Rent with Option	Renter pays "option fee" for right to purchase property at specified time and agreed-upon price. Rent may or may not be applied to sales price.	Enables renter to buy time to obtain down payment and decide whether to purchase. Locks in price during inflationary times. Failure to take option means loss of option fee and rental payments.
Reverse Annuity Mortgage (Equity Conversion)	Borrower owns mortgage-free property and needs income. Lender makes monthly payments to borrower, using property as collateral.	Can provide homeowners with needed cash. At end of term, borrower must have money available to avoid selling property or refinancing.
Zero Rate and Low Rate Mortgage	Appears to be completely or almost interest free. Large down payment and one-time finance charge, then loan is repaid in fixed monthly payments over short term.	Permits quick ownership. May not lower total cost (because of possibly increased sales price). Doesn't offer long-term tax deductions.

Appendix D
Some Pointers On Condo/Co-Op Buying (Or Selling) Process

As a growing number of renters in most major cities all across the United States are probably so well aware by now, recent years, more particularly the 1980's, have seen a tremendous growth in the number of condominium (condo) and cooperative types of housing units, either from conversion of existing stock of rental and commercial units, or from entirely new constructions. In deed, at one time in the mid 1980s so rapid was the growth, especially since 1977, that some authorities came to seriously believe that within twenty years, half the housing stock in the nation would consist of condos alone. In any event, whatever may ultimately turn out to be the case, one thing is already a fact: condo and coop housing are already a substantial force in the real estate world of the modern times in America. As one analyst summed it up,

> "Condos [and coops] are everywhere. They are here to stay. Directly or indirectly, they are becoming a part of everyone's life. Yours, too." Adding that: "There will continue to be young people and empty nesters who want the security and pride of homeownership without excess space to clean and maintain. There will continue to be people attracted to homes that give them recreational facilities they could never otherwise afford ... a sense of belonging and community.... And for the investor ... there is a source of wealth and security no simple annuity could ever match."*

---

*Robert Natelson in "How To Buy and Sell a Condominium" pp. 15 & 160.

Hence, in this chapter, we'll highlight a few facts and procedures of home transfers that particularly relate to the condo/coop type of housing. For, true, the procedures involved in the buying or selling of a condo or a coop are by and large identical to those outlined in Chapters 5 and 6 of the manual concerning the buying or selling of 'regular' dwelling homes. There are, nevertheless, some important differences of concepts and details between them that are worthy of elaboration.

A. What is a Cooperative Apartment?

A cooperative apartment (commonly called "co-op" for short) is an apartment (or a housing unit) located within a building that is owned by a ***Cooperative Corporation.*** The system essentially works this way: When a building is "converted" into a cooperative, the converted building is sold by the building's owner to a cooperative corporation—a new or separate corporation formed to take over the ownership of the newly converted building. The Cooperative Corporation now becomes, in other words, the landlord (owner) of the entire building and the coop apartments within it. Now, as is the case with any corporation, the Cooperative Corporation (the new landlord) is, in turned, owned by its stockholders—that is, by those who elect to buy shares in the corporation. The shares of the corporation which each shareholder would own is the proportion of the total shares of the corporation he or she buys or owns.

How do you buy or get to become an owner (tenant) of a cooperative apartment? *In a cooperative, you do not actually "buy" your particular apartment. Rather, you merely buy a certain number of shares in the cooperative corporation that is allocated to a particular apartment and that apartment then becomes yours.* (Factors such as the location and size of each apartment unit are used to determine how many shares an apartment should be alloted). Once purchased, ownership of the shares of the cooperative corporation entitles you, the purchaser, to a long-term lease *(a "proprietary" lease)* for your new apartment. The proprietary lease document, in turn, is what defines your rights and obligations regarding the possession, use and occupancy of the apartment.

The governing and policy-making body in a co-op situation is ***the Board of Directors*** of the cooperative corporation. This Board is composed of a group of people elected by the owners of the shares of the corporation, with each cooperative apartment owner having a vote proportional to the number of shares he or she owns. Basically, it's the board's primary responsibility (or, more typically, the responsibility of the real estate management firm the board hires for that) to operate the building and collect the maintenance charges from each unit owner, and to see to the overall day-to-day functioning of the co-op complex.

The rules, regulations and procedures for conducting the affairs of the cooperative, and for defining the rights and obligations of each apartment owner (and of board members), are detailed in two basic places:
   i) in the tenant's **proprietary lease,** and
   ii) in **the By-Laws** of the cooperative corporation.

> **NOTE:** These two key documents should always be painstakingly read, re-read and analyzed by every would-be co-op buyer before deciding to sign up.

B. What is a Condominium?

In a word, a condominium unit (commonly called "condo" for short) is an apartment (or a housing unit) within a building wherein each tenant <u>owns</u> his or her particular unit or apartment. Technically speaking, when a building is "converted" into a condominium ownership, the entire complex or development is a condominium. The buyer of an apartment unit within that complex buys basically two things: i) the apartment itself; and ii) an undivided interest (a fractional portion) of the common areas and facilities of the complex, such as the land on which the building stands, the lobby, stairways, and hallways, the tennis courts, the clubhouse (if any), and the heating, electrical and mechanical systems.

Unlike the situation with a co-op, there is no intermediary corporation which "owns" the apartment units in a condominium set-up, and there's no proprietary lease for each apartment. *The buyer in a condo situation directly OWNS his or her apartment.*

Here's how a condo (or co-op) conversion system generally works: The landlord of a rental apartment or commercial building who rents out the units to individual tenants soon discovers (or believes) that he's finding it difficult to meet the costs of maintaining and keeping up the building at the prevailing rent levels. And, given the rental laws, he knows he can't just raise his rents at will to a level he feels he needs to match such costs. So, what does he do? He simply files a document with the appropriate state authorities that changes the building into a condominium (or, as the case may be, a cooperative). This, then, enables him to sell each apartment as a separate entity (often at a handsome profit), and to turn over the management of the building to a "condominium association," thereby relieving himself of the responsibility of being a landlord.

The governing and policy-making body in a condominium situation is called the ***Board of Managers.*** This Board is composed of a group of people elected by the shareholders or owners of the individual apartments in the building. This Board functions in a manner very similar to the Board of Directors of a cooperative corporation, and must act in accordance with the powers granted it under a document called the ***"Condominium Declaration."*** The Declaration, which the condominium developer is usually required to have on file with the local county clerk's office, is considered the most important document in condo purchase deals. It's an elaborate document: it sets up the condo project, defines the common elements, describes how the development is to be managed, etc. Basically, the board's primary responsibility (or, more typically, the responsibility of the real estate management firm the board hires for that) is to handle the day-to-day operations of running the building—that is, to see to the maintenance of the public parts of the condo complex, to provide heat, hot water, electricity for the hallways and elevators, remove garbage, and provide other services pertaining to the common areas.

The rules, regulations and procedures for conducting the affairs of the condominium, and for defining the rights and obligations of unit owners, are detailed in the By-laws of each condominium. *(**Any would-be condo buyer would be well advised to read, re-read and analyze this document and the Condo Declaration most painstakingly before deciding to sign up).***

C. The Main Differences Between Co-ops and Condos

Cooperatives and condominiums are different from each other in many important ways. *Here are some of the most important differences:*

1. In a cooperative, it is the Cooperative Corporation (or, at times, the homeowners association) that officially owns the entire building complex, not the tenants; but in a condominium, it is the tenants themselves that actually own their individual apartment units (plus, of course, a fractional portion of the building's common areas and facilities).

2. In a cooperative set-up, each tenant is a stockholder in the cooperative corporation and merely holds a "proprietary lease" on his apartment from the corporation. The corporation (not the individual occupants) holds the building mortgage; the occupant pays enough "rents" to the corporation to meet his share of the common "maintenance charges"—real estate taxes, the mortgage expenses on the building, fuel charges, payroll for the building employees, and other costs of operating the building, in addition to his share of the loan financing expenses on an individual apartment.

A condominium resident (or owner), on the other hand, directly obtains and holds in his own name, the mortgage to his unit, and is directly responsible to the lender for repaying the mortgage loan. All of the apartment owners in a condominium are responsible, each for a proportional share, for the "common charges" for operating the building—the fuel costs, payroll for building employees and the like.

3. In a cooperative set-up, the cooperative corporation being the official owner of the complex, is the entity that directly pays the real estate taxes. In a condominium situation, on the other hand, each condominium owner is separately responsible for paying his or her own separate share of the real estate taxes on the entire building, based on his proportionate interest in the common areas.

With respect to income tax planning, owning a co-op apartment is commonly viewed by tax experts as a device that provides some unique tax advantages—advantages similar to those enjoyed by owners of single family homes. The cooperative apartment owner (who shall have, of course, met the relevant federal tax law require-ments) could deduct the following expenses in his annual tax returns: i) that part of his maintenance charge costs which went to pay the interest on the building's mortgage; ii) his part of the real estate taxes paid by the cooperative corporation; and iii) the interest (not the principal) he pays on a loan he took out to purchase the shares for his co-op apartment.

The condominium owner may, also, deduct from his taxable income the real estate taxes he pays on the build-ing, as well as the interest.

5. Overall, owning a condominium is said to involve a little less risk to the tenant than owning a co-op apart-ment. This is because, since each condo owner has direct title to his own apartment, and is separately responsible for his mortgage and taxes, the financial misfortune of one apartment owner (such as his inability to pay his mortgage, taxes or rent) does not threaten everyone else's apartment unit. With a co-op, on the other hand, one unit owner may encumber the entire property; when a few tenants are behind in their rent, everyone else's unit can be threatened by foreclosure. (As a practical matter, when co-op tenants are not able to meet their monthly charges, it's customary for the management to require the remaining tenants to absorb an extra charge to make up for the non-paying tenants, as a way of avoiding placing the entire co-op complex in jeopardy).

6. Finally, there are some differences in the process by which tenants of the two types of accomodation could be evicted. To evict a tenant from a cooperative (say, for failure to meet his monthly charges), the board of directors playing the role of the landlord's representative, would have to take the tenant to the housing court for a Warrant of Eviction—the same as in any regular eviction case in a landlord-tenant situation. To evict a dweller in a condominium situation, on the other hand (for failure, for example, to pay his mortgage), the move would generally come, not from the governing board, but from the banks or other lenders in a *"foreclosure"* action—as in any regular foreclosure case where the object for a lender of the mortgage money is to seize the borrower's house itself, and to sell it to satisfy the outstanding mortgage.

D. Buying a Co-op Apartment

Increasingly, conversion of rental buildings into co-ops or condos in an already tight rental market like New York City is becoming a major area of contention between tenants occupying the building to be converted and the landlord who seeks to convert. To protect tenants from being unduly subjected to displacement hardships or sudden forcible evictions by developers who might be bent on making a quick financial killing from conversions, the governments of most localities have often enacted certain laws and procedures to control the conduct of developers in conversions.

For New York State dwellers, for example, the statute provides that a detailed prospectus be furnished to prospective buyers, and that a "full and fair" disclosure of all relevant facts be made. It requires that the "spon-sor" (same thing as the "builder", "developer" or "landlord") of a plan to convert a building must first furnish each tenant in present occupancy with the offering plan, commonly called a preliminary ***Prospectus*** or a *'red herring'*. This preliminary prospectus* is basically a preliminary application to covert to which the sponsor attaches the various supporting legal documents and financial details explaining the terms of the proposal; it basically alerts the tenants that the proposed conversion plan has not been accepted by the government for filing and, more importantly, that the information contained in that conversion plan is still subject to suggestions by tenants and others alike to supplement or modify it.

---

*The Preliminary Prospectus is usually a long, detailed report with several supporting documents, running at times to over 150 pages. The N.Y. version of the law requires that certain information must be included in such documents, for example: a schedule that lists each apartment as to whether it is rent stabilized, rent controlled or decontrolled, as well as the purchase price and the estimated monthly maintenance charges and tax deduction for each apartment; an inspection report of the building from an independent licensed engineer or architect; details of the 'subscription agreement' (the contract to purchase the apartment which each prospective purchaser will get); a description of the various rights of tenants who reside in the building for each category of tenants; a statement as to whether the plan is an "eviction" plan or a "non-eviction" one; the proposed legal documents by which the converted building will be governed. e.g., the proprietary lease (in the case of a co-op), and the by-laws, etc.

Hence, if you are making the purchase of the coop apartment directly from the developer, and it is not a resale, then *the single most important thing you must do is to carefully and thoroughly examine the prospectus*—on information about a variety of matters, such as the corporate charter, the by-laws, contract of sale by the promoters of the corporation, ground lease, construction contracts, management agreements, mortgages, etc.

And in situations where the purchase is a resale case? Additionally, review the official corporate minutes *of* the Cooperative Corporation for at least the last 2 years. You'll find planned or contemplated expenditures for improvements or other proposals which might cause a rise in maintenance charges in the future; and you might find other facets of the corporation's management which might be of interest to you.

Examine copy of the proprietary lease to be given, or to be assigned to you, and look particularly at those provisions concerning assignment and subletting.

There'll probably be restrictions on both without a prior consent of the corporation. There might be buy-back provision, giving the corporation the privilege of first refusal.

Closely allied to the matter of restrictions on transfer, is the matter of restrictions on mortgaging the buyer's interest. These could be crucial and should be examined carefully. Is corporate consent required for the possible sale on foreclosure? Is corporate consent required for the mortgaging?

The tax status of the corporation should be investigated since one of the buyer's objectives will be the deduction on his income tax of real estate tax and interest. Is 80% of its gross income derived from tenant-stockholders—one of the requirements for qualification as a "cooperative housing corporation" under IRS Code Section 216. [Get a certification from the corporation in the form of an Affidavit, stating, among other things, that the corporation is not in default in the payment of taxes, interest, or any other obligations.]

As a purchaser, you'll be purchasing shares of stock in the coop corporation; the number of shares is allocated to the apartment according to its relative value. With ownership of this block of shares goes the right to a proprietary lease of the specific apartment to which they appertain. As a Buyer, then, you'll be both an assignee of the stock and of the lease. Hence, you must *order a combined title search to be made on each of these elements:* **1)** the title to the securities; 2) the underlying title to the apartment building; 3) the land on which it stands; and 4) the title to the leasehold.

[A standard, pre-printed form used for coop sales, is "Contract For Sale of Cooperative Apartment," on pp. 172-4.]

NOTE: Readers may order a copy of this form (or an equivalent one for your state) directly from Do-It-Yourself Legal Publishers. To order, turn to p. 191 for an Order Form.

E. Buying a Condo Housing Unit

One obvious significant distinguishing feature—and an advantage—of the condo over the coop, is the fact that the condo unit, being that it is separately owned, can be separately financed. The owner has to apply independently for his own mortgage, and he has only his own mortgage payments to keep up—no blanket mortgage for the entire housing complex.

A condominium unit is transferred from one owner to another by an ordinary deed (such as the ones on pp. 175-8). However, the deed (the same also, as to the lease of the condominium units) must include a description of the land on which the building is located, and the liber, page, and date of recording of the Condominium Declaration, and the like.

[A standard, pre-printed form used for condo sales, is "Contract For Sale of Condominium Apartment," on pp. 175-8. Blank copies of the form may be obtained from The Legal Publishers, see the Order Form on p. 191.]

W 123—Revised Contract of Sale of Cooperative Apartment.
Approved by The Cooperative Housing Lawyers Group.

COPYRIGHT 1972 BY JULIUS BLUMBERG, INC.,

[NEVER MIND THIS LAWYERS' IDEA] CONSULT YOUR LAWYER BEFORE SIGNING THIS INSTRUMENT

CONTRACT OF SALE—COOPERATIVE APARTMENT

CONTRACT OF SALE OF
COOPERATIVE APARTMENT

Agreement made as of the _____ day of _____ 19___

between _____

residing at _____

and _____ hereinafter called "Seller"

residing at _____

hereinafter called "Purchaser".

WITNESSETH:

SHARES
1. Seller agrees to sell and transfer and Purchaser agrees to buy (i) _____ shares (the "Shares") of

(the "Corporation") allocated to Apartment _____ (the "Apartment") in the cooperative apartment building located at

LEASE
and (ii) the Seller's interest, as tenant, in the proprietary lease, as amended (the "Lease"), for the Apartment, which Lease is appurtenant to the Shares.

PERSONAL PROPERTY
2. (a) Subject to the rights of the landlord under the Lease and any holder of a mortgage to which the Lease is subordinate, this sale includes all of the Seller's right, title and interest, if any, in and to:

Strike out Inapplicable Items (i) the refrigerators, ranges, dishwashers, kitchen cabinets and counters, lighting and plumbing fixtures, air-conditioning equipment and other fixtures and articles of property attached to or appurtenant to the Apartment, except those listed in subparagraph (b) of this Paragraph 2;
(ii)

(b) Excluded from this sale are:
(i) furniture and furnishings, and
(ii)

The property referred to in Paragraph 2(a)(i) and 2(a)(ii) may not be purchased if title to the Shares and the Lease is not closed hereunder.

PRICE
3. The purchase price is $
payable as follows: $
by check, subject to collection, on the execution and delivery of this agreement; $_____ in cash, cashier's check or by unendorsed certified check of Purchaser drawn on a local bank or trust company, to the order of Seller, to be delivered at the closing.

WARRANTIES
4. Seller represents, warrants and covenants that: a) Seller is the sole owner of the Shares, the Lease and the property referred to in paragraph 2(a)(ii); the same are and will at closing be free and clear of liens, encumbrances and adverse interests, subject to the matters, if any, affecting the title to the real property of which the Apartment is a part; and Seller has the full right and power to sell and transfer the same; (b) the Shares were duly issued and fully paid for and are non-assessable; (c) the maintenance (rent) payable on the date hereof is at the rate of $_____ a month and at the date of closing will be fully paid to said date; (d) Seller has not received any written notice of any intended assessment or increase in said maintenance (rent) not reflected in the figure set forth in subparagraph (c); (e) the Lease is and will at closing be in full force and effect; (f) Seller is not and will not become indebted for labor or material which might give rise to the filing of a notice of mechanic's lien against the building in which the Apartment is located; (g) there are and will at closing be no violations of record which the tenant would be obligated to remedy under the terms of the Lease; (h) Seller is not a Sponsor or a nominee of a Sponsor under any plan of cooperative organization affecting this Apartment.

The representations and warranties contained in this Paragraph 4 and in Paragraph 14 shall survive the closing but any action based thereon must be instituted within one year from the date of closing.

NO OTHER REPRESENTATIONS
5. Purchaser has examined and is satisfied with the certificate of incorporation, the by-laws of the Corporation and the form of the Lease, or has waived the examination thereof. Purchaser has inspected the Apartment, its fixtures, appliances and equipment and the personal property, if any, included in the sale, and knows the condition thereof, and agrees to accept the same "as is", i.e., in the condition they are in on the date hereof subject to normal wear and tear. Purchaser has examined or waived examination of the last audited financial statement of the Corporation, and has considered or waived consideration of all other matters pertaining to this agreement and to the purchase to be made hereunder, and does not rely on any representations made by any broker or by Seller or anyone acting or purporting to act on behalf of Seller as to any matters which might influence or affect the decision to execute this agreement or to buy the Shares, the Lease, or said personal property except those representations and warranties which are specifically set forth in this agreement.

—OVER—

REQUIRED APPROVAL

6. This sale is subject to the approval of the directors or shareholders of the Corporation as provided in the Lease or the corporate by-laws. Purchaser agrees to submit to Seller or to the Corporation's managing agent, within five (5) days after the execution and delivery hereof the names and addresses of persons to whom, or banks or corporations to which,

REFERENCES reference may be had as to Purchaser's character and financial standing, and thereafter to attend [and to cause Purchaser's spouse to attend] one or more personal interviews, as requested by the Corporation, and submit to the Corporation or its managing agent such further references and information as are commonly asked for in such transactions. If any of the aforementioned references are submitted to Seller, Seller shall promptly redeliver same to the Corporation or its managing agent. Seller may, but shall not be required to, take any steps in connection with the procurement of such approval. Seller shall promptly notify Purchaser of such approval or of the refusal thereof upon receipt of notice thereof. In the event of such refusal, this agreement shall thereby be deemed cancelled. If approval or refusal be not received by Seller or Purchaser at or before the closing, either may by notice given to the other on or before the date fixed in paragraph 10 for the closing, adjourn the closing for a period not to exceed thirty (30) days for the purpose of obtaining such approval, and if the party who has adjourned the closing is unable to obtain approval of this sale within said period of time, this agreement shall ipso facto be deemed cancelled. If this agreement is cancelled as provided in this Paragraph, all sums theretofore paid to Seller by Purchaser on account of the purchase price shall be returned without interest to Purchaser and both parties shall be relieved from all further liability hereunder.

SALE AFTER APPROVAL; ASSUMPTION

7. If approval of this sale be granted, Seller agrees to transfer and assign to Purchaser the Lease, the Shares and the personal property, as in this agreement provided, and Purchaser agrees to pay the purchase price and to assume, with respect to obligations arising from and after the time of the closing, all of the terms, covenants and conditions of the Lease on the part of the lessee thereunder to be performed, and to be bound by the by-laws of the Corporation and the rules and regulations, if any, from time to time promulgated by the Corporation. To that end Purchaser shall execute and deliver to the Corporation at the closing an agreement containing such assumptions in the form requested or approved by the Corporation, and, if requested by the Corporation, a new proprietary lease for the balance of the lease term shall be executed by Purchaser and the Corporation and the Lease being assigned by Seller shall be surrendered for cancellation.

REMOVAL OF SELLER'S PROPERTY

8. Seller shall, prior to the closing, remove from the Apartment all the household furniture, furnishing and other personal property not included in this sale, and shall repair any damage caused by such removal, and shall deliver possession of the Apartment at the closing, broom-clean.

RISK OF LOSS, ETC.

9. (a) The risk of loss or damage to the Apartment, or to the property included in this sale in accordance with Paragraph 2, by fire or other cause, until the time of the closing, is assumed by Seller, but without any obligation on the part of Seller, except at Seller's option, to repair or replace any such loss or damage. Seller shall notify Purchaser of the occurrence of any such loss or damage within five (5) days after such occurrence or by the date of closing, whichever first occurs, and by such notice shall elect whether or not Seller will repair or replace the loss or damage and if Seller elects to do so, that he will complete the same within the sixty (60) day period hereinafter referred to. If Seller elects to make such repairs and/or replacements, then Seller's said notice shall set forth an adjourned date for the closing, which shall be not more than sixty (60) days after the date of the giving of Seller's notice. If Seller does not elect to make such repairs and/or replacements, or if Seller elects to make them and fails to complete the same on or before said adjourned closing date, Purchaser shall have the following options:

(i) to declare this agreement cancelled and receive a refund, without interest, from Seller of all sums theretofore paid on account of the purchase price; or

(ii) to complete the purchase in accordance with this agreement without reduction in the purchase price except as provided in the next sentence. If Seller carries hazard insurance covering such loss or damage, Seller shall turn over to Purchaser at the closing the net proceeds (after legal and other expenses of

collection) actually collected by Seller under the provisions of such hazard insurance policies to the extent that they are attributable to loss of or damage to any property included in this sale; if Seller has not received such proceeds Seller shall assign (without recourse to Seller) Seller's right to any payment or additional payments from Seller's said insurance which are attributable to the loss of or damage to any property included in this sale, less any sums theretofore expended by him.

(b) If Seller does not elect to make such repairs and/or replacements, Purchaser may exercise the resulting option under (i) or (ii) of (a) only by notice given to Seller within five (5) business days after Purchaser's option arises. If Seller elects to make such repairs and/or replacements and fails to complete the same on or before the adjourned closing date, Purchaser may exercise the resulting options within five (5) business days after the adjourned closing date.

10. The closing documents referred to in Paragraph 11 shall be delivered, and payment of the balance of the purchase price shall be made, at the closing to be held on

19   at   M., at the office of

CLOSING DOCUMENTS

11. At the closing: (a) Seller shall deliver to Purchaser:

(i) Seller's certificate for the Shares, duly endorsed for transfer, or accompanied by a separate duly executed stock power, with necessary stock transfer stamps attached and in either case, with any guarantee of Seller's signature required by the Corporation;

(ii) Seller's duplicate original of the Lease and a duly executed assignment thereof to the Purchaser in the form requested or approved by the Corporation;

(iii) Certificate of the secretary of the Corporation or other evidence of the consent of the Corporation or its directors to the transfer of the Shares and Lease to Purchaser in accordance with the applicable provisions of the Lease or the corporate by-laws;

(iv) If requested, a statement by the managing agent that the maintenance and any special assessments then due and payable to the Corporation have been paid to the date of the closing;

(v) If requested, a bill of sale in customary form transferring the property referred to in Paragraph 2(a);

(vi) Keys to the outer doors of the Apartment.

(b) Purchaser shall deliver to Seller and the Corporation, together with the payment of the balance of the purchase price, the duly executed agreements and/or new lease referred to in Paragraph 7 hereof.

PROCESSING FEE

12. (a) Seller shall, at the closing, pay the processing fee, if any, charged by the managing agent for its services in connection with the approval of this sale and the transfer of the Shares and the Lease and the legal fee of the Corporation's attorney, if any, in connection with such transfer. Purchaser shall pay (i) the sales and transfer taxes, if any, on this sale, other than the transfer stamps provided for in Paragraph 11 (a)(i) and (ii) the cost of title search if required by the Corpora-

APPORTIONMENTS tion. (b) The parties shall at the closing apportion, as of midnight of the day preceding the date of actual closing, the rent under the Lease, and utility charges, if any, due the Corporation. Assessments will not be apportioned but will be payable by the party who is the Owner when the same become due and payable.

PRIOR LEASE TERMINATION

13. If prior to the closing the Corporation shall elect to cancel and terminate the Lease under any option or privilege reserved therein for any reason except Seller's default, this agreement shall thereupon become a nullity and Seller shall be deemed to be unable to convey the Lease and the Shares and Seller shall refund to Purchaser, without interest, all sums theretofore paid on account of the purchase price.

BROKER

14. Purchaser represents to Seller that Purchaser has not dealt with any brokers in connection with this transaction other than

and Seller agrees to pay said broker a commission.

DEFAULTS, REMEDIES

15. If Purchaser defaults hereunder, Seller's sole remedy shall be to retain as liquidated damages the down payment mentioned in Paragraph 3, it being agreed that Seller's damages in case of Purchaser's default might be impossible to ascertain and that the down payment constitutes a fair and reasonable amount of damages in the circumstances. If Seller willfully defaults, Purchaser shall have such remedies as he is entitled to at law or in equity, including but not limited to specific performance because the Apartment and possession thereof cannot be duplicated.

ENTIRE AGREEMENT

16. All representations, understandings and agreements had between the parties with respect to the subject matter of this agreement are merged in this agreement which alone fully and completely expresses their agreement.

NO ASSIGNMENT BY PURCHASER

17. This agreement cannot be changed, discharged or terminated orally. Purchaser may not assign this agreement or any of his rights hereunder.

SELLER'S EXCULPATION

18. Notwithstanding any contrary provisions of this agreement, express or implied, or any contrary rule of law or custom, if Seller shall be unable to transfer the Lease and the Shares in accordance with this agreement and any conditions hereof, then the sole obligation and liability of Seller shall be to refund to Purchaser, without interest, all sums theretofore paid on account of the purchase price, and upon the making of such refund this agreement shall be deemed cancelled and shall wholly cease and terminate, and neither party shall have any further claim against the other by reason of this agreement. However, nothing contained in this paragraph shall be construed to relieve Seller from liability due to a misrepresentation or wilful default.

NOTICES

19. All notices or demands ("Notice") that must or may be given or made hereunder shall be in writing and sent by certified or registered mail, return receipt requested, to the address above set forth for the party to whom the Notice is given, or to such other address for such party as said party shall hereafter designate by Notice given to the other party pursuant to this paragraph. Each Notice shall be deemed given on the next business day following the date of mailing the same.

MARGIN HEADINGS

20. The margin headings are intended only for convenience in finding the subject matter and do not constitute part of the text of this agreement and shall not be considered in the interpretation of this agreement or any of its provisions.

Note:
Either strike this paragraph because there is no financing condition to the transaction or complete the paragraph as required.

FINANCING CONDITION

21. A. The obligations of Purchaser hereunder are subject:
(a) to the issuance of a commitment letter by   a commercial bank, savings bank, savings and loan association or insurance company doing business in the State of New York to Purchaser, on or before   , 19   (a copy of which letter shall be furnished to Seller promptly after receipt thereof), pursuant to which the institution agrees to lend not less than $, at a rate of interest not to exceed   % per annum, for a term of at least   years solely upon the security of a pledge, security interest or assignment of, and/or mortgage on, the Shares and the Lease, in order to enable Purchaser to consummate the transaction provided herein;

(b) to the consent of the Corporation to the loan if such consent is required by the terms of the Lease or the by-laws of the Corporation and to the execution by the Corporation of an agreement, in form and substance satisfactory to the institution and the Corporation, for the protection of the institution's rights as a lender; and

(c) to the closing of the loan on or before the date fixed in Paragraph 10 for the closing.

B. Purchaser shall apply for the loan, shall furnish to the institution, within five (5) days of the date hereof, accurate and complete information on Purchaser and members of Purchaser's family, as required, shall advise Seller of the name and address of the institution to which such application has been made and the date upon which it was made and shall cause to be furnished to the Corporation, for its consideration, as soon as practicable, the agreement proposed to be made by the institution with the Corporation. Purchaser shall pay or reimburse Seller the fees charged by the Corporation and its counsel for reviewing and negotiating the aforesaid agreement.

C. Purchaser shall accept any commitment letter complying with the terms of subparagraph A(a) hereof, if issued, shall pay any application, appraisal, commitment or other fees in respect of the loan, and shall comply with the requirements of the commitment letter other than those relating to the Corporation.

D. Provided that Purchaser shall have fulfilled all of Purchaser's obligations under subparagraph B hereof, if the aforementioned commitment letter is not issued by the date provided for in subparagraph A(a) hereof, Purchaser shall have the right to terminate this agreement on Notice given not more than five (5) days thereafter, or if the other conditions provided for in subparagraph A   hereof are not met, Purchaser shall have the right to terminate this agreement on Notice to Seller, and in either such event all sums theretofore paid on account of the purchase price shall be returned without delay and without interest to Purchaser, and all parties hereto shall be relieved of and from any further liability hereunder.

IN WITNESS WHEREOF, the parties hereto have duly executed this agreement the day and year first above written.

....
Seller

....
Seller

....
Purchaser

....
Purchaser

CONSULT YOUR LAWYER BEFORE SIGNING THIS INSTRUMENT

NEVER MIND THIS — THE LAWYERS' IDEA!

CONTRACT OF SALE OF RESIDENTIAL CONDOMINIUM UNIT

Contract of Sale of Residential Condominium Unit, dated [1] _____

between [2] _____

("the Seller," whether one or more)

and [3] _____

("the Buyer," whether one or more).

1. The Parties

1.1. More than one buyer. If there is more than one buyer, their interests shall be as [4] joint tenants with right of survivorship, unless they are husband and wife, in which case their interests shall be as tenants by the entirety.

Unless otherwise specified in a notice mailed no less than 5 business days prior to the Closing, the deed shall be drawn in accordance with the provisions of this paragraph.

1.2. Assignability. The Buyer's interest in this contract is [5] assignable. In any event, no assignment shall be effective unless it expressly includes all interest in the Down Payment as well as any claim arising from the negotiations leading to this contract. Any otherwise ineffective assignment shall be effective at the Seller's option.

1.3. Successors. Except as otherwise stated, (a) this contract is for the benefit of and binding on all successors in interest of each party, and (b) any reference to a party includes that party's successors in interest.

2. The Property Sold

2.1. Sale of Unit. The Seller sells to the Buyer, and the Buyer buys from the Seller, the residential condominium unit ("the Unit") designated as Unit [6] in the building known as [7] in the [8] condominium ("the Condominium"), together with its [9] per cent interest in the common elements of the Condominium, as described in the declaration recorded on [10] in [11] County at [12] liber(s) page(s) [13] ("the Declaration"). The unit includes [14] rooms [15].

2.2. Appliances, etc., included in sale. The sale includes the following as now located in or used in connection with the Unit ("the Personal Property"):

All installed carpeting
All installed drapery hardware
All mantels and wall and door mirrors
All shades and venetian blinds
All screens and screen doors
All storm windows and doors
All chandeliers and lighting fixtures, including bulbs

[16]	Refrigerator(s)
[17]	Freezer(s)
[18]	Range(s)
[19]	Wall oven(s)
[20]	Garbage disposal unit(s)
[21]	Dishwasher(s)
[22]	Clothes washer(s)
[23]	Clothes dryer(s)
[24]	Window air conditioner(s)
[25]	Through-the-wall air conditioner(s)
[26]	Dehumidifier(s)
[27]	Fan(s)
[28]	Pump(s)
[29]	Sauna(s)
[30]	

2.3. Other items included in sale. Insofar as related to the Unit, the sale also includes whatever ownership interests the Seller may have in (1) plumbing, heating, electrical and other central systems, (2) non-escrowed funds and other property held by the board of managers, (3) unit-owners associations, (4) beds of streets, highways, lakes and streams, and (5) unpaid awards due to any change of grade or other taking or damage by governmental authority.

2.4. Items not included in sale. The sale does not include:

Contents of the Unit that are neither attached to it nor included under Paragraph 2.2.
[31]

2.5. Existing Mortgage. The sale is subject to a mortgage ("the Existing Mortgage") originally in the amount of [32] $ [33] , now held by and the present principal balance of which is stated in Subparagraph 3.1.2. If that blank is not filled in, all references to "the Existing Mortgage" shall be disregarded. As to the Existing Mortgage, a current full copy of which has been supplied to the Buyer, the Seller shall (a) agree to no modification, (b) make all required payments, and (c) make no other payments. If required payments reduce the principal balance below the amount stated in Subparagraph 3.1.2, the amount of that reduction shall be paid to the Seller at the Closing.

2.6. Title exceptions. The sale is subject to the following, none of which shall constitute a ground for rejecting title, for canceling this contract, or for an abatement in the purchase price:

2.6.1. Zoning and other laws and governmental regulations, unless violated by the Condominium's existing structures or their present use.

2.6.2. Any state of facts an accurate survey would show.

2.6.3. Consents for the erection of any structures on, under or above any street or highway.

2.6.4. Encroachments (a) upon other units or the common elements due to settling and (b) of fences, stoops, areas, trim, cornices and similar items upon any street or highway.

2.6.5. Customary utility easements.

2.6.6. The Declaration and all matters referred to in the Declaration.

2.6.7. The by-laws and rules and regulations of the Condominium and any power of attorney given to the board of managers.

2.6.8. Any matter that a title insurance company would ordinarily insure against without additional premium.

2.6.9. Any lien for which the Buyer is allowed a credit under Paragraph 3.4.

2.6.10. Any matter of which the Buyer or the Buyer's attorney shall have received knowledge and shall not have specified in a notice mailed by the later of (a) the 10th business day after receipt or (b) the 10th business day before the Closing.

2.6.11. [34]

—OVER—

2.7. Seller's obligations. Unless otherwise stated, the [41] by the Seller's attorney on forms then customarily in use. The Seller shall see to it that:

2.7.1. At the time of the Closing:

2.7.1.1. The Condominium shall have been validly formed under Real Property Law article 9-B and the Unit shall be legally occupiable for residential purposes.

2.7.1.2. The Existing Mortgage (if any) shall be in good standing and not callable as a result of the sale, and there shall be no other liens on the Unit.

2.7.1.3. No right of first refusal applicable to the sale shall be outstanding, provided that the Buyer, if requested to do so, shall have submitted applications, attended interviews and otherwise fully cooperated in seeking to bring about a waiver or termination of any right of first refusal.

2.7.1.4. The Personal Property shall be fully paid for and free of encumbrances.

2.7.1.5. No pre-contract violation shall be outstanding against the Unit.

2.7.1.6. All required approvals shall have been received from the board of managers and governmental agencies for any alterations or additions to the Unit.

2.7.1.7. No assessment or major increase in common charges shall be established or pending against the Unit due to improvements, acquisitions, claims against the board of managers or otherwise. However, the Seller shall not be responsible for any matters of which the Seller was not, and upon reasonable inquiry would not have been, aware prior to the date of this contract.

2.7.2. At the time of delivery of possession:

2.7.2.1. The Unit shall be broom clean, reasonably odor free, empty of all contents not included in the sale, and free of occupancies.

2.7.2.2. All appliances included in the sale and, to the extent within the Seller's control, the plumbing, heating, electrical and other systems shall be in good working order, faucet drips and similar minor items excepted.

2.7.2.3. There shall be no unpaid obligations affecting the Unit under the emergency repairs provisions of the New York City Administrative Code.

2.8. Transfer expenses. The Seller shall bear the following expenses of the sale (payment to be made in the required form, and both parties to execute any applications, tax returns or other required documents):

2.8.1. Documentary stamps on the deed.

2.8.2. Any other sales or transfer taxes.

2.8.3. Any payments required by the board of managers, its agents or attorneys, except that the Buyer shall bear any portion that would not be required if the sale were all cash.

2.9. Access. Upon reasonable notice to the Seller, by telephone or otherwise, the Buyer shall be afforded access at reasonable hours, up to 3 times, in order to inspect the Unit and the Personal Property, to take measurements, and for similar purposes.

3. Payments

3.1. The price. The purchase price is the total shown below and is payable as follows:

3.1.1. On signing of this contract by check subject to collection delivered to the escrow holder ("the Down Payment")   [35] $........................

3.1.2. By taking subject to the Existing Mortgage (which amount may be reduced as provided in Paragraph 2.5)   [36] $........................

3.1.3. By promissory note secured by a mortgage of the Unit   [37] $........................

3.1.4. At Closing (which amount may increase if the Existing Mortgage is reduced)   [38] $........................

3.1.5. Total ....   [39] $_____

3.2. Form of payment. Unless otherwise agreed to in writing by the Seller or the Seller's attorney: (1) payments shall be made (a) in cash (but not over [40] $1,000   ), (b) by check drawn by the Buyer, or (c) by official check of a lending institution; and (2) any check shall be either (a) payable to the order of the Seller or (b) only if the Buyer is one or more individuals, payable to the order of the Buyer and endorsed to the order of the Seller in the presence of the Seller or the Seller's attorney. Except for checks aggregating not more than [41] $500   , all checks drawn by the Buyer shall be certified.

3.3. Purchase money mortgage. Any note and mortgage to be given as part of the purchase price shall be drawn

by the Seller's attorney on forms then customarily in use. The Buyer shall pay all the expenses of that mortgage, including (a) recording charges, (b) mortgage recording taxes, (c) any additional fees imposed by the board of managers, its agents, or attorneys, and (d) a fee in the amount of [42] $150 to the Seller's attorney. If the Buyer's interest in this contract has been assigned, the note shall be signed by both the Buyer and the original Buyer.

3.4. Credit for liens. The Buyer shall be allowed a credit for liens on the Unit as provided in this paragraph. This paragraph shall apply to a lien only if (a) in favor of the board of managers, a governmental authority or a lending institution, (b) immediately satisfiable by the payment of a sum of money, and (c) specified in a notice mailed by the Seller not less than 5 business days before the Closing. The notice shall be effective only if it sets forth a computation of the credit to be allowed to the Buyer and is accompanied by official bills or other supporting documents sufficient to establish the applicability of this paragraph. The computation shall (a) be based upon the assumption that payment will be made on the third business day after the Closing and (b) include all interest, penalties, recording and filing fees, title company charges, fees payable to the lienor's attorney, and other amounts that must be paid in order to discharge the lien.

3.5. Credit for payments for Seller. If requested to do so by notice mailed not less than 5 business days before, the Buyer shall at the Closing (a) pay on behalf of the Seller any items specified in the notice and (b) be allowed a credit therefor.

3.6. Limitation on credits. Paragraphs 3.4 and 3.5 shall not apply to the extent that the credits would exceed the amount payable by the Buyer at the Closing.

4. The Closing

4.1. Time. The Closing shall be at [43]   .M. on [44]   Time is [45] not of the essence.

4.2. Place. The Closing shall be at [46] the office of the Seller's attorney.

However, if the Buyer is financing part of the purchase price by a mortgage on the Unit, the lender may designate any place that is not more than [47] 90   minutes in one-way driving time from the Unit.

4.3. Possession. The Seller shall deliver possession at and as a condition to the Closing. However, if the following blanks are filled in, (a) possession need not be delivered until noon of the [48]   day after the Closing, (b) the purchase price shall in any event be reduced by [49] $, (c) the Seller shall refund to the Buyer an additional [50] $ for each day or portion of a day that the Seller fails to deliver possession after that time, and (d) in order partially to secure (but not in limitation of the amount of) that refund, [51] $ of the Down Payment shall be retained in escrow after the Closing, to be paid in accordance with the foregoing to the Seller, the Buyer or both. Nothing contained in this paragraph shall be construed as creating a landlord-tenant relationship. The Seller shall at the time of delivery of possession turn over all keys relating to the Unit and associated use of the common elements.

4.4. Apportionments. Insofar as related to the Unit, (a) the Seller shall show to what extent the following items have been paid and (b) they shall be apportioned as of the midnight before the Closing:

4.4.1. Interest on the Existing Mortgage (if any).

4.4.2. Real estate taxes, on the basis of the fiscal period for which assessed (unless a different method is established by local custom). If the Closing takes place before the tax is fixed, the apportionment shall be based on the latest rate and the latest assessed valuation.

4.4.3. Water charges and sewer rents, on the basis of the applicable fiscal period, except that, if there is a meter for the Unit, the Seller shall obtain a reading not more than 30 days before the date then fixed for the Closing and it shall be assumed that consumption continued at the same rate.

4.4.4. Common charges and unit-owners association dues.

4.4.5. Fuel, if any. A letter from the supplier shall be a sufficient basis for estimating the amount on hand and its value, including sales tax.

4.4.6. The following transferable memberships, rights, guarantees and service contracts: [52]

4.4.7. [53]

–OVER–

176

4.5. To be done by Seller. At the Closing, the Seller shall:

4.5.1. Deliver a usual [54] bargain and sale

deed sufficient to convey to the Buyer the fee simple of the Unit, free of all encumbrances and defects except as specifically otherwise provided. The deed shall comply with Real Property Law §339-o and shall contain [55] a covenant against grantor's acts and the covenant required by Lien Law §13(5). If a corporation, the Seller shall establish compliance with Business Corporation Law §909.

4.5.2. Deliver bills of sale, stock certificates, guarantees and other documents sufficient to transfer to the Buyer all other ownership interests provided for in this contract.

4.5.3. Turn over to the Buyer all certificates of occupancy, permits, Board of Fire Underwriters certificates and similar documents in the Seller's possession relating to the Unit and, if available, a certificate of insurance under any master policy insuring the Condominium.

4.5.4. At the option of the Seller, assign to the Buyer any transferable escrow deposits pertaining to the Unit made with the board of managers or the holder of the Existing Mortgage.

4.5.5. Furnish a recordable certificate (or, as provided in Real Property Law §274-a, a letter), signed not more than 30 days earlier by the holder of the Existing Mortgage (if any), setting forth the interest rate, the maturity date and the amount unpaid principal and interest.

4.5.6. Supply the necessary forms for any powers of attorney and other documents required by the board of managers.

4.5.7. Deliver such affidavits as to names, judgments, bankruptcies, and other matters as may reasonably be requested.

4.6. To be done by Buyer. At the Closing, the Buyer shall:

4.6.1. Make on behalf of the Seller any payments required by Paragraph 3.5.

4.6.2. Pay to the Seller the portion of the purchase price set forth in Subparagraph 3.1.4, adjusted as follows:

4.6.2.1. There shall be added the amount of (a) any amortization paid on the Exisiting Mortgage (if any) as provided in Paragraph 2.5 and (b) any assigned escrow deposits as provided in Subparagraph 4.5.4.

4.6.2.2. There shall be subtracted the amount of (a) any credits for unpaid liens and payments made on behalf of the Seller under Paragraphs 3.4 and 3.5 and (b) any price reduction provided for in Paragraph 4.3, assuming that possession will be delivered at the required time.

4.6.2.3. There shall be added or subtracted, as the case may be, the net amount of apportionments under Paragraph 4.4..

4.6.3. Deliver any note and mortgage to be given as part of the purchase price.

4.6.4. Deliver (and pay the costs of recording) any powers of attorney and other documents, and make any escrow deposits, required by the board of managers.

5. Remedies

5.1. Buyer's lien. All amounts paid by the Buyer under this contract, as well as costs incurred for title examination, searches, inspections and surveys, are made a lien on the Unit. The lien shall be automatically discharged if the Buyer materially fails to perform obligations under this contract.

5.2. Right to cancel for breach. If either party materially fails (whether by reason or inability or otherwise) to perform obligations under this contract, the other party shall have the right, by notice mailed within 10 business days of learning of such failure, to cancel this contract. If the canceling party is the Seller, the Down Payment shall belong to the Seller free of any claim by the Buyer. If the canceling party is the Buyer, the Seller shall pay to the Buyer all amounts referred to in Paragraph 5.1. In either case, neither party shall thereafter have any further rights under this contract.

5.3. Abatement of purchase price. If the Seller fails (whether by reason of inability or otherwise) to perform obligations under this contract and this contract is not canceled by the Buyer, the Buyer may accept such performance as the Seller shall give (whether voluntarily or under legal compulsion) and the purchase price shall be abated accordingly. If the parties are unable to agree on the amount and source of the abatement, those matters (but no other) shall be determined by arbitration under the rules of the American Arbitration Association in effect at that time. Unless otherwise agreed by the parties or provided for in the arbitrators' award, the abatement shall come first from the money portion of the purchase price (including the Down Payment) and next from any purchase money mortgage.

5.4. Impairment of common elements. If, as to the common elements, at the time of the Closing (a) there is a substantial title defect or encumbrance not referred to in this contract, (b) there is outstanding a substantial pre-contract violation

not disclosed in this contract, (c) a material portion has been taken by governmental authority after the date of this contract, or (d) there is substantial uninsured or unrepaired damage that occurred after the date of this contract, the Buyer may cancel this contract and receive a return of the Down Payment, after receipt of which neither party shall have any further rights under this contract. The right to cancel under this paragraph shall be the Buyer's exclusive remedy as to matters pertaining only to the common elements and not to the Unit.

5.5. Notice of right to cancel. Except as expressly provided, this contract is subject to the Uniform Vendor and Purchaser Risk Act (General Obligations Law §5-1311). If it appears that the Buyer will have a cancelation right under that Act or under Paragraph 5.4, the Seller may mail a notice setting forth the facts and advising that there is an immediate right of cancelation. If the Seller does so, the Buyer's right will be deemed to have been waived unless exercised by notice mailed within 10 business days thereafter.

5.6. Limitation of Seller's obligations. In the absence of fraud, no claim shall be made by the Buyer on account of (a) any matter that would ordinarily be covered by title insurance if obtained or (b) any other matter under Paragraph 2.7 unless asserted in a notice mailed on or before the [56] 180th day after the Closing.

5.7. Right of first refusal. The Seller has advised the Buyer that the board of managers does [57]   have a right of first refusal applicable to the sale. If the preceding sentence states that there is a right of first refusal, (a) the Seller shall take all necessary steps to secure an early determination as to whether or not it will be exercised and (b) if it is exercised, the Down Payment shall be refunded to the Buyer, after which neither party shall have any further rights under this contract.

5.8. Other remedies. Except as expressly provided, this contract shall not preclude any remedy available to either party.

6. Mortgage Contingency

6.1. Buyer to apply for loan. If the blanks in this paragraph are filled in, the Buyer shall promptly and diligently attempt to obtain a satisfactory mortgage commitment. "Satisfactory mortgage commitment" means a commitment in customary form issued by a lending institution to make a [58] conventional mortgage loan to the Buyer (a) in the amount of [59] $ (or any lesser amount stated in an application made by the Buyer), (b) bearing interest at an annual rate of [60]   per cent (or any greater rate stated in an application made by the Buyer), (c) payable over a period of [61]   years (or any lesser period stated in an application made by the Buyer), and (d) secured by a lien on the Unit. At the time of making each application, the Buyer shall send the Seller a copy.

6.2. Contingency period. "Contingency period" means the period ending [62]   or any other period established under Subparagraph 6.4.1.

6.3. Buyer's obligation. If the Buyer has not obtained a satisfactory mortgage commitment by the end of any contingency period, the Buyer shall within [63] 5 business days thereafter mail notice of that fact. If the Buyer fails to do so, it shall be conclusively presumed that the Buyer obtained a satisfactory mortgage commitment on the last day of that contingency period.

6.4. Seller's options. Within [64] 5 business days after any notice given under Paragraph 6.3, a notice may be mailed by the Seller electing to do one of the following:

6.4.1. Establish a new contingency period to end on a date stated in the notice, which date shall be not less than [65] 2 nor more than [66] 4 weeks after the notice. However, the Seller may not establish more than [67] 3 additional contingency periods.

6.4.2. Elect to accept a purchase money mortgage on the terms described in Paragraph 6.1.

6.4.3. Attempt for up to [68] 60 days to secure a satisfactory mortgage commitment on behalf of the Buyer, in which event the Buyer shall pay all application costs and otherwise fully cooperate with the Seller. If unsuccessful, the Seller may, by notice mailed within [69] 5 business days after the end of the period, elect to accept a purchase money mortgage on the terms described in Paragraph 6.1.

6.5. Seller's failure to elect. If the Seller fails to make an election under Paragraph 6.4, this contract shall automatically terminate and the Buyer shall be entitled to a refund of the Down Payment, after receipt of which neither party shall have any further rights under this contract.

6.6. Satisfaction of contingency. If a satisfactory mortgage commitment is obtained, this contract shall be binding as if this Article 6 had not been written. Either party, upon learning from the lender that a satisfactory mortgage commitment has been obtained, shall promptly mail a notice so stating.

7. The Broker

7.1. Buyer's representation. The Buyer represents that the Buyer dealt with no broker in connection with the sale [70] other than

("the Broker").

7.2. Seller's obligation. The Seller shall pay the Broker as the Broker's sole compensation a commission of [71] $, or, if the preceding blank is not filled in, as provided in a separate agreement. However, no commission shall be payable unless the Closing either takes place or is prevented by the Seller's wilful default.

7.3. Broker's agreement. By signing below, the Broker (a) agrees to Paragraph 7.2, (b) represents that the Broker is the sole broker that brought about the sale, and (c) agrees to indemnify the Seller against any loss caused by the assertion of claims by other brokers, including reasonable attorney fees.

8. Escrow

8.1. Acceptance of escrow. The escrow holder is [72] the Seller's attorney.
By signing below, the escrow holder agrees to hold and disburse all escrow amounts in accordance with this contract.

8.2. Responsibility of escrow holder. All escrow amounts shall be deposited in a noninterest-bearing special bank account in the escrow holder's own name and not commingled with the escrow holder's personal funds. The escrow holder is acting as a stakeholder only and in the absence of bad faith shall not be liable for any action or inaction. In the event of a threatened dispute, the escrow holder may be relieved of responsibility for the disputed amount by paying it into court.

8.3. Payment after Closing. Except for any portion remaining in escrow under Paragraph 4.3, the escrow holder shall pay the Down Payment to the Seller promptly after the Closing.

8.4. Payment upon direction. The escrow holder shall make prompt payment to either party in accordance with any notice received from the other. If either party is entitled to receive any amount and the other party without good cause and after proper demand refuses to direct the escrow holder to pay that amount, the refusing party shall be liable for all damage caused by the refusal, including reasonable attorney fees.

9. Other Provisions

9.1. Attorneys. The name and address of the Seller's present attorney is [73]

and the name and address of the Buyer's present attorney is [74]

If there is any change in the identity or address of the attorney for either party, that party shall promptly mail the other party notice of that fact. Until actual receipt of such notice, the other party shall be entitled to rely upon previous information as to such matters.

9.2. Notices. Unless otherwise stated, all notices shall be (a) in writing, (b) signed by either the party (or one of the persons constituting that party) or the attorney for that party,

(c) dated on the day actually mailed, (d) addressed to the attorney for the other party, (e) sent by registered or certified mail, return receipt requested, and (f) deemed given on the day mailed.

9.3. Documents. All documents shall be delivered to the other party fully executed and, where appropriate, acknowledged and otherwise in proper form for recording. In addition to documents specifically referred to, each party will, at or after the Closing, deliver any further documents reasonably requested to carry out the intention of this contract, provided that they are either furnished by the requesting party or already in the possession of the delivering party.

9.4. Proof of entitlement. A party required to satisfy a condition or seeking a payment, credit or apportionment shall provide satisfactory proof. Except to the extent that that party has already received a benefit, a party need give no payment, credit or apportionment on account of any expenses incurred, or any escrow deposit or other payment made, in bad faith or in an excessive amount or at an unreasonably early date.

9.5. Meaning of certain words used. Unless otherwise clearly indicated by the context, as used in this contract:

9.5.1. "This contract" includes any annexed schedules and riders.

9.5.2. "Sale" means the transaction agreed to in this contract.

9.5.3. "Closing" means the date of actual closing of the sale, whether the date originally fixed or any advanced or adjourned date.

9.5.4. "Business day" means any day that is not a Saturday, a Sunday or a holiday under New York or Federal law.

9.5.5. "Lending institution" means an organization doing business in the State of New York that is a bank, trust company, savings and loan association or insurance company.

9.5.6. "Unit-owners association" means any organization, whether or not incorporated, whose membership is essentially limited to owners of units in the Condominium or in condominiums located in the vicinity.

9.5.7. "Pre-contract violation" means a violation of law or municipal ordinance, order or requirement recorded or otherwise noted in writing by a governmental agency before the date of this contract. It shall not include any other violation, whether or not due to conditions existing before that date.

9.5.8. "Includes" means "includes (but is not limited to)" and "including" means "including (but not limited to)."

9.5.9. The plural includes the singular and the singular includes the plural.

9.5.10. Words defined in Real Property Law §339-e have the meanings therein set forth.

9.6. No other agreements. All prior understandings and agreements between the parties are merged in this contract. The Buyer has inspected the Unit and other property included in the sale, is acquainted with their present physical condition, and, except as otherwise stated in this contract, agrees to accept them in that condition, "as is," subject to reasonable use, wear, tear and natural deterioration prior to delivery. Neither party is relying upon any statement whatever, made by any person whatever, unless set forth in this contract. Neither party shall be entitled to rely upon any change in this contract unless contained in a writing signed by the other party.
[75]

The Buyer

....

....

Article 7 is agreed to.

_____
                                      Broker

STATE OF NEW YORK, COUNTY OF [76]   ss.:
On [77]   before me personally
came [78]

to me known to be the individual(s) described in and who executed the foregoing contract of sale, and the individual(s) duly acknowledged to me execution of the same.

....
                                      Notary Public

The Seller

....

....

Article 8 is agreed to. Receipt of check for the Down Payment is acknowledged.

_____
                                   Escrow Agent

STATE OF NEW YORK, COUNTY OF [79]   ss.:
On [80]   before me personally
came [81]

to me known to be the individual(s) described in and who executed the foregoing contract of sale, and the individual(s) duly acknowledged to me execution of the same.

....
                                      Notary Public

Appendix E
GLOSSARY OF REAL ESTATE TERMS

Abstract of Title	A short history of a piece of property, tracing its chain of ownership (title) through the years, plus a record of all liens, taxes, judgments or other encumbrances that may impair the title. Your title insurance company reviews the abstract to make sure the title comes to a buyer free of any defects (problems).
Acceleration Clause	A provision in a mortgage or trust deed that may require the unpaid balance of the mortgage loan to become due immediately, if the regular mortgage payments are not made, or if other terms of the mortgage are not met.
Access Right	The right of an owner or lessee to freely go to and from his or her property.
Accord & Satisfaction	An agreement or a document settling a claim or a suit.
Acknowledgment	A declaration before a person qualified under the law to administer oaths, to the effect that a document or a deed is the act of the person who signed it.
Acre ft.).	A piece of land measuring 43,560 square feet (i.e., about 208.71 ft. by 208.71
Act of God	An accident which could not have been foreseen or prevented, such as those caused by earthquakes, severe storms, and the like.
Ad Valorem	A latin phrase meaning "according to value."
Advance Commitment	A written offer by a lender to make a mortgage loan at a stated interest rate over a specific number of years.
Adverse Possession	The physical occupancy or possession of property in spite of, and in defiance of, someone else's legal title. If such possession continues for twenty years, legal title can be claimed by the one in possession.
Affidavit	A written statement, sworn to before a notary public or other officer authorized to administer oaths.
Agreement of Sale	A contract between seller and purchaser stating the terms and conditions of sale. (See also Purchase Agreement)
Alienation	The transfer of property from one person to another.
Amortization	A method of paying off the principal owed on a loan in regular installments (as opposed to making the entire payment in one lump sum on a certain date).
Appraisal	An estimate of the market value of a home—that is, what it would sell for under normal conditions. 'Market value' is almost never the same as replacement cost, so an appraisal made by a lender is not adequate for insurance purposes.

Appraiser	A professional who charges to estimate the market or replacement value of a house.
Appreciation	An increase in the value of a piece of property, not including the added value of the property made by extensions and improvements. A property may appreciate in dollar value simply because of inflation, or in real value because of limited housing availability, improved neighborhoods, etc.
Assessed Value	The value of a property as determined by the tax assessor for the purpose of collecting property taxes. The assessed value is usually a fixed percentage of either the market value or the most recent purchase price.
Assessment	A special tax due for a special purpose and charged to a specific group of homeowners who are benefiting from a municipal improvement (for example, a sewer tax, street tax, etc.); may also refer to the value placed on property for purpose of taxation.
Assumption of Mortgage	The promise by the buyer of property to be legally responsible for the payment of an existing mortgage. The purchaser's name is substituted for the original mortgagor's (borrower's) name on the mortgage note and the original mortgagor is released from the responsibility of making the mortgage payments. Usually the lender must agree to an assumption.
Attachment	The seizure of property by court order.
Balloon Payment	When the final payment on an installment loan is larger than the preceding payments and it pays the debt in full, it is called a balloon payment.
Bench Mark	A permanent marker placed in the ground by the city to help surveyors establish property lines. Also known as a 'monument.'
Binder	A simple contract between a buyer and a seller which states the basic terms of an offer to purchase property. It is usually good only for a limited period of time, until a more formal purchase agreement is prepared and signed by both parties.
Blanket Mortgage	A simple mortgage which covers several pieces of real estate.
(Real Estate) Broker	A person licensed by the state to arrange the purchase or sale of land or real property, acting as intermediary between buyer and seller, and often between buyer and lender. Also known as a real estate agent.
Buy-down	See p. 163 of the manual.
Carrying Charges	What it actually costs for a homeowner to maintain his home—including the mortgage payments, taxes, and general maintenance.
Certificate of Title	A written opinion by an attorney that his examination of land records has established a clear ownership of property.
Chattel Mortgage	The creation of a loan on personal property as security for payment on a real estate loan.
Chattels	Goods, or any other type of property, which are not real property (real property generally includes land, and whatever is erected or growing upon it).
Closing	The final step in the sale and purchase of a property, when the title is transferred from the seller to the buyer; the buyer signs the mortgage, pays the settlement costs; and any money due the seller or buyer is handed over.

Closing Costs	The various expenses, over and above the actual sale price of the property, involved in arranging a real estate transfer.
Cloud on the Title	Any condition which may affect the title to property, usually a minor matter which can be settled with a quitclaim deed or court judgment. (See Title Defect)
Commission	A real estate agent's or broker's compensation for his services, usually a percentage of the selling price or rental and is spelled out in the Purchase (Sales') Agreement.
Community Property	In some states, a form of ownership under which property acquired <u>during</u> a marriage is presumed to be owned jointly unless acquired as separate property of either spouse.
Conditional Commitment	A promise to insure (generally with FHA loans) payment of a definite loan amount on a particular piece of property for a buyer with a satisfactory credit rating.
Condominium	Individual ownership of an apartment in a multi-unit project or development, and a proportionate interest in the common areas outside the apartment.
Contractor	A person or company who agrees to furnish materials and labor to do work for a certain price.
Conventional Loan	A mortgage loan which is not insured by FHA or guaranteed by VA.
Conveyance	The transfer of the title (that is, evidence of ownership) of property by deed from one person to another.
Cooperative (Apartment)	An apartment building or group of housing units owned by all the residents (generally a corporation) and run by an elected board of directors for the benefit of the residents. The resident lives in his unit but does not own it—he owns a share of stock in the corporation.
Covenant	A promise or agreement between two parties usually applied to specific promises in a deed.
Credit Rating	A rating or evaluation made of one's financial standing by a person or company (such as a Credit Bureau), based on one's present financial condition and past credit history.
Credit Report	A report usually ordered by a lender from a credit bureau to help determine a borrower's credit rating.
Deed	A written document by which the ownership of property is transferred from the seller (the grantor) to the buyer (the grantee).
Deed of Trust	In some states, generally those west of the Mississippi River, a document used instead of a mortgage. It transfers title of the property to a third party (the trustee) who holds the title until the debt or mortgage loan is fully repaid to the lender, at which time the title (ownership) passes to the borrower. If the borrower defaults (fails to make payments), the trustee may sell the property at a public sale to pay off the loan.
Deed (Quitclaim Deed)	A deed which transfers only that title or right to a property, if any, that the holder of that title has at the time of the transfer. A quitclaim deed does not warrant (or guarantee) a clear or definite title.
Deed (Warranty Deed)	A deed which guarantees that the title to a piece of property is free from any title defects.

Default	Failure to make mortgage payments on time, as agreed to in the mortgage note or deed of trust. Generally, if a payment is 30 days late, the mortgage is technically in default, and it may give the lender the right to start foreclosure proceedings.
Defeasance Clause	The clause in a mortgage which gives the borrower the right to regain clear ownership of his property upon full payment of his obligation to the lender.
Defect of Record	Any lien or encumbrance upon a title which is part of the public record.
Delinquency	The state of a mortgage payment being past due.
Deposit	A sum of money given to bind a sale of real estate—also called **'earnest money.'**
Depreciation	A loss or decrease in the value of a piece of property due to age, wear and tear, or unfavorable changes in the neighborhood; opposite of appreciation.
Discount	The difference between the normal dollar amount of a loan and the lesser amount which is actually given to the borrower. This difference is usually charged in "points" to the borrower.
Documentary Stamps	In some states a tax, in the form of stamps, required on deeds and mortgages when real estate title passes from one owner to another. The amount required differs from one state to another.
Down Payment	The money a buyer must pay in cash on a house before being granted a loan.
"Due on Sale" clause	A provision often stipulated in a mortgage loan contract, which gives the lender the right and option to require full and immediate repayment of the entire balance you still owed on the loan—at any future time when you ever sell or transfer the property. Here's an example of a typical due-on-sale clause: "If all or any part of the property or an interest therein is sold or transferred by Borrower without Lender's prior written consent.... Lender may, at Lender's option, declare all the sums secured by this Mortgage to be immediately due and payable."
Earnest Money	(See Deposit)
Easement	The right to use land owned by another. For instance, the electric company has easement rights to allow their power lines to cross another's property.
ECOA	Equal Credit Opportunity Act—a federal law that requires lenders to loan without discrimination based on race, color, religion, national origin, sex, marital status, or income from public assistance programs.
Eminent Domain	The government's right to acquire property for necessary public or quasi-public use.
Enroachment	The building of a structure or improvements which trespass on the property of another person.
Encumbrance	Anything that limits the interest in a title to property, such as a mortgage, a lien, an easement, a deed restriction, or unpaid taxes.
Equity	A buyer's initial ownership interest in a house and the increases thereof as he pays off a mortgage loan. When the mortgage is fully paid, the owner has 100% equity in his house.
Equity of Redemption	The right of an owner to regain his or her property during a foreclosure action for nonpayment.
Escalation Clause	A clause in a contract which allows the adjustment of certain items (such as the size of a monthly mortgage payment) in certain circumstances.
Escrow	Money or documents held by a neutral third party until all or certain specified conditions of a contract are met.

Escrow Agent	The third party responsible to the buyer and seller or to the lender and borrower for holding the money or documents until the terms of a purchase agreement are met.
Escrow Payment	That part of a borrower's monthly payment held by the lender to pay for taxes, hazard insurance, mortgage insurance, and other items until they become due. Also known as **'impounds'** or **'reserves'** in some states.
Exclusive Agency Listing	A document giving one agent the right to sell a piece of property for a certain period of time, but reserving the right of the owner to sell the property himself without paying a commission.
Exclusive 'Right to Sell' Listing	A document which gives an agent the right to collect a commission if the property is sold by anyone during the term of the agreement, regardless of who found the buyer.
Fee Simple	The most complete ownership of land, one without any known limitations on the owner's right to dispose of the property as he or she chooses.
FHA	Federal Housing Administration—a division of the U.S. Department of Housing and Urban Development (HUD). Its main activity is to insure home mortgage loans made by private lenders.
FmHA	Farmers Home Administration—a government agency (part of the Department of Agriculture) which provides financing to farmers or other qualified buyers (usually in rural areas) who are unable to obtain loans elsewhere.
Finance Charge	The total of all charges one must pay in order to get a loan.
Firm Commitment	An agreement from a lender to make a loan to a particular borrower on a particular property. Also an FHA or private mortgage insurance company agreement to insure a loan on a particular property for a particular borrower.
Forbearance	The act of delaying legal action to foreclose on a mortgage that is overdue. Usually it is granted only when a satisfactory arrangement has been made with the lender to make up the late payments at a future date.
Foreclosure	The legal process by which a lender forces payment of a loan (under a mortgage or deed of trust) by taking the property from the owner (mortgagor) and selling it to pay off the debt.
Grantee	That party in the deed who is the buyer.
Grantor	That party in the deed who is the seller.
Guaranteed Loan	A loan guaranteed to be paid by the VA or FMHA in the event the borrower fails to do so (defaults).
Guaranty	A promise by one person to pay the debt of another if that other person fails to do so.
Hazard Insurance	Insurance which protects against damage caused to property by fire, windstorm, or other common hazard. Required by many lenders to be carried in an amount at least equal to the mortgage.
Hidden Defect	Any encumbrance on a title that is not given in the public record (e.g., unknown liens, forged documents, etc.).
HUD	The U.S. Department of Housing and Urban Development.
Impound	(See Escrow)

Installment	The regular payment that a borrower agrees to make to a lender on or by specified dates.
Instrument	A written legal document.
Insurance Binder	A document stating that an individual or property is insured, even though the insurance policy has not yet been issued.
Insured Loan	A loan insured by FHA or a private mortgage insurance company.
Interest	A charge paid for borrowing money, usually set as a percentage of the amount borrowed. Also used to refer to a right, share or title in property.
Joint Tenancy	An equal, undivided ownership of property by two or more persons. Should one of the parties die, his share of the ownership would pass to the surviving owners (right of survivorship).
Land Contract	A sales contract which allows the seller to retain title to the property until the buyer has paid the full purchase price.
Late Charge	An additional fee a lender charges a borrower if his mortgage payments are not made on time.
Lien	A hold or claim which someone has on the property of another as security for a debt or charge; if a lien is not removed (if debt is not paid), the property may be sold to pay off the lien.
Life Estate	Taking ownership of property for the lifetime of a given person (a "life estate"), after which the property goes, after the first person dies, to another designated person; an estate (property) meant for the use or enjoyment of the designated beneficiary only for the lifetime of the person.
Listing	Registering of property for sale with one or more real estate brokers or agents allowing the broker who actually sells the property to get the commission.
Loan Disclosure Note	Document spelling out all the terms involved in obtaining and paying off a loan.
Margin of Security	The difference between the amount of the mortgage loan(s) and the appraised value of the property.
Market Value	The amount of money that serious prospective buyers are likely to offer to pay for a piece of property at a given time.
Marketable Title	A title clear of any encumbrances or objectionable liens that might adversely affect an owner's ability to sell.
Mechanic's Lien	A lien which building contractors, suppliers, and workmen are allowed by state law to invoke for unpaid bills.
Monument	A fixed object established by surveyors to mark land locations.
Mortgage	A loan given especially for the purpose of buying real property; a lien on real property which home owner (borrower) gives his lender as security for the borrowed money.
Mortgage Interest Subsidy	A monthly payment by the Federal Government to a mortgagee (lender) which reduces the amount of interest the mortgagor (homeowner) has to pay to lender to as low as 4%, if the homeowner falls within certain income limits.
Mortgage Origination Fee	A charge by the lender for the work involved in the preparation and servicing of a mortgage request. Usually 1 percent of the loan amount.
Mortgagee	The lender who makes a mortgage loan.
Mortgagor	The person borrowing money for a mortgage loan.

Multiple Listing	A system in which a group of brokers (as opposed to one broker) have a right to sell a property which has been exclusively listed with them. The broker who had the original right to sell receives a portion of the commission if one of the others sells the property.
Net Listing	A listing arrangement which allows a broker to keep as compensation all sums received above a net price.
Note	A written and signed document in which a borrower acknowledges a debt and promises repayment.
Offset Statement	A statement by an owner of property listing the present status of all liens against that property.
Open-end Mortgage	A mortgage which allows a borrower to borrow additional money at a later time without paying the usual financing charges.
Open Listing	An arrangement which gives a broker the non-exclusive right to sell an owner's property. Open listings may be given to several agents and only the agent that sells the home is entitled to a commission.
Option (to buy)	An agreement granting a potential buyer the right to buy a piece of property at a stated price within a stated period of time.
Perfecting Title	The elimination of all claims against a title by payment or court judgment.
PITI	Principal, interest, taxes, and insurance (in FHA and VA loans paid to the bank each month).
Plat (or plot)	A map of a piece of land showing its boundaries, length, width and any easements.
Point(s)	An amount equal to 1% of the principal amount of a loan. Points are a one-time charge collected by the lender at closing to increase his return on the loan. In FHA or VA loans, the borrower himself is allowed to pay only a limited and designated number of points.
Prepaid Items	An advance payment, at the time of closing, for taxes, hazard insurance, and mortgage insurance, which is held in an escrow account by the lender.
Prepayment Penalty	A charge made by the lender if a mortgage loan is paid off before the due date. FHA does not permit such a penalty on its FHA-insured loans.
Principal	The amount of money itself borrowed, as differentiated from the interest and other finance charges which must be paid back on a loan.
Purchase Agreement	A written document in which a seller agrees to sell, and a buyer agrees to buy a piece of property, with certain conditions and terms of the sale spelled out, such as sales price, date of closing, condition of property, etc. The agreement is secured by a deposit or down payment of earnest money.
Quiet Title	A court action taken to establish title, often used to remove a cloud on the title.
Quitclaim Deed	(See Deed, Quitclaim)
Real Estate	Land and the structures erected or growing upon it. Also anything of a permanent nature such as trees, minerals, and the interest and rights in these items.
Real Estate Agent	An individual who can show property for sale on behalf of a seller, but who may not have a license to transact the sale and collect the sales commission.

Real Estate Broker	(See Broker-Real Estate)
Realtor	A real estate broker or an associate holding active membership in a local real estate board affiliated with the National Association of Realtors.
Recording Fees	The charge payable to a local or county land registry to put on public record the details of legal documents such as a deed or mortgage.
Redemption	Buying back one's property after a court-ordered sale.
Refinancing	The process of paying off one loan with the money (proceeds) from another loan.
RESPA	Real Estate Settlement Procedures Act—A federal law that requires lenders to send to the home mortgage borrower (within 3 business days) an estimate of the closing (settlement) costs. RESPA also limits the amount lenders may hold in an escrow account for real estate taxes and insurance, and requires the disclosure of settlement costs to both buyers and sellers at least 24 hours before the closing.
Restrictions	A legal limitation in the deed on the use of property.
Right of Rescission	That section of the **Truth-in-Lending Law** which allows a customer the right to change his/her mind and cancel a contract within 3 days after signing it. This right to cancel is in force if the contract would involve obtaining a loan, and if the loan would place a lien on the property.
Right of Way	An easement on property, where the property owner gives another person the right to pass over his land.
Sales Agreement	(See Purchase Agreement)
Sale-Leaseback	An arrangement in which the owner of a piece of property sells his land to another but retains the right to continue occupancy as a tenant under a lease.
Secondary Financing	A loan secured by a second mortgage or trust deed.
Security Agreement	The agreement between the lender (the secured party) and the debtor which creates the security interest (see below).
Security Interest	The interest of the creditor in the property of the debtor in any credit transaction.
Section	A piece of land in a government survey which contains 640 acres.
Settlement Costs	(See Closing Costs)
Severalty ownership	Owned by one person only; the sole owner.
Sheriff's Deed	A deed granted by a court as part of the forced sale of property (foreclosure) to satisfy a judgment.
Stamps	(See Documentary Stamps)
Subordination Clause	A clause in a second lien which recognizes the priority of prior (first) liens. First liens often have subordination clauses allowing prior claims by mechanic's liens.
Surety	One who guarantees the performance of another: a guarantor.
Survey	A map or plat made by a licensed surveyor showing the measurements of a piece of land; its location, dimensions, and the location and dimensions of any improvements on the land.
Tax Sale	The sale of property for non-payment of taxes.
Tenancy-by-the-Entirety	The joint ownership of property by a husband and wife in such a manner that if either one dies, his or her share of ownership goes to the remaining survivor.

Tenancy-in-Common	When property is owned by two or more persons with the terms creating a joint tenancy, but in such a manner that in the event one of the owners dies, his share of the property would not go to the other surviving owner automatically, but rather to his (the decedent's own) heirs.
Title	The rights of ownership of a particular property, and the documents which prove that ownership (commonly a deed).
Title Defects	An outstanding claim or encumbrance on property which affects its marketability (whether or not it can be freely sold).
Title Insurance	Special Insurance which usually protects lenders against loss of their interest in property due to legal defects in the title. An owner can protect his interest by purchasing separate coverage.
Title Search	An examination of public records to uncover any past or current facts regarding the ownership of a piece of property. A title search is intended to make sure the title is marketable and free from defects.
Truth-in-Lending	A federal law which provides that the terms of a loan (including all the finance charges) must be disclosed to the borrower before the loan is signed. It also contains a provision for the Right of Rescission.
Trust Deed	(See Deed of Trust)
Trustee	One who holds property in trust for another to secure the performance of an obligation.
Trustor	One who deeds his property to a trustee.
VA	Veterans Administration—The VA guarantees a certain proportion of a mortgage loan made to a veteran by a private lender. Sometimes called GI loans, these usually require very low down payments and permit long repayment terms.
Valuation	Estimated worth or price.
Vendee	A buyer.
Vendor	A seller.
Void	To have no effect; something that is unenforceable.
Waive	To relinquish a right to enforce or require something.
Warranty Deed	(See Deed, Warranty)
Wraparound Mortgage	A secondary mortgage arrangement in which the home buyer reimburses the seller for the seller's continuing pay off of his mortgage (presumably at a lower interest rate than would currently by available to the buyer).
Zoning	The legal power of a local municipal government (city or town) to regulate the use of property within the municipality.

Appendix F
HUD's Regional Offices

The Department of Housing and Urban Development (HUD) is the agency responsible for administering federal programs concerned with the nation's housing needs. HUD is divided into two sections: the Office of Fair Housing and Equal Opportunity, and the Office of Neighborhoods, Voluntary Associations and Consumer Protection. The Fair Housing office administers the fair housing program authorized by the Civil Rights Act of 1968, and is chiefly concerned with the housing problems of lower-income and minority groups. The Office of Neighborhoods exists to protect consumer interests in all housing and community development activities, and to enforce the laws regarding interstate land sales, mobile home safety standards, and real estate settlement procedures. For information, publications, advice, referrals, or complaints about local housing practices, contact the regional office nearest you.

Region I
(Conn., Maine, Mass., N.H., R.I., Vt.)
Tel. (617) 223-4066
Dept. of Housing and Urban Development • John F. Kennedy Bldg., Room 800 • Boston, Mass. 02203

Region 11
(N.J,N.Y., Puerto Rico, Virgin Islands)
Tel. (212) 264-8068
Dept. of Housing and Urban Development • 26 Federal Plaza • New York, N.Y. 10007

Region III
(Del. Md., Pa., Va., W. Va.)
Tel. (215) 597-2560
Dept. of Housing and Urban Development • Curtis Bldg.• 6th and Walnut Sts. • Philadelphia, Pa. 19106

Region IV
(Ala., Fla., Ga., Ky., Miss., N.C., S.C., Tenn.)
Tel. (404) 526-5585
Dept. of Housing and Urban Development • 1371-1375 Peachtree St., N.E. • Atlanta, Ga. 30309

Region V
(Ill., Ind., Mich., Minn., Ohio, Wis.)
Tel. (312) 353-5680
Dept. of Housing and Urban Development • 300 South Wacker Dr. • Chicago, Ill. 60606

Region VI
(Ark., La., N.M., Okla., Texas)
Tel. (214) 749-7401
Dept. of Housing and Urban Development • 1100 Commerce St. • Dallas, Texas 75242

Region VII
(Iowa, Kan., Mo., Neb.)
Tel. (816) 374-2661
Dept. of Housing and Urban Development Federal office Bldg. • 911 Walnut St., Room 300 • Kansas City, Mo. 64106

Region VIII
(Colo., Mont., N.D., S.D., Utah, Wyo.)
Tel. (303) 837-4513
Dept. of Housing and Urban Development•Executive Tower Bldg. • 1405 Curtis St. • Denver, Colo. 80202

Region IX
(Ariz., Calif., Guam, Hawaii, Nev.)
Tel. (415) 556-4752
Dept. of Housing and Urban Development • 450 Golden Gate Ave. • P.O. Box 36003 • San Francisco, Ca. 94102

Region X
(Alaska, Idaho, Ore., Wash.)
Tel. (206) 442-5414
Dept. of Housing and Urban Development•3003 Arcade Plaza Bldg. • 1321 Second Ave. • Seattle, wash. 98101

For General information
Office of Public Affairs • HUD • 451 7th St., S.W., Room 10132 • Washington, D.C. 20410

Appendix G
Some Relevant Bibliography

William R. Allen, *New York Real Esate Practices* (National Real Estate Institute, Redmond, Washington)

American Homeowners Foundation, *How To Sell Your Home Fast* (Arlington, VA)

Harley Bjelland, *How To Sell Your House Without A Broker* (Cornerstone Library, N.Y. 1979)

Richard F. Gabriel, *How To Buy Your Own House When You Don't Have Enough Money!* (Signet, New America Library, N.Y. 1982)

Federal Trade Commission, *The Mortgage Money Guide* (Washington, D.C.)

Earl C. Gottschalk Jr., "Picking the Wrong Mortgage Broker Can Become A Homeowner's Nightmare." *The Wall Street Journal,* 26 March 1992: C1, C18.

Kiplinger's Personal Finance Magazine, "Selling Your Home Do It Yourself?" (Feb. 1995), p. 86-9.

HALT, *Real Estate* (Washington, D.C.)

HSH Associates, *How To Shop For Your Mortgage* (Butler, N.J. 1989)

Robert Irwin, *The For Sale By Owner Kit* (Dearborn Financial Publishing, Chicago, IL)

Danielle Kennedy, *Double Your Income in Real Estate Sales* (John Wiley & Sons, N.J.)

Andrew J. McLean, *Investing in Real Estate* (John Wiley & Sons, N.J.)

Peter G. Miller, *How To Save Money When You Hire A Real Estate Broker,* (The Springhill Press, Silver Springs, MD)

Robert G. Natelson, *How To Buy and Sell A Condominium* (Simon & Schuster: 1981)

N.Y. Times, "Picking The Best Broker," Sunday Section 10, June 12, 1994; "Your Home: Haggling Do's and Dont's," Sun. Sec. 10, Aug. 7, 1994; "An Appellate Ruling Rekindles Disclosure Debate," Sun., April 24, 1994, Sec. D., p. 9.

Frank R. Pajares, *For Sale By Owner* (New Trend Publication, Tampa, FL)

Pete, Marwick, Mitchell & Co., *RESPA: The 1979-80 Evaluation, Vol. I: Executive Summary* (October 1980)

Alex Rachun, *How To Inspect The Older House* (N.Y. State College of Human Ecology, Cornell University, N.Y.)

Robert Schwartz, *The Home Owner's Legal Guide* (Collier, Macmillan Publishers, N.Y. 1965)

Martin M. Shenkman and Warren Boronson, *How To Sell Your House In A Buyer's Market* (John Wiley & Sons N.Y. 1990)

Edward Siegel, *How To Avoid Lawyers* (Ballantine Books, N.Y.: 1989)

Paulette Thomas, "Federal Data Detail Pervasive Racial Gap in Mortgage Lending," *The Wall Street Journal,* 31 March 1992: A1, A12.

U.S. Department of HUD, *House Buyer's Information Package: A Guide For Buying and Owning a House* (Washington, D.C.)

U.S. Department of HUD, *Questions About Condominium: What To Ask Before You Buy* (Washington, D.C.)

U.S. Department of HUD, *Wise Home Buying* (Washington, D.C.)

Appendix H
PUBLICATIONS FROM DO-IT-YOURSELF LEGAL
PUBLISHERS/SELFHELPER LAW PRESS

Please DO NOT tear out this page. Consider others!

The following is a list of publications from the Do-it-Yourself Legal Publishers/Selfhelper Law Press of America. (Customers: For your convenience, just make a photocopy of this page and send it along with your order. All prices quoted here are subject to change without notice.)

1. How To Draw Up Your Own Separation/Settlement Agreement Without, Before, Or During Marriage.
2. Tenant Smart: How To Win Your Tenant' Legal Rights Without A Lawyer (New York Edition)
3. How To Probate & Settle An Estate Yourself, Without The Lawyer's Fees ($35)
4. How To Adopt A Child Without A Lawyer
5. How To Form Your Own Profit/Non-Profit Corporation Without A Lawyer
6. How To Plan Your 'Total' Estate With A Will & Living Will, Without A Lawyer
7. How To Declare Your Personal Bankruptcy Without A Lawyer ($29)
8. How To Buy Or Sell Your Own Home Without A Lawyer Or Broker ($29)
9. How To File For Chapter 11 Business Bankruptcy Without A Lawyer ($29)
10. How To Legally Beat The Traffic Ticket Without A Lawyer (forthcoming)
11. How To Settle Your Own Auto Accident Claims Without A Lawyer ($29)
12. How To Obtain Your U.S. Immigration Visa Without A Lawyer ($29)
13. How To Do Your Own Divorce Without A Lawyer [10 Regional State-Specific Editions] ($35 each)
14. How To Legally Change Your Name Without A Lawyer
15. How To Properly Plan Your 'Total' Estate With A Living Trust, Without The Lawyers' Fee ($35)
16. Before You Say 'I Do' In Marriage or Co-habitation, Here's How To First Protect Yourself Legally
17. The National Home Mortgage Escrow Audit Kit (forthcoming) ($15.95)

Prices: Each book, except for those specifically priced otherwise, costs $25, plus $3.00 per book for postage and handling. New Jersey residents please add 6% sales tax. ***ALL PRICES ARE SUBJECT TO CHANGE WITHOUT NOTICE.***

- -

(CUSTOMERS: Please make and send a xerox copy of this page with your orders)

Order Form

TO: *Do-It-Yourself Legal Publishers* (Books Division)
60 Park Place,
Newark, NJ 07102

Please send me the following:

1._____copies of_____
2._____copies of_____
3._____copies of_____
4._____copies of_____

Enclosed is the sum of $_____to cover the order. *Mail my order to:*

Mr/Mrs/Ms/Dr._____
Address (include Zip Code please):_____
_____Zip_____

Phone No. and area code: (   )_____Job: (   )_____

*New Jersey residents enclose 6% sales tax.

IMPORTANT: Please do NOT rip out the page. Consider others! Just make a photocopy and send. And have you please completed our 'Readers Opinion Sheet' on p. 192?

Appendix I
ORDERING YOUR HOMEBUYING/SELLING FORMS

IMPORTANT: Please do NOT rip out the page. Consider others! Just make a photocopy and send.

For our readers' added concenience, the Do-It-Yourself Legal Publishers, the nation's original and leading self-help law books publisher, makes available to its readership an assortment of standard forms used in real estate sales and purchases.

Customers: For your convenience, just make a xerox copy of this page, and send it along with your order. All prices quoted here are subject to change without notice. **Only orders placed by mail will be honored, please.**

Order Form

TO: Do-it-Yourself Legal Publishers, *(Legal Forms Division)*
    60 Park Place #1013,   • Newark, NJ 07102

Please send me the following of the Legal Publisher's printed forms: [Prices: $11.50 for set of 2 copies, per form]

	Quantity	Price

Contracts/Agreements
B122 Purchase Offer & Acceptance (Binder) .... _____ x _____
P1125 Contract & Sale (Purchase)—Short Form .... _____ _____
A125 Residential Contract of Sale (Purchase)—Long Form...... _____ _____
3125 Contract & Sale (Purchase) for office, commercial & multi-family premises (all states)..... _____ _____
A311 Contract & Sale, with Subordination of Mortgage .... _____ _____
W123 Contract of Sale—Cooperative Apartment .... _____ _____
M124 Contract of Sale—Residential Condominum Unit .... _____ _____
T486 Real Estate Listing Contract Between Broker & Owner .... _____ _____

Deeds
M290 Warranty Deed (long form with Basic Covenants) .... _____ _____
P620 Warranty Deed (Basic Covenants, Mortg. Assumption) .... _____ _____
A291 Bargåin & Sale Deed, with covenant: long form .... _____ _____
T691 Bargain & Sale Deed, with covenant: short form .... _____ _____
A293 Quitclaim Deed: long form .... _____ _____
P694 Quitclaim Deed: short form .... _____ _____
A278 Executor's Deed: short form .... _____ _____

Mortgages and (Mortgaging) Notes or Bonds
A283 Mortgage: long form (1st Mortgage) .... _____ _____
P670 Mortgage: short form .... _____ _____
M671 Mortgage: long form .... _____ _____
A673 Mortgage, financial institution .... _____ _____
A367 (Subordinate) 2nd or 3rd mortgage .... _____ _____
M674 Mortgage, subordinate .... _____ _____
P676 Mortgage note, financial institution, escrow provisions .... _____ _____
T677 Mortgage note, FNMA/FHLMC .... _____ _____
P675 Mortgage note .... _____ _____
T174 Bond .... _____ _____
P686 Combined bond and mortgage: short form .... _____ _____

Enclosed is the sum of $_____ to cover the order, which includes $2.50 per set for shipping, plus local sales tax,* as applicable.

*New Jersey Residents enclose 6% sales tax.

Total...................... $_____
Shipping @2.50 per form...$_____
Sales Tax*.................$_____
Grand Total.............. $_____

Send this order to me:
Mr/Mrs/Ms/Dr_____ Address:_____
City & State_____ Zip_____ Tel. # ( )_____

READERS OPINION

The author (the Publisher as well) is interested in serving **YOU**, the reader, as he's deeply of the view that **YOU**, the consumer, are the KING or QUEEN! He'd love to know: Did this book meet your needs? Did it answer the more general, basic questions that you had; was it to the point? Most importantly, did it get the job done for you—of letting you make the sale or purchase on your property at a reasonable price? Are there other subjects you'd like him to write about? If you would like to express your views directly to the author, *please complete and return this sheet to: the author*, in care of the Publisher. And we'll make sure your opinion promptly gets directly to him. *Please use the reverse side, if you need extra space.* [**Please do <u>NOT</u> tear out the sheet; just make a photocopy and send that**]

1. The areas (subject matters, chapters, issues, etc.) this book covers that were of interest to me were:
_____

They were ____ were not____ covered in sufficient depth. _____

2. Areas not covered by this book that I would like to see are:
_____

3. The most helpful chapter(s) were: The Intro 1 2 3 4 5 6 Appendix A B C D Other:_____

4. The least helpful chapter(s) were: The Intro 1 2 3 4 5 6 Appendix A B C D Other:_____

5. The organization of the contents and writing style make the manual easy to read and use? Yes__No__
  (Explain/Elaborate:)
_____

6. What did you like the best about the book?_____
_____

7. The concept of do-it-yourself, self-help law you champion is: An excellent idea ____ A bad idea____ Why? *(Please elaborate)* _____

8. How would you improve the manual? _____
_____

9. My job/profession is: _____

10. I have completed 8-12____ 13-16____ over 16____ years of school.

11. My primary reason for reading this book was: _____

12. I bought or learned about the book through this bookstore or library (address in full, please):
_____

13. The book met my primary need in purchasing the book: Yes____ No____

14. It saved me appx. $_____ using the book to buy/sell a home without hiring a broker and/or lawyer.

My Name & Address are: _____

_____ Zip _____ Tel. # _____

Send it to: *Dr. Benji O. Anosike, author • c/o Do-It-Yourself Legal Publishers, "Tell It To The Author" Program,* **60 Park Place** *Suite 1013, Newark, NJ 07102*

INDEX